PROLOGUE

One winter's evening while dinner was simmering on the stove awaiting my husband's arrival home, I heard the garage door open and his car pull in, getting both of them out of the snowy night. As Ron burst into the kitchen, I knew without a doubt something big had happened at work and he couldn't wait to tell me.

It took all of his inner strength to contain himself until he could slowly tell me his news. He was so excited and wanted me to be excited with him. That afternoon his boss had discussed the real possibility of Ron taking a foreign assignment in England for eighteen to twenty-four months.

As he was so excited, I tried to be excited with him. We had had the chance of two other assignments but they had fallen through due to financing problems. This time he felt it was a "done" deal. I said, "It sounds great" although my heart wasn't in it. He said we could travel and spend quality time together since I would no longer be teaching. It sounded fabulous: Ron, travel, and freedom from my heavy teaching load.

As I had time to consider this "opportunity", I realized what I would be giving up: my family, friends, and my home. What upset me most was the prospect of leaving behind my beautiful two-year old granddaughter, Jennifer. She and I had a special bond, as she was the little girl I never had. My "daughters" came to me fully grown when they married my sons.

Uneasiness filled me as the prospect of this assignment became more and more real. Fear struck me. I kept hoping it wouldn't become reality but it did. Ron's company, *Comco*, needed an emission's expert to oversee its catalytic programs in Europe and Ron was the one selected for this assignment. There was no way of stopping this move eastward.

I was crushed and angry that this event was being heaped onto me while trying to be excited about the prospect of living in England and exploring Europe and all the nuances of living abroad. As Charles Dickens's so appropriately said it in, *The Tale of Two Cities*, "It was the best of times and the worst of times". I was in for a roller coaster ride of highs, lows, sunshine, rain, happiness, and tears for the next year and a half or so.

Life on international assignment, like any life, is filled with encounters to experience, learn from, live through, and enjoy. From the moment Ron accepted *Comco's* offer, I knew my life would never be the same. This time abroad would open me up to new horizons to discover, adventures to be taken, people to meet, and a whole new way of life for me to experience. Living across the "pond" (the Atlantic Ocean to international travelers) in England and Europe would change me into the person I am today and I am grateful for that time.

Come along with me and remember to bring your sense of humor with you for the ride of a lifetime. Experience it for yourself first hand. It's quite a ride.

ACKNOWLEDGMENTS

Many thanks go to my friends and especially to my initial readers, Pat Knudsen and Suzi Peterson, who nursed me through all the lapses and overlays of my thinking and writing. To my illustrator and friend, Boyce Collins, without whom this book would never have come to life. To a British friend, Derek Eade, who provided a better book title than my own. To my friend, Edward Czarnecki, who kept me focused and level headed. To Pete Ross for getting in touch with Hazel Proctor, my publisher, who has been invaluable to me in polishing and publishing this book.

To my husband, Ron, my sons, Ron and John, my "daughters" Nancy and Laura, I thank them for supporting me through the emotional throes of this endeavor.

To my beloved grandchildren, Jennifer, Christopher, Patrick, and Ronald III, I dedicate this book. For it is for you, I wrote this book about some of my life encounters, so you could get to know me more intimately than ever before.

Table of Contents

Close Encounters of the European Kind

1. My Adventure Begins

In the months following Ron's acceptance, he and I were prodded with tongue depressors, needles vaccinated us from everything from tetanus to hepatitis A to typhoid, and stethoscopes checked our hearts and lungs for any problems. The doctors and nurses needed to make sure we were in perfect health before certifying us as excellent health specimens. I suppose the company didn't want to send anyone on assignment with any health issues, even a hangnail. Did they find anything wrong with me? Never. I was as healthy as a horse, and I had my medical documents to prove it.

Decisions came at us like lightning bolts. What about our home? Ron and I talked about renting or selling our home. We decided to sell it. We had been discussing this for a while because it was too large for just the two of us. This adventure made that decision for us. I also didn't want to return to our home after someone else had lived in it for an extended period. I had heard horror stories about people returning home to trashed houses and having to redecorate them before they could move back into them. That was not for me! Although I hated to sell my home, it was the best choice for us.

By mid-May our house was on the market and my classes were winding down to semester exams and final grades. Our home sold within two weeks, leaving me time to finalize my school year. At the same time I told my department heads that I would not be returning in the fall which didn't please either of them. I guess they didn't like losing a good teacher to England or anywhere else. My next major job was to finish my classes and calculate my students' grades. Once that was done I needed to turn not only the grades in but also my textbooks and grade books to the respective college registrars and department heads.

After all that was completed, I realized a monumental job lay ahead of me. We had to be out of our house on June 14. Since I hadn't been able to take a week out of my teaching schedule to go to England on one of Comco's pre-visit tours for housing, I had to make decisions on what furniture and things we would take to England and what we would leave in local storage here. Not knowing how large or small our place would be I was in a pickle to figure out what we would need. Oh well, with a little bit of this and a little bit of that, we should be all right. If I missed something, I would just buy it there. Right? Yes, right! I love to shop and this would give me an excuse to do what I love most. Shopping!

During our orientation sessions into living abroad, Comco told us with moving we would have to decide just what we were taking and what we were storing locally. We had a lot, so choices had to be made. After thirty years of marriage we had a lot of "stuff" – some that had meaning to us and we would keep and some we would have to part with. Questions such as; what is no longer wanted, needed, or valued? What do we sell outright? What do we take with us? What will be stowed until we return?

The next hurdle was to sort everything into three groupings: local storage, sea shipment, and air shipment. Air shipment (a maximum of ten boxes) included those essential things needed to begin housekeeping while the sea shipment would be the bulk of our furniture and clothing needed for our duration in England. The air shipment would arrive in about ten days and the sea shipment would arrive in about eight weeks. Each group then had to be thoroughly inventoried onto customs forms: furniture, clothing, dishes, appliances, and even the number of socks, bras, slips, and skivvies we owned. Comco and its insurance company needed these forms so if anything went missing or damaged we could get reimbursed. The triplicate forms for each of the sea and air groups needed to be readied for the respective crates so the British customs officers could check the lists against the crate contents. Believe me, they did go through each crate to check for accuracy. Wow, I couldn't believe it. The third set belonged to the local moving company to be held until our return.

As I thought of this task that lay ahead of me I thought, "Well, here I go. I've done everything expected of me – why not this? I can do it without problem." I didn't realize the hours and hours that went into this. I was exhausted just counting the number of underclothes we had and I had just started on the forms. This could take months to finish. Oh, well, I didn't have anything else to do. I knew I had a deadline of June 14th to be out of the house. So to my task I proceeded.

Once the forms were finished, a local moving company known to deal with both local and international moves came to assess our needs for packing, storage, and crating materials. The boss on the job suggested we put everything for one group in one room – all the air shipment in the living room, the local storage small items in another room, the sea shipment little things in another room – then we would deal with the big furniture items at the end. That weekend Ron and I placed things as they wanted. I thought we had done a bang up job. Just wait till the movers come on Monday, won't they be thrilled with us.

My only problem was I didn't put signs or Post-its on each door. All day I was running up flights of stairs from the basement to our second floor answering questions about what was to be done with this?

Was it sea, air, or local? It seemed so simple to me but to them it wasn't. Oh, well, I got through the first day.

That night after Ron and I had a pizza and a glass of wine, I took a long soaking bath and had another glass of chardonnay just to relax my pulsating muscles. I had just started but knew the evening hot bath would revive me for the next day's onslaught of questions and problems. I had to be a stalwart of energy and strength to make it through this process. "This too shall pass – I'll muddle through somehow," I said to myself.

The second day finalized the packing. With the third day came the large sea containers to be filled with the crates of our things. Our air shipment boxes were placed in a small van so they wouldn't get confused with the local storage boxes and crates. By the end of the fourth day our house was empty of everything – bare to the walls. It looked so lonely without our things and us in it.

My prayer was that I had chosen correctly and hadn't taken too much or too little with us. For a yardstick, I used my cousin Vernon and Margaret's semi-detached house (duplex for us Americans) for a blueprint of what to take. It was a medium sized place which I figured was the right size. Ron and I had taken my Dad to visit his Scottish relatives the summer before he died and we had stayed with them. If I had brought too much, well, I would just have to find some storage place to put the additional until our return Stateside.

On June fourteenth we said goodbye to our home. I cried to think of all the happy memories of wonderful parties, family times, and our granddaughter Jennifer we were leaving behind. It had been a wonderful house to live in. The following evening we boarded a British Airways plane bound for London. We were on the company's pre-visit to find housing which we desperately needed now that our furniture was on the way. What a backwards way to live!

Twelve hours later we arrived at Ron's new office building where we found out that there had been some haggling over the "pond" about which side was going to pay for his assignment and in the interim no one had pursued his British work permit so he didn't have one and couldn't work here until he had been assigned one. My thoughts ran to what happens if he isn't given one? What about our furniture that was on the sea and air? What do we do next? Ron had thought this was a done deal and it hadn't proven to be. We only had a matter of six to eight weeks to accomplish this. What about housing in England and the States? We were to find housing while we were here. They would have that time to paint and fix it up before we came. "Ok, but what do we do for housing in the States?" we asked. The answer was simple. The company will put you up in the States until you can return and begin work. I couldn't believe how hard we had worked and a clerical error or something had muddied up the water for us. What does Murphy's law say, "If anything can go wrong, it will." It did.

I will never forget the day we began looking for a place to live. Trevor Banks, the real estate broker for the company, was to take us to see five places we were eligible to rent. The first three were unworkable floor plans. One even had half floors included in it. After seeing the third, I innocently asked Trevor, "What happens if we don't like any of the showings?" Taking affront to my question, he said dogmatically, "Well, you don't have to come." I thought not only have I given up my family, home, and career to come to this foreign land with Ron to help your country out – you're going to be hostile and uninviting as well. What if the last two rentals aren't something I can live with either? My heart sunk. Fear set in.

We drove to the fourth offering. As Trevor's car pulled into the driveway and front garden, we noticed the straggly, unkempt shrubs and flowers. This didn't make us feel terrific about what we saw. Oh, my what a lot of gardening I have to do to put this garden back in order. Ron and I just looked at each other and shrugged our shoulders. The house's exterior design included white stucco walls with traditional mahogany beams. Entering the house through its thick wood door, we both knew this was the place for us. To the right of the foyer was the lounge (living room to us) with a huge bay window overlooking the front garden and street. The sun radiated through the window giving the room as well as the house a warm, cozy atmosphere. What a glorious welcome. The right wall was filled with built-in bookcases. I was excited about this becoming a wonderful showcase for our library of books and knickknacks, giving this room a sense of hominess and dimension. In the middle of the opposite wall was a gas fireplace surrounded by beautifully hand-painted floral tiles. On either side of the fireplace were additional built-in bookcases. The peach and aqua marbled wallpaper as well as the peach and aqua fleur de lis carpeting would be perfect accents for our traditional ivory furniture.

From the lounge we walked down the hallway. On the left we found a half bath with parquet flooring and plain cream walls and fixtures. At the end of the hall was a magnificent gourmet kitchen. The floor was deep red brick linoleum. From the floor to halfway up the walls was red brick tiling and the remainder of the wall was papered in a green Laura Ashley fleur de lis print. The cook area contained many wood cabinets and gray marbled Formica countertops which surrounded the hob (countertop gas stove), the built-in wall oven and grill (broiler) with temperature choices of gas 1, 2, 3, 4, and 5 that made no sense at all to me, and the sink area. Next to the sink was a built-in dishwasher which required not only dishwasher soap but dishwasher salt to run.

What a kooky thing to operate but I knew I would get the hang of it sooner or later. Over the sink was a three-piece window overlooking the back patio and garden.

The dinette alcove contained another three-paned window along with French doors leading to the outside. This would be great for our brown Formica wood–looking kitchen table and four dark brown leather chairs. The only problem was they were in the States. Oops. I wondered if we could get the movers to go into our storage, retrieve them and ship them with the next sea shipment to England. All we could do was ask. No harm in asking, I thought. All they could say was yes or no.

To the back of the kitchen was a small pantry filled with a compact refrigerator/freezer unit, compact washer and dryer set, and wood shelving for storing boxed and canned items. I thought how wonderful that would be for storing things.

Returning to the kitchen I saw another set of French doors leading to the dining room. The top of the walls were decorated with another Laura Ashley green crested wallpaper; below the paper was a light green chair railing followed underneath by hunter green paint. The carpeting was a mousy brown. This room's centerpiece was another gas fireplace surrounded by hand painted floral tiles. Trevor explained that before central heating was put in these two fireplaces were the only means for heating this house. I knew our dining room furniture would fit perfectly.

Before inspecting the upstairs, Ron and I wanted to explore the back garden. We strolled through the kitchen's French doors out onto a small wood deck leading to the stone patio floor. A lovely stone trellis with blooming yellow roses on it separated the patio and the garden area. Laurel trees separated our property from our neighbors. The garden itself was divided into two parts by a tall overwhelming oak tree and a rundown wood storage shed. The initial section was filled with multi-colored flowers around its perimeters. Additionally, separating the patio from the garden and yard area were clusters of peach, white, and pink azaleas and pink and purple rhododendrons. The square grass area in the first section was so small Ron would need less than five minutes to mow. The former tenants had used this back section for a vegetable, fruit, and flower garden. Since there was a large glass hothouse along the back wall, we decided to continue the practice and produce our own vegetable and fruit plants for spring planting. Next to the hothouse was a carpentry shed complete with its own electrical supply. I doubted Ron would use it, as he's not into carpentry projects.

Returning indoors we went upstairs. Climbing the stairs was a little tricky for us as the depth of each step was about two-thirds that of American staircases. Once upstairs we saw the bathroom. The room consisted of a freestanding washbasin, toilet, and a bathtub totally enclosed in a wood paneled alcove. Paneling extended halfway up the walls around the room then topped with a pretty medium blue floral print paper. We asked where the mirror or medicine cabinet was. Trevor said, "Only Americans need that luxury but we'll put one in if you really need one." I said, "Ron needs a mirror in the morning to shave." We would settle for the mirror not wanting to be too forward to ask for a medicine cabinet. I had to hedge my words so I wouldn't appear too bold to him.

Just outside the bathroom was our bedroom. The walls were painted and wallpapered in salmon colors and the window dressing were rust–colored Austrian pull-up curtains. The wall opposite the entrance was filled with built-in closets. Immediately I knew I was in trouble as we had shipped more clothes than this space afforded us.

Oh, what am I going to do now. They're already on their way.

The remaining two rooms were in the front of the house. The room next to ours had cream wallpaper with tiny red rosebuds all over it. The exterior wall consisted of a large three-paneled window allowing more sun to warm and brighten this room. We decided this would be our guest and television room. The other room was so small we named it our "half room". Since it had a full-length built-in desk and cabinet area along the outside wall, we decided this would be our office. This room's only light, outside of the ceiling light, was its window. Entering this room I became aware of a large storage cabinet to the right. I must have said, "Oh, my clothing dilemma is over. I can use this space to store our off-season clothes." Trevor said, "This is where your hot water heater is. The wood slating above and below it allows you to store your towels and linens on the slats so you can keep your towels warm for after baths." It was a great idea. Let's see how well it works in reality.

After seeing the house, we knew we would be happy here for the next two years. The street in front of our home was called Priests Lane, so named because early priests walked this lane on their pilgrimages to Canterbury. An adjoining street was named Friars Avenue for the same reason.

After four days of house-hunting and work related meetings, we returned to the States. We moved into a two-bedroom apartment at *Comco's* disposal. I wondered how many others might have had the same problem as we were experiencing. During those eight weeks I spent a lot of time with Jennifer as well as our family and friends. Not knowing what to expect in Britain's food stores I stocked up on large containers of needed cinnamon, cardamom, garlic powder, onion flakes, and also flour, sugar, and Mexican staples. I had to be prepared for any cooking and baking needs.

The fateful night came when the real goodbyes had to be said. It took all the strength and energy I had not to burst into a torrent of tears. Saying goodbye to Jennifer and my family tore me apart. As we boarded our British Airways 747 bound for London, Ron and I knew we were finally beginning the new life that lay ahead of us.

As I looked back through the darkness, pouring rain, and fogged-up window to the window where I knew my family was, the tears began to flow like there was no tomorrow. I was leaving everything I loved behind except Ron.

As our plane roared down the runway toward its destination, I settled into my seat. I let my mind remember what we had been through these past nine months to get to this moment – the medical tests, the orientation sessions, and the venting of concerns about going on this assignment. My mind returned to the young couple who sat across from us in one of the orientation sessions. They were taking their three-month old son and were heading for three years in Japan. I shuddered as I thought of them trying frantically to find an English-speaking pediatrician or doctor in the middle of the night when their son had a temperature of 102 or more. I did not envy them in the least but they looked so eager for their new way of life.

I just thought of the completely new life we were beginning. We felt excited as well as nervous about this new life. I knew we would make it because we had each other and our love. Come with me on this exciting encounter with life.

2. Arrival in London

As our 747 approached London Heathrow Airport at 6:05 AM British time, Ron and I tried to wake our bodies up but they didn't want any part of it. "Hey, wait a minute!" they screamed, "it's only 1:05 AM." Adjusting to this new time zone would take effort. Our international friends had recommended we stay awake throughout our arrival day, then go to bed at our normal time. This way our bodies would adjust to British time. How would we keep ourselves awake? We were so tired after a sleepless night crossing the Atlantic, but decided to follow our friends' recommendations. We knew we had to keep active or we would be asleep in a moment's notice.

After departing the plane, we went to British Immigration where Ron presented his work permit to the inspector. Ron and his paperwork were entered into British immigration records then both our passports were stamped with the official British work permit stamp which would allow us to travel within and outside England at will for the length of his permit.

Completing that task, we moved to the baggage area. Retrieving our bags, we pressed on to customs. Since we did not have anything to declare, we simply followed the green channel or line and exited the area. If we had had something over our allowed limit, we would have had to follow the red line and stop at the customs office and pay the duty on our excess.

With all the nitty-gritty things done, we quickly moved to outside activities. Ron hailed one of England's vestiges of British tradition – the famous black taxi. As we sat in the back seat watching the airport traffic jostle into and out of spaces leading to the motorways, Ron and I looked at each other then squeezed each other's hands. Ron said, "You ready??"

I said, "I am game," controlling my apprehension. The taxi took us to Comco's headquarters where security was to loan us a car.

Watching the motorway we realized we would have to learn a new way of driving – driving on the left side of the roads. What a scary thing to think about. We needed to make those adjustments quickly or we could be in some serious problems before we knew it and that wasn't something we wanted or needed.

The sun was rising to full strength as we traversed the green, pristine countryside full of grazing cows and sheep. About an hour later we were at our destination. Ron took our luggage out of the taxi's boot (trunk) then paid our fare. Fortunately, we had the fifty pounds (about $75) for the fare leaving us little money to start our bank account. Oh, well, this too will pass. I had known this feeling before when we were in grad school so I knew we would work it through.

After signing for our navy blue Sierra automobile, Ron placed our baggage in the boot. We hopped into the car only to realize we were on the wrong sides; I was sitting with the steering wheel while he was on the passenger side. Quickly, we changed. With a trusty area map and directions to our flat we started off. We would live in the flat until our home was ready, our sea shipment had passed customs, and our things were ready for delivery.

As we pulled out of Comco's car park (parking lot), I realized Ron was on the wrong side of the road. I screamed, "You need to be on the other side of the road!" He quizzically looked at me silently saying,

"You mean I'm suppose to drive over there!" Getting acquainted with a right side steering wheel, a left gearshift, and a left-sided emergency brake would take some time getting used to. Fortunately, the gas pedal and brake were on their usual sides only in this car they were on the right side. We would need a lot of practice before this would become normal to us and we could proceed with accuracy.

We proceeded to our flat without incident. I was glad it was Sunday morning as there was little traffic to maneuver. The complex manager, George Squires, welcomed us and showed us our temporary home. It was a typical British flat: a lounge-dining room area, a bedroom, a full bath, and a compact kitchen which his wife, Barbara, had stocked with eggs, thick sliced bacon, cereal (corn flakes), bread, butter, tea, and some new oddities – long life orange juice and milk. Fresh dairy products have short refrigerated lives so the dairy and juice industries devised the idea of long life products. These products are manufactured in wax boxes and can sit unopened on a pantry shelf for up to three months. Once opened, they must be refrigerated and used within three days just like their fresh counterparts.

After George left, our first half hour was spent unpacking our baggage. We estimated being here for approximately two or three weeks until our home was cleaned and our furniture was ready for delivery. With the unpacking done, Ron began reading the *Sunday Times (The London Times)* he had acquired before leaving the plane. My, it was massive – must have been at least a hundred pages – it looked larger than the Sunday *New York Times*. While he did that, I wrote the family telling them we had arrived safely. We didn't know we could use the phone in our flat for international calls so I did the next best thing – I wrote. Ron said he would call the family from the office in the morning. Later, feeling the need for sleep we decided to get active and investigate our little village. Sunday in England meant all the shops were closed but that was all right as we had little money with us. Walking out of the complex, we turned left and began walking toward town. In the first block we passed Black Horse Estate Agency (real estate), Chris Evans the Florist (looked expensive), Thresher's Wine and Spirits (whiskey) shop, Rose's, a bakery (I better not get too friendly here or my body might quickly show its breads and pastries), Wheatcliffs (a paper and design shop), then the corner bookshop with lots of good books advertised in its front window.

The next block contained Ree's Pharmacy, Midland Bank where we would do our banking, a Seven-Eleven shop, Claire's, a collectibles and china shop (I must investigate this one), an Indian Tandoori (restaurant), Land and Land Butchers, Smithers, a greengrocer (fresh fruits and vegetables), and a fishmonger (fish shop).

The following block contained Sketchley's, a chain dry cleaner. I remembered it as we looked at the flat above it in June when we were house hunting. It would have been perfect if it had had a parking space for our car. None was available. The next shop was the village co-op market then a newsagent's shop (newspapers, magazines, stationery, sweets); it also included a branch office of the British Postal Service.

Further down the street were two hardware or DIY's (Do It Yourself) shops then Shenfield Travel with large posters in its front windows enticing everyone to visit places like Morocco, Paris, Tenerife, and places eastward.

On the opposite side of the street was the British Rail station from which customers could travel to nearby villages or London (35 miles southwest of us) or connect with other trains traveling to places throughout the United Kingdom. Wow! Just a five-minute walk from our flat to the train station and I could go anywhere. What an overwhelming thought. All this and LONDON, too!

As we were finishing our walk, we saw a second Indian Tandoori that said it would be open for dinner. Dinner! I didn't have to worry what to feed us on our first night here. Tomorrow I would worry about groceries. Not tonight.

We watched a little BBC television. What a change to have only four stations: BBC1 and BBC2 are state run while ITV and BBC4 are two commercial rivals of the BBC. All displayed that dry British humor.

Early evening found us eating Indian curry, rice, and condiments. After a walk back to the flat, a hot soaking bath, and a tired "I love you," we fell exhausted into our comfortable bed with its enveloping duvet lulling us to sleep.

3. Getting in Sync with Life Here

Our first morning came early. Ron showered, shaved, and dressed while I made breakfast: corn flakes, toast, and long life orange juice and milk each having their own distinctive tastes. We watched the morning news on the "tele" (televison); such a change from Charlie Gibson or Matt Lauer. I loved hearing the British accent. We tried to make sense of the cities and news bits but we were so new we struggled to keep up. I knew in time the news would become second nature to us. Once breakfast was over, Ron gathered up his trusty map to guide him to his new office. With a reminder to drive on the left side, a wave goodbye, and a mouthed "I love you", he drove off to his new, uncharted world.

I washed up our few breakfast dishes, made the bed, showered, and dressed for the day. My job for the day was to investigate the village shops and find something for dinner. Since the shops didn't open until 9:30 or so, I curled up in our cozy dusty rose velvet chair to finish reading *Body Count* by William Kienzel, one of my favorite writers. I had bought it at Easter, his usual time to issue a new book. I had not touched it, as I wanted to save it for this trip. I love this mystery-writing priest's work. His first book, *The Rosary Murders* with his priest sleuth, Father Robert Koesler, hooked me at once. During his previous book signings I had been fortunate to meet and talk with him about writing and what it took to write a publishable book.

About 10:30 I began my walk into the village. Coming around the street corner, my nostrils recognized the incredible aromas of baking breads. Oh, yum, yum. Rose's was definitely a shop I needed to stay away from; especially after seeing all her breads, pies, and biscuits (cookies) on her shelves waiting for me to come in and purchase. This shop would give me some weighty problems if I didn't abstain from stopping inside. As I was about to pass Ree's Pharmacy in the third street, I noticed a doctor's office above it. How convenient. Next to Ree's was the Midland Bank branch. Following it was Claire's. Venturing inside, I found an amazing array of collectibles (china and crystal) and paper products from cards to wrapping paper. I felt like a little kid in a candy store wanting to sample everything in sight. Claire stocked everything from *Royal Doulton* china and *Waterford Crystal* to endearing *David Winter* and *Lilliput Village* houses and shops. *Dunoon* bone china beakers (tea mugs) came in sets of three or four each with its own theme and designs. I inspected her *Beatrix Potter* animals, as I wanted to create a collection for Jennifer. This shop was overwhelming. "I had to get out of here," I thought, "before I could get into financial chaos."

Once outside I passed Lands and Lands Butchers and was dumbfounded to see meats hanging on hooks or laying in stainless steel display trays in the shop's sunny front window. Hadn't they heard of salmonella? I decided to pass them by for now. Next came Smithers with produce bearing labels from Israel, Spain, Italy, and France. I gazed at European white asparagus, red juicy strawberries, casaba melons, bananas, and honeydew melons as well as fruits and vegetables grown locally. What a selection. Since I was on a tight budget until our first paycheck a month away, I moved on to the next store. The fishmonger on the corner was closed so I would have to wait to see his fish.

The village co-op market was next on my list and seemed like an oversized 7-11 to me. What an amazing shopping change I was to encounter in products and measurements. I saw cleaning products, tinned (canned) products, dairy and bread items I had never seen before. Adding to my confusion everything was in metric measurements. A gallon of milk was 3.8 liters.

Catching my eye as I walked down one aisle were five different types of British flour (white, wheat, plain, self-rising, and strong). I thought I'd figure that out in no time only to be bombarded with another sight and problem – five different kinds of sugars (caster, brown, golden caster, icing, and demurra). In the dairy case I found both regular and soured milk (similar to a weak sour cream) along with single and double creams. I realized I would need a British cookbook or encyclopedia just to decipher what to use – this would mean a whole new way of cooking and baking. On the bread shelf laid loaves of white, brown, grain breads and something called Scottish cakes (pancakes). Potato chips were called crisps. Eggs were either brown, white, or free-range each in their own container boldly sitting out on a store shelf. They weren't refrigerated like I was used to. The British had butter – no margarine. Sliced bacon was either smoked or unsmoked. Advertisements for washing up soap puzzled me. What did that mean? Was it for the dishwasher or the washing machine? I knew I would soon get on intimate terms with these new fangled items. I purchased some minced (ground) beef, chips (French fries), baps (hamburger buns), ketchup, British mustard (ouch, a sharp taste to it), cokes (American variety), British ice cream, and some bananas for our breakfast cereal. When I came out with my purchases, I realized how overwhelmed I was from all I had seen and what I would have to come to terms with. I resolved I would not be daunted by this new wrinkle in my life.

After finishing my grocery shopping, I spied a Boots pharmacy,

Britain's largest chain of chemist (pharmacy) shops. I was curious to see what medicine changes I would have to make. We were well stocked as we had been told during orientation meetings to purchase all the medicines we would need before coming here. I had complied. I may even have overdone it a bit but I was ready for our two years.

Next was the Shenfield Travel shop where sugarplums danced in my head seeing posters of places I had only visited in my dreams. Maybe living here I might be able to visit some. Across the street I saw the British Rail station and felt it beckoning me to come in and ride its trains to destinations I wanted to explore. Soon, I would go in and find out how to do that, but my ice cream was getting soft in my carry bag so I had to forgo that investigation. That would give me something to do on another day.

As I crossed the street from the travel shop to the train station, I saw Tower Cleaners with its own shoe repair shop then came Becham's, the other market in town, more cosmopolitan but fewer food choices. Hurrying on, I passed Hanleys, the second and larger green grocer specializing in local produce. After that came the Shenfield branch of Barclay Bank, Francine's, a ladies clothing shop with shoes, and Shenfield Wine and Spirit shop. At this point I wished I had waited to buy my groceries so I could have spent more time checking out the shops and their prices. Oh, well, I have lots of time to get acquainted with them.

On the corner of the next block was the Shenfield library, open Tuesday through Saturday noon to seven. Further up the street was the local Friend's Meeting place which reminded me that Ron and I needed to find a church as well. Sunday would begin our search.

Once "home" I put away my goodies. "Now, let's check out this new fangled stove and oven," I thought. Halogen burners – fast, efficient heat but what is this on the oven/grill – Gas 1, Gas 2, ... Gas 8? What do these gauges mean? Where are the temperatures I know like 350 and 375 degrees? Another learning situation. Hopefully, soon, I would have enough money to buy a British cookbook explaining all these new flours, sugars, creams, temperatures, and grill distinctions. I shuddered to think of all the burnt or undercooked meals we would have until then. Oh well, just another encounter with my new life. I was beginning to feel lost and overwhelmed with all the new things coming at me. I knew things would get easier; or at least I hoped so.

4. Extending my Horizons

The first few days passed like a blur – I was still attempting to get my emotions under control. Reality had begun to set in – I was a long way away from the people I loved and no way was I going to dispel those lonely feelings quickly.

About nine-thirty on my first Thursday morning I heard a knock on my door. Who could that be? Ron had a key and we knew no one else here. Although I felt uneasy, I opened the door and saw a woman with a warm, welcoming smile. She said, "Hello. I am Loraine Meadows. I have come to collect you for the weekly international wives' coffee hour if you want to come."

"Oh, yes," I said. "Just give me a minute to change into something more appropriate." She was an answer to a prayer. People.

At the coffee I was asked to introduce myself to the gathered group of ladies. I said, "I am Nancy Hurley. My husband is Ron and he works at the *Comco's Research* facility. We have two married sons and one granddaughter." The women asked how long our assignment was and whether we had found housing yet. I said, "We would be here for 18 to 24 months and yes, we had a place on Priests Lane which we were waiting to move into." They said having your own place would make the adjustment easier.

The women discussed various group activities I might want to get involved in while on assignment. They told me what doctors and dentists to go to and where to go shopping. If I needed any information, all

I had to do was ask one of them.

Leaders from each group made themselves known to me. Barbara Nielsen was the leader of the weekly Bible study group. This group met Tuesday mornings in the members' homes; they were discussing major women of the Bible. "Our group is very small and quite close – almost like extended family," she said. Since I felt the need for expanding my spiritual life, I said, "Yes." Barb said she would pick me up for their next meeting. Loraine spoke of "Questers", a group that met on the first Fridays of the month. Speakers came to discuss British landmarks, architecture, painters, writers, bone china manufacturers, silver hallmarking, women's costuming during various historical periods, manor homes and gardens as well as anything concerning royal heritage. After their meetings a light lunch and dessert was served; the members provided the food on a once a year rotation.

Sharon Kooch asked if Ron and I were card players as there were two monthly Pinochle groups (an afternoon one for us gals and a Friday night one for couples) each grouping met in member's homes. Peggy Mason talked about her book discussion group. Since I needed to catch up on my reading, this group sounded like a winner also.

Mary McShane discussed the weekly knitting, cross stitching, and needlework group that met on Wednesdays. Since I had time on my hands and wanted to start knitting and cross stitching again, this would be another group to consider. Loraine described the group as warm and friendly. Another group that interested me was The Grapevine, the monthly international wives' newsletter keeping everyone abreast of group activities, shopping, recipes, things to see and do, and any information pertinent for our group. With my years as an English teacher I thought I was well suited to this activity. Pam Knight was delighted to include me in her group.

The Grapevine also sold their own cookbooks filled with much needed information as well as wonderful member recipes. I was in seventh heaven finding a cookbook that not only gave me new recipes but explained all these new flours, sugars, metric measurements, and temperature gauges on my hob and grill units. Relief came over me as I paid my £5 ($7.50 American) for this kitchen bible. Upon opening it, I found a wealth of cooking and baking information. Whoopee! Now, I could cook and bake competently again. Running through its pages I wondered which recipe I'd try first. All the recipes sounded wonderful: orange and ginger chicken, five hour stew, smothered pork chops, garden quiche along with chocolate cheesecake, oatmeal raisin cookies, and tapioca pudding. "Oh, boy," I thought, "there goes my waistline." I began to feel more at ease not only with these new culinary skills but also with the camaraderie I was feeling with these new women in my life.

After the meeting we walked to the Rose and Child, a large Tudor pub around the corner from our meeting place. Walking inside I found a large bar area surrounded by men sipping their noontime pints while watching us girls invade their territory. We ordered our lunches and beverages with the barmaid then went into their dining area. In there the wood walls, flooring, tables and benches made the room feel a bit cold and uninviting. The girls and I sat talking at our tables waiting for our numbers to be called so we could pick up our food; I had ordered the Ploughman's lunch: sliced ham and cheese on a half baguette and a pint of coke. Served with my sandwich was Branston relish, almost like a chutney. It was diced cauliflower in a dark sweet and sour sauce. Quite tart but tasty. My lunch cost me only £1.80 ($2.70). Not bad. I discussed the high price of food and clothing I had found in the village shops. They said, "It's best not to exchange pounds for dollars in your head as the prices will be staggering then you won't buy anything. Remember you are paid in pounds so buy in pounds and you'll be all right."

Some of the summer holiday returnees talked of Paris, Madrid, Rome, Amsterdam, Tenerife, and Munich. My head spun thinking of all the places I wanted to visit. I needed to make a wish list of places I wanted to see, then create a timetable to accomplish as much of it as I could. At the top would be France, Germany, Italy, and Austria as well as familial places in England, Scotland, and Ireland.

I talked with several women at different stages in their assignments; some had just come on assignment like me, others had been here for a year or more while some had been here for five plus years, initially coming for 18 to 24 months like us. I didn't like hearing that as it scared me to think our assignment could be extended like theirs. That night Ron and I discussed all I had heard, especially about extensions. He said that wouldn't happen to us.

Sunday morning we attended St. Mary the Virgin Anglican Church, the small 11th century church in Brentwood, a neighboring village. It looked so inviting with its white stucco and dark wood exterior Tudor walls, its lovely cream interior walls and dark wood struts and beams, and its beautiful hand-painted and gilded reredos behind the altar. I felt at home the minute I walked inside it. I wandered how the parishioners would react to us "intruding" into their church and service.

5. Our First Exploration – London

All week I had been excited as Ron and I were going to venture into London to have a look around. It was my favorite city. It had such a magical atmosphere to it. On the appointed Saturday, we were greeted with a warm, bright, and sunny morning. After showering and dressing I made Ron a quick breakfast, as I was too excited to eat.

Within a half hour we were walking to the exotic place called the British Rail Station to begin our first trip into a new uncharted territory or one of those *Close Encounters of the European Kind*. Inside the station Ron and I stepped up to the ticket agent asking him a myriad of ticket questions. "How do we get into London? What train(s) do we take? How do we get around when we're there? How do we get back to Shenfield? What tickets do we need? How much do they cost?" We found out a day pass allowed us to go into London and return home as well as having full use of both the underground and bus services at no additional cost. The ticket did not allow us to use the taxis at no charge; we would have to pay for them ourselves. We paid £4.80 ($7.20) for each ticket then climbed the stairwell to the upper train level.

Within ten minutes, our train came barreling into the station coming to a screeching halt before us. Passengers got off then we boarded along with others going into London or to smaller market villages along the route to do their weekly shopping. Quickly, we moved through the cars until we spied two empty seats together and sat down. I sat next to the large picture window. As the train pulled out, the excitement rose in me. We were actually going to London – mystical, magical London. The foggy London town Frank Sinatra crooned about for years.

As the train traversed the picturesque countryside, we saw quaint little villages with their traditional churches, rugby and soccer playing fields, fish and chip shops, red telephone and postal boxes while house exteriors, merchant shops, and schools lent a different style or color variation to the scenery. Excitement filled me as I saw our new life unfolding, surrounding, and enveloping us.

Thirty-five minutes later we arrived in London's Liverpool Street station – a mammoth maze of train tracks and passengers hustling and bustling hither and yon in search of connector trains or exits to London streets and businesses. Ron and I realized we were ducks out of water. All we knew and cared about was we were in LONDON. We couldn't wait to investigate all her splendor.

We bought a map of the Tube, London's underground system, and studied it to see what lines and stations we needed to use to get to the Piccadilly Circus (circle to Americans). Mapping out our route, we searched for the stairs to take us to the Central Line. We would train to Holborn Station where we would change to the Piccadilly Line for the Circus.

Mustering all our courage and fortitude we started down the first set of stairs leading to the Central Line. Reaching the bottom we noticed a turnstile and wondered what procedure we needed to use to get through it. We watched as the other commuters put their tickets into the front slot, retrieve it from the top then push through the stile. "Ok, let's give this thing a whirl," I said and off we went. Once we were through we found a pair of escalators; one descending into what seemed the bowels of the earth and the other ascending from that destination. What an eerie and almost scary feeling came over me. "Oh, well, we have come this far; let's go all the way. Let's not let a simple thing like an escalator keep us from wonderful London," I thought.

At the bottom we saw two mammoth metal maps. One detailed the Central Line's eastbound route with all its stops while the other mapped out the westbound route. Studying the maps we realized we needed to take the westbound train to Holborn Station where we would change to the Piccadilly Line.

Within seconds we heard the rumbling of the approaching train coming through its sooty tunnel then screeching its brakes as it came to an abrupt halt. Once stopped, the passenger doors opened rapidly letting out a massive number of passengers. When they were off, other commuters pushed us into the train before the doors would close again and the train push off on its appointed route. I felt like animals herded onto trains for points unknown.

After the doors closed, the train lurched forward and away we went. Thank goodness I was sitting down or I would have been sprawled all over the train's floor. We moved along the rails from Liverpool Street to Bank, St. Paul's, Chancery Lane, finally stopping at Holborn Street station where we needed to change underground lines. Our next challenge!

Once out on the platform we watched the throngs of people move up the stairwell. We followed suit finding the next level where we spotted the stairway to the Piccadilly Line. What a relief! We were gaining on our objective. We followed the others like little puppies. Again we proceeded into the depths of the earth until we found our Piccadilly connection. After studying our map we knew we needed the westbound train. Another screech, push, and forward lurch we were on our way to Piccadilly by way of Covent Garden and Leicester Square stations. After disembarking the train, we ascended the escalator then climbed two flights of stairs. Finishing our last stairs we found ourselves in front of another turnstile, we repeated our initial turnstile process and moved on. Once outside we were bombarded by sunshine, blue skies, and fresh "clean" air; no more of that black, sooty, dead air of the underground caverns. Even London's "clean" air was polluted from all the gas fumes of its cars, buses, and commercial vehicles. The reason Ron was assigned here – to design catalysts to solve that problem.

After all the fears and diligence getting to this place, we knew it was worth the effort. We had arrived! When I visited here forty years ago, this was an actual circus or circle where only tourist buses and taxis were allowed to let off or take on passengers. At that time tourists would venture here just to visit quaint shops or hotels for their traditional British high teas, pubs for their pints, or just to sightsee. Today, the Circus is much different. The circus is surrounded by multi-leveled chain stores or businesses. Additionally, there are hustling and bustling red double decker buses, black taxis, passenger cars, and lorries (trucks) all impatient to get to their destinations. Blaring horns sound their masters' impatience at having to wait an extra second or two before moving on. Oh, what a difference. I was aghast at what I was seeing. I didn't like it at all.

In the center of all this mayhem stood the famous golden Eros statue in all its finery. People sat around on its base talking to each other or just eating their lunches in the blissful sunshine and warmth. Photographers of all experience levels maneuvered people and camera lenses into awkward places and positions to get the best shots.

I couldn't believe the number of people swarming around us. What we didn't know was British families take their summer holidays in August when school is out for the month. August is not a good time to come into the City. Finally, we found an open spot, jumped into it, and took in all the sights, sounds, smells, and colors of this wonder of wonders. The Sony billboard was touting its newest products for all unsuspecting customers to see while Burger King across the way was trying to entice shoppers to come inside and sample its gourmet delights. Jewelers' windows displayed fascinating arrays of diamonds, rubies, and other precious gems. Clothing stores presented fall clothes lines in their front windows to seduce shoppers to come in and buy. Even the Tower Record store was awaiting our arrival with all its records, CD's, and videos. Street vendors promoted their magazines, worldwide newspapers, and various jerseys, hats and scarves from famous British soccer league teams. Even the West Side theatres invited us to come and savor all their stage treats. We looked at each other and said, "Where do we begin?"

We decided the best way to get to know London was to take one of her purple or red open-air tour buses. After purchasing two 24 hour tour tickets so that we could get on and off the bus to investigate important landmarks, we boarded our red bus at the Hippodrome. Along our tour, our guide, Fiona, gave us detailed historical information about each landmark just before we passed by them so we were able to see them in their full importance. She even had her driver slow down in certain places so we could get better snapshots of something.

Our bus began its tour on Jermyn Street that adjoins Leicester Square where the half-off theatre ticket booth stands. Fiona told us to buy tickets at this stand and not from the scalpers who say they have the best prices when in actuality they sell them at above theatre prices. It's best to wait the time in the half-price line or go to the particular theater office where good seat tickets can be bought for reasonable prices. Caveat emptor! We had been warned.

Following along Haymarket we entered Trafalgar Square, designed by John Nash, creator of many London buildings. Over the years Trafalgar Square has been the scene of many rallies, demonstrations, and outdoor public meetings as well as the congregating place for many pigeons and tourists.

On the south side of Trafalgar Square stood the 165-foot column with Admiral Lord Nelson standing atop it. Nelson was Britain's most famous sea lord who died in the Battle of Trafalgar in 1805. Rumor says that the night before Nelson's statue was placed atop his column, the fourteen stonemasons who had created the column ate dinner on its flat top. I am not sure that I believe the story or that I would do such a thing, but they did.

Behind this column stood Admiralty Arch built in 1918 by Aston Web as a tribute to Queen Victoria. The Arch separates the city business traffic from the royal traffic going down the Pall Mall to Buckingham Palace, Clarence House (the Queen Mother's residence) or St. James Palace (Prince Charles's office and residence).

The National Gallery takes its residence on the north side of Trafalgar Square. In 1824 George IV had the government purchase 38 major paintings including some Raphaels and Rembrandts in order to begin a national collection. Over the years benefactors have donated paintings and endowments to further the museum's international status and prestige. Each floor contains a different age of art from Early Renaissance (1260) to High Renaissance (1520 - 1600) to the Dutch, Spanish, Italian, and French painters of the 1600 - 1700 period including Van Dyck, Cermeerm, Carracci, Champaigne, and Murillo then the 1700 to 1920 period with the Venetian painters including Canaletto, French artists Chardin and Watteau as well as the 19th century English artists Gainsborough, Turner, and Constable. I decided I would immerse myself inside getting to know intimately the greats and their works over the next two years.

On the east side of Trafalgar Square was the beautiful, little church called St. Martin's in the Fields as it was the only structure on this land when it was built in 1726. This little church's design became the architectural blueprint for many early American churches. Over the years St. Martin's has given shelter to returning soldiers and homeless civilians. During World War II it has served as an air-raid shelter. Even today it continues to serve hot soups and foods to the needy. Charles II's mistress, Nell Gwynn, as well as painters William Hogarth and Joshua Reynolds are buried within its walls.

From Trafalgar we traversed up the Strand to the theatre district. The Strand contains the world famous Savoy Hotel, opened in 1889 on the site of the medieval Savoy Palace. It was the first hotel to have en-suite bedrooms (bedrooms with their own bathrooms) and electric lighting. Next came Simpsons-On-The-Strand that daily serves its world famous roast beef fare to its elite clientele.

From there we sped off to the Royal Courts of Justice and Fleet Street, once the newspaper/journalism street. Scrunched between two rather tall buildings was one of Christopher Wren's best-loved churches, the little St. Brides Church. On its walls commemorative plaques pay tribute to famous journalists and painters. On rare occasions the church holds memorial services for newly departed journalists. One thing that caught my eye was its octagonal, layered spire which resembled a wedding cake for which the church was named. I wanted to go inside but there was no stopping. The more I saw, the more I knew I had to see and explore this beautiful city. Ironically, I said to myself, "Will I have time to see and do everything I want in our two years here?"

A few minutes later Ye Olde Cheshire Cheese pub came into view. Over the years such literary greats as Samuel Pepys, Ben Jonson, and

Charles Dickens frequented here; eating, drinking, and critiquing literary works and plays with their groups of friends. Even Mark Twain visited when he came to London. I wonder what they would have discussed? Just to be a little mouse in the corner or under the table to hear what they talked about would have been a joy for an English teacher like me. What revelations and techniques would I have learned? To be privy to that kind of intellect, literary knowledge, and writing advice would have made my head spin with delight.

Since my visit to this pub forty years ago, I remembered how I wanted to return here and be able to scoot my feet across its sawdust floors, have a pint of bitter (ale or beer), and indulge in one of its succulent beefsteak and kidney pies. Oh, what heaven. People entering this pub are transformed into another time and place. I wanted to return and relive that experience.

After turning another corner, we came face to face with the magnificent St. Paul's Cathedral, my favorite one. This grey edifice is so impressive with its massive columns and outdoor chandeliers. After being built in 604 AD, it was reduced to rubble during the Great Fire of 1666. Christopher Wren was commissioned to rebuild it although the authorities did not generally accept his ideas. Using all his creativity and fortitude he created what is now this elegant cathedral. Thank you, Christopher Wren, for your determination and creative talent.

Our next landmarks were the Tower of London and Tower Bridge; remember London Bridge now resides in Arizona. The 900-year-old Tower of London has served as a prison for perpetrators of heinous crimes or those who defied the royalty. Many prisoners were transported here by boat under the veil of darkness through the Traitor's Gate and placed in the Tower's turrets or a cell within its walls. They stayed until their sentences were pronounced, usually a public beheading on Tower Hill, so spectators would think twice before breaking the law or defying the royals or government.

The Tower's Jewel House displays all the royal jewels, tiaras, necklaces, rings, and crowns daily for throngs of visitors. The Royal Armory contains over 40,000 weapons as well as sporting pieces. The Queen's House serves as the private home of the Tower's governor as well as the overnight residence of a monarch on the eve of his or her coronation. The entire Tower grounds are continuously guarded by the revered Beefeaters (distinguished retired military personnel), who live in their own apartments on the Tower's grounds. They have their own chapel as well as chaplain who holds daily and nightly services. Other revered residents here are the eight ravens that are cared for by the Ravenmaster. Legend says that should they desert the Tower walls, the kingdom will fall; therefore their wings are clipped so they cannot fly away.

From the Tower we drove down Cornhill past the Bank of England, a massive grey building, then to Newgate Street and the Holborn area where Charles Dickens lived and wrote.

The bus pushed on to Shaftsbury then to Trafalgar Square. This time we drove through Admiralty Arch and onto the Mall passing through both St. James and Green Parks. At the end of the Mall was the forecourt to Buckingham Palace, the monarchial home of the government. When the Queen's flag is not hoisted above the Palace, it means she is not in residence. She could be out of the country or visiting one of her two favorite residences: her beloved Windsor Castle located in Windsor or her Balmoral Castle in Scotland where she spends her August holiday. Since her flag wasn't up, I said, "I guess I can't stop in for tea today." We circled around the Palace in order to exit onto Whitehall leading to the Houses of Parliament with its booming Big Ben and adjacent Westminster Abbey. My excitement grew when I heard Big Ben booming out its eleven strikes telling everyone it was eleven o'clock.

Since 1512 the Palace of Westminster has been the seat of government consisting of the House of Lords and the House of Commons. The House of Commons is the people-elected branch of government with its leader being the British Prime Minister. The other branch, The House of Lords, is not elected by the people. Its members take their seats due to his or her family's royal lineage or manorial titles. There are three major political parties within both houses: Tory, Liberal Democrat, and Labor. Many heated debates have occurred within these hallowed halls over the years. Although both houses debate issues, new and old, only the House of Commons can create the new laws and regulations.

Every November the Queen rides to the Parliament in her ornate Irish state coach pulled by four beautiful horses. Here she is escorted through the corridors into the House of Lords where she ascends her throne. She officially opens the new parliamentary year and presides over its initial session. Both houses are in attendance for this ceremony as she outlines her proposals for the coming year.

Around the corner is the regal Westminster Abbey, London's oldest and most important church and home to many royal celebrations and burials. Some of the most memorable, recent events taking place inside have been the coronation of Queen Elizabeth II in 1952 and the 1981 marriage of Prince Charles and Princess Diana. While it provides the final resting place for many monarchs as well as some important military and literary personages, the Abbey serves both as a church and a national museum.

The final part of the tour took us from Whitehall to Haymarket and back to the Hippodrome, our disembarkation point. The two-hour tour gave us a rich overview of the city and showed us what we needed to explore to get the real flavor of the city. After getting off the bus and thanking Fiona, we walked around the corner to Piccadilly Circus and found the Burger King. We stepped inside and each of us ordered a delectable whopper, bag of fries, and a tall Coca Cola. A piece of home to us. We sat for a while talking about all we had seen and experienced. What a magical city this London is.

After we had revived our energy, Ron and I walked up Regent Street looking into windows bearing such names as The Scottish Shop (tartans and wool sweaters), Hamleys (the British equivalent to the American FAO Schwartz), Lamleys (major retailer and discounter for English bone china, sterling silver, and crystal), Liberty's (signature upholstery, drapery, and clothing materials, dress wear, scarves, and sundries), then Laura Ashley (children and women's clothing). Soon, we found ourselves on Oxford Street walking toward stores named Selfridges (a modern Harrods), John Lewis (large department store), Marks and Spencers (Marks and Sparks to the British: why, I don't know), Richards (women's clothes, hats, and shoes), Clark's Shoes, The Sock Shop, various accessory and hat shops, and the usual greasy spoon eateries.

Being almost 5 o'clock and tired from our day of excitement and exploration, Ron and I retraced our steps back to Piccadilly tube station. Feeling more confident about the commuting process, we worked our way through the maze of tunnels to the correct trains until we found ourselves back in Liverpool Street station where we boarded our British Rail train for home.

It had been a wonderful day of exploration in a town we hoped to become intimately acquainted with soon. The more we would venture in, the more we would learn about it and ourselves. All I could think about was the beauty and history of London. We knew we would investigate it more fully during our time here as well as other cities in the United Kingdom (England, Scotland, and Wales). What an invigorating, exhilarating day in a wonderland full of heritage and tradition.

6. Lost in No Man's Land

Our first dinner invitation came. One of *Comco's* suppliers asked Ron and me along with Tim and Janice Mills, one of Ron's British co-workers, to dinner at The Pontland Park Hotel in Galleywood. Where was Galleywood? We had never heard of the town much less the hotel.

Ron's British friend, Arthur Gillmore, whom Ron had met a few years before while Arthur was on assignment in the US, drew us a detailed map complete with roundabouts and roads to take. We felt there would be no problem finding this place. Arthur told Ron the trip should take only fifteen minutes.

The evening came with all the anticipation and anxiety of finding a new place and meeting new people. I wore my double breasted navy suit with a crested two toned costume pin and matching earrings while Ron wore his navy suit, light blue button down Oxford shirt, and an international flag necktie. I thought we looked quite spiffy for our evening out.

With our map in hand, we started out. Within minutes we pulled onto the A-127 heading for Galleywood. We cruised through the correct roundabouts and watched each road sign making sure we didn't veer off the designated roads. We were quite pleased when we arrived at the Pontland without any incident. We amazed ourselves by making it in thirteen minutes, not Arthur's fifteen. What a feat we had accomplished.

The Pontland was a renovated grey brick Victorian country house, quite impressive as well as imposing. As we walked through the front door, the receptionist thinking we were in the wrong place asked us our names and who we were meeting. Most Americans didn't know about this hotel. Ron said, "We are the Hurleys. We are dining with Peter Frankel and party."

With a nod and a smug smile she lead us through an anteroom that I believe once served as the house's library then was transformed into a lovely bar and before dinner meeting area. The bar and the shelving behind it were made of carved mahogany wood. The bar shelves were filled with various sizes and shapes of glassware and a wide variety of wines, spirits, cordials, and mixers to delight anyone's taste buds. The room's walls, about 12 feet tall, were painted a warm, inviting yellow. The floral cream draperies complimented the yellow and gold striped and floral overstuffed sofas and armchairs. The side tables were beautiful hand carved mahogany wood pieces.

Passing though this room we entered a small intimate meeting room similarly decorated. Peter greeted us then introduced us to the assembled party. I was pleased we had dressed well, as the others were as smartly (chicly) dressed. The bar waiter served a round of drinks along with trays of the most luscious canapés – stuffed mushrooms, phyllo dough wrapped snails, cheese mini-tarts, and mini spring rolls (egg rolls).

About half an hour later, the maitre d' announced our table was ready. After being seated and surveying the menu I was stunned by the variety of starters (appetizers), salads, and entrees to choose from. This was no slouch restaurant; it definitely was first rate!

Being in a quandary about what to choose, Peter recommended the escargots as a starter followed by either the broiled salmon or the Dover sole for entrees. Peter suggested we save room for dessert, as their hot soufflés were fantastic. They had to be ordered along with dinner so the chefs had enough time to make them and have them arrive at our table at just the right moment. I took note of the hotel's other entrees that included steak, pigeon, quail, spring chicken as well as a number of vegetarian and pasta dishes. I had never seen such a conglomeration of things from which to choose. Making choices would be difficult. Ron and I followed Peter's lead with the escargots and the Dover sole.

Over our starters the group asked how we were adjusting to life in England and how our family and friends were dealing with our assignment. We explained life here was different and we were slowly getting used to it although some of our family was quite upset with us. We felt our life would be better once we moved into our permanent housing and had our own things around us. We wanted to experience everything, especially the British way of life. We had heard from Ron's British co-workers that usually Americans stayed together in a closed community and didn't mingle outside their group. Both Ron and I thought they were missing out on a rare opportunity to learn a whole new way of life by being part of the British people, their culture, traditions, and environment. They would never extend their own horizons and grow from the experience if they stayed in an American group setting. What a shame! What a loss to them as well as the British as we could learn so much from each other.

As our meal progressed, the men began talking shop leaving us wives out in the cold. We tried to work them out of it but to no avail until the waiter removed the dinner dishes.

Within moments, the waiter returned carrying a silver tray filled with our twelve hot Grand Marnier soufflés. The soufflé presentation was spectacular to say the least. As he placed each soufflé, he delicately opened its center with a large tablespoon then poured warm Anglais sauce inside. Talk about ambrosia for the gods – this truly could have been it. I could not believe how absolutely divine it was.

After dinner, the gentlemen treated themselves to a glass of 1963 vintage port. The dinner had been exquisite. It had been a good evening for me as I met some of the men Ron worked with as well as their wives. I knew I would see them at future social functions. It was a fabulous evening; one I would not forget in more ways than I realized.

After dinner we said our thank yous and goodnights and took our leave. We restudied Arthur's map so we could easily maneuver our way home as quickly as possible as it was getting close to the bewitching hour of midnight. A late night for us.

As we returned to the A-127, we realized road signs had changed. Names we had not seen before were on road signs. We expected the signs would list the towns and villages in reverse order. No such luck. Not in England. Arthur had failed to give us the village names we would encounter on our return home leaving us in the dark in more ways than one. Without the names we knew from our original trip, we were lost. Lost was the operative word. Each time we came to a roundabout we looked for a name we knew but found none. What confusion and frustration.

We drove through the village of Chelmsford near the hotel three times. The final time Ron stopped at the only petrol station open to get directions. The attendant tried to help but Ron couldn't understand his British brogue through three layers of protective glass. We left no more enlightened than when we turned into the station.

To help calm our nerves, Ron said, "We have a full tank of petrol and we can drive all night if we have to in order to find our way home. If we don't, in the morning I will call the office and have someone come out and rescue us." We kept driving then by accident or Providence we found the road we needed to lead us back to Shenfield and our little flat.

At half three (three thirty), four hours after leaving the Pontland, we pulled into our building's car park with a vacant parking place waiting just for us. Usually, our complex had more cars than spaces. Exhausted to the bones, we quickly took off our clothes letting them drop wherever they fell and flopped into bed for a short catnap before the workday would begin once again. But oh, what a wonderful evening we had.

7. At Last – Moving-In Day

After living out of suitcases and temporary housing on both sides of the "Pond" for nearly four months, we were finally MOVING into our new home. Our air shipment had been delivered to our flat. Since I didn't need those things yet, I had the men stack the boxes along the lounge's far wall until we actually moved.

From the time we arrived, Ron and I took nightly strolls up Priests Lane peering in our windows to check progress of their getting our place ready for us. The Monday before we moved in, Jim Petersen of *Comco's* relocating office called Ron to tell him our sea shipment had passed British customs and our new abode was ready for us. The move was scheduled for that Friday. As the days passed, our anticipation grew to new heights. A place to call home!!

Friday came. Our alarm clock's wakeup call put us into action. We showered, dressed, and ate a quick breakfast. After driving into our driveway, we walked up to the front door. Using the key housing had given him the afternoon before, Ron opened our door. As I looked across the street, I noticed a house bearing a cement plaque just under its roof declaring it was built in 1897, a fairly new home by English standards. In that amount of time Americans would have torn down and built new homes on that spot two or three times. After walking into our home, I thought to myself, "I will have this place looking like home in no time."

The removers (movers) were due at 9:00 AM. Over the past weeks, I had been planning where every piece of furniture would go hoping there would be no leftover pieces. I decided to make one more survey before the removers came to make sure my decorating plan would work. I wanted everything to be just right. I knew I had a lot of work ahead of me but I was excited to get about my task.

After my tour, Ron and I went outside to wait for the lorry (truck). While we were waiting, the neighbor on our right came out to put her rubbish (trash) into her dustbin (trash can). During one of Comco's orientation sessions we were told the British do not initiate conversation, as they didn't want to appear nosy or intruding. To our astonishment, she asked if we were moving in. We said, "Yes." She introduced herself, "I am Jennifer Knight." She said that she, her husband, Graham, and two teenaged sons, Christopher and Jon, were leaving that evening for their annual two week holiday in the south of France. They camp, taste-test all the wines of the region, and have a jolly, good family trip. She asked if we would like a cuppa (cup of tea). We said that would be wonderful. Within a few minutes she returned with two large beakers (mugs) full of inviting tea. What a welcome treat! Jenny excused herself to do some final holiday packing leaving us to await our furniture and things. It seemed like only minutes and a couple of swallows of tea before we heard the sound of our removal lorry barreling down the street. It came to a screeching halt in front of us. Does every conveyance here come to a screeching halt?? It doesn't seem to matter if it is a train or lorry. What is it about speed and stops with these drivers?

Within minutes the driver ascertained we were the rightful owners of his delivery and had Ron move his car out of the driveway so he could reverse his lorry in. Once the lorry was in place he began rolling up the canvas siding. Another note: most British as well as European lorries have heavy canvas siding, not metal siding as in the States. Goods loaded onto these lorries are strapped to the flat bed then the canvas sides are lowered and secured. The reverse procedure takes place at the delivery site.

Once his canvas sides were rolled up, we saw five gigantic wood crates. Each crate was as tall and wide as the lorry. Within moments Alex, the driver, and his three helpers began cracking open the first crate with a crowbar. He gave me his clipboard with directions to tick (check off) the label numbers on each box and piece of furniture as it came through our front door against the manifest sheets. Simultaneously, I was to direct the positioning of everything. A daunting task but I knew I was up to it. At that point seeing I had everything under control, Ron decided he had done his part and took off for work. By one o'clock the five crates were unpacked. Most of our furniture was giving our house that lived-in look. Then I looked around and realized our bed, chest of drawers, sofa bed, and desks were not here. Alex said he had to return to the warehouse for the three remaining crates containing those items.

While the driver and one of his helpers returned to their London warehouse, the other two men stayed to help me unbox and put away the kitchen and dining room bits and pieces (dishware, glasses, bowls, utensils, etc.). I knew some of my placement decisions would change once I got a feel for those rooms.

About two hours later the driver returned with our remaining three crates. By then, both the dining room and kitchen were about half complete. During the next three hours our bedroom furniture, wood office desk set, and hideaway sofa were put into place. Oh, how the men grunted and growled having to take that heavy furniture up the stairs. With our furniture in place, we checked to see how much damage had been done in transit or during the customs checks. Our only problems were a broken centerboard leg in the coffee table, a crack in an old entertainment center, and a few broken everyday dishes. I believe our American packers wrapped and crated things so well that nothing could happen to them. "Thanks, guys!"

At six, Alex said they were finished. I asked when they would be back in the morning to finish the unpacking; part of their contract. He said, "We have done all we are going to do." I guess with it being Friday they didn't want to work on Saturday. I had forgotten it was Friday. I was upset – although in the long run I was glad. I needed time to think where the remaining things would go. It wasn't until they left that I realized how tired and hungry I was. I had worked all day without a break or a bite to eat. It had been a rewarding but exhausting day of accomplishment.

Now, my work lay ahead of me – the unboxing, sorting, and placing everything in their new places so we would feel at home. That evening when Ron walked through the front door, he looked around and saw all the opened and unopened boxes surrounded by reams of crumpled shipping paper, he said, "What a mess."

I said, "It will come together – just give me a few days."

Now all I wanted was something to eat, a long, hot, soothing bath, and a good night's sleep in my own cozy bed. Ron drove us to The Harvester, a local pub just on the outskirts of Brentwood for dinner. We were told it had a well-stocked salad bar and good food. After a large salad, baked chicken, roasted potatoes, and steamed vegetables, we returned home. Once more we surveyed the boxes and began unpacking a few more.

By midnight, we were both ready to collapse. After opening a number of boxes labeled "master bedroom", we found some sheets for our bed. After the bed was made, Ron took a hot shower, then I lounged in a hot bath trying to soothe my strained, tired muscles. With that we fell into the familiarity and security of our own bed. Oh, what a glorious feeling of contentment. We were finally home!!

8. Reality Sets In!

A few days after we moved in we were told we had to register with the local police as aliens. I couldn't believe we had to do that. At noon the next day we drove to the Brentwood police and registered. They had to take down all our passport information, work permit number, along with his business and our residence address. We also had to give them our next of kin at home in case of an emergency here, or if there was one in the States the police could find us here. I really felt like an alien. I knew I was now a part of this whole experience. We were on record not only with the British government as working here but also now with the local constabulary. What was next?

After a week of organizing furniture, books, and knick-knacks, finding out that I needed special nails to mount our pictures on the plaster walls, and just getting settled, Ron and I decided "we" needed a few additional things to make life here more livable. The first thing on our list was a television to keep us abreast of the news, weather, and sports as well as needed nightly entertainment shows.

That Saturday morning we drove into Brentwood and found a television and appliance rental shop, Radio Rentals, where we made arrangements to rent both a television and a VCR. In order to do that, we had to have our monthly payment debited directly from our bank account to theirs. That irritated me as I felt they didn't trust us to pay our monthly installments. I had always paid our bills on time before but that did not satisfy them. Rules were rules; debit our bank account or no rentals.

After Ron signed the contract and debit authorization, the salesman said, "Don't forget your television license." I said, "What is that and where do we get one?" He told us a television license was required to use any television in a home or business and any postal office could sell us one. We needed to do that before plugging in our television. This fee probably enabled the government to run two of their television channels without commercials. The other two channels had to pay for themselves through advertisements. He said the annual fee for our color TV would be £65.

"Do I need to get one for the VCR as well?" I asked.

"No, just for the TV." he said. He added if the government found us using the television without a license, we could be fined £1000.

I also wanted some small kitchen appliances, as I couldn't use ours in their 220 voltages. I had placed our alarm clock plug into a British adapter not thinking their wiring was for 220 not 110 voltage. Within seconds our clock spun in a wild frenzy and finally died from exhaustion. Since moving-in I had been making toast in our grill, boiling water for instant coffee, and the ironing was piling up in the pantry waiting for an iron to make them look pretty.

With a £250 advance on Ron's first pay, we drove from Brentwood to the Lakeside Shopping Mall (Britain's largest) only 15 minutes away. Lakeside's interior and exterior resembled Toronto's Eton Center – simple, straight architectural lines with bright lighting and light grey walls. What surprised me were all the major store chains [Dixon's (electrical and computers), Rosebuds (linens), British Telecommunications (telephones and equipment), Clark Shoes, and Clinton's Cards (British Hallmark] having more than one shop here. Each, owned and operated by different people, sold the same products at similar or different prices.

So unusual. I had never heard of that before. Weird!

As we moved through the throng of perambulators (baby carriages) and pushchairs (strollers), we priced the items we wanted so we could make our money go as far as it could. We were on a tight budget until our first paycheck when the pay advance had to be repaid.

Walking around seeing all the moms and dads with their children reminded me of my little Jennifer. At that moment reality hit me like a ton of bricks. My heart sank. This foreign assignment was not an excursion or pleasure trip. We were here for 18 to 24 months. In all my organized preparations for our move, I had neglected to deal with the reality of what was about to happen to me and us. I had denied my true feelings and concerns about this adventure for fear I would not be able to handle them. Now, I could feel those tears welling up in me like a geyser demanding to be released. I sat down on one of the marble benches where my tears flowed freely and uncontrollably out of me. People stared at me wondering what was the matter. Although no one came to ask, I could see the questions in their minds. "What terrible thing has happened to her? Is she all right?" They wanted to know but didn't want to get involved. Ron and I just sat while I continued sobbing. Since Ron didn't know what to do with me, he just sat and waited for the deluge to subside. His embarrassment made me feel worse as I couldn't control my emotions.

After I collected myself, Ron and I continued our search purchasing a coffee maker (no more boiling water for coffee), a toaster (no more broiling toast), an iron (no more wrinkled work shirts for Ron), a hand mixer (no more hand mixing of cakes or mashing of potatoes), and an answer phone (no more missing "important" calls). Satisfaction flowed as we took our purchases to the car. Things would be more like home now.

On our drive home we sat in virtual silence; neither of us wanting to discuss my crying jag. We stopped at Brentwood's Sainsbury's market (an English chain), small store by American standards, where I picked up our week's groceries. For years I had made out weekly menus that made easy work of my shopping list. Well, I was about to learn a few new lessons. Their grocery stores do not employ baggers – subsequently customers must bag their own groceries. Watching the people in front of me I learned to place like things such as dairy, breads, cereals, meats, and produce together in piles on the cashier's conveyer belt. Bagging them that way would make putting them away in the refrigerator, freezer, or pantry much easier. I realized I liked this plan of action. Yea, Brits – a brilliant idea!

While putting the grocery items away, I was about to learn another lesson. British refrigerators and freezers do not have the room American ones do. Therefore, I needed to adjust my shopping lists to only two or three days of groceries instead of my usual week. I rationalized that shopping frequently would mean fresher produce and meats. I would get to know my green grocer, baker, fishmonger, and butcher on a first name basis since I would see them about every other day. This would also give me exercise walking to the shops then back home. Another good idea! I was so glad I had brought along my grocery cart so I could pull my foods, newspapers, and magazines without having my arms weighed down with packages.

My next reality check came after British Telecommunications opened our telephone line and put in our kitchen telephone. Oh, how excited and nervous I was to make that first call to the "kids". I actually had been dreading it – just thinking about hearing their voices made me shutter and shiver realizing how far away they were.

After dinner Sunday night, we placed the calls. I prayed I would not break down making it even harder on both sides of the telephone line. Fortunately, I steeled myself and got through both calls without tears. Quite a feat for emotional me!

After the calls my thoughts ran to, "What am I doing here? Parents don't leave home. Children leave home and venture out into the big world outside, not the other way around." Then came, "How am I going to manage being here for the next 18 to 24 months? What am I going to do with all this time on my hands and no family, friends, or job?" These were troubling thoughts; thoughts I didn't want to deal with, as I knew tears would soon follow. I told myself, "Just take it one day at a time." That's what I set out to do. It made logical sense but now I had to put it into action. As the days passed, I hoped to make this adventure work for Ron and me.

9. A Day on the Thames

Ron thought a diversion was in order after all the work I had done putting the house together. He had overheard some of his co-workers talking about a planned barge trip on the River Thames. Sounding like a great experience, he purchased two tickets.

That Sunday morning, we woke up to a cold, overcast, misty morn. I thought this would have been a great day for staying home with steaming beakers of tea, a roaring fire in the fireplace, and a good book from our library of unread books.

As we dressed for our outing, the BBC weatherman said it was going to be a cold and blustery day, so bundle up. With that in mind, we pulled on our thermal underwear along with our warmest trousers, turtlenecks, wool sweaters, heavy socks, and thick boots to brave all the elements. I even found our heavy winter jackets just in case we needed them. We could take things off if we got too warm but we couldn't put on clothes we didn't have with us.

We drove to Ron's office building where our coach (bus) would pick us up. The group had decided it would be easier to hire a coach than for each of us to drive into London's pier area where the barge was docked. Some of us did not know how to get there either. This plan was best.

At eight o'clock the coach arrived and everyone piled in filling her to the brim. As we lumbered along the A-127 to the M-25 and London proper, we watched the scenic countryside give way to more villages then London's industrial section and finally London proper. As the neighborhood streets passed, I peered out my window and saw only a few lone people out and about. Some were braving the wind and rain elements in their long trench coats, wide brimmed hats, and black brawlees (umbrellas). I visualized them back in their flats, sitting in an overstuffed easy chair or at their breakfast table enjoying their freshly baked scone smothered with clotted cream and lemon curd or strawberry jam along with their beaker of hot tea or cocoa while they devoured their *Sunday Times*. Others braced themselves against the elements wearing only a sweater while huddling against buildings or shop fronts hoping to keep as dry as possible while getting their Sunday necessities. They probably weren't going back to a warm hearth to read or munch on wonderful morsels of food. A twinge of sadness came over me for those cold, lonely people trying to survive in this hostile environment.

As the coach neared where our encounter with the Thames was to begin, Ron and I saw the high, austere Tower Bridge. Close by was the Hay's Galleria, a glass enclosed mall full of boutiques and eateries. I wished I had some time to explore the shops but today was not the day. Within seconds of that sighting, our coach pulled into the pier car park where our barge was moored. We retrieved our belongings from the overhead bins, zipped up our jackets, and then covered any remaining exposed parts of our anatomy with hats and gloves.

The barge crew met our motley group of forty; most of us were bundled up to the eyelids. Since our barge, Miss London, was the furthest out, the men escorted us over three wood pylons making sure none of us fell in or had any other mishap beset us as we boarded her.

The barge looked like an old, used, oversized tugboat with large black tires hanging alongside her outer midsection to help ease her in and out of her berth without damaging her sides or jolting her passengers. She was painted red although she had some white stripes on her smokestack and tire areas.

Inside her lower level we found long wood picnic tables topped with red and white-checkered oil tablecloths. Long wood benches were underneath them for people to sit on. On the back wall was a long, narrow serving table with two large urns of hot coffee sitting on it and another urn filled with hot water for making tea. Along with the hot beverages were plates of biscuits (cookies) and scones. Later in our excursion the crew would serve sandwiches, crisps, and sweets (desserts).

When Miss London was ready to leave her berth, we all came on deck for the push away and the beginning of our trek up or down the Thames whichever way she proceeded. We waved to all the curious dockside spectators who wished they could join us. What an amazing feeling. The Thames and all its accoutrements lay ahead of us to glimpse and enjoy. The feeling of being one with the city was growing on me.

In order to document this event I had brought my trusty camera and had our group huddle in the ship's prow amongst the ropes, anchors, and other ship's paraphernalia while a crewmember took our picture for posterity. I have a thing about making sure the history of each event in our lives is well documented with photos, even if it takes rolls of film and time to document each and every event. Ron had repeatedly said to me, "I guess you think you won't get arthritis in that "trigger" finger of yours if you exercise it by taking all those snapshots." I guess I had to agree with him.

Progressing along the water we cruised to the Thames Barrier, the largest, movable flood control device in the world. Our tour guide explained that after two disastrous floods in 1663 and 1928 as well as a tidal surge in 1953 killing 300 people, the Greater London City Council decided some preventative measures had to be taken to protect the city from any further floods and surges.

The Council knew building higher dikes would not suffice so they called for architects to put together designs for their consideration. Nine years later a plan was approved with work beginning soon after. The Barrier's expanse is 1,700 feet from one end to the other. It has ten pivotal gates to direct and control incoming water. The design of the gates is unique – underground cylindrical cement foundations and pedestal bases hold large, curved metal fan structures. These can be rotated, day or night, to control the water levels.

After viewing the structure, our barge made a wide u-turn starting back up the Thames passing the HMS Belfast then the Tower of London and Tower Bridge. To me, both the Tower and Bridge looked completely different from this vantage point than from the top of the double decker tour bus we were on a couple weeks before. From the waterside, I could clearly see Traitors' Gate where prisoners were brought into the Tower to await their trials and more than likely their beheading. As we passed under Tower Bridge housing merchant shops, I decided one day Ron and I must walk across it to explore its contents.

Next, we passed the County Hall, once the seat of London's government now renovated into a hotel. Following our agenda we moved past nearby Mansion House, the official residence of the Lord Mayor of London since the 1740's. Within minutes, I was able to make out the beautiful dome and spire of St. Paul's Cathedral. Proceeding further, we passed Somerset House, a civil service office building.

Next in view was Cleopatra's Needle, a misnomer since it had nothing to do with her. Carved with the heroic deeds of Thothmes, the needle was to be presented to England by the Egyptian Viceroy, Mohammed Ali, in 1819. Its amazing journey to England took many twists and turns. First, it was mislaid in Egypt, then lost at sea but was later salvaged, then finally reconstructed on the Thames sixty years later.

Within moments we passed the ships, the HMS's President, Chrysanthemum, and Wellington. At long last we sailed under Westminster Bridge with its magnificent view of Parliament, Big Ben, and Westminster Abbey. Parliament has withstood the ravages of time. After the 1834 fire destroyed the building, two architects were commissioned to design and rebuild it. Londoners wanted a new look from John Nash's gothic architecture. Sir Charles Barry designed the exterior while French architect Augustus Pugin created the interior. Further rebuilding had to be done after the May 10, 1941 Nazi bombings nearly destroyed it. It was totally rebuilt to Barry and Pugin's original designs. The mustard-yellow coloring of the exterior walls transforms the building into its elegant, royal look even on the most misty, rainy, overcast day.

Within minutes our barge made its final turn and passed in front of Lambreth Palace, the residence of the Archbishop of Canterbury. Further down we passed London County Hall where London's governmental officers go about their business of running this large, world capital city.

Next on our itinerary was The Royal Festival Hall where world-class orchestras perform because of its acoustical excellence; this hall is home to both the London Philharmonic and the London Symphony. Last on our agenda was the proposed site for the Shakespeare Globe Center.

About noon we returned to Miss London's berth where our coach and driver were waiting for us. After boarding our coach Ron and I talked about exploring London more fully now that we had seen her both by bus and by boat. Our next encounter with her would be on foot so we could fully experience her finery and beauty. We also decided before returning to the States we must drive into London proper at least once. We knew we would have to do it on an early Sunday morning when the city and its traffic would still be asleep. Maybe just at daybreak, not under the cloak of darkness, so we could see the road and roundabout signs. The London Centrum traffic is unforgiving of the novice driver who must literally take his or her life and limbs into harm's way.

As the coach moved swiftly back to the our drop-off point, Ron and I savored the beauty of all we had seen; we knew the city would have been even more dazzling in the sunshine rather than today's rain and bitter wind. When does the sunshine happen I wondered? Most of our first weeks here had been drizzly and overcast. I knew the sun must come out sometime but when? Even with the rain and cold, it was a wonderful day. One we would long remember.

10. A Red Letter Day

Some of my coffee morning friends as well as some of Ron's co-patriots had told us how absolutely marvelous the play "Miss Saigon" was. We decided to go and see it on a weeknight since tickets were cheaper then than on the weekend.

Theatre day arrived amid other goings on. When our previous tenants decided to vacate the premise, they didn't give a hoot about taking care of either garden area. What a mess! Broken branches, overgrown shrubs, and weeds lay everywhere. The garden needed some serious help. Just by accident, I found Charlie Payne, a retiree who loved gardening, and fit my pocketbook. I could not believe the work we did the first day he came. We worked most of the day making progress only in one section of the front garden. I realized that this project was going to require a lot of TLC before the front and back gardens were back into apple pie order.

The wood trellis on the front of the house was full of the most fragrant yellow and pink climbing roses, but they needed pruning. Weeds in the garden bed overwhelmed the shrubs and plants and needed to be pulled out. If that didn't happen soon, the life in them would be choked out. Once that was done, I would need to remulch the beds, then buy some new plants, roses, and shrubs to make the gardens look healthy and producing again. I had to find some way with my limited budget to finance this recreation of our gardens. Charlie said he had a nursery friend who would sell him the things we needed at cost. I hoped so.

After Charlie finished for the day, I posted some letters home. What amazed me was the postal service van emptied the red post box at the end of our little street four times a day. Another change for me: the British postal service only delivers mail; it never collects it from its customers and posts it for them. How strange.

Returning from dropping off my letters, I knew I had to hurry and get ready for this special evening. After Ron arrived home, we walked to the train station, purchased our tickets to Liverpool Street station, and rode into London. There we took a taxi to Theatre Royal on Drury Lane arriving in plenty of time for the play. Wanting to make it a special evening for us, Ron had decided to use our newly arrived plastic money and splurge on an after-play dinner at Michael Caine's Longnan's Brasserie off of Piccadilly. What a treat!!

"Miss Saigon" was outstanding. The acting, singing, and dancing were extraordinary. The sets moved flawlessly. Thin, wispy, gauze-colored hangings created the illusions of rooms. To add to the play's authenticity, set designers made use of an actual helicopter to give credibility to the evacuation of American soldiers from Vietnam. In another scene an authentic 1959 pink Cadillac, symbol of the American dream, was used by "The Engineer".

"The Engineer" was the conduit to all the play's themes. Five major themes intertwined within the play: the love story between Chris and Kim, the Engineer's hope of living the American dream, the plight of the American-Vietnamese children left behind by their American fathers, the feelings the American servicemen had about the Vietnam War, and the Vietnamese resentment towards the Americans when they left.

The Engineer hoped to use his nightclub and prostitutes to blackmail American servicemen (especially Chris and his Army buddies) into getting him an American visa so he could live the American dream.

Chris and Kim, the Engineer's favorite girl, fell in love which the Engineer hoped would work in his favor. He said to Chris, "You get me a visa and I will let you have Kim. You can't have her unless I get my visa." However, Chris had a problem. Although Chris loved Kim, he was already engaged to an American girl and felt obliged to honor that commitment.

The final heartrending scenes with Chris and Kim as he returns to his new life in the States, the life Kim and subsequently her son are forced to live after Chris' departure, the Engineer's acknowledgement that he will never get to live the American dream, Chris's return to Vietnam, Kim's sacrifice of herself to give her son a life in America with Chris, Chris' agony over Kim's suicide, and his first meeting with his son were gut-wrenching. I was glad I had a small packet of tissues in my purse, as I needed them.

After the theatre we hailed a taxi to Longnan's Brasserie. What a beautiful place. Cream and light peach walls were filled with pictures of film and theatre personalities adding to the restaurant's ambience. I longed to look at each one but with the after-theatre crowd it was impossible. I wished Michael Caine would have come in as he is one of my favorite character actors. The tables were covered with peach tablecloths, white napkins, silver dinnerware, and bone china place settings. Brass railings separated sections and tables.

Ron and I shared a mushroom pate and crackers, a chateaubriand with freshly steamed carrots, cauliflower, broccoli, and red potatoes. Topping off this incredible dinner we delved into a sinfully rich white chocolate mousse. What a fabulous evening - another evening not to be forgotten.

We took a taxi back to Liverpool Street Station then boarded the last train for home. After arriving in Shenfield we walked home in the moonlight. It was so romantic. When I looked at my watch, I could hardly believe it was 2:30 AM. Another short night of sleep before the reality of daylight and work dawned on us again.

11. Things Get Better

As days became weeks, we had found a home in our little parish, *St. Mary The Virgin Church*. Every time I came out of church and shook hands with Roderick Withnell, our curate and his wife. I will never forget the first time we attended there; it became a most embarrassing moment.

During the service I had become aware of all the children in the congregation especially two little girls who reminded me of Jennifer. It took all I had to keep my tears in check. When we were leaving the church, Ron and I stopped to say hello to the clergy as was our custom. All Roderick had to say was hello and I burst into tears. I was so embarrassed. He was concerned that I was so upset. He then said to Ron, "Homesick?" to which Ron said, "Yes." At that moment Roderick understood the feelings I was dealing with, as he and his wife had just moved away from their families in Scotland to take this position here. He suggested when we were fully moved in he would like to come and visit with us one evening. We were to call when we were ready. Both Ron and I could tell Roderick was a gentle, caring shepherd of his flock – we took to him immediately.

The following Wednesday evening he bicycled up to our place saying he needed the exercise to control a cholesterol problem. He wanted to know how we were settling into our new community as well as the church. We said things were slow but we were making progress.

We sat and talked a bit then I offered a pot of hot tea and some

American fig newtons I had brought with me. Baking was not my forte yet and I wasn't going to embarrass him or me with hockey puck cookies or sweets. The fig newtons were a hit, as he had never had such a "delicacy".

The evening was delightful. We "talked of many things" as the walrus said in *Alice in Wonderland*. We discussed the differences in the Anglican and Episcopalian liturgies, lay-reading procedures (both Ron and I were licensed in Michigan), and other church practices. Peter Mason, the rector, wanted a "high" church – all pomp and circumstance – while Roderick preferred a "low" church for its pure, simple services. He talked of his hope of having his own church one day. He and his wife, Allison, were excited about the expected arrival of their first child in two months.

He was interested in knowing about life in the United States, as there was only one other American at St. Mary's. We reminisced about our sons, Ron and John, their families, their jobs, and our feelings about England and Ron's job here. Being an avid environmentalist he was quite interested in the catalytic converters Ron was designing. With the pollution problem in Britain and Europe as grim as it was, Roderick was happy someone had come to change the emissions problem.

We discussed how Ron and I could become more involved in St. Mary's. Roderick said he would write the Bishop of Chelmsford to have us licensed here as Eucharistic ministers. In the Anglican Church, lay readers must take a two-year course on social care, ministrations, and religious services; this course equals what Episcopalian deacons have to do. The American lay reader's course lasts about four months and is much less intense.

We discussed how we could get more involved in the Shenfield community and asked his help in doing so. He was quite surprised at this request, as he had been told the Americans stick together and don't venture out of their own little conclave. I said, "What a shame! They miss the whole encounter of getting involved and living a new way of life as well as getting to know their British counterparts who had so much to offer them. Getting involved could only maximize their experience here, not diminish it. Why were they so reticent about becoming involved? I didn't understand it." We left that question unanswered.

Roderick talked glowingly of his seminary days at Cambridge along with his graduate studies there. He wanted to make a date to take Allison, Ron, and me on a guided tour of his illustrious alma mater. The problem was the incompatibility of his and Ron's schedules along with the impending birth of their first child; we decided to put off the trip for a while. That was OK for us – we could explore it on our own then get his guided tour later.

As the weeks moved on, my homesick feelings began to subside a bit. Ron and I spent weekends picnicking and sightseeing neighboring villages and areas. Before venturing out and about on Saturday or Sunday, we would stop at Rose's for a French stick (French baguette or bread) then the grocer for some sliced ham, cheese, the spirit shop for a bottle of wine, and the greengrocer for some fresh apples, grapes, pears, or nectarines.

Upon arriving in a village green, we would find a grassy place, place our trusty blanket at our feet, set out our basket of goodies, then bask in the sunshine while eating our sumptuous feast. These joyful days went a long way to healing some of the loneliness inside of me. I was beginning to feel good and warm inside again.

12. A Lesson Learned

Ron and I had been in our new home for a month when I noticed Jennifer and her family had returned from their holiday in southern France. I wanted to thank her for the beakers of hot tea on our moving-in day so I decided to bake some cupcakes for them. After the gift was finished, I knocked on her door and said, "I just wanted to thank you for your kindness. I know from experience growing boys like a snack when they come home from a long day at school and thought you might like these for them." She accepted them graciously.

I couldn't believe she remembered my name. She said she had told Graham we were Ron and Nancy and he had said to her, "Oh, the Reagans" and that was how she remembered us. It is interesting Graham had connected us with them. I told her we had gone to costume parties as them.

She asked me in for a cuppa. We discussed the British school system, grade levels, and curriculum, as we were both teachers. Their grade levels were so strange to me. She also explained that all sixteen-year-old students take GCSE exams; these tests measure each student's expertise in various study areas, then determine who is university material and who isn't. Students with low grades are directed into trade or technical schools or apprenticeships somewhere. Those with high marks continue in their areas of expertise for an additional two years. After that time those students take their "A level" exams (college entrance exams); those securing top grades will be assured placement in the most prestigious universities. Those with lesser grades enter lesser-known colleges. Many test takers put themselves under so much pressure to get top marks that they become emotionally distraught, even suicidal, waiting for their test results. The stress is extreme.

She told me how courageous she thought I was to come here – to pick up house, leave my family behind, come to a whole new world, then pick up and return home after the assignment was over. She said she couldn't imagine doing it.

Before long, I realized how late it had become. I also sensed I had overstayed my welcome so I quickly excused myself and made my exit.

A few days later, Graham trimmed their tall evergreen trees that bulged on both sides of our mutual front garden wall. Ron had offered to help him but Graham said it was his responsibility since they were his. He thanked Ron for the offer. Later, I took over a plate of homemade peanut butter fudge to thank him for all his hard work. Jenny accepted it but I realized I had overdone it with her. Graham was pleased but she wasn't. After that, she kept her distance. A lesson learned – I was a guest here and was not to go overboard with the natives.

13. Cambridge

After church one Sunday Ron and I decided to stop by Rose's for a French stick then stopped at the house for some cheddar and brie cheeses, some ham, lettuce, tomato slices, pickles, and a bottle of chardonnay. With these goodies in our picnic basket we drove through Brentwood on our way to the M-25.

As we drove down Brentwood's High Street (the same as Main Street USA), we passed all the shops closed due to Sunday closure laws. The public houses or pubs were overflowing with patrons waiting to have a pint or two of bitter or ale, chat with their neighbors, then leisurely walk home later in the afternoon. Homes and pubs serve as the only socializing places within a village where families, friends, and neighbors can congregate, play darts, or share a meal together. Sunday pub fare usually contains roast beef, roasted potatoes, peas, and sweets. Some patrons only want a Ploughman's lunch, a bag of crisps, and a pint or two.

On occasion when we ventured into one of the pubs the regulars knew we were not one of them. Some took it as an affront to them that we had invaded their private domain while in other pubs the regulars accepted us without note. One such pub was The Artichoke, a white stucco and mahogany timbered pub where we would go for dinner some evenings. Its British-American fare carvery (buffet table) made us feel more at home. The chef sliced portions of ham, roast beef, and roasted chicken for us while we served ourselves roasted potatoes, steamed broccoli, cauliflower, turnips, rutabagas, peas, and cabbage from large steaming Le Crouset casseroles. Their sweets included the British staples of bread pudding, apple pie slices topped with ice cream or an Anglais sauce (a rich custard sauce), trifles layered with wonderful fruit, rum drizzled sponge cake, and rich custard, as well as ice cream sundaes with chocolate, butterscotch, or strawberry toppings finished off with minced (chopped) nuts and real whipped cream, none of that aerosol stuff for them. The cost of all this was only £6.95 each (about $10.50).

As we continued our drive down High Street, we passed our usual petrol station (Esso) where a gallon of petrol ran approximately three dollars or more depending on the particular oil costs. What a difference from the prices at home! We would have to watch the amount of driving we did.

Following along, we made our way to the M-25. I was pleased Ron was driving as the roundabouts still scared me. I knew I would soon have to master them, as I had to take the British driving test. Anyone living in the country for more than a year had to take and pass that test. Since we would be in England for more than a year, we had to take and pass it also. I didn't look forward to taking it as I had heard how terrible it was. Many failed it and had to retake it until they passed.

Entering the M-25, we had to catch up with other drivers doing 80 plus miles per hour. Motorists drive quite fast (70 to 90 miles per hour). If the police catch anyone doing 100 miles per hour or more, his or her driver's license is revoked and given an astronomical fine of £1000 (at least $1500). This was not uncommon. English drivers have a propensity for speed. Cruising along the byways, we turned onto the M-1, a major motorway to the North. The countryside was so lush with green pastures filled with cows and sheep, as well as fields of beans and potatoes. Interestingly, hedgerows or stone fences, not wood and barbed wire fences mark off British property lines.

We turned on our cassette player listening either to the voice of Frank Sinatra, the saxophone tones of Kenny G, or the trumpet music of Chuck Mangione while riding along the thoroughfare. Some of the tunes we sang along with, hoping no one could hear us. Ron and I are great shower singers. Believe me – I know the truth.

Within an hour we were ready to turn off onto the two-lane road for Cambridge, a wonderful, tight-knit university town. Driving into the city center we saw tree-lined streets dotted with massive old Victorian homes – some had been turned into apartments for students and others into fraternities. Being a bright, warm Sunday, students, professors, and families were bicycling two by two while others were bowling on the green or walking their babies in baby carriages or pushchairs. All were enjoying the sunshine and a breath of fresh air from their daily or scholarly endeavors. I felt relaxed just watching them.

We drove along the University buildings until we found a parking place near an engaging pond. We took out our blanket and picnic basket filled with our lunch. I had even made some cookies. I felt such a sense of accomplishment baking again.

We sat and watched other couples with their families. A bit of nostalgia hit me but I refused to let it get the best of me. Afterwards, we walked around the pond then watched a game of bowling on the green, similar to American bowling except the bowler uses grass rather than a wood alley for his ball rolling. After watching them for a while, we began our walk into Cambridge's center. The city streets were lined with the usual British shops. The closer we got to the center; the more it felt like a university city. The bookshops presented window displays of textbooks, artist's sketchbooks and brushes, engineering equipment for creating architectural designs as well as the classic works of Byron,

Keats, Dickens, Austen, and Thackery. It made me want to be a part of university life again.

We walked through the byways and pathways to the various colleges within Cambridge. We were told Cambridge University's colleges were entities unto themselves although each taught special disciplines or specialties. When applying for admission to a particular college, the applicant must also apply and be accepted by the University as well as that particular college. Once accepted by both, he or she must pay admission and course fees to both the University and the respective college. I learned it cost nearly ten thousand pounds (fifteen thousand dollars) a year to attend there. I wanted to work on my PhD but it was financially impossible for me. I would need a grant or loan but with Ron's work and our citizenry I felt it would be an impossible feat. In addition, graduate students had to live within ten miles of their respective college and professors for at least one year. That was out of the question – Ron in Shenfield and me in an apartment in Cambridge. Oh, no. Way too expensive. I wondered if there was a college near me where I could take some courses. It wouldn't have the distinction of Cambridge but at least I could work on my degree. It would give me a goal. I needed to investigate this possibility.

As we walked further, we came to the River Cam where some students and tourists were "punting". What an amazing feat a punter or captain had to do to make that thing move and stay upright. First, he had to push a long pole into the water then lean on it so that the flat bed boat or glee would move along the river while the passengers could just sit, relax, bask in the sunshine, or have a glass of wine while enjoying the scenery. We watched various glees maneuvered by both novice and advanced punters. Some went perfectly straight while others skidded sideways making their punters frantically try to right it before an oncoming boat appeared. I overheard a young couple say glees, with novice drivers, sometimes capsize with everyone going in for a swim. One day, not that day, we would do that. Maybe we would engage a seasoned punter to take us for a ride.

As it was almost four, we decided to begin our drive home to avoid the peak Sunday traffic on the M1 and the M25 when the motorways had a tendency to become jammed up parking lots slowing things down to a snail's pace. We wanted to get home before dark as driving from unknown places at night left us uncomfortable since our journey home from Galleywood.

As we pulled off the M25 onto the A12 leading to Brentwood and home, the evening traffic was just beginning to build. I was glad we were almost home. We were home by half five just as the sun was going down for its nightly sleep. It had been a wonderful, relaxing day.

14. Our First Trip Abroad

One evening Ron came home and asked if I wanted to go to Brussels and Germany with him. Jonathan Craine, who worked for him, would be going with us as the two of them had meetings with Ron's catalyst suppliers in both places. Ron thought I could use a change of venue for a few days. "Yes, oh, yes," I said without a moment's hesitation. I was so excited.

The next two days were filled with washing, ironing, and packing. The night before we were to leave, I placed the suitcases near the front door to make it easier to load them into the car. That night when Ron came home, he looked at the suitcases and said, "How long do you think we're going to be away?" I explained that I didn't know whom we would be with and what we might do so I packed for all contingencies of dress and weather. I knew with more travel I would become more adept at light packing. This was only our first trip.

The following morning we left home at half five to pick up Jonathan at work and drive to Dover before our ferry to Calais, France was to load. The morning was picturesque, as the sun was just coming up to its full force. The closer we came to Dover, the more excited I became. Europe! France, Belgium, and Germany all lay ahead of us – new and uncharted places to encounter and explore.

Following the road signs and roundabouts into the harbor, we arrived at Stena Line's check-in building. We were an hour ahead of schedule and were able to rebook our crossing for the eight o'clock ferry instead of the nine.

Because we had American passports, Ron and I had to go through the non-European resident Immigration Office where our passports were examined, our numbers placed in their books as being out of the country, then each passport was stamped with their official stamp allowing us to return to England. Jonathan, a British subject, only had to wave his passport in front of the immigration personnel and move on.

With that accomplished Ron pulled our car into Lane 16 and we waited for the boarding procedure. At seven forty-five, the gangways were put into place. Row by row the cars moved, taking their places behind us in order to board the ferry. When the boarding steward motioned to us, Ron drove us into the ferry, The Spirit of Bruges. We circled around and around until we arrived in the ship's belly or lower automobile parking area. Once finding a parking spot, we locked the car and proceeded up the nearby stairwell to the open-air deck. Walking back to the stern, I looked back at Dover. What a magnificent sight! The white cliffs of Dover just as the picture postcards portrayed – stoic, marble-like stone ridges saying to the world, "We are here as a sign to any intruder that we will protect our homeland at all costs." We took multiple pictures of the three of us with the cliffs as the backdrop.

About 8 o'clock, still standing at the stern, we felt a jolt and tug then saw our ferry pull away from her berth. We were on our way! Seventy-five minutes and we would be in Calais. One of the things I love to do when traveling is people-watch. I learn so much about people by just watching them. The Spirit was full of British, French, German, and Dutch truckers along with the usual tourists, small family groups, and business people just like us. I prayed our Channel crossing would be smooth.

Since we had time to waste, we decided to go to the breakfast buffet for some fresh fruit, rolls, and coffee. As we sat and ate, I learned that Jonathan was born and raised in Uganda. He was a gentle, kind-hearted man with a fabulous sense of humor. While a child in Uganda he had learned Royal British English by listening to BBC Radio programming from London. His wife, Margaret, was a revered Ugandan obstetrician-gynecologist. She was in the process of taking the medical examinations to become certified to practice in England. They had two young sons, Peter (8) and Jon (6).

A few minutes before nine fifteen the captain came on the loud-speaker telling us "to man our vehicles" as we were coming into Calais. After the ship docked, we followed the lines of cars, lorries, and motorcycles to the surface and onto French immigration. Once again, Ron and my passports had to be stamped. "My," I thought, "before we return to the States, our passports will be filled with the stamps of all the marvelous places we have visited." I was duly impressed.

As we exited the port area, a new challenge presented itself. One we never thought about but should have. We were driving a British car with right side equipment on French roads where motorists used left side-driving equipment and drove on the right not left side of the road. As long as we were driving along we were all right but when Ron wanted to pass he could not see the oncoming cars as he was sitting on the opposite side of the car. Jonathan and I said we would act as his eyes. With our help he got the hang of it.

The sun was aglow as we drove through the industrial areas of Calais on our way to Brussels. Once out of Calais, we traveled through some quaint French villages. As we moved past their homes, I tried to visualize families sitting at their tables eating hot homemade croissants, butter, jams, fresh fruits, and coffee before beginning their workday. Driving along the ripe farmlands, I watched farmers harvest their crops then load them onto long bed wagons that would be pulled by a tractor to market. Women were hanging their newly washed shirts, trousers, and undergarments on clotheslines while others carried crocheted fishnet bags that would be filled with fresh fruit, vegetables, and possibly some fish or meat for their evening meals. Being curious or nosy, I wished I could be invited into one of their homes to watch how they went about their day keeping house and preparing their meals.

I loved seeing the reality of France instead of looking at French tour book pictures. It was all laid out in front of me in vivid color. Architecturally, French homes were different from English Tudor ones. The French homes had whitewashed stucco exteriors, the windows were accented with pastel shutters, and the long roofs were triangular in design with brown tiles or slate atop them. Their white churches glistened in the sunlight while their towering spires seemed to be reaching toward the heavens. Their gardens were not as smart or full as English ones, as they didn't seem to have the same interest in that venture.

The roads were in exceptional condition. No road work or detours were encountered. Somewhere between Lille and Brussels we stopped for a picnic. I had brought some ham and turkey sandwiches, crackers with sliced cheese, fresh fruit, and bottles of mineral water and Coca Cola.

Since Europe was now under one rule, we did not have any more border checks. Most of the checkpoints were boarded up or unmanned. Moving from country to country or nation to nation was much like driving from state to state in the States. The only thing I hated about this situation was not getting all those country entry and exit stamps in our passports as we traversed their countries. I was amazed that within one hour's time we had driven through three different countries, each with its own language and road signs. With the help of my trusty word translator and road sign indicator we moved through them without incident. It was mind boggling to me, but I knew with more trips to Europe these things would become commonplace to us.

Driving into metropolitan Brussels was a nightmare. I was now driving. Somehow I had veered off the outer ring road and ended up in one of the city's multi-cultural areas. After two hours of frantically driving up and down roads, we still didn't know where our hotel was. Street intersections had few if any traffic lights or directional signs. Some streets we had planned to use to get to our hotel were closed off because of a protest demonstration by international lorry drivers against the European Community. Cars, buses, and masses of bicycles were racing at top speed in every direction. I didn't know enough road rules to know who had the right of way or when to move so I did just as the other drivers did – I "closed my eyes" and went full speed ahead. It was so confusing as well as terrifying.

Finally, I stopped a policeman checking parking meters for violators. He said, "Go down this street, turn left, then another left and it will be on your right." No dice. I found him again and he gave me different instructions. Still no hotel. Finally, I spotted a female policeperson and asked her for directions. She said, "Turn left here, you can't miss it." She was right. We were never so happy to see anything, as our hotel. It had taken us four hours to drive to Brussels and another two to find our hotel. Oh, well, we got the scenic tour. Brussels is a city filled with many cultures and a bright future as the forthcoming mecca of world trade and finance.

The Royal Windsor had a typical British and international flavor much like the Grosvenor House in London but on a much smaller scale. After checking in and locating our room without the need of a map, we laid down for a rest after our long drive.

About half four we decided to explore the area as is our usual custom in a new place. We walked into the Grand Place, the heart of old Brussels. We sat down at one of its little sidewalk cafes. Using my limited ancient high school French I ordered cokes hoping my French wouldn't fail me. While waiting for our order, I listened to the conversations at nearby tables. I heard everything from the locally spoken French to German, Dutch, English, and possibly Flemish. When the waiter returned with our cokes, without a moment's thought, I asked him in French why the streets were full of madrigals and street festivities which reminded me of the New Orleans Mardi Gras with its stilted, costumed men and skeletal figures walking around in the crowds. He rattled back in French an explanation some of which I understood; some I didn't. What he told me was the French were celebrating their entry into Belgium many years ago. I was astounded I was able to understand parts of the history he was telling me.

After drinking our cokes and watching the tourists, we moved further into Grand Place. Its central square was cobbled making it difficult for trucks as well as pedestrians to get around. The buildings around the square were tall, slender and gothic in design. The top floors of each contained the offices of the guild that owned them while the sidewalk floors were leased out to various boutiques or beergartens. The little boutiques touted local laces and tapestries while the beergartens and outdoor cafes advertised the local beer, Jupilier along with their daily menu hopefully enticing customers inside. Since, it was Saturday, the flower merchants filled the Place with a wonderful montage of colors (pinks, purples, yellows, blues, and oranges) and the numerous types and shapes of hibiscus, palms, sculpted dwarf bonsai trees, salvia, ivies, azaleas, rhododendrons, heathers, and junipers. What a magnificent sight. Some had even brought spring bulbs to sell. We were told that on certain holidays or celebrations florists worked together to create a collage design to commemorate the event. Artists of various experience levels tried to get us to let them sketch us but we said, "No, maybe another time." They seemed disappointed. Why do I need a picture of myself or Ron; I know what we look like.

A few tour groups moved along the perimeter wall of guild buildings. Tour guides discussed the history of each. Each guild's roof displayed its own particular shield or symbol. With the sun shining brightly, the guild halls took on a magical golden luster creating the wonderful ambiance of days long gone.

Historically, Brussels began with its founding in 580 by St. Gary, Bishop of Cambria. It continued to develop until the eleventh century when walls had to be erected to protect it from invaders and marauders. Many of the guild buildings were not built until the eighteenth century.

That evening Ron and I were too tired to dress for dinner or even to go back into the Place to eat at one of the little outdoor cafes. Instead we called room service and ordered hamburgers with sliced tomatoes, lettuce leaves, pickle and onion slices, French fries, along with bottles of coke. The best beef we had had since leaving Michigan. The burgers were a bit rare but had a wonderful taste of home. British beef was rather tough and tasteless which was the reason we had became chicken and fish eaters since arriving in England. The other and more important reason was the European Community had banned British beef for containing Mad Cow Disease; something the Europeans didn't want and neither did we. European beef was disease free.

On Sunday we slept in then walked to a little sidewalk café. We ordered orange juice, croissants, and coffee. We had heard European coffee was quite strong; the rumor was correct. One small cup seemed like a turbo charge of caffeine and we were poised for the day. I couldn't believe breakfast cost us ten dollars. An expensive repast! The sun was shining and crowds of people walking around making it all worthwhile. The sun warmed our bodies so we jettisoned our sweaters.

As we sat eating, the square again began to fill up with a menagerie of blooming plants and flowers as well as bins made of wood or metal filled with spring bulbs ready for planting. I wanted to buy some but I thought I couldn't get them back through customs. One amazing sight was a chrysanthemum plant that had been pruned into a "tree". It had one bare main stem and its top was a ball of leaves and buds just ready to open and display its beauty for all the world to see. Extraordinary to say the least.

Most of the boutiques and shops were closed but we didn't care. We just wandered around the area wanting to take in every bit of splendor we could.

In the afternoon Ron and I became tourists, taking a three-hour bus tour of old and modern Brussels. The old part we had investigated on our own while trying to find our hotel the day before. The new part of the city consisted of modern buildings where international legal, financial, and business affairs took place. Brussels was definitely part of the present as well as the future of Europe.

On our tour we saw Leopold II's castle along with monuments to various religious, political, and military personages. One park displayed the atom symbol or obelisk from the Brussels World Fair. We passed St. Michael's Cathedral. I hurriedly wrote down all the landmarks so I could find my way back to see it inside. I knew it would be beautiful.

That evening we met up with some British friends, Nikki and Alex, who took us to a little French restaurant, "Benjamins", they frequented. We had six courses of fish and lamb, all the chef's specialties.

Why the royal treatment? Nikki and Alex were personal friends of Chef Homme; we felt special just being invited into his domain. After welcoming us, he said he would come out as each course was served to explain the ingredients and preparation process for each item. He would answer any of our questions as well. Would you believe I even tasted brains? What a culinary education! I don't know that I would ever eat brains again but I was game to try them once.

From the brains we sampled various fish dishes then braised lamb accompanied with a puff pastry filled with spinach and scalloped potatoes. Interesting combination, but good. For dessert Nikki and I split two desserts: one with phyllo leaves filled with coffee mousse and the other a thin slice of sponge cake topped with chocolate mousse then a Kahlua chocolate sauce. Ron and Alex finished off their meals with hot passion fruit soufflés with Anglais sauce poured into their centers.

After all that food, Chef Homme brought us a selection of his favorite pastry tidbits to have with coffee. Before we knew it, we had spent four hours enjoying some of the finest food we had ever eaten. Being able to talk openly with Chef Homme made the evening quite spectacular. As we left, we gave him a huge hug and thank you; he was most impressed. With that, I thought the special evening was over. But it wasn't. As we walked out of Benjamin's front doors, we walked into a star filled night. Magic was definitely in the air.

The next morning Ron, Jonathan, and I had a breakfast of fresh fruits, poached eggs, bacon, and toast, then they drove to *Comat Industries* for their meetings and a tour of their Belgium production facilities. I decided to busy myself with shopping. What else was I to do? I just love shopping. I also wanted to look for the statue of the Mannikin-Pis Nikki had referred to the evening before. I could hardly wait to get started on my own little tour of the area. Leaving the hotel, I strolled down the Rue du Chene past the various boutiques with their front windows beckoning me to come in and purchase some of their specialties: locally handmade lace tablecloths, blouses, little girls' baptismal gowns as well as wool tapestries.

Since it was only nine o'clock and European shops do not open until ten, I strolled around the Place studying the goods and shops I wanted to revisit and possibly make a purchase at. I hoped to purchase a lace tablecloth and napkin set for each of my girls and myself as a memento of Brussels. I knew if they were too pricey, I would have to forgo them. I hoped I could squeeze in a lace dress for Jennifer.

Walking along the alleyways I found all sorts of shops from bookstores to clothiers. Some merchandise looked too expensive for me even to look into their windows. I loved all the sleek, sophisticated European fashions made for all nature of moods and occasions. Black skirts and trousers topped off with bright colored blouses or blazers decorated with lace or sequins and some just plain and reserved, just ready for any sort of situation whether career, social, or evening. The bookshops displayed books for all age groups and reading preferences; some were published in foreign languages. I thought to buy Jennifer some children's stories in French but realized she might be just a bit too young yet. Now, thinking back I wish I had so she could have had exposure to another language. Isn't it true that hindsight is 20/20?

Walking back into the Place, I was overwhelmed by the grandeur of its tall, slender guild buildings along the square's perimeter. Although the guild buildings were built during the seventeen hundreds, the guilds existed for hundreds of years before. The only distinguishing differences between the guild buildings were their roofs. Each roof displayed the shield or statue of the guild inside its boughs. The buildings were gothic in design – quite ornate and gilded from gold extracted from

Belgium mines.

First built and used as a covered bread market, the King's House is now used as a national museum for earthenware and porcelain. Dark brown stucco with mahogany wood beams and archways make this medieval-looking building look like a dark and forbidding place. That day it was not open to the public so I put it on my list of things to do later. Across the courtyard was the town hall, the ancient seat of the government. Even with its lighter paints, woodwork, and archways, it too seemed ominous. Today, it is used as a concert hall and theater.

As I stood there admiring the scene, I watched the lorry drivers bounce around in their conveyances trying to navigate the square's cobbled area while making their beergarten, restaurant, and boutique deliveries. This area was not only difficult for them but also on us pedestrians.

That evening Colin Hanley from Comat came to take us to dinner about 6:30. Walking through the Place to our restaurant, the day's lingering sunshine accentuated the square's beauty. The night was young and our reservations weren't for a half hour, so we stopped at one of the beer cafes. The beergarten was designed and decorated in true Belgian decor from its wood floors to its side panels. Cream colored walls with brass sconces, wood tables with matching chairs or benches, and waitresses dressed in the traditional white blouses, black pinafores, and white starched aprons tightly drawn around their waists greeted us. We decided to try a glass of Stella Artoris beer. Quite crisp yet mellow to the palate. After finishing our liquid libation, we walked through the narrow alleys leading to the famous fish market area. Here its restaurants are known for their gastronomic delights; some even have five star Michelin chefs. In front of each restaurant were ice-ladened wooden carts filled with samples of their daily seafood offerings of mussels, oysters, clams, and lobsters along with the fresh catch of fish for the day. I understood why people called this area "a seafood lover's paradise".

Upon entering Colin's favorite restaurant, Victor's, we were escorted over the sawdust wood floors filled with tables covered with white and peach tablecloths topped with brass candlesticks. Brass chair railings and steps up or down divided one dining section from another. Waiters bustled around bringing patrons large buckets of steamed mussels and clams or platters of oysters. The marvelous smells emanating from the kitchen enticed and overwhelmed us. I wanted to be seated quickly so we could begin feasting on these delicacies.

Once the rest of Colin's co-workers arrived, he ordered bottles of a light, tingly Chardonnay. Not being wine connoisseurs, his choice was perfect for us. Our table ordered combinations of mussels, clams, and oysters along with large garden salads and hard French rolls. It was absolutely divine. Since our dinners were fairly light in calories, Colin said we needed to treat ourselves to Victor's luscious white mousse parfait. Oh, how sinfully rich it was. I felt badly as I could only eat a few bites of mine. I hated leaving it but I couldn't force another spoonful down. Being full from dinner we decided to walk to our hotel, about ten blocks away, hoping to walk off a few of the calories we had just enjoyed.

The following morning I slept in and had breakfast alone as the guys had already left for their meetings. I decided to find St. Michael's Cathedral. Using my Brussels's city map I walked up and down streets until I found myself in front of the church. After climbing up two long flights of steps I entered the church. The sun shone through its stained glass windows enhancing the already magnificent religious scenes and personages created in deeply hued panels of yellow, blue, red, green, and orange. Above each window was a rose window placed there to add dimension and contrast to the window below. Implanted in the four corners of the cathedral proper were mighty statues of the four apostles. On the far wall a deeply carved frieze depicted Christ carrying his cross to Calvary surrounded by his followers and the Roman soldiers.

To the right of the altar in an integral part of the nave was the marble sculpture of Mary in pain after Jesus' crucifixion much like the Pieta in St. Peter's Basilica in Rome. It was a breathtaking reminder of the agony of this moment. The altar and the lectern were carved in the baroque design.

While standing admiring the church, I could hear in the background the organist practicing his music for the next service. About that time visitors were told the next service would begin in fifteen minutes. Those wanting to attend mass should take a seat in one of the front pews while those not planning to attend should move out of the altar area. I moved away and took some pictures before leaving. I hoped the window ones would come out, as the windows were gorgeous.

After walking down the front steps, I turned for another look at the Cathedral. The sun was shining on it, illuminating its twin cream marble front towers, carved marble arches, and heavy wood doors. What perfection this was. I knew I had to bring Ron here.

On my way back to the hotel, I purchased three homemade lace tablecloth and napkin sets for the family and myself. Continuing on, just by accident, I found in his own little cubbie the statue known as the Mannequin de Pis. I had been searching for him since Nikki had told me of him. Two versions of this story are told. The first tells of a little boy and his father coming to Brussels to do some business. They became separated with each searching in vain for the other. Later the little boy has a call of nature and not being able to find a toilet anywhere stands against a stonewall relieving himself to the horror of his approaching father and onlookers. The other tale tells a very different story of this little boy. He had become separated from his father during an invasion of Brussels. Marauders had set little fires everywhere. The little boy wanting to help save the city used the only device at his disposal to douse the fires. Today, he remains standing in the place where this all took place still spraying the area down with his bodily fluids. He was hailed as a little hero, a symbol of courage and helpfulness in time of crisis.

Meandering down another side street I found a fairly large glass-enclosed mall or galleria with more expensive boutiques. High society types frequented here as they could purchase anything they wanted at whatever the cost and the shopkeepers were more than willing to take their money. One shop I did venture into was Neuhaus Chocolate. Ron loves chocolate so I thought I would treat him to some on our trip to Germany. Samples of this delicacy were placed in strategic places throughout the shop. I had no objection to trying some. Talk about heavenly. The richness of the chocolate to a non-chocolate person like myself caused me to rethink my position on eating chocolate. I splurged, buying six bars that were on sale for a total of $12 American.

As I approached the other entrance to this galleria, what did I see but a Hagen Daz shop. Since I had not eaten lunch yet, I decided to indulge and say this was lunch. The coffee ice cream was as luscious as ever. I definitely knew this would add to my waistline but I didn't care for the moment. I was enjoying myself too much. I rationalized that I had walked almost three hours so I thought this "little" indiscretion could be gotten away with. Right? Yes, right! Who was to know but me? No one – so I enjoyed every slurp and bite of it. Cone and all. Oh, what a treat.

Continuing my walk, I peered into different boutiques. At one point I came upon a corner antique shop displaying a conglomeration of Victorian jewelry as well as antique furniture, dolls, and lamps. As I looked around the shop, I caught sight of a porcelain college professor who reminded me of my idea of what a European professor would look like. One I would like to take a class from. He seemed flamboyant in his ruffled white shirt and black straight pants. Over this he wore a flowing lecturer's robe. On his head he wore his scrunched black miter. He held his Lex (textbook) in one hand while his other arm was flung in the air dramatizing the point he was making. His black hair and stern face lent to his posturing and demand for respect and admiration from his indentured students. I fell in love with him the moment I saw him but I refused to go inside to check his price as I yet had more family gifts to buy before indulging myself with him.

I returned to the hotel about three o'clock. I showered and lay down for a short nap as another supplier Redesigns, was taking Ron and me to dinner. Before I knew it, Ron was waking me asking me how my day was. I said, "I'll have to take you on a tour tomorrow after your meetings if you have some time before we leave for Germany."

We dressed, met Jonathan in the lobby waiting for Steve Ardleigh to pick us up. He took us to an upstairs tavern overlooking the Grand Place and introduced Ron and I to Jupiter beer – a light crisp beer. Ron, usually a non-beer person, and I both liked it. Jonathan who did not imbibe alcohol had orange juice. We then walked to the seafood market area. Once again I felt uneasy with all the icy displays of seafood and fish in front of the restaurants. I wondered, "Haven't they heard about botulism?"

The restaurant Steve frequented had a long queue (waiting line) in front of it so he took us to Les Fruites de Mer instead. The seafood was delicious but the service left a lot to be desired. From the escargots to the buckets of clams, shrimp, and mussels to the crepes suzettes, the meal was magnificent! After walking back to our hotel, we fell into bed exhausted after two rather late nights.

I awoke to another glorious morning. In the dining room I sat near a window so I could people-watch and plan where I would go and what I would see. After breakfast, I returned to the room to retrieve my sweater as the morning air was crisp. I knew I would be cold in only my white long sleeved blouse and blue jeans. I was excited to search out new things but sad as I knew we would be leaving this extraordinary city in the afternoon. I had fallen in love with Brussels.

Starting out I decided to go in the opposite direction from the day before. Once again, the bricked streets were narrow and wound around in what appeared to be a semi-circle design. As I progressed past unopened cafes and restaurants, I noticed new shops featuring women and men's clothing while others were filled with silk scarves, leather shoes and handbags, or books.

As I moved along, I came to a major thoroughfare. I was stunned by the change of venue. This street housed large department stores, small and large appliance stores, and bookstores including W. H. Smith, a British entity. I stopped in Smith's and purchased the new Tom Clancy book for Ron and a few magazines for myself. Furniture stores displayed all kinds of styles hoping someone would decorate his or her abode with their things. Classical or modern music wafted out of music shops hoping to entice people to come in and take them home.

As I stood on the street corner, I saw something that shocked me – a McDonald's restaurant and down the street to the left was of all things a Dunkin Donut shop. I marveled at finding Americana in Europe. I guess I never thought of either being international entities. I would not use either food shop that morning but decided to remember them for future reference.

As I returned to the hotel, I spotted the antique shop where my porcelain professor was. He was still there waiting for me to return for him. I looked longingly at him through the shop's window like a little girl pressing her nose against the window longing for that special piece of candy. I paced back and forth weighing whether to buy him or not. Wanting him so badly, I rationalized that this might be my only trip to Brussels, therefore, if I wanted him I had to buy him now. I walked in and asked the elderly proprietor what she wanted for him. She said thirty-five American. At that moment I broke a promise to myself that I would not use my new plastic money unless it was an emergency. I said that this was one of those shopping emergency moments. I told her to wrap him up in lots of paper so he would not break on the remainder of our trip. I was in seventh heaven. I could have danced my way to Germany.

After returning to the hotel, I finished repacking our suitcases. Ron and Jonathan packed them into our car, paid our hotel bill, and with that we were off to Germany. We stopped to fill up on petrol as in Germany a car out of gas incurs hefty fine and towing charges. Not something one wants to have happen to them. While they were doing that, I bought us some sandwiches and crisps in their deli shop.

The journey to Germany was fast due to the autobahns where speeds become whatever drivers want them to be. You have to keep your eyes on your rear and side mirrors all the time, especially when deciding to pass another car. A speck in a mirror (usually a Mercedes in Germany) one second could be passing you at upward of 120 miles per hour the next second. We were told, "Watch out for that speck because it could be on your bumper flashing its lights demanding you get over and let it through if you are in his passing lane."

The meandering Rhine River countryside was filled with stoic castles, little villages, and hillsides saturated with rows and rows of ripe grapes waiting to be harvested. Vineyards are planted in rows on the hillsides in order to protect them from winter's strong breezes, heavy rains, and snows that could break branches lessening the following year's harvest. During the spring, summer, and early fall the sunshine along with the gentle, misting rains can easily share their products with each row of grapes making them a rich bounty for each wine producer and connoisseur of the nectar.

About eight o'clock we arrived at our destination, The Dorint Hotel. The hotel was positioned on a hillside overlooking the city of Kaiserslauten. The hotel's white, tall, straight exterior walls made it look formidable. I almost shuddered as I entered. The interior walls were cream with portraits of German personages and landscapes strategically placed around. Accentuating the cream and black-specked marble floors were beautiful cream, navy, black, and burgundy Oriental rugs that lay on top of them. Burgundy leather wingback chairs and sofas further decorated the room. The ambience was warm and inviting.

After freshening up, Ron and I met up with Jonathan and some men from *Catalyst Design* who Ron and Jonathan had come to see in order to discuss their catalyst coating methods. Our dinner included steak, fries, garden salad, and for dessert a wonderful fresh fruit salad. After saying good night to the gentlemen, we turned in for a restful sleep after a full day of travel.

After breakfast the next morning, Ron checked with the hotel about arranging a late departure as I wanted to wash my hair, finish reading my Maeve Binchy book, *Light a Penny Candle*, and just relax before our side trip to Heidelberg, then home. The hotel registrar rather indignantly said, “That’s impossible as we have an engineers’ convention taking over the hotel and all the rooms need to be ready for them within two hours.” What was I to do? I thought. Ron and I returned to our room and repacked all our things.

We telephoned Jonathan saying we were on our way to the garage and he could join us there to put his bag into the boot. He amazed me as he carried only a small black satchel with all his clothes and toiletries. How he packed everything he needed for four days in it astounded me. Maybe as I get more proficient at the art of packing I could do that also. I would need more practice to perfect that art.

Since I couldn’t stay in our room, I decided to sit in the lobby and read or knit while the guys held their meetings. I kept my Binchy book and my knitting bag with me. I had begun knitting a sweater for each of my daughters-in-law for Christmas: a sky blue and black tweed for Laura and a fire engine red and black for Nancy. I was quite pleased with myself, as these were my first knitting ventures in more than ten years. If I got tired of reading or knitting, I could people watch. I love doing that.

About nine o’clock Uwe Gunderson from *Catalyst Design* came to pick up Ron and Jonathan. He asked me what I was going to do all day while they had their meetings. I said, “Read and knit.”

He said to me quite matter of factly, “Why don’t you go into Kaiserslauten?” I said to him, “Uwe, I don’t know your language or your city, and you want me to go in there?”

“You won’t have any problems and you will enjoy yourself,” he said.

I replied, “We’ll see,” meaning there was no way I was leaving the security of this hotel for his city.

An hour later, surrounded by a mass of engineers enveloping me with their cigarette and cigar smoke, I decided I had to go somewhere, anywhere, but where? I thought about doing what Uwe said. Maybe I would go into Kaiserslauten. I found a young waitress who spoke English. I asked her rather nonchalantly how I could get into the city. She told me I could to go out the front doors and take the Number 2 bus into the city center for 5 marks each way. Or, I could get a taxi into the city for 10 marks. Since Ron had left me fifty marks, I knew I had enough money for the taxi and a bite of lunch.

While depositing my book and knitting in the boot, I saw a taxi drive into the garage. A woman got out. Without thinking, I jumped into the taxi asking him to take me into a shopping area.

About seven minutes later the driver stopped me at what looked like a glorified open mall area with some boutiques and two or three department stores. I paid him his 10 marks then he gave me his taxi card and told me to phone him when I wanted to return. I said, "Thank you" and got out of his taxi.

Timidly, I walked around the area window-shopping in order to get my bearings. I needed to take time to calculate the German prices into English pounds so I would know the American equivalents. The German fashions were chic, Vogue or GQ magazine front cover clothes, and quite pricey. I had my eye on a three-piece black wool suit (blazer, skirt, and white linen sleeveless blouse underneath) until I converted the 245 marks into dollars. When I finished converting, I realized the suit would cost about 750 dollars. I quickly got rid of my desire for it.

Walking along a main walkway, I spotted a little boutique displaying a beautiful Kelly green long sleeve silk blouse that would be perfect for Laura for Christmas. I walked in and attempted to sound worldly – "English?" I said. The charming, well-dressed saleslady immediately went to the back of the shop returning with a young woman who spoke broken English. We managed to converge our two languages enough so I could purchase the gift with little problem. I left quite content and a bit more courageous about entering the next shop.

With my confidence up, I decided to tackle a large department store. After meandering through the jewelry counters and finding nothing I liked, I moved on to the perfumes, hats, then up the escalator to the kitchenware department. I love kitchen gadgets. I was shocked when one of the saleswomen asked if she could be of assistance. I said, "Thank you, no, I am just looking" much to her disdain and she shuffled off.

After finding nothing I wanted, I left the store deciding to move onto another shopping venue. I walked down one of the side streets finding a small glass and stationery shop. I went inside to see what they had to offer me in the way of gifts. Looking around I found various odd shaped vases hand painted with brightly colored flowers. In the center of their two-roomed shop the owners had placed dinnerware sets. Some sets were the basic or pastel sets while others contained hand painted animal, flower, or geometric motifs each hoping to catch the eye of the beholder.

A multitude of colors infiltrated silk hibiscus, roses, crocuses, tulips, gladiolus and irises along with accompanying varieties of silk greenery that had been strategically placed throughout the store in glass vases to accentuate their existence and presentation.

Along the wall in the second room I found delicate, clear-glass candlesticks fitted with different silk floral rings. I thought what an elegant gift for my girls (my daughters-in-law) as well as Kelly, Laura's middle sister, for her new apartment in Germany. I bought three sets and had the clerk wrap and secure them well in a heavy box so they wouldn't break. I said my thank you and left.

All of a sudden I looked at my watch and realized it was almost two o'clock. I had to be back to the hotel by three as Ron and Jonathan would be back from their meetings and we would be leaving thereafter. I stood on the sidewalk where my taxi driver had deposited me and waited for a taxi to buzz along. Since I had used plastic money for my two purchases, I had not created any coinage for the telephone therefore I couldn't call my trusty taxi driver to drive me to the hotel. I was stuck.

I waited for a taxi or even a number 2 bus to happen along. No such luck. What was I to do!! No one knew where I was and neither did I but I knew I had to get back to the hotel and quickly. I waited another five minutes with nothing but personal cars and motor scooters passing me. Time was moving and I was still there. I began feeling panic running through my veins. How would I get back? If I found a taxi and driver, would the driver understand English? What was I to do?

As the seconds and minutes raced on, I took hold of myself. I said, "You are an intelligent woman – what would any intelligent, rational woman do in this situation?" I thought I must find a main street as a number of the taxis and buses must run there. Regaining my composure I began walking toward what I thought must be a main street.

Eight city blocks later I saw what appeared to be a major intersection. Just as I was getting to the intersection, I happened to look to my left and saw a taxi stand with not one but five taxis waiting for customers. I raced to them and jumped into the first one. The startled driver looked at me. Fortunately, I remembered the name of our hotel. I said, "Dorint Hotel" but he didn't seem to understand me. My blood pressure skyrocketed as I calmly repeated, "Dorint Hotel." He looked at me and pronounced it a different way. With that, we were off maneuvering through the traffic. I prayed he would take me to the correct hotel.

About ten minutes later, I paid him his ten marks and got out of my chariot. Racing into the hotel I was thankful Ron had not returned. Quickly, I went into the garage, opened the car boot, put my purchases inside, and took out my knitting.

No more than ten minutes later, the guys entered the lobby where I was sitting. Uwe asked, "Did you have a nice day of knitting and reading?"

I said joyously, "Yes, thank you! I went into Kaiserslauten."

Ron's mouth must have dropped ten feet. I immediately noticed the anxiety that came onto Uwe's face when he realized I had taken his suggestion and what might have happened because of it.

Without giving him a second to respond I said to Uwe, "You have given me a marvelous gift. You gave me the courage to go into a city where I did not know the language, and I managed to get around, do what I wanted, and return to my starting point. I will no longer have that fear and I have you to thank for that."

He still looked ashen but seemed a bit relieved. I don't think he will ever make that suggestion to another client's wife. Maybe I was just lucky or brazen but it was the beginning of a new Nancy: one who could tour on her own, watch out for herself, and go where she wanted. What a marvelous feeling! I had Uwe to thank for that!

A half hour later Ron, Jonathan, and I followed Uwe to the Frankfort airport where Jonathan had an evening flight back to London as he had meetings the following morning. Ron and I had decided to take a couple days holiday before returning home. After dropping Jonathan off, Uwe directed us onto the correct road for Heidelberg. The sun was still shining but the temperature was dropping quickly.

Old Heidelberg lay inside the larger industrial part of Heidelberg. Our hotel, Zum Rutter, sat on a knoll underneath the fifteenth century Heidelberg Castle. Navigating the twisty brick streets and pedestrian walkways through the town to our hotel was tricky. Winding around we noticed international sidewalk shops and cafes selling coffee, wine, but mostly steins of beer. Each shop sold its own country's home products such as steins from Germany, lederhosen from Austria, and abacuses from China or Japan. I must look into this international fantasyland of shopping as soon as possible. I might just find a special gift for someone in the family.

We found our room on the top floor of this eleventh century edifice. Our bedroom furniture consisted of a heavy, dark planked mahogany bed, chest, dresser, and rocking chair; it reminded us of a medieval bedroom. From our bay window we could see the Church of the Holy Spirit founded by a monastic order living here around the eleventh century. Later it became Heidelberg University, one of Europe's finest universities. Nine Nobel Prize winners in chemistry, physics, and mathematics have taught and researched here.

After refreshing ourselves from the day and drive, we walked down the long wood and tapestry staircase to the ground level and the dining room. We asked the waiter what dinner selection he would recommend. He said emphatically, "By all means the wiener schnitzel with fried potatoes and onions." He was quite correct; the veal and vegetables complemented each other perfectly.

The next day Ron and I climbed the hillside to see the castle. What a hike! We both were so winded half way up we had to stop and catch our breath before continuing on. We realized we were definitely out of shape. The walk was worth it. The castle's old, darkening blonde masonry and brick castle was in good shape considering it had been ransacked many times due to invasions and civil war times. In addition, in 1763 all but the perimeter walls were damaged when the castle's powder magazine was struck by lightning causing an enveloping fire everywhere.

The castle had maintained its aura of dignity and charm. We walked around its perimeter walls to view the city and river below. The courtyard walkways were made of tile stones. In the center courtyard late fall flowers were readying themselves for their winter sleep. Walking around we thought what a formidable fortress this must have been with its turrets, walls, and hillside advantage. A few rooms were open for the public. They displayed the weaponry, family shields and coats of armor along with the flags of vanquished marauders as well as those of the victors. A history lesson in and of itself.

Walking back down the hill was easier but also trickier as we were moving at a much faster pace. Once at the bottom, we decided to have a sandwich and a pot of hot tea before checking out of the hotel. We wanted to drive onto Mainz and hoped to meet up with Laura's sister, Kelly, who was stationed at a nearby Army base.

Almost into Mainz we realized Kelly's apartment telephone number still sat on our desk at home. We stopped at a McDonalds close to the base where we talked to some soldiers about how we could contact her. Because I didn't know which company or work department she was in, they couldn't help us. Remembering numbers, whether telephone, street address, or credit card number, has never been a problem for me; it has been a real gift of mine. Ron just asks for whatever number then shakes his head when I come up with it correctly. Taking a minute, I sloshed around in my head and remembered her home number. After two unsuccessful tries and no answer box to leave a message on, we drove on to Mainz hoping later in the evening or following morning to get her.

Mainz was a real change for us. Our hotel room overlooked the local train, bus, and trolley station. I felt like we were in Poland or

Russia. As I looked into the faces of the people, they seemed so much older than their actual years. They hustled and bustled on foot or whatever conveyance needed to get to their appointed destinations, work or home. I noticed many beleaguered workers pedaling or carrying their meager baskets of food home for their evening meals. Watching them gave me a deep sense of their poverty and possible despair – most worked fifteen to eighteen hours, seven days a week just to make ends meet. The gloom of the impending rain only added to the sight I was viewing. No happiness or light seemed to transcend into this scene.

When I got up at half five the following morning, the day was just dawning for Ron and I while these workers were already dressed, hopefully fed with some kind of food, and hurrying on their way to work. To me, life for them seemed like an everyday struggle to survive. I was thankful I was not one of them.

Before checking out we tried Kelly again with no answer. Maybe she was out in the field on maneuvers or something. Whatever the reason, we couldn't stay to see her. What a shame.

At nine we checked out of our room, repacked the car, and headed for Bruges, Belgium, our last stop before home. The six-hour drive along the Rhine River revealed more hillside vineyards where harvesters gathered their fall grapes. With each kilometer we drove north, the colder the air became.

About three that afternoon we drove into Bruges. Within minutes we realized our map didn't show us how to get to our hotel, The Europa. Fifteen minutes later, we were quite lost and with no petrol station or tourist bureau in sight to give us directions. It seemed hopeless. Pulling into a side street, Ron and I scoured the map trying to find any street that would take us back to a main one.

All of a sudden a woman came bicycling past. Noticing our British car plates she recognized we were lost. She tapped on the window and said in Flemish, I think, "Are you lost?" I pointed to the name of our hotel; she tried to explain how to get there. Realizing we did not understand her, she motioned for us to stay right there. I thought she was going inside to get a sheet of paper to draw us a map. Instead, she got on her bike and motioned for us to follow her. Trusting her, we followed her across Bruges to The Europa. We tried to get her to have a pot of tea or something for her help; we even tried to pay her for her time but she refused. Our guardian angel and Good Samaritan all wrapped up in one wonderful woman on her bicycle. We have never forgotten her kindness to us. Good people do exist in this world of ours.

Wonderfully romantic, Bruges is a large village situated on canals and waterways with homes built right alongside them. The homes have gabled rooftops and intricate brickwork. The houses seem "glued" together. The reason for this: the less house and yard footage, the less property taxes to pay. Along the canals, overflowing trees, shrubs, and greenery transformed the homes as well as the city into a picturesque scene. It was a garden of beauty.

After unpacking our overnight duffel bag, we walked to the town center much like that of the Grand Place in Brussels. This square was filled with glued together two story buildings housing businesses on the street level and rental apartments on the upper level. Many of these buildings were not built until the eleventh or twelfth centuries. The exteriors were pastel in nature while the shutters were painted in complementing colors. Its cobbled center was filled with bicycles, pedestrians, and cars. Again, I watched as delivery trucks, pedestrians, and tourists tried to balance and navigate the stones with varying degrees of difficulty.

On the square's one side, seafood restaurants and sidewalk cafes proudly displayed their names on red, white, and black striped awnings. Outside each establishment waiters coaxed any potential customers to come in and have a drink or a bowl of their famous Belgium mussels. Intoxicating smells emanating from this area made Ron and I quite hungry. We declined all offers, as we wanted to visit more sights before stopping for dinner. We told the café barkers we would return later.

Walking along the tree-lined waterways hand in hand like other couples around us reminded us romance was in the air. We watched as horse drawn carriages meandered leisurely through the streets while the drivers recounted Bruges' history from medieval days to the present. They described the architecture and told of their culture and traditions.

As we strolled along, we spotted a rather large building with six or seven limousines parked in front of it. We stood wondering what occasion would bring such luxury here. Within moments our question was answered when a bride and groom alighted from the main double doors and got into the first limousine. From talking to a couple sitting on a nearby bench we learned the building was the town hall. In Europe all couples must be married in a civil service before their marriage is legal. Couples can have a religious service and reception but the town magistrate first must marry them. A European rule. We watched as the radiant, newly married couples came out and got into their limousines to go either to their religious ceremony or their receptions or both. I wished them much happiness in their futures.

We kept walking through the streets until we found some city tour boats. Ron said, "You want to take a tour?" I said, "Yes." Each flat-bottomed boat could seat up to twenty tourists. As we moved from the dock, I felt this is what it must be like to take a gondola ride in Venice.

It was a lovely canal trip. Benjamin, our guide, explained that Bruges in the medieval days was the gateway for trade and commerce in Northern Europe. Soon, he pointed out the convent built many years ago. The nuns served as nurses for the St. Michael Hospital founded in the eleventh century; today it serves as its museum. Benjamin said we must tour the hospital, as it had been a working hospital for centuries. Now it displays its original medical implements, logbooks, and pharmacy.

It was late afternoon when we concluded our tour. By then we were starved, as we had not eaten since breakfast. We looked at all the sidewalk cafes and picked one. We ordered two number three combinations on the menu – a fish soup, a bowl of mussels, and a dessert. Well, the bowls of soup would have been enough dinner for us. The soup, a combination of mussels, shrimp, and clams in a delicious tomato stock, was served in small soup tureens. It was filling to say the least. Our mussels came in a delicious wine and garlic sauce; we literally had to force them down as we had little to no room for them. To top the meal off, our waiter served us chocolate mousses. We ate a few bites not to offend them. By the time we waddled outside, we noticed the temperature had dropped significantly. We put our jackets on to keep us warm on our way back to the hotel.

After a continental breakfast the next morning, we set off to find St. Michael's Hospital. Down one of the side streets I caught a glimpse of its dome so we turned in that direction. Once there, we were just in time to take the next tour. We learned of the barbaric medical procedures and hospital care dispensed here over the years. Patients slept on short, cramped cots with little or no room to stretch their arms or legs. The surgical and optical instruments the doctors used were crude to say the least. I shuttered to think of them being used on me. I was glad I was alive today and not then. The local brewery also had tours with one just beginning. We thought of hopping in line but since it was almost noon and we had a five fifteen ferry to catch we decided to wait until our next trip here.

The drive to Dunkerque was uneventful. The weather was still sunny but cold now. We were glad we had brought our heavier Land's End jackets with us. We stopped to shop at the Hyperstore. Ron's British co-workers had told him that the prices were cheaper than in England and sold everything from "soup to nuts." They were right. This Hyperstore was three times the size of any all-purpose/discount store I had ever seen in the US. We bought some cases of cokes along with some salmon fillets, cheeses, and French breads. I could not buy any of their wide frozen food items as I didn't have a freezer bag with me. I needed to put that on my packing list for our next trip.

We made the ferry on time and arrived in Dover at half six. Returning in the dark, we could not see the White Cliffs of Dover. We maneuvered our way into the non-EC line for immigration and passport control. Once through we attempted to get into the customs line but with the glut of cars and lorries, our little blue Sierra couldn't get us into that lane so we had to bypass it. Oh, well, that's how it goes. We would have been okay anyway as we didn't have anything to declare.

The night had become quite cold and rainy. As we entered Brentwood, we realized that again we hadn't eaten anything since breakfast and were hungry. We decided to break down and try a delivery from the new pizza shop in Brentwood – Pizza Hut. When we got home while Ron was unpacking the car, I telephoned in an order for a large pepperoni. The pizza, interestingly enough, was delivered by a young man on a motorized bicycle. I couldn't believe it tasted like the Pizza Hut at home. We were thrilled.

We were so excited about our trip and finding a good pizza place that that was all we could talk about. It was late before sleep came upon us.

15. Long Days with Nothing to Do

With our adventures over for a while, I settled back into my life in Shenfield. I was finding the days were getting shorter and shorter and the nights were getting longer and longer. With the change in the seasons, my mood became more somber. I had trouble dealing with too little sunshine as well as too much unused time on my hands.

My days were filled with fixing breakfast and packing Ron's lunch, making our bed, and doing routine dusting and cleaning. A couple days a week just to pass the time I washed clothes as each wash and dry cycle took an hour. This took up the better part of the morning. I spent time tending to my flower gardens and planting winter flowers.

As my frustration and moodiness rose, I tried to find other things outside of the house to do. Oh, I could hop on the train and go into London but I had done all the touristy things. Now, what was I to do. I needed more to do. Since I could not work or teach, under Ron's work permit, I was stuck. I had to find something to do with my days, anything would do. We had been told in orientation that an assignment was harder on professional women and the women without children as they had nothing to do. Women with children had their children and schedules to manage. The orientation leader nailed it on the head. I began reading and going to more wives' activities but fulfillment didn't come along with them. They were just "filling in time" for me. There was nothing substantial for me to do to make me feel good inside.

Men have it easier as they are stimulated by their business friendships and contacts. Many are overworked by their jobs and European business travel. Wives don't have that luxury. *Comco* frowns upon wives accompanying their husbands on these trips.

As the days grew shorter and the nights grew longer, my mood deepened. When the "girls" told me that within the month "daylight" would only come from half eight or nine in the morning to half two or three in the afternoon, I felt my world closing in on me. I began traveling into London more for shopping and plays when I could afford them. I had to do something to brighten my mood and activities.

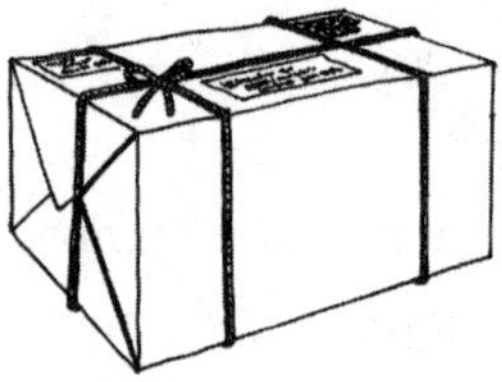

16. A Suspect Package

Bob Steele, one of Ron's co-workers from the States, and his wife, Molly, were on assignment for the company and living in Aachen, Germany. He had meetings with Ron and some other departments and they both were coming for a few days. The four of us planned to do dinner and a play on their second night in town. As I had never met either of them, I was edgy.

Molly phoned the night they arrived in Brentwood and we decided to meet at the train station there as it was near her hotel. Since she knew London like the back of her hand, she promised to give me the royal tour of London with all its shopping opportunities. She accompanied Bob to England this time, as it was a driving trip. We decided to go into London, do some shopping, have some lunch, and then take in a matinee. What a treat. Something fun for me.

The next morning I took the train into Brentwood where I met her. She was lovely. We took the train into Liverpool Street Station then made our way through the maze of the subway until we made it to Oxford Circus and its shopping area. Wanting to get a wool shawl for her landlady, we went to John Lewis first. We worked our way through the perfume and handbag sections until we arrived at the scarves and shawls. Hanging from large chrome hangers was a vast array of various sized solid black, royal blue, hunter green, hot pink and purple scarves along with a myriad of plaid combinations and floral prints. Molly perused them all until she found just the right one – a bright purple and fuchsia plaid. We moved on to the fabric department where she looked for some yellow material to create a dress for her daughter's upcoming spring wedding. She styled most of her own clothes. What talent. Unfortunately, she didn't find anything she liked.

After her purchases, we moved on to Debenhams, another department store, then Richards, a lovely women's clothing and shoe shop. I found myself the perfect navy broad-brimmed hat for keeping my head warm in the blustery English winds.

We popped onto the underground heading for Piccadilly. Being lunchtime she took me to her favorite deli and sandwich shop, Ponti's. The queque (line) was long but she said it was worth the wait. We gave our order which was shouted to the next available sandwich creator, just like one of the New York delis. Within moments we had our ham and cheese sandwiches, packets of crisps, and cokes.

Finding a table with two chairs became our next task since the deli was full of lunchtime customers. We saw two chairs together under a long shelf on the back wall and gave chase to them before someone else might spot them as well.

We leisurely ate our sandwiches while getting acquainted. She told me about her months in Germany. Aachen did not have an international women's group which made it hard for her to make friends or traveling companions. Since she had passed her German driving test, she was free to travel anywhere her little car could take her. She had taken train trips into neighboring countries while Bob was traveling elsewhere on business. I did not feel brave enough to travel in Europe on my own yet. Molly's parents had traveled extensively with her while she was growing up so she did not share my fear of it. I envied her. Living in Europe made travel easier for her as she didn't have to ferry across the Channel just to get to Europe. She could train or drive anywhere she wanted.

After lunch we walked to Leicester Square where we purchased two half-price tickets for the afternoon performance of "The Passionate Husband". At the same time we bought four half-priced tickets for the evening performance of "It Runs in the Family". From there we walked through the side streets filled with outdoor cafes and expensive boutiques on our way to the theatre. At this time of day many cafes were filled inside as well as outside with coffee aficionados.

We arrived at the theatre about twenty minutes before the performance was to begin so we took a moment to refresh ourselves in the ladies room. I overheard two women critiquing the play as being quite good.

With the help of an usher we found our seats; two end seats on row two, stage left. The seats would have been great if they had been a little further back from the stage, as we could have seen more. Just before the play began, it was announced the female lead had taken sick and another actress, not her understudy, would stand in for her. That had an ominous ring to it.

My fears were not without reality. The replacement was the understudy for another actress and did not know the lead's lines. I am sure she knew the lines of her actress but definitely not the lead. What a mess! Routinely, she asked for offstage cues or lines to be given to her. This was disconcerting for the actors who had to wait for her to get her lines before moving on. Their rhythm broke down as lines were dogged with impatience. The audience waited frustrated and impatient with this situation. By intermission I was ready for a nice diversion to this terrible situation. That diversion was not what I expected it to be.

As the steel safety wall lowered from the stage's ceiling and the stage drapes closed ending Act One, the theatre manager quickly ascended the stage. He told us not to leave the room, as there was a suspect package in front of the theatre; the bomb squad had been called and was on their way. A tremor of fear struck me. The IRA was up to no good once again.

Ron and I had only been in England for three months before the IRA bombings came into full view. Their bombings were intended to disrupt the daily business of London and hopefully make England listen to their demands for independence. They didn't intend to hurt or kill anyone in their bombings. To make sure of that, an hour or so before one of their devices would go off, they would call the building or area that was their target to tell them of the bomb's timing. This would give time for the occupants to vacate the premise. That didn't do anything for my sense of security. The reality this might happen while Ron and/or I would be in London sent chills up and down my spine. Now, standing inside the theatre the danger of what might happen became acutely evident not only to me but to the rest of the audience.

About fifteen minutes later, the manager returned to the stage saying the bomb disposal squad had removed the package. We could now move around the building at will; the play would begin again in fifteen minutes. Relief spread all over my body. The remainder of the play was just a continuation of missed or slaughtered lines. Toward the end of the play, all Molly and I wanted was for the play to be over so we could leave.

We had two hours before the guys would meet us for dinner so she decided to show me her favorite store, Fortnum and Mason. It did not have the name and reputation of Harrods but was an old establishment of tradition and style. As we walked through their front double doors, we were greeted by their tea, chocolate, and food sections, each in itself a dynasty. Since I loved tea, I checked that section first. Teas, bagged and loose, came from all over the world, China, India, and other exotic destinations. I purchased some of Fortnum and Mason's breakfast tea as well as a box of Queen Anne's tea, said to be a bit milder and would be good for my afternoon readings.

The store's meat and deli sections full of game, beef, pork, chickens, pigeons (a delicacy), sliced meats and cheeses as well as blocks of cheddars and Stilton amazed me. Behind that section was one devoted to imported goods such as Betty Crocker cake and frosting mixes, Kellogg cereals, tins (cans) of various vegetables, bottles of maple and blueberry syrups, boxes of Oreos and Keebler chocolate chips cookies, and condiments such as ketchup, mustard, and real pickle relish. I was astounded not only that they were there but their price tags. The Oreos were £3.75 ($8) a package; cake and icing mixes were £2.50 and £3 ($5 and $6) each. I wouldn't pay those prices even if I wanted them. I decided to have the "kids" bring those things over when they would come for a visit.

Molly and I walked upstairs and looked at the women's and men's clothing departments. Gorgeous,but price tags were two to three times that in America. They were outside my budget and I did not plan to buy anything from here.

At six we waited outside Piccadilly Station for the men to join us. After twenty minutes, we went inside to find out what the delay was – another suspect package in one of the stations along their train line. Now, I was really uneasy. An IRA bomb placed and detonated within a tube station would wreak havoc killing many passengers and employees working and traveling the Tube. The afternoon package and now this unnerved me even more. About a half hour later the guys stepped off their train and into our waiting and anxious arms.

The four of us walked into Chiquita's Mexican restaurant in nearby

Leicester Square. The eatery was busy so we waited for our table in the upstairs bar. A strawberry margarita later the maitre d' called our names and we followed him downstairs. We told our waitress we had theatre tickets. She said she would try to hurry the kitchen staff for us. We ordered a variety of tacos, burritos, enchiladas, and nachos. It was like homemade spicy Mexican with lots of cheese, chilies, and sauces.

Since we only had forty-five minutes before curtain time, we ate our meals quickly. Once outside, we hailed one of London's finest black taxis to take us to the theatre. The driver buzzed through the back streets to The Old Vic Theatre just in time for the opening scene. "It Runs in the Family" was a hilarious comedy about a physician-father who attempted to cover-up his numerous affairs with the hospital nurses from his family, and especially from his son. The hilarious thing was the son was following in his father's footsteps hoping to cover his tracks as well. The extent each went to conceal his activities left our sides sore from all the laughing we did. Even at one point the actors began laughing when another actor flubbed his lines making the situation even more hilarious.

After the show, we boarded a Circle Line train to take us to Liverpool Street station. Once there, we had a wait for our train home to arrive so we purchased some warm raisin scones and coffee to take with us for our thirty-five minute journey. All the way home we chuckled about the play's amusing plot and the antics used. The item on our minds we didn't want to think or talk about was the IRA's flexing its defiant muscles. This made me think twice about going into London for the day to shop or even take in a matinee when Ron was out of town and I had time on my hands. I knew the IRA could place a package anywhere I went (a shopping area or even the underground) and I didn't like that thought. I knew from time to time a station would be shut down for a security alert when a package or parcel was found without an owner. The bomb squad would be called, the station checked for any other packages, then the package would be taken away. After an all clear had been raised, the station would reopen for business.

One evening I said something to Ron's friend Arthur Gilmore about my fear and he said, "Nancy, if the IRA keeps you from going into London, they have won. They are attempting to send fear into people so they don't go into London which will hurt the economy and thereby the British government. Don't let them scare you off." At that moment I resolved I wouldn't let them scare me anymore; I had to believe Arthur was right. The IRA hadn't hurt anyone yet. I had to believe they didn't want to take lives just to send their message of defiance. I resolved to be self-confident but vigilant about what and who was around me and what people were carrying. Prime Minister John Majors as well as the police kept saying, "Be vigilant and report anything out of the ordinary" which I determined to do. An uneasy state of affairs but one I would have to learn to live with.

17. Normandy

Ron had always talked about wanting to go to the allies' invasion beaches at Normandy, France. As long as I have known him, he has been a World War II buff. His Uncle Chester arrived on Omaha's beachhead on his eighteenth birthday. Although Ron and his uncle have always been close, Chester would not talk about those agonizing days with Ron or anyone. Ron's desire to see what Chester and the other soldiers had lived through had always been on Ron's mind.

For some unknown reason since we came to England, I had been designated the Hurley travel agent. One evening Ron told me he had some vacation days he had to use up, I decided to go into Brentwood and check the possibility of going to Normandy the first week in November. I talked with Lisa, a travel agent with the Lunn Polly Travel Shop, about my idea or to get ideas for something else. She was shocked we wanted to go off-season especially since the weather had turned cold and wet. I explained Ron had vacation days he had to use or lose them. The destination we wanted was Normandy.

Lisa looked through a number of travel brochures before finding a "drive yourself" tour. We would take the ferry from Newhaven, England to Dieppe, France. The first two nights we would stay in a French farmhouse bed and breakfast and the other two nights in a renovated French chateau near St. Mere Eglise. Since we wanted to go within two weeks, she would have to call each place personally and find out if they would be open or closed at that time. She told me she might have trouble contacting them but give her a couple of days. She would get back to me as soon as possible but she told me not to get my hopes up. A few days later Lisa called saying the trip was all arranged. Ron would be ecstatic and I was pleased.

Our trip began on a cold, rainy, and windy November morning. It did not seem like a day even for ducks to be on the water. I was uneasy but undaunted. After two hours of bracing the car against the winds and rain, we arrived in Newhaven about half eight. Checking in with Stella Lines, the ferry company we were using, we learned the ferry from Dieppe had not come in – we would be delayed at least until noon because of the weather. That sounded ominous, especially since the wind and rain had not abated and seemed to be getting worse. The ticket steward suggested we eat little for breakfast, as the crossing might be a bit rough. We decided on toast, butter, marmalade, and beakers of hot tea.

About eleven our overdue ferry came in. Within an hour all the cars had been buckled into their deck parking slots and the passengers had taken their seats. Fifteen minutes later the captain came over the loudspeaker and said he would "give it a go" to get out of the harbor. A harbinger of doom! All I wanted to do was pick up our car and get off that "bloody" ship as quickly as possible. Since that wasn't possible, unless the captain couldn't get out of the harbor, I'd have to make the best of it until the ferry arrived in Dieppe.

Rough wasn't the word. I felt like I was riding a bucking bronco. I kept waiting for the mayhem to subside. Seeing that wasn't going to happen anytime soon, I decided to go to my favorite place, the duty-free shop. Ron said he would come with me.

As we started our trek, the ship heaved. We clung onto the wall railings for dear life as we made our way through the corridors and stairwells hoping soon to find the top floor and duty-free. Steadily we moved forward until I spied my goal. We were finally there.

Upon reaching the shop, I should have taken notice the cashiers were buckled into their seats because of the ship's pitching. I was oblivious, as my only thought was to shop. Without thinking I let go of the rail's security to cross the hallway to get to the shop just as the ship heaved once more sending me flying through space. I grabbed onto a jewelry carousel thinking it was bolted to the floor. To my great surprise and shock it wasn't. There I was trying to upright myself holding onto this unattached column while trying to keep the earrings and other jewelry from falling off and making a mighty mess. I must have looked like some Laurel and Hardy comic scene. Everyone including the cashiers tried not to laugh at my comical distress but couldn't help themselves. After I got things stabilized and let go, I felt the warmth of my embarrassment burning in my cheeks. Even I couldn't help laughing at myself when I realized how funny I must have looked to one and all. I knew this would be a story I would one day tell my grandchildren.

We arrived in Dieppe six hours late. Now, what do we do? The farmhouse bed and breakfast expected us early afternoon. Night had settled in. The rushing winds and rain were still with us. We had no directions to the farmhouse, as we were to pick them up at the Dieppe port offices of Stella Lines when we arrived. They were now closed for the evening.

Ron walked to one of the port office personnel and asked her to call our hosts and explain our lateness and get directions to their farmhouse for us. The couple gave her the information we needed. They also said they would be away for the evening. Our room was on the last part of the cottage section to the side of the farmhouse. They would leave the door unlocked and a light on so we could find it.

An hour into our drive, we were about to add a new wrinkle to our encounter with France. We came to a tollbooth. I looked at Ron and said, "What are we going to do, we don't have any French francs yet?" We had not been able to exchange monies at the port as the booths were closed for the night. Ron kept telling the official that we didn't have any francs. He kept asking for his ten francs so we handed him a five-pound note. Seeing we meant business, he waved us on. What a relief!

The last hour of our drive was on rural roads in pitch-black darkness. It was like driving in pureed black bean soup. We meandered in and out of villages. We looked into lighted houses longing for the warmth of family, food, and hearth. Oh, if only we could find ours. At times driving along we could not see the few and far between road signs for the rains.

Finally, we found Pont L'Eveque, the village where we were to make a hard left onto a small farm road leading to the farm. We inched our way past the first three farmhouses on the left side then turned down the next road hoping to find our farmhouse. We were a bit frightened as the dirt road was hard to follow. As we pulled up to the farmhouse, we could see a light lit in the end room past the farmhouse. Ron said, "I hope this is right. I would hate to face an angry farmer armed with a sharp pitchfork or a loaded rifle in the middle of the night."

As we reached "our" door, we found it unlocked. The room was frigid, as the heating in this section had been turned off for the winter. The cement floor was ice cold. The room was inviting with its rather large bed filled with a number of feather comforters topped with a beautiful burgundy and cream diamond patterned quilt. Two rose embroidered chairs were on each side of the bed. The bath was furnished with a large Victorian step tub, toilet, and wash area with a large antique hand-painted rose pitcher and accompanying bowl. On the far wall were a white wicker table and two matching chairs as well as an armoire. On the table we found two mugs and a thermos of hot coffee. What a wonderful welcome! We felt this must be the right place.

We wanted a bath to revive us but decided against it due to the chill in the room. Next, we realized how hungry we were, as we had not eaten anything since our toast and tea in Newhaven. Fortunately, I had packed our small Coleman ice chest with some leftovers from the previous night's dinner. We dined on Italian meatballs, hard rolls, fresh apples and bananas, and healthy slices of cherry pie and hot coffee. What a feast!

We slept soundly until the morning sunlight came streaming in through our window and woke us. After quickly dressing in the cold atmosphere, we went outside which felt much warmer, especially standing in the sunshine. The sun was burning off the hovering morning fog and drying the dew from the grass and driveway. What an eerie picture it made of the farmhouse and its surroundings. The farmhouse was a blended mix of French and English styles. The roof was tiled. The exterior walls were white stucco with upright mahogany Tudor beams and elongated double pane windows.

As we walked to our car, we saw our hostess. She was a slender woman of 65 years, wearing a simple gray dress with a black pinafore on top, and she had twisted her long gray hair into a long rope that cascaded down her back. Once she noticed us; she beckoned for us to come into her dining room – a small room with modest tables and chairs. Our table was covered with a white linen tablecloth and napkins. Her eyes sparkled as she spoke to us in her broken English although she broke into her French when she spoke too quickly. Madame Le Corneur gave us no menu so we waited to see what would come. Using my broken French I discussed with her the sun warming up the crisp morning and evaporating the fog. I thanked her for the thermos full of hot coffee. Pleased with my complement she felt more at ease with us. Madame was a delightful woman although her elder husband was aloof. I presumed he could not speak English and our French was not up to par so he stayed away. Breakfast was something to behold. The travel brochure said we would be treated like royalty and so we were. She served us freshly squeezed orange juice, poached eggs, crisp bacon slices, triangles of buttered toast, her homemade jams, and huge wedges of rich chocolate cake and lemon pie. I couldn't believe my eyes. We couldn't eat everything. We ate the eggs, bacon, toast and jams while drinking our juice and coffee. I felt she was a bit upset with us for leaving so much untouched but the breakfast was way too large for us. Our usual breakfast consisted of hot or cold cereal, orange juice, and coffee or tea or maybe a poached egg, toast, juice, and coffee. She had placed before us a feast for eight people or more. Afterwards she showed us a picture of her beloved granddaughter, Thresa; Madame was a very proud grandmama.

After breakfast the bright sunshine made us feel warm. We felt all was right in God's heaven on earth as we drove through the beautiful French countryside with its flowing pastures and grazing cows, inviting farmhouses and residences hugging their hillsides, encasing stone fences defining property lines, and bicycling singles, pairs, and groups. A moment of reality came when we saw the first German gun turrets and pillboxes that were used against the Allied forces; most of them were now covered over with grass. The area looked so peaceful, as if the ravages of war had never touched it. Carl Sandburg once wrote about green grass covering over the horrors of war; his poem described this phenomenon we were seeing right outside our car windows. I didn't have any sense of the actual traumas that happened here so many years ago.

As we drove to LeMans, Alencon, and Caen, we realized we needed to exchange some of our English pounds for French francs. Stopping at a large bank in Caen, Ron made the necessary exchanges. Without the francs we wouldn't be able to buy petrol and food since few places took the yellow and red Master Card or the silver and blue Visa cards.

We had planned to see the beautiful Caen tapestries on our first day here but found the shops closed so we decided to drive into the resort and art areas of Trouville and Honfleur. By the time we arrived in Trouville, the sky had clouded over and the wind had picked up making us shiver from the cold. Walking into the Trouville Tourist Office, I asked for pamphlets about the area. Following one map we walked through the winding side streets and alleyways looking for open art shops but all were closed for the season. Instead of displaying prints or paintings in shop fronts, the proprietors had large posters announcing the following year's calendar of events. We got back in our car and moved on.

Honfleur was a quaint, picturesque fishing village with a marina filled with some yachts but mainly fishing boats. The ship buildings nearby were grey weather-beaten structures; fishing nets, ropes, and tackle held themselves on the building walls by nails. Walking through the streets, friendly faces and nods from the villagers surprised us making us feel good to be there. Since it was off-season, no restaurants were open so we decided to return to our farmhouse room.

Although I didn't know it, I was about to encounter a new experience in the French way. Before the long drive back to our room I wanted to find a toilet. I found one open in the nearby park marina. It was quite unlike any I had ever encountered before! As I entered, I saw open holes in the cement floor. No stalls for privacy or no toilet paper. I was shocked to say the least. I needed to go but had difficulty getting my mindset engaged to do what I needed to do. I knew I couldn't wait for our room so I said to myself, "Well, here goes." Another first for me.

On our way back we realized how late it was getting and how hungry we were. Working our way back to Pont L'Eveque, we spotted a little village restaurant nestled between two shops; it looked inviting. To our surprise it was open; probably because the villagers frequented it year round. As we entered, we found the dining room warmed by a blazing fire in the fireplace. The tables were covered with white linen tablecloths and erect, fanned napkins. The staff welcomed us warmly. Looking at the menu I managed to order us a fish soup and a garden salad. The soup with its various whitefish, shrimp, and clams, finely chopped vegetables simmered in a white wine broth was magnificent. From my first spoonful, I savored every taste hoping I could recreate this wonderful dish. The salad needed a bit of seasoning for me but the soup certainly made up for the salad.

Saying goodbye to the staff, we jumped into our car. Our return to our room was easy as it hadn't turned completely dark so we could see and follow the roads.

The next morning Madame Le Corneur served us fresh orange juice, coddled eggs, croissants, and her homemade butter and jams. She asked if we wanted tea or coffee. I said tea while Ron said coffee. Within minutes she was pouring the hot liquids in our cups. We thanked her for her thoughtfulness about a smaller breakfast; she beamed.

After saying "au revoir" to her and her husband, we began our drive to the beach areas. Within an hour my tumultuous day was about to begin. Driving along we saw road signs pointing out the roads and the number of kilometers to Sword, Juno, and Gold beaches. Moving along the coastline we finally got in touch with what the Allied forces faced on that morning of June 6, 1944. It must have been an indescribable torment for all those boys and men to face. The Sword beachhead was a barren landing area now but some of its barbed wire battlements still stood intact, rusted but still ready for another war.

We stopped in Arromaches to tour its war museum. The memorabilia returned us to the feelings and horrors of that day so many years ago. The uniforms of all armies, their boots, unused and aged weaponry, mess kits, company flags, deployment and engagement maps, newspaper and magazine articles along with military films making that day so real to us that we shivered to think of what had happened on those beaches.

As we continued on along the beach area, we marveled at the imbedded and corroded flatbed boats which were supposed to become bridges and roadways for the Allied machinery and supplies. The cement blocks that ships dragged in to make an Allied harbor area were still intact along the beach.

As we advanced further west toward Omaha Beach, we began to feel the tremendous significance of this area. The eerie juxtaposition: a place of war years before with a place of peace and serenity of today.

After the War the French government designated ground on Omaha Beach as a cemetery to all those American soldiers who gave their lives here for France. Getting out of the car, we felt overwhelmed by what had happened here. As we were starting into the cemetery proper, we saw the memorial "building" with its altar area. On its charcoal marble walls were the engraved names of those who had died here. In the center of the memorial, carved marble sculptures of soldiers reenacted a portrait of what had happened here. The sense of loss and grief could really be felt here and this feeling was only beginning to build in me.

As we walked up the knoll leading to the cemetery itself, we saw those perfectly lined rows of white marble crosses, each engraved with a soldier's name, his company, the state from which he had come, and his dates of birth and death. This only added to the gravity of their sacrifice for our freedom. The grounds were perfectly groomed; I pictured gardeners taking scissors and manicuring each blade of grass around each white cross.

I thought the trauma of seeing those white monuments to our fallen men who had sacrificed so much for us was over but I was totally mistaken. The closer to the beaching area I came, the more intensity I felt. As I stood on the crest of the coast looking out into the Channel, I visualized all the landing craft bringing in our young boys and men, the sacrificial lambs to the slaughter. I could only envision what they must have seen and felt as they watched the German guns blasting their fire out at them. I can't begin to think of the terror they must have felt about what lay ahead for them. Some never made it off their landing craft. Even if they did, they had to make it onto the beachhead then up its forbidding cliff with the German guns spraying bullets and mortar shells coming down on them wounding, maiming, and killing even more of them that June day.

It wasn't until I watched "Saving Private Ryan" some years later that I glimpsed what they faced: the German guns, barbed wire fences, mortar shells, and bullets whizzing around their heads killing their friends and fellow soldiers – many they did not even know but could only empathize with.

The loneliness and sadness I felt for all of them was deep and unending. I stood there sobbing for those lives lost in the pursuit of my freedom from tyranny. Many young men were never given a chance to live or experience life. I thanked God my sons never had to face this horror; they weren't born yet. I selfishly realized that I never wanted to go through the daily terror of the Western Union man bringing me a telegram telling me that Ron or John had been killed – knowing I would never be able to hold, comfort, or cradle either of them again. I thanked those men for their sacrifice and prayed that this would never happen again. Cowardly, all I wanted at that moment was the safety and refuge of my car while these brave men never had that shield of security.

We decided to go on to Point du Hoc. Along the coastal road we encountered more scenes where war played itself out with Allied ships battering large shells into the French landscape creating huge holes now covered by grass that hid the devastation that had occurred. Again that eerie, sad feeling came over me as I began to think of those lost here. How fierce the fighting must have been. I thought of the French citizens on whose land this war had been fought and the devastation the German occupation reeked upon them, their families, homes, and villages. I thought of the brave resistance groups whose courage saved many of the Allied soldiers. What they must have gone through. I felt overwhelmed and empty.

About one that afternoon we decided to find our next "home". The idea of sleeping in a chateau intrigued both Ron and I. We drove along the N-13 until we reached the village of Carentan; here we turned off onto a less used road to our chateau. As we got to the end of the road we got our first glimpse of Le Bel Enault, surrounded by its tall, inviting black wrought iron fencing and gate.

After driving up its long circular driveway, we parked in front of its main doors. Le Bel Enault stood majestic in the afternoon sun. The two-story chateau with its grey-brown stucco exterior and black tiled roof seemed to shine for all to see. Its exterior still displayed some shelling holes from the German bombing runs during World War II.

Our hosts, Jacques and Thresa Pauvel along with Sandy, their brown and white sheltie, rushed out to greet us. They had two sons; one was away at school while the other lived at home and went to a nearby public school. Thresa's English was adequate while Jacques struggled with his. He attempted to use his English with anyone he could and took pleasure when people let him know he was doing well. Taking us inside we saw additional bomb and shell damage. Jacques and Thresa were in the process of reconstructing their main fireplace and chimney that had been blasted away during one German strafing run. They hoped to find similar stones to replace the ones lost or broken.

Going upstairs we found a completely different world. Each of their four guest rooms was named and decorated after different botanical plants or trees. We had our choice of the Jasmine, the Lotus, the Sequoia, or the Chine room. Our room, the Lotus, had murals of palm trees and pink hibiscus flowers along with exotic parrots painted on the walls befitting a Lotus garden. Our room and private bath contained little furniture but all we needed.

St. Mere Eglise was on our agenda for the remainder of the day. It would prove to be another unnerving experience. As we drove into the town, I recalled the film, "The Longest Day". Its depiction of the German slaughter of our airborne forces here on the morning of June 6th vividly replayed in my mind. The Germans controlled this little village as well as the surrounding area. I watched as our planes overshot their drop points by five miles. Our men floated down not into their proposed drop zone but into the courtyard of the burning St. Mere Eglise. I relived the moments when the residents, the mayor, and the priest formed bucket brigades to pass water from one person to another in hopes of putting out the fire in their beloved church which the Germans had just bombed on one of their runs through the area. When the

German commander heard the Allied planes and noticed all the white parachutes floating down, he ordered his spotlights be turned into the sky so his men could see and easily shoot every descending parachutist. Many were killed in mid air while others died with their chutes hooked onto a church buttress or tree limb. It was like skeet shooting. What trauma was wreaked on those young soldiers! Again, pain and sadness overwhelmed me. I didn't want to believe people could kill or maim without a second thought as those soldiers did. It gave me an additional sense of what our countrymen went through for my liberty and the world's freedom from tyranny.

Driving back to the chateau we decided to have dinner. Our hosts had recommended four restaurants: L'Escapade (traditional French cuisine), Viopel (fish and seafood), Aubrenge Normandy (very expensive), and Le Creperie (creperie with many different fillings from seafood to dessert). They highly recommended the Viopel for its seafood and reasonable prices. The restaurant, unknown to tourists yet, was off the beaten path but not difficult to find. Ron ordered mussels and scallops while I ordered salade du mer. When it came, I had a tray with enough mussels, shrimp, scallops, and clams to feed both of us. It was absolutely wonderful. A cup of fresh fruit complemented the dinner.

When we arrived back at the chateau, Jacques and Thresa asked if we had had a good day. We told them about all we had seen and eaten. They were pleased. They told us they had placed a booklet in our bedroom they had written about the chateau's history. They hoped we would enjoy reading it. I was afraid it would be in French making it difficult for us to read or translate. To our surprise, they had written it in not only French but also English and German.

We learned that this property had been part of the French crown until 1548. It was then that King Louis XIV wanted to give his highest ranking officer a gift for all his years of excellent service. Having little money, he gave him this parcel of land instead. The officer built this chateau then decided to create a fantastic botanical garden with all kinds of exotic plants, trees, and shrubbery from all over the world. In order to defray the mounting costs of his dream garden, he bred and raced champion horses. As the botanical costs mounted, he was forced to sell off the horses one by one to pay off his debts.

As his debts grew, his horses and monies dwindled until he was bankrupt. Finally, he was forced to sell the chateau. The man who purchased it was Jacques' great, great uncle. He attempted to maintain the gardens but it became too much for him. The uncle then passed it on to his son who sold it to his son. When World War II broke out, the chateau was part and parcel in the war zone. In a scene from "The Longest Day" two parachutists, dropped short of their designated spot, came crashing down through the roof of the chicken coop inside the vegetable garden. In actuality it was the chicken coop and garden of this very chateau. The lady of the house (who was Jacques' great aunt) and her maid were whispering and giggling on their way to the outhouse. As they passed where the men hid, the paratroopers stood up and put their fingers to their mouths and said, "Shush", scaring the two women almost to death. The men were afraid that if the women saw them they would scream and alert German soldiers of their presence. The aunt and maid ran quickly back into the chateau. It was a piece of history to be remembered.

A few years ago Jacques' uncle sold the place to Jacques, as it was too much for him to maintain. Jacques saw its potential as a bed and breakfast hotel and the gardens would bring people from all over to see them. Since purchasing it, Jacques had spent time and money restoring both the chateau as well as the garden areas. "What a magnificent place it will be when it is finished," I thought. Ron and I decided to come back for another visit before returning to the States.

The following morning Thresa asked where we planned to travel. We said we were off to Villedeux then onto Mont St. Michael. "Quite ambitious," she said. Her orange juice, hot, homemade croissants, butter, preserves, and coffee were just right for our appetites.

By the time we reached Villedeux, known for its copperware, it was drizzly but the sunshine was trying to overcome the clouds and make a day of it. Since it was only half nine and the shops didn't open until ten, we walked along the main and some side streets checking out what was being offered. We thought to purchase a memento of our trip, as a return trip here was doubtful.

At ten we returned to the shops containing the pieces we were interested in, hoping the prices would be affordable. We purchased a lovely umbrella holder as well as a coal bucket for our lounge fireplace. I was pleased with our purchases.

We returned to our car and drove onto Mont St. Michael catching a glimpse of it as we drove along the coastline. What a sight! A monastery atop a "mountain" isolated from the world by the tides surrounding it. Building here, the monks and the religious ones knew they wouldn't be encumbered by daily secular entrapments that could divert them from their days of study and religious life. It was alone by itself – a true cloister for the devout, devoted men of God.

As we drove closer, we noticed the clouds encasing the Mont giving it the appearance of the Lord surrounding it. What a wonderment and sense of peace came over me. The Lord in all his glory was there with them and us.

Driving into the car park we were told to position our car so if we returned late our car would still be there. The incoming tide was swift and had been known to take cars out to sea in its wake. If we didn't watch our time, we could be stranded here overnight.

As we walked across the sandy beach from the car park toward the cloud-encompassed island, I felt the cloud's affect on me. I wanted to be a part of its serenity and peace. After passing through the entry gates we walked along an alleyway filled with tourist shops selling all manner of maps, postcards, historical pamphlets, and souvenirs. I purchased some postcards and two historical and pictorial booklets.

At the walkway's end we began our climb upwards passing three levels of enclosed apartments and residences. The monastery itself took charge of the entire top floor. Reaching the summit we walked around the parameter wall taking in all the sights for miles around in every direction. The isolation of this place from the world became even more evident to us. In seeking a place for solitude, religious studies, and reflection time for their godly endeavors, they certainly found it here.

We wanted to visit the chapel but the religious were holding services so we were not permitted inside. The "guard" told us we could come back later; the chapel would be open then. I wasn't sure I could climb those steps again so I read the information and looked at the pictures instead.

Returning to the second level, we were surprised to find a rather large stone hotel. Being curious we walked inside. On entering we saw along one wall a line of rustic wood benches covered with overstuffed cushions and a roaring fire in the fireplace. A group of people milled around the lobby sipping something that smelled like wassail while other people relaxed or read books in the warm, cheery environment. It was so inviting that I wished we had known about this place so we could have spent the night here as well.

Becoming aware of rattling cups and saucers, we followed the sounds until we found a rather busy café. The hostess walked us to a table with two chairs. We ordered a large pot of tea and some biscuits for fortification. Once finished, we pressed on our way back outside to the sandy car park and our car.

As we returned to Carentan, we stopped once again at Viopel's for another wonderful seafood meal. Both of us ordered smaller salade du mer plates to celebrate our wonderful vacation knowing that the next day we had to drive to Cherbourg for the ferry to Southampton where we would spend the night before returning home. We finished our glorious feast by splitting a perfect white mousse parfait.

Once, back in our room I realized how thirsty I was from all the seafood and began drinking glasses of water from the bathroom sink. Without thinking it might be well water, I drank probably a half dozen glasses of the liquid. I should have gone to the car and brought in our bottled water but I was too lazy to get them. What a mistake.

The next morning Thresa presented us with breakfast. As we packed and began our goodbyes, Jacques said we couldn't leave without visiting his pride and joy, his garden. We walked alongside the tennis court he was also refurbishing then into his Garden of Eden. Looking at this masterpiece of palms, redwood trees, yucca plants, arborvitaes, ivy and seedlings, we could see his dreams for this paradise emerging before our very eyes. He strategically placed gazebos so guests could sit and enjoy the scenery. It was a restful, spiritual place for guests to commune with nature and God. It was breathtaking. His dream was becoming a reality.

As we said last goodbyes, our once happy Jacques came out of the chateau quite distressed. We asked, "What was wrong? Could we help in some way?" He said he had just opened a letter from the French Department of Transportation saying that the new N-13 throughway would not be built close to their chateau as originally planned but about 25 miles south of them. This meant the tourists they were hoping to attract would be routed away from him and his dream. I felt defeat for them. What a blow after all their work. Ron and I promised to return again as soon as we could manage it. We enjoyed our two days with this hospitable and caring couple. What a tragedy for them and for those who might never know or see this wonderful chateau and couple. As we were pulling out of the chateau, I felt a bit queasy and the closer to Cherbourg the queasier I felt. I first thought it must have been something I had eaten the night before. Then it dawned on me – the water. Well water to boot. By the time we arrived in Cherbourg, I was quite ill.

After checking in with Stella Line, I searched for the closest bathroom. Once I used its facility, I thought I would be okay until we boarded but that was only a pipe dream. Waves of nausea riddled my body. I fought them until I realized I was fighting a losing battle.

Looking for help I walked down one of the corridors in the port building and noticed a pharmacie. I went in and with my limited French explained my illness. The pharmacist realizing the truth of how ill I was gave me a restricted opium derivative for the diarrhea and cramps along with some anti-vomiting pills. I could have kissed him for his help but I didn't.

He told me to take a dose of the opium immediately and another dose just before boarding the ship. I become concerned when the initial dose did not seem to have any effect. About a half hour later, its effects began to take hold and the diarrhea and cramping began dissipating. Ron was concerned at my demeanor. He was ready to find a doctor or even a hospital. I said, "No, I will be all right. The pharmacist gave me some medicines and I just want to get home. I don't want to attempt medical care here as I do not know the language well enough to negotiate it. Let's just get home and if needed, I'll call Dr. Richardson."

As the ship pulled out of her slip, I had second thoughts about my decision. The boat's movement upset my stomach. Reaching for the opium medicine, I took my second dose along with one of the anti-vomit pills. By the time both had entered my stomach and blood stream I was feeling little of anything. I was in and out of sleep for the entire seven hour Channel crossing.

After realizing how out of it I was, Ron decided against staying overnight in Southampton. He drove us directly home so I could get in touch with my own doctor.

I am the one known in our family for having a heavy foot but Ron must have pushed the pedal as hard as he could because the trip took the record time of five hours. Arriving home just after midnight Ron wanted to call Dr. Richardson but I said it was too late to bother him. I had my French medicines. I would sleep. If I didn't feel better in the morning, we would call him.

By morning I was better and didn't bother Dr. Richardson since it was Sunday morning. I decided if I wasn't any better in the morning I would call and see him. I drank pots of hot tea to wash the toxins and opium out of my system. By Monday morning I was better, just a tad on the weak side from the experience. It had been a wonderful holiday filled with much emotion but the harrowing trip home was one I did not want to relive again.

18. Something called Guy Fawkes Day

What was all the hubbub of the last weeks about? England was getting ready to celebrate a day named for Guy Fawkes. Who was he? Why was he so important in England to have a day named after him? I had never heard of him. Was he a little known politician who had done something extraordinary or was he a famous British industrialist, banker, or journalist I had never heard of? In England Guy Fawkes Day is full of celebration and fireworks just as the Fourth of July is in the States.

About a week before this day Ron came home and said that Clive and Juliette Dornby, his English supervisor and his wife, had invited us to come for dinner then go to their village's Guy Fawkes' bonfire and fireworks display with them. What a treat.

On the appointed evening we followed Clive's map and arrived at their home precisely at half six. Clive and Juliette greeted us warmly and introduced us to their two daughters, thirteen-year-old Bethany and ten-year-old Angelica. While sipping a glass of white wine, I asked about the significance of Guy Fawkes. Clive explained that on November 5, 1609 Guy Fawkes lead a conspiracy against the British government; the intent of the Gunpowder Plot as it was called was to blow up the Parliament.

Fawkes' plan was to hide in the lower dungeon area of Parliament until eleven o'clock when he would set off the dynamite charges bringing down the seat of government. His hiding place was crucial as he could hide his equipment and gunpowder as well as himself before setting off his plan. His only problem was one of his accomplices grew afraid of what might happen if Parliament was still in session debating something when Fawkes' plan went into action. Not wanting anyone to be in the building when the blast would be detonated he spoke in confidence to one of his friends in the House of Commons warning him to be out of the building by eleven o'clock. This representative at once went to one of the Lords advising him of what he had heard. An all-out search of the Parliament building ensued. Just before eleven the door to the last dungeon was opened and Fawkes was found sleeping along with his equipment ready for use.

His explosive plan put him on trial for treason and later he was hung. Each year the country celebrates this day. Many village soccer fields are used as sites for huge bonfires that burn Fawkes in effigy. Afterwards, mammoth fireworks celebrate his failure to complete his dastardly deed to bring down the British government. What a night!

After the explanation, we sat down to roasted chicken, potatoes, carrots, and peas. We all decided to go to the bonfire and firework celebrations before having our dessert.

After the evening events we walked back to their home filled with all we had seen then finished off the evening with a wonderful fruit trifle and a glass of port. What feasting.

Taking our leave about ten o'clock we thanked them for the wonderful dinner and history lesson along with all the fireworks that were still lighting up the skies. They still couldn't believe Ron and I had never heard of Guy Fawkes.

19. A Thanksgiving Treat

What a wonderful treat. Kelly, Laura's sister, wrote saying she would come for Thanksgiving. She was stationed at an Army base near Wiesbaden, Germany. We had not seen her since John and Laura's wedding the October before. This would be the first overseas Thanksgiving for all of us. She planned to fly into Heathrow Thanksgiving morning and stay for the weekend. I hoped to create an American Thanksgiving meal for us.

As the time came closer, I began to think of what I would serve for dinner. I wanted turkey, potatoes, stuffing, and all the trimmings. No turkeys were available. My butcher said, "Turkeys are Christmas fare." That made sense, as the British do not celebrate Thanksgiving. Ron planned to take a vacation day in order to spend the day with us.

I settled for a large roaster chicken from my trusty butcher, Mr. Land, some new potatoes, peas, fresh salad greens along with tomatoes, mushrooms, and cranberries from my greengrocer man, Mr. Pace, and a nice bottle of Chardonnay from the local wine shop. My real headache was the pumpkin for the pumpkin pie. I couldn't find a pumpkin or a tin of pumpkin anywhere. None of the local markets had it. The next best thing – a sweet potato pie. That would have to do; with some pumpkin spices maybe I could get it to taste like pumpkin.

The day before Kelly arrived, I baked some yams, a delicacy here. After they cooled, I mashed them, adding some eggs and some evaporated milk I had brought with us from the States, then I added the usual spices and a lot of hope. I poured the mixture into the piecrust. Within an hour our house contained the holiday aromas of cinnamon, cloves, and nutmeg in it.

I washed a bag of fresh cranberries and put them in a saucepan with a bit of sugar and water. Soon the traditional cranberry sauce was finished. After placing it in the refrigerator, I walked down to our favorite bakery, Rose's, to buy some whole grain bread, a French stick, and some bagels. I stopped at the local market for more eggs, real strawberry and red raspberry preserves from Tiptree, and fresh orange juice, not the long life kind. I had laid in sliced meats and cheeses for sandwiches along with crisps and biscuits for lunches. With a big roasting chicken I figured we could have hot "turkey" sandwiches one evening. I had prepared and frozen a lasagna and an enchilada casserole for us so we could visit London and other interesting places without worrying about meals. I also thought Kelly might enjoy trying a pub meal at one of our locals as a diversion from my cooking and her German cooking.

As time for her arrival got closer, our excitement grew. Soon we would have our first houseguest and a family member to boot. Who could ask for a better present?

Thanksgiving morning arrived with sunshine and crispness in the air – all reminders of fall and Thanksgiving to me. Ron and I had a cup of coffee and a piece of toast before jumping into our little blue Sierra for our journey to Heathrow.

Her plane arrived precisely at ten. She advanced quickly through immigration and customs then came outside to our awaiting car. She looked great sans uniform, her red hair pulled back in a black ribbon, and her smile outshone the sun itself. We were all so happy to be together.

We talked all the way home about her assignment and the villages we passed through. The TV room was ready to receive her and her things. While she was unpacking, I made breakfast. Not tired, she and I talked while I put the chicken into the oven. Having that accomplished, we decided to tour around our village, my local grocery markets, our little eleventh century church as well as Ron's work building. It was strange to see the shops open on Thanksgiving and no church services.

After two hours of touring we returned home to the beginning smells of dinner cooking. I proceeded to peel the potatoes, organize the peas, put the rolls on the baking sheet, and set the table with tablecloth, napkins, and candles. I wanted this to be a real celebration.

Before eating we gave thanks for the blessings of family, friends, Kelly's safe arrival, and life itself. We toasted the day with a glass of chilled Chardonnay then Ron began carving our "turkey". Everything tasted absolutely wonderful and having Kelly with us only enhanced our meal. The sweet potato pie sufficed for our pumpkin pie taste buds but they knew it was not the real thing. Oh well, we can't have everything.

Afterwards we were so full all we wanted to do was read or talk. Kelly told us of her love for classical music. She had even purchased a keyboard for her apartment that she played whenever she had a spare moment. Her job kept her quite busy; she was the deployment officer for all military vehicles, equipment, and personnel in Germany. A huge responsibility but she had the ability to do all that was required of her.

The following morning Ron, Kelly, and I took the train into London. Since Kelly had been here before and had seen all the important and traditional sights, we decided to show her some of our favorite places. First, we took her to Fortnum and Mason. She was especially amazed to see all deli meats, blocks of cheeses, plus quail, pheasant, beef, chicken, and sausages. She couldn't believe the prices on the

American products such as Betty Crocker mixes, American tinned foodstuffs, cookies, cereals like cornflakes and grape nuts that she could buy through her base PX for a fraction of our cost. When she saw the tea department, she zoomed in purchasing several different types and flavors of teas to take back with her. She bought some chocolate truffles for gifts for her friends.

After Fortnum and Masons, we walked up Regent Street browsing in the shop windows of The Scottish Shop, Jaeger, Liberty's, Dickens and Jones, then we turned onto Oxford Street where we found the British Home Store, John Lewis, one of my favorite department stores, Debenhams, D. H. Evans, and finally the overwhelming Selfridges, the ultramodern "Harrods". It never ceased to amaze me that Selfridges was a subsidiary of Sears and Roebuck.

Finishing that part of town we made our way to Bond Street Station for the train to Knightsbridge and the traditional landmark – Harrods. What a wonderful stop. Anyone entering Harrods knows it is THE place in London. You don't need to see the black taxis, the Mercedes, or the limousines lining up outside its doors to realize this is a place of importance. You feel it from the moment you walk by its doormen then through the entrance doors. Their security personnel check your parcels as well as your attire. Without shirts, long pants (no Bermudas or shorts) and shoes on, you are not allowed in. Once inside you feel all its tradition and elegance enveloping you. It is a place of excellence. I don't believe anyone spending a month within these walls could see everything on display or sale. Harrods contains everything from clothes, china, silver, crystal, inside as well as outside furniture, large and small kitchen appliances, hats, shoes, and toys for all age groups. In addition, on the ground floor, shoppers can treat themselves to a complete food hall with everything literally from soup to nuts and probably a whole lot more. If customers don't find what they want, all they have to do is ask. People say, "If Harrods doesn't have it, no one does."

After touring the store, we made our way back to Piccadilly and one of Ponti's wonderful deli sandwiches. Later, we walked to Leicester Square then through the West End Theatre district and Soho. Tired to the bone, we knew Kelly's tour of London needed to be shortened and quickly jumped on the underground back to Liverpool Street Station then the British Rail for home.

We each took hot showers to take the soreness out of our bodies from all the walking. Sitting around the lounge's fireplace, we ate turkey sandwiches and chips; beakers of hot tea washed everything down and also warmed us. We lingered with our memories of the day's events.

Saturday brought a real change in the weather. We woke to cold breezes and rain. I had planned a beach picnic at South End, a coastal village about thirty minutes from home. I thought it was a no go on our program but Kelly wanted to see it even with the inclement weather. We packed ham and cheese sandwiches, crisps, fresh fruit, biscuits, and a large thermos of hot chocolate then off to the seaside we went.

We arrived about noon, found a parking place alongside the sea, and then pulled on our heavy sweaters and jackets. Buffeting the winds and rain we walked the length of the wharf. Many small boats were moored just off the beach area while oil tankers sailed full or empty along the horizon.

Finishing our walk and feeling cold and damp, we saw a wonderful little tea cafe waiting for us to come in. Seeing we were in need of reviving, the short, rotund proprietor asked, "What can I do for you folks?" "Cups of hot chocolate and some warm scones would do nicely," we said. With a huge smile, a twinkle in his eye, and a song in his heart he went about getting our energy builders. Since we were the only ones in his shop, he struck up a lively conversation with us about the States and our reason for being here. Ron explained we were on assignment for a couple of years and Kelly was in from Germany on Thanksgiving leave.

We talked about his little shop and the years he had worked to make a go of it; it had been a struggle but he had afforded his family with an income. He said as we were leaving that he hoped we would return and have another chocolate with him. We said we would. Americans say the Brits are unfriendly; I strongly disagree with that. If we just give people a chance, they usually are warm and charming. You get what you give is my motto.

Sunday morning came much too soon. We had a big American breakfast full of melons, strawberries, eggs, bacon, toast, strawberry preserves, and coffee as Kelly had a full day of traveling ahead of her. It still amazed me the variety of fruits from all over Europe I could purchase here: strawberries from France, melons from Israel, and so on.

The drive to the airport was a somber one, as we didn't want our time together to end. She promised to visit us again. We said if we were close to her, we would stop in as well. Many tears flowed as she got out of the car and said goodbye. I felt as if I had lost a part of me.

20. Driving Tuition Begins

When Americans think of taking driving lessons, they enroll at their local high school or driving school. In England, the driving programs are called driving tuition – not driving lessons. I assume that's because one pays tuition for the lessons, not a fee. With *Comco* any employee as well as any driving age dependent on assignment for a year or more are required to take the British driving test before the end of their first year. If they did not do this, *Comco* would not issue them lease cars or insure them. Since Ron and I filled that bill, we knew we had to take the test. Passing this test was no sure thing I had heard from my international friends who had taken it. Some employees and their dependents had to take this test two or more times before passing it. With each passing day, I became more nervous about taking and passing this test.

At one of our usual coffee klatches in November, I was urged to take the necessary driving instructions and the test as soon as possible. The sooner, the better; then I could relax. The longer I waited, the more I would get into the rhythm of my own way of driving rather than the British way I would be tested on. Once passing the test I could revert to my old driving habits. The British have specific ways of driving that drivers must learn in order to pass the test. Included in those procedures were making sure both hands were on the steering wheel at all times, continuously checking all the mirrors (rear as well as side), clutching in a certain way, and learning to execute three mandatory maneuvers. It seemed like a overwhelming task.

The women gave me the name of a particularly patient and understanding instructor, Steve Barber, at the British School of Motoring with an excellent pass rate. It took every ounce of courage and true grit for me to make that call. After the receptionist asked my name, address, and telephone number, she asked if I wanted to use a manual or automatic car. The type car I used for the test made a significant difference in the license issued. If I used an automatic drive, I could only drive an automatic but if I took the test in a manual drive, I could drive either a manual or automatic vehicle. If an automatic licensed person was found driving a manual car, the fine was quite hefty.

Since Ron had ordered a manual car for me, I needed to take the manual instruction and test. I became even more unglued when I learned few American women passed the manual driving tests. I was determined to pass the first time, as I knew I couldn't or wouldn't take it a second or third time. The final question she asked me was did I have an instructor in mind. Since the "girls" had told me to use Steve Barber, I said "Steve Barber."

The day came when Steve drove up to our place. He was the "All-American Boy", the son mothers love to have. This red-haired, tall, lanky, personable young man presented himself at my door on the bright sunny afternoon of November 23rd. He was young enough to be my younger son, John, and reminded me so much of him. I instantly felt at ease with him.

As we approached the car, my whole body began to shudder and quake. My nerves were raw with fear and anticipation. Could I really learn to drive on the left side of the road? Even though I had practiced in local school car parks, it was still foreign and confusing to me. I needed to remember I was in a foreign environment and I had to learn to adapt to it. I had three choices: I could remain at home, find someone who would drive me around to where I wanted to go, or learn to drive this bloody thing. I was and am too independent for the first two ideas so I had to put my mind into the set of learning to drive here.

My head pounded with the thoughts of: Will I be able to learn to do this? Will I be able to prove to the British examiner I can execute those three required test maneuvers with precision? I had been told the test required applicants to reverse around the corner, parallel park on the left, and do something called a three point turn as well as the usual emergency braking technique. This would require a lot of time and practice on my part.

As I opened the car door, Steve said, "Nancy, if you expect to drive, you need to be on the other side of the car." My face must have turned a thousand red shades of embarrassment. After I got in the proper side, Steve and I sat getting to know each other and talking about what each of us expected from these lessons. I said, "To PASS the first time." He said, "My students do pass; I haven't had a failure yet." That was reassuring but also unnerving. I felt the pressure not to be his first failure. We set up an initial series of five lessons with an extension series if we decided I needed more work. Afterward he discussed some test requirements I needed to begin using as the inspector would be looking for them; such as using all three mirrors and raising the hand brake at each complete stop. These must become second nature to me.

My first lesson (forty-five minutes) was mainly to assess my British driving expertise. I was thankful Ron had taken me out a few times to get me used to driving on the left side of the road. I didn't want to look like a complete klutz on my first lesson.

I felt safe driving as long as I was moving forward and didn't have to deal with any roundabouts. I remembered the Chevy Chase movie, *"National Lampoon European Vacation"*, where he was caught in a roundabout at Buckingham Palace and didn't know how to get out. After a few minutes or hours he finally managed to maneuver himself into an outside lane and exit the roundabout. I didn't want that scene.

Steve explained roundabouts made exiting busy intersections easy. You just have to be in the proper lane. He explained that there were usually three or four exits from a roundabout. I should think of it like the face of a clock. If I wanted to exit from one of the first two exits, I should stay in the outermost lane so I could turn easily. Wanting to make a later exit, I should stay in the inner lane until I could move to the outside lane and make my turn. Sounded so easy coming from him but my stomach was not accepting that theory at all. The dive-bomber brigade was working overtime for my benefit.

Steve had me drive into our little village. I felt good cruising along until I saw a dreaded roundabout before me. My knees became jelly and my palms began to sweat. My thoughts ran, "Oh, Steve take over and get me out of this predicament. I can't do this; you have to do it for me." Steve immediately noticed my reticence and began talking me through every motion to get me in and out of that dreaded menace. Once through it, a sense of accomplishment hit me and I almost returned to feeling normal. I still had a half hour left in my lesson that only meant more driving and roundabouts. I kept saying to myself, "You can do this. I know you can. You did it once; you can do it again and again."

Steve had me drive some less used country roads just to give me a sense of confidence behind the wheel. If I was going to pass that test, I had to be confident. I knew that and so did Steve.

After another thirty minutes I drove through the dreaded village roundabout and home. I wasn't as lily-livered as before but I still wasn't comfortable with roundabouts. Fortunately, I didn't know that I would have to negotiate a double roundabout in order to pass my test. Thank goodness that information hadn't come up yet.

After Steve drove away, I walked into the house and fell into a discombobulated lump on the couch. One down and how many more would I need! I figured a thousand more, maybe even more. Steve had said, "Practice" and that I would. Another thing I thought strange was Steve hadn't discussed any of the procedures I needed to learn in order to pass the test. Oh, well, one lesson at a time!

When Ron came home for dinner that night, he asked me how the lesson went and whether I liked Steve. I said I liked Steve and for a beginner I felt good about the first session. I said I needed a lot of practicing. He said how about tonight after dinner. Oh, great another session!

Ron had learned quickly how to drive, as he had to get to and from work. I could only practice when he was home as I didn't have a car of my own yet. How many times had I heard – don't learn to drive with a family member. No truer words were ever spoken. It seemed everything I did he said was wrong. All I heard was "Now watch the curbs, watch your mirrors, get in the left lane, and turn on your signal." By the time I got home twenty minutes later I never wanted to see his car and maybe him again. I was crushed and thought childishly I'll just stay home and let him drive. But I realized the coward's way out was not for me. I knew I could do this and I would show both him and myself I could.

A few days later Steve returned and out we went again. We drove through Shenfield's roundabout, then the back roads and on to the A-127, a heavily traveled road. I felt like a duck taking to water, and my confidence rose. An interesting side point – in England the roads bear no posted speed limits except the 25 mile per hour speeds in towns, villages, and school areas. Motorists drive up to 90 miles per hour on the motorways (interstates to Americans).

With each minute I drove with Steve, the stronger I felt with my driving ability. Steve was patient and reassuring. Down the A-127 he wanted me to exit onto a large roundabout the A-127, then return. While I was negotiating the turn, I noticed a large Sainsbury supermarket. I needed to investigate it later and see how much more variety it had than the one in Brentwood. Finishing the roundabout I reentered the A-127 and thought I was on my way back home. I was amazed how easy this was becoming. My confidence rose.

On our return, we entered Brentwood where Steve had me negotiate another but smaller roundabout. This is a piece of cake I said to myself as I sailed through it without incident. Next, Steve asked me to pull into one of the side streets and stop. He told me to pull over about 200 feet past the next corner. I could not figure out why but I was soon to learn. I was about to learn the first of my required maneuvers – reversing around the corner. "You want me to do what?" I heard my mouth say.

With reversing procedures, first, I was to unbuckle my seat belt then check my mirrors for traffic. With no approaching traffic either way, I was to release the emergency brake. (In Britain with any complete stop the emergency brake must be engaged – the inspector would check that as well.) Once the brake was off I could begin my reversing. He told me I had to stay within a foot of the curb at all times. Reversing; I needed to move slowly backwards using my side and rear mirrors to direct my path. After making the turn I was to continue the maneuver for approximately 200 feet. The cardinal rule: Don't touch the curb at any time with either of your wheels. After the fifth try I accomplished the feat with only one tap on the curb.

Steve said, "Remember, the test inspector will fail you if you touch the curb." My confidence level went spiraling down. Not much pressure to be perfect, I thought. More practice was needed.

As we drove home, my thoughts ran to the idea of parallel parking and that thing called a three-point turn. I knew the mandatory emergency stop presented no problem; I would be able to do that in my sleep. Executing the perfect reversal and the three point turn scared me.

The next lesson concentrated on reversing around the corner and roundabouts. The more I practiced them, the more confidence I acquired. Usually when I got overconfident, something brought me back to reality. For example, one time I entered a single roundabout planning to make my exit from the last turn but stayed in the outer lane. All of a sudden I noticed a small black Austin-Martin on my back bumper expecting me to exit so he could also. He flashed his lights and beeped his horn to remind me I was in the wrong. At that moment I wished I had one of those big red L signs on my boot letting others know I was a learner. British law requires all beginner drivers to display a large red L on the car's boot and bonnet (hood) to let other drivers know he or she is a learner. Once the test is passed, the red L is changed to a green L signifying the driver has passed the test but is still under probation for six months. Since I already had my U.S. license, I wasn't required to display the L logo. I was glad, as the embarrassment would be mortifying to me. I moved on and made my turn late. This reminded me to be aware of everything around me and what I was doing. I learned a valuable lesson. Although I had gotten myself into a bad situation, I had kept my cool and got out of it. I felt pleased with myself.

The next time Steve and I went out he had me pull into a less used road. He wanted me to pull up alongside a parked car on the left side of the street. He then said, "Ease yourself back using your side and rear mirrors to reverse yourself in the open space behind that car." I thought, Oh, this will be a piece of cake as I am getting good at reversing around the corner; this is no different. Well, to my surprise, it was a bigger deal than I had estimated. Parallel parking on the left with a right side wheel was near impossible. "Oh golly, Miss Molly. This is not easy." I must have taken more than five minutes just to get even with that space and not touch the curb. Ten tries later I felt more at ease though I wasn't good at it. Again, I knew I needed to get out and practice to get it right. Steve then said, "Now open your door and check to see how close you are to the curb." Well, let me tell you I must have been two feet from the curb. Steve said, "You can only be 10 centimeters away and no more." With that I knew this test was going to take work and time – daily work and no sluffing off either. Thinking of daily practicing unnerved me, as I had not soloed yet. I knew I had to do this test solo with the test inspector. Fear gripped me. I can do this; all I have to do is get myself ready for this driving encounter.

The next day I got my courage up and took Ron to work. The morning commute could be just as nasty and congested as in any major U. S. city. "Oh, boy. Here we go." I thought. As long as I drove in the little villages or on country roads I had no fear but when it came to the drivers on the A-127 fear struck me. I knew other drivers would not barter with me. I had to do it right.

I drove confidently to his plant and dropped Ron off then realized I was all alone in his little car. Retracing our drive would take work and time, as I was unsure of the route. Well, I decided to make an adventure of it. Out of the car park I moved toward the main thoroughfare and felt fine. All of a sudden I faced my first roundabout without assistance. I eased into the outer lane as I was using the first exit. I moved with traffic and proceeded out, just as I should. Accomplishing that, I felt more in control. I cautiously watched my speed and the other cars as I moved right along. Cool, calm, and collected was I.

The first real test came when I pulled up to the traffic light needing to make a left turn. After waiting for all the oncoming cars in the left lanes to pass me, I said to myself, "It's like making a left hand turn at home except you're doing it in reverse." As the light began to turn yellow, I remembered what I had to do. With my turn signal on, I released the emergency brake and made my turn. I was pleased with my precision and no horns blew at me for a faulty maneuver. I felt confident again.

After making the turn and moving down the long winding street I saw our home. Relief poured out of every pore, as I pulled into our driveway safe and sound. I hurried into the house and put the teakettle on for a soothing cup of hot tea. I decided to wait for the morning traffic to subside before going out to practice my driving. Practice would fill my days until I could do them in my sleep and effortlessly for the actual testing. I knew I had to find some deserted streets so I wouldn't be bothered and could practice without gawkers standing and watching me saying to others, "Oh, look at her; she's practicing. I wonder if she will get it right? Oh, she hit the curb that's not good. Oh, she turned into that parking space too late or quick. She'll never do it. I'll bet a pint on it." I wasn't ready for their remarks so I decided to look for the loneliest road. If I was to pass, I needed space and no eyes watching me. Practice, practice, practice would be my motto until I passed that "bloody" test.

Later after a nice cuppa I set out to begin my practice session – the first of many I suspected. I took to the back streets of Brentwood looking for the loneliest road I could. I didn't want any unforeseen complications in my way.

I made a right turn onto Park Lane, a little used street with a number of OAP (old aged pensioners) apartment buildings there. Not many cars or children to concern me there.

First, I began with reversing around the corner. Although I felt comfortable with the procedure, I knew I needed to build my confidence. I spotted an open corner about a block down the lane. I pulled over to the curb making sure I pulled in close enough but not too tight so I could perform the procedure. I pulled on the emergency brake and took a few deep breaths before beginning. I checked all my mirrors making sure all was safe for me to begin. Once that was assured, I unlocked my emergency brake and began inching my way around. My first attempt began well but I overcompensated on the actual turn and touched the curb. Returning to my original starting point, I muttered, "This is hard. I will literally have to put blinders on and feel my way around the curb, just like Luke Skywalker did when he was learning to use his light saber. He had to practice and practice with his saber to be proficient with it just as I will have to with my car. The more practice, the better I will become." After a number of failed attempts I decided not to frustrate myself further and moved onto parallel parking.

I decided to first work on pulling alongside a parked car with nothing behind it. After the full stop, I released the brake and moved backward turning into the curb; once again I hit the curb. "No tap or hit allowed. Well, let's try that again," I thought. This time I went much slower and negotiated the reverse without a tap. Now, I must move on to the next part of the procedure – parking between two parked cars. Finding two cars not too close together, I decided to practice with them. That worked out well. Now, I was pumped. I thought I had one procedure under control. A couple more tries led to more successes. Hooray!

I decided to go back and practice that corner thing. Shouldn't have; as I still was having trouble feeling my way around the corner even with the use of my side and rear mirrors. Becoming frustrated I decided enough for today; I would wait for Steve to give me pointers to finesse this technique. I drove home without incident and put the teakettle on for another reviving cup of tea, nothing better after a practice session. I felt more in control of my driving as I had experienced it alone and was able to work through some of the test requirements.

The next day Steve and I worked on the corner problem and got it closer to perfection – still not passing but I was getting a better feel for it. With parallel parking, both Steve and I were pleased.

I then asked him, "What is this thing called a three point turn?"

He said he had left that for last, as it was the most difficult. My confidence dropped again. "The three point turn means you pull up to the left side of the road," Steve said.

"There's nothing to that," I said.

"Then you look to check for no traffic, release your brake, then pull across the street to the right stopping just before the curb there, reverse back around to the other side's curb and stop without touching the curb, then advance forward."

"Oh, that is a bit more trouble," I said. I attempted it a number of times without success. That curb always got in my way. "Oh, well, practice makes perfect," I said to myself. I had plenty of time to get these maneuvers down pat before the test.

"Oh, hey, when is the test??" I wanted to ask, although I really didn't want the answer. I was happy enough to just do my practicing for now.

21. A Night Dickens' Tour

Our international women's group decided to make the Christmas season a little more festive and realistic. London City Tours take groups on various tours in London proper. Their guides are costumed for the tours they lead. Some tours have ghoulish themes, some go backstage at West End theatres and explain their histories, others visit main points of interest, and others follow a certain theme. The "girls" decided to take the Friday night Charles Dickens tour. It sounded like fun as well as informational. I signed Ron and myself up. We were to meet our group outside St. Paul's Station at half six.

That Friday had been busy with a morning trip into London for some last minute Christmas gifts and decorations. Harrods was chocker block with people especially in the Christmas shop. I bought some tree ornaments and greenery for the lounge mantle. After finding a box of Neuhaus chocolates, I bought a bar of the delicious confection for myself. Since I had little time, I had to quickly make my stops at Debenhams and John Lewis on Oxford Street for final Christmas purchases for the "kids". I took the half four train then hopped into a taxi home. Arriving home, I found Ron dressed to leave. I quickly changed into my warm boots, trousers, and coat. Within minutes we arrived at the train station for our half five train into the City. We needed to meet our group in an hour which we could do with time to spare.

We rode in with Mark and Barb Neilsen, a lovely couple whose assignment had been extended twice. When we arrived at Liverpool

Street, we heard the announcement that the Central Line was on hold because of a security alert meaning the bomb squad would have to go in and dispose a suspect package. Oh, great.

With the delay we missed our group at St. Paul's, an agitated Barb asked a nearby newsagent if he knew the route our guide would take so we could catch up with them. He said, "Go to St. Bartholomew the Lesser Church, that's where he would be." We put on our "running shoes" and caught up with them.

Our guide called himself Mr. Macawber, reminiscent of the jolly, humorous, and lively character from *David Copperfield*. I didn't believe our Mr. Macawber had any of the financial difficulties the Dickens' character had. He was dressed in the Dickensian theatre apparel: heavily starched and ironed white shirt with a ruffled center panel, burgundy and navy paisley cravat, grey pinstriped waistcoat with a gold-plated watch fob and chain, long, grey morning jacket, black knickers and long stockings, and black leather shoes with silver buckles representative of the times. He finished his costume with a long, black theatrical cape and smooched black velvet hat befitting of an actor in performance. Not only was his costume perfect but he portrayed his character well. His tour would take us through the areas where Dickens lived and wrote.

Macawber gave us the history of St. Bartholomew the Lesser Church and its connection with its hospital, St. Barts. In *The Tale of Two Cities* the resurrection men (body snatchers) dug up bodies so they could sell them to St. Bart's for its research purposes. These men resurrected bodies to give them new life and purpose.

Moving on we traveled through the Smithfield Central Market, the slaughter area for chickens, pigs, and cattle in Dickens's days. Continuing our tour we walked through the Holborn district where Dickens lived much of his life. He gave us some of Dickens's biography. After Charles married Catherine Hogart at the age of seventeen, they lived in a small apartment with her mother, brother, and younger sister, Mary, whom he deeply loved but couldn't marry. Mary edited all his writings and helped him develop his characters. Returning home one evening from the theater, Mary complained of being quite tired. Within minutes she collapsed and died in his arms. He never got over her death or his love for her. He and Catherine had seven children; two sons died.

We passed the area and street where he wrote *Bleak House* and *Little Dorrit*. Macawber explained that in Dickens time as well as today this area had its own police or security force since London's Metropolitan Police refused to patrol this area. For that reason the homeowners erected two masonry pillars on both ends of the street, then put in wrought iron fencing and double gates to protect the homeowners from any kind of dangerous folk. On the gates, wrought iron wreaths of holly were embedded to remind people of the wreath of thorns our Lord wore and its encrusted holly berries represented the drops of blood from his head. Another interesting tidbit. At that time, most London streets were unpaved, so the servants of the house had to carry their masters from their homes to their waiting carriages and visa versa in studio chairs so the owners didn't get dusty or dirty.

We pressed on to the Mitre Pub built in 1576; Dickens frequented here after theatre nights and openings. The interesting thing about this pub was at some point in time someone planted a tree in his honor. As it grew, it became incorporated into the pub's sidewall. What an amazing sight. No one ever had the heart to cut it down so there it remains today and has become a point of notoriety or interest for all.

Macawber guided us through Fagin's areas. His lair of operation ran between the slaughterhouse and the booksellers. The wealthy came here to buy meats and books. Their rich clothing alerted Fagan's gang that these people were ripe for the picking. The boys pocketed wallets and watch fobs which Fagan took to a pawnshop and turned into ready cash.

Our tour ended at the Barnaby Rudge Pub known for two reasons: having the longest bar in England as well as its down drafting fireplace. This fireplace heats not only the upstairs but the downstairs cellar bar as well. Dickens wrote about this pub in *Barnaby Rudge* hence its name. Our group said, "Goodbye" to Macawber giving him an additional stipend for the wonderful evening he had given us.

Our group remained at the pub having a pint of their libation. We shared all we had learned and seen so we could fill in any lingering questions anyone had about what we had seen along the way. We felt having all the information we would be able to enjoy the revisited sites even more in the daylight.

A little later we walked to Trafalgar Square where an enormous Christmas tree was decorated and around it various choirs or singing groups sang beautiful carols of the season. What a beautiful night – the sky was clear, the stars were out like a fireworks display, and the moon shown brilliantly. The lights on the tree only added to the richness and magic of the evening as well as the upcoming season.

Loraine and Gavin Meadows and Peggy and Ray Stern said they were going to TGI Fridays for a bite to eat. They asked us to join them. We were delighted. Ron had an enormous cheeseburger with fries, imported US beef, while I had chicken fajitas which were wonderful and filling. After dinner we took the Tube to Liverpool Street and then British Rail home. What a treat. Another unforgettable night.

22. The House of Lords

John Bergan, a business associate of Ron's, as well as Lord Straithcairn, had gotten us an invitation to lunch with the Lord. Included in that we would watch part of the House of Lord's session in the afternoon. What a spectacular day.

We caught the 10:21 train to London then a cab to Lord and Lady Straithcairn's Mayfair townhouse; something that never, ever happens to us commoners. We arrived about fifteen minutes late which caused a bit of aggravation as the Lord had reserved a table in the Lord's dining room for precisely 11:30.

Lord Straithcairn introduced himself to us as David and his wife as Eve. What a wonderful regal couple they were. I took to them in a second. He was a spry and energetic 69 years old. He had been a member of the House of Lords since he became 21. He still rode his beloved motorcycle to Parliament everyday through London's morning traffic. Ron and I were amazed at his prowess and courage to do such a feat especially since he had had an accident the year before. He wasn't seriously hurt, just bumps and bruises but he and Eve realized he needed to wear a helmet when cycling.

The Lord drove Ron, Carol, (John's wife) and me in his black BMW to Parliament while John followed with Eve in her car. How very honored we felt and knew we should be. After parking, David walked us through the Lords' entrance where the security force checked us over before he could take us into the Lords' coatroom where we deposited our coats, hats, and gloves. He pointed out the hangers for His Royal Highness the Prince of Wales, the Duke of Edinburgh, and the Duke of York as well as other important personages. Each day David hangs his coat or jacket along with his motorcycle helmet here before going to his office. Recently, he was featured in *Motorcycle Magazine*.

He talked a little about himself, telling us during the 1940's he had trained in Arizona as a Royal Air Force pilot for six months but was glad to get away from the hot desert and its food. He held onto his pilot's license after the war and continued to fly until five years ago. During a routine medical checkup, the doctors found an irregular heartbeat and the civil aviation board revoked his license. He was still bitter about it, saying he felt great and had had no problems with his heart. He talked about his and Eve's upcoming Caribbean cruise in January or February and a possible March holiday to Madeira where they would enjoy their relaxation time in the sun and surf. Sounded like heaven to me.

While David took us on a short tour of the House of Lords, Eve excused herself. Recently she had had leg surgery and walking came hard for her. She said she would meet us for a pre-lunch glass of sherry or wine in the lounge bar. We quickly said goodbye to her and began our tour.

First, he showed us the Lord's Abbey where all state funerals are held. In its ceiling is a sun window so the sun can shine down upon the casket. While the casket is lying in state and during the funeral, Beefeaters and the Queen's Guard rotate turns standing in precision for twenty minutes which is the most anyone can stand perfectly erect and on guard.

As we walked the chamber where the Lords conduct their business, I saw their red leather chairs with their gold button studs. Anyone could tell this was the regal part of Parliament. The Lords gain their seats in this chamber by their lineage or title while members of the House of Commons must be elected into their green leather chairs by the British people. What an awesome place – to be able to see and feel the importance and majesty of this chamber. I felt so privileged that goosebumps ran all through my body. Not many people are allowed this honor and privilege to do what we were doing. He pointed out the Speaker's Chair where their ruling officer, like our Speaker of the House or Vice President, oversees the day's agenda and discussions along with their voting on bills. Microphones and television cameras are positioned all over the chamber to allow the media to record each day's events and arguments. David found the House of Commons boring and their use of degrading mannerisms rude and disgusting.

He took us through the Hall of Divisions (the voting area for the Lords) where the yea and nay votes are counted. The Lords vote by hand ballots then place their individual votes into the Hall's wall cabinet. When voting is concluded, two people, one from the consenting side and one from the dissenting side hand count the votes then deliver the results into the House of Lords.

After our tour we joined Eve. Lunch in the Lord's dining room was spectacular – I had potted shrimp, grilled lamb chops, fresh steamed carrots, cauliflower, broccoli, and finished off with a wonderful steamed pudding for dessert while Ron had the shrimp, a filet mignon, the steamed vegetables, and the pudding. Ron said the beef was wonderful, tasted just like USDA Grade A beef. Couldn't say that to David or anyone else at our table or in earshot of us.

During lunch the table discussion turned to Prince Charles and Princess Diana's marital dismay. David was quite upset with the situation saying Charles should have married a royal as they were trained from birth to be a royal instead of trying to make a royal out of a commoner. That just couldn't happen. Eve was sympathetic with Princess Diana making David even more upset.

On the way to the Lord's spectator gallery David wanted us to purchase postcards and postage at their "post office". By mailing them there they would have the House of Lord's stamp. What a great collector's item.

At 2:20 the bell rang to tell the Lords to go into their chamber for their afternoon discussions. He handed us signed and stamped invitations for the upper spectator pews of the Lord's chamber where we would have a bird's eye view of everything going on; those in the lower viewing area would not have that privilege. After taking us to the stairs leading upward, he said goodbye.

Once in the spectator area we had to be perfectly still, no talking, whispering, sneezing, or coughing. We were mesmerized as the opening questions and discussions began. On the docket was the discussion about President Clinton's coming to the United Kingdom to study while the Vietnam draft was in full force. Also, later in the agenda the Lords would discuss a statement about the previous weekend's European Community conference. Just sitting there one could feel the power of this house as the Lords, Ladies, Baronesses, and Earls debated their views on various issues.

At half three a recess was called, unfortunately Baroness Thatcher had not made her appearance so we did not see her. David came up motioning for all of us to come out. Ron and I said our goodbyes and thanked him for the wonderful opportunity he had afforded us. A once in a lifetime experience.

Carol and I excused ourselves and went to the Baroness's room to freshen up. The retiring room (bathroom) had a pull-chain toilet and a wood bench lid cover. While we were in there, Lady Coussins came in.

She was interested in the discussion about the issue of Northern Ireland and how it would affect England. She asked if we had seen Lord Snowden, Princess Margaret's former husband. We said, "No."

David had the guard at the entrance door flag a taxi for us. Ron and I drove off for Liverpool Street station and our train for home. What a glorious day – one that could never be repeated. I will never forget David and Eve and all their kindness to us.

23. Christmas Party Villain

One early December afternoon as I sat at our kitchen table, the telephone rang. Putting down my beaker of tea and the mail I had been sorting through, I answered, "Hello." On the other end of the line was Nikki Parker, the friend of Chef Homme and a salesperson from *Comat*, one of Ron's suppliers.

Comat held an annual Christmas du (party) to which we would be invited. This year's theme was a murder-mystery. It sounded like a fun evening until Nikki asked me a fateful favor. She was coordinating this event and had engaged a group of West End actors to create and enact the murder-mystery play. She was putting together a group of actors from *Comco* and *Comat* to work with the West End group to bring the play to life. One major character role eluded them: the murderer.

I said, "I think Ron would be happy to be involved," – only to be told, since I was the newest and most unknown person to both groups, no one would suspect me of "murder."

"Me!" I said shocked.

"Yes, you will be perfect for the part," Nikki replied.

Feeling guilty to refuse her, I agreed. She would drop off my part of the script one afternoon when Ron wasn't home. She swore me to secrecy about the play and moreover, my part in it. My involvement had to be a complete surprise.

I kept imagining how I would keep a straight honest face with Ron, as I had never been able to keep a secret from him. I had to play it cool. The morning after Nikki's call, Nick Geoff of the West End group telephoned to discuss the plot, characters, and my role in the play. He said I had been chosen because of my free spirit since I was driving around town in my new cabriolet, a little red convertible with a black top.

Nick told me that during the drinks segment of the du evening I was to introduce myself to a blonde waitress, Monica, whom he would be playing in drag. He called himself a master of disguise. He would also play Inspector Holmes who would unravel the murder mystery. I was now excited. It sounded like fun. I was looking forward to seeing Ron's astonished face if I could pull this off without a hitch. Nick gave me some costume pointers, dress stylishly but not so people would be aware of my comings and goings, as I needed to "kill" two people in secret.

Two days later Nikki called asking if I was alone so she could drop off my part of the script. I said, "Yes."

As we discussed the plot and characters, I was shocked to learn who I was to "murder." One was Ron's new boss, Jeremy Long, even though he was already in the play. "Oh, dear, how will that look?" I thought to myself. People knew I was not thrilled about this assignment but now I was to murder his boss. What would Freud say about that??

I was stuck with it and had to work it through. The lines were simple enough but I feared I would get stage fright and not be able to carry this off. As the day of the party grew near, my fear mounted.

Party night we dressed festively. Ron dressed in his double-breasted navy pinstripe suit and I wore my red suit with black lapels. Boy, I didn't think how showy that would be trying to sneak out to do my dastardly deeds. I just wanted to look Christmasy.

As we left the house, the initial butterflies in my stomach became divebombers. Could I really pull this off? I wished I had an understudy to step in for me. All the way to the Green Manor, an elegant manor home turned into a hotel and restaurant, I talked to Ron about his day trying to keep my mind off the evening ahead as well as block any questions about it. As we walked through the front doors, the fragrances of holly and balsam came wafting through to greet us. Surrounding the blazing fire in the large fireplace, set large red and white poinsettias that added to the evening's festive mood.

Nikki found us and led us into the anteroom next to the dining room for a drink before dinner. I hoped a glass of wine would calm me; it did, but only momentarily. Within moments of our arrival, the mystery began unfolding before the assembled group. Never having met any of the London performers or those from *Comat* or *Comco* who would be in the play, I was at a total loss to know who was in the play, their roles in it, or the progression of events. I had only seen my part in the play in order to keep everything in the play top secret.

During drinks I was introduced to Rico Frangelico who said he was from Michigan but really looked Italian and spoke with an Italian dialect. I could tell he enjoyed the company of women.

All of a sudden two of Jeremy's "mistresses" were having a rather heated argument about a third woman who had eyes for him. The women talked louder so all could hear their distain for each other and this new woman. The third woman wrapped herself around Ron saying she liked him hoping to defuse their attention on her. But the other women saw through her plan. Within moments the first two were into a catfight over Jeremy. I eased my way out as I was supposed to in order to murder Alice, his new mistress.

Just as dinner was announced, the assembled throng heard a bloodcurdling scream. A passerby had found the dying Alice moments before she died and reported valuable clues about her murder to the dinner attendees. Since I was out of the room "murdering" Alice, I didn't hear the murder clues. Returning to the group, some people noticed I had been gone but didn't think anything about it as I had gone to the ladies room. With that, Act I was completed.

Entering the dining room, Nikki directed us to find our place cards. During dinner each table was to decide who the killer was and compose a song about that person using the tune from a popular song. Our meal consisted of Christmas fineries: seafood cocktail with avocado and prawn sauce, Beef Wellington, and freshly steamed vegetables.

As we were eating, Inspector Holmes began interrogating some of his suspects in Alice's murder in an attempt to give us novice detective's clues about "who done it".

The first to be questioned was Clive Dornby, Ron's supervisor. He was shocked to hear his name called as a suspect. The inspector inquired about Clive's suspected drug ring and his use of catalytic converters to transport his drugs. Was Alice a part of his dealings with the drug cartel, Blissful? Next, he turned to Jeremy Long, Clive's supervisor, questioning him about his numerous office affairs especially with Alice. He said he did not have an affair with her – he didn't even like her. He left the room in a real huff demanding to telephone his barrister and put a stop to this invasion of his privacy.

Moments later I excused myself from the table to go to the Ladies room in order to "murder" Jeremy.

While I was gone, another suspect, John Collings, was questioned about his running a suspected pornographic video business from his office computer in Clive's department. Was Alice one of his women models? How did she fit into his work area?

"I am not running any business but company business; how dare you accuse me of anything dishonest," he resonated throughout the room. He was infuriated to be a suspect of porno trafficking but much more upset being a suspect in Alice's murder.

Nikki was questioned about her providing the girls for John's extracurricular venture. Each suspect provided additional information and clues about the identity of the killer. Just before the intermission, I sheepishly returned to my table and chair. Within moments a woman's shriek came from the stairwell. Jeremy was dead.

With dessert served, the Inspector told the assembled diners additional clues lay on the back table for all to peruse. We could use the clues to further decide who the killer was. Our table decided we didn't need to do that, as we knew John was the culprit. He knew Jeremy could link him to the pornographic business he was running. I even interjected false information to further help them suspect John and turn the light off me. We began writing our song about who and why. Later we learned each table was to sing its song for all to hear.

Our group wrote a silly song about John and his business dealings then put it to the tune of "I Could Have Danced All Night." As each table's song was sung, it was evident that tables one, two, and five had no clue to the killer's identity. The other tables sang about their choices. Table four pinned me perfectly. Ron looked at me and said, "Now, what reason would they have to suspect you?" I looked him straight in the eye and said, "I don't know." When table seven nailed me, Ron said, "I don't understand why they keep picking you. You don't even work with these people." I said. "I haven't a clue" hoping to keep a straight face so he wouldn't know the truth. I managed it but I didn't know how.

Toward the end of the cherries jubilee Inspector Holmes took the podium to announce the winners of the evening. He said, "Two tables correctly solved the murders." At this point I was to stand up, grab a large spoon that had been placed there for me, and put it to the neck of the man sitting to my right. I was to use him as a shield to exit the room. With the Inspector's clue-in I stood up and said, "You won't take me in alive," and took hold of the spoon and put it to Ian Gardnier's neck. After a tussle with Holmes, I was taken into custody and charged with murder. If tables four and seven hadn't figured the mystery out, I might have gotten away with two perfect murders.

Turning around, I saw Ian's shocked face then I turned to Ron. The look on his face was worth a gram of gold. Ron couldn't believe I had pulled my part off without a hitch and he didn't know anything about it.

After the dinner was over, the London ensemble presented me with one of their stage shirts for my part in the play. They said I should have gotten an Oscar for what I pulled off. I felt honored just to be a part in their performance.

All the way home Ron just could not get over that I had accepted the part much less kept it a secret. I totally loved this special night. I knew I would do it again if asked.

24. Our Christmas Present

The day we had waited for so long had finally arrived. Ron, Nancy, and Jennifer were coming for Christmas. The house was ready. The holly garlands were wrapped around the banister, the Christmas tree was trimmed, the cookies and sweets were baked, casseroles were frozen, and an evergreen wreath even hung on our front door, a sign an American lived inside, as one wasn't seen on anyone else's door.

When our alarm clock buzzed at half four in the morning, we knew it was time to dress, have a quick bite of toast and juice, and be on our way to Gatwick for the "kids". Just as we closed the door, Ron asked, "Do we have any coffee left?" I said, "Sure, I'll put some in our travel mugs."

With little on the radio, I put in a Christmas cassette and we sang all the traditional songs of the season. We sounded like two magpies singing *The Christmas Song, White Christmas, Joy to the World*, and *Good King Wenceslas* as we motored down the M-25.

About an hour later, we pulled into the airport parking structure then proceeded up its levels looking for a parking place. Finally, someone pulled out and we drove in. Alighting from our Sierra we searched for a lift (elevator) to take us to the plane arrivals level.

By six we were gazing at the arrival's screen only to find their plane had arrived fifteen minutes early with its passengers already in the immigration process. Wouldn't be long now before they would come out. We waited as close to the exit door as we could. Passengers started trickling out looking exhausted from their nine-hour overnight flight.

Finally, we saw them come through. We waved and waved to get their attention. Seeing us, their faces turned to smiles and waved back. It was great to see them. Nancy announced, "You'll never get me to do that again! Nine hours on an airplane is way too long." In only four months Jennifer had changed so much; she looked older and taller.

Pushing the luggage trolley to the car we plopped their things into our car and off we drove for home. Having them here was like opening our Christmas present early. Santa was certainly good to us.

After sandwiches, crisps, and sodas, we gave them a foot tour of our little village. Like us, they expected Christmas decorations and trees in homes but none were found. The terrible British economy meant people couldn't afford the trimmings. Being an English teacher I envisioned a Dickens' wonderland manifested everywhere. Trees filled with candles, tinsel, and ornaments. To my amazement, shops did not decorate either. I guess a Hallmark Christmas only pervades the States, not here. The only signs of Christmas here were the lighted decorations hanging from village lampposts.

Two weeks prior to the family's arrival the village hosted a festive Dickens' evening. All the lit village shops stayed open until nine o'clock. Some shops served hot cider for the adults and biscuits and chocolates for the children. What a lovely evening, especially with twinkling overhead lights, the smells of hot cider and cinnamon, and Christmas songs sung by groups of carolers in the crisp, night air.

Ron and Nancy couldn't believe the small shop sizes, the lack of commercialization, as well as the limited grocery choices. I took Nancy into Clare's, my little china shop, to show her the china beakers which she might like for family gifts back home. While we were in Clare's, the guys took Jen next door to the Seven-Eleven for some candy. Regrouping we passed Mr. Land's where they were aghast to see cut meat along with feathered and footed turkeys hanging upside down in his sunlit front window. The greengrocer was just as they had expected. Their next eye-opener proved to be our village "grocery". Seeing the long life milk and juice products, the small selection of tinned items, the limited choices in meats, frozen products, cereals and laundry products, along with the unlimited amounts of breads, crisps, and candies dumbfounded them. Nancy said, "How do you manage here?" I said simply, "You learn to adjust." Another adventure for them was the newsagent shop filled with newspapers, magazines, candies, and cards as well as our local postal office.

They spent the rest of the day unpacking and readjusting to the new time difference. Five hours ahead definitely does people in, especially the first day. We kept them moving so they didn't have time to sit down and doze off till bedtime.

The following day the effects of Jen's long flight caught up with her. All she wanted to do was lay on the floor and do absolutely nothing. For her, she was still moving with the plane. Ron took young Ron golfing at a friend's course. In England golfers can play year round as it never gets cold enough or snows enough to stop them.

One of the things Nancy wanted to see was *"The Phantom of the Opera"*. Fortunately for us, one of my coffee buddies couldn't use her tickets so I purchased them for Ron and Nancy's Christmas gift. To see it at Her Majesty's Theatre would be a treat in and of itself.

A day later we bundled up in our winter heavies and walked to the train station and London. This was Jen's first train ride. She was glued to the train window peering out at all the cows and horses. While riding in, I explained to Jen she had to hold onto one of us at all times. People rushing to their destinations could push her out of our sight and she could get lost. Continuing on, I told her, "In London some trains travel under the ground. They move very quickly and carry many people on them so again she needed to stay close to us." I explained the air in the tunnels they traveled reeked of dirt. She was not to be afraid but just stick with us. If something scared her, she was to let us know. She seemed to understand and went back to watching the countryside.

Screeching into Liverpool Street Station we took hold of each other. The station's expanse, number of trains, and the hustle bustle of the commuters, train personnel, and shopkeepers overwhelmed Ron, Nancy, and Jennifer. Inside the station proper they spotted newsagent shops, two pubs, a bookshop, and sundry clothes shops for those items people might have forgotten on their way to work. The amazing thing for them proved to be the McDonald's on the upper level. A piece of home away from home.

Maneuvering our little flock into the Central Line walkway, we approached our first ticket turnstile. Jennifer noticed people putting their tickets into the lower part of the stile and retrieving them from the top. She wanted to do hers herself – being an independent little lady of three and a half. We let her, even though she wasn't supposed to. Down the forthcoming elevator and another flight of steps we arrived on the platform waiting for the next oncoming train. We took the westbound passing Bank with its station loudspeaker saying, "Mind the Gap". Ron and I always loved hearing that as it alerted people getting on and off the train to look for the gap between the platform and the train. The train slid past St. Paul's, Chancery Lane, and onto Holborn where we changed to the Piccadilly line for the Circus.

Jumping off at the Circus, we pushed our way through the throngs of commuters, then the exit turnstile finally finding ourselves outside in the sunny, cold day. To see their faces in awe of all they perused was a treat in itself. We walked down Piccadilly so I could show them Fortnum and Mason. Bad choice! F and M was inundated with the Christmas deluge of shoppers searching for special Christmas goose and country pates, roasting turkeys, Stilton and cheddar cheeses, and spirits. It was wall-to-wall people without an inch to breathe. We pressed forward as I wanted them to see this wonderful establishment. Christmas holly and evergreen garlands encircled posts and doors, and the flavor of international cuisines could be found in each food department.

We lunched at my favorite Ponti's. Their selection of sandwiches (corn beef, ham, cheese, roast beef, any kind of cheese), salads (tuna, chicken, garden, pastas), huge jacket potatoes (enough baked potato for two or three), and desserts (tortes, éclairs, mousses) could make even the most stuffed individual hungry. Ron and the kids had ham and cheese sandwiches with crisps; Jen ate part of my potato and a part of Nancy's sandwich. Afterwards we walked them to Her Majesty's Theatre for the matinee performance of *"The Phantom"*. Nancy was excited like *"A Cat on a Hot Tin Roof"*. She couldn't believe she was going to see the play she had wanted to see for many years. I was thrilled for both of them. After depositing them at the theatre, we took Jennifer to see the *"The Muppets' Christmas Carol"* with Michael Caine. With bags of popcorn and cups of Coke we slid into our seats. For the next hour and a half she was glued to the story on the screen. She loved it.

After our show we walked up to the theatre to retrieve Ron and Nancy who were just coming out. Overjoyed understated their mood. Nancy said, "I can't believe the scenery, the costumes, the boats in "water", the singing, and the candelabra. I can't thank you enough for that. It was absolutely the best gift I've ever gotten." From her beaming smile and euphoria, I knew she loved every minute of it.

All five of us walked back into Leicester Square only to find a Christmas carnival going on full blast with ferris wheels, merry-go-rounds, clowns, calliopes, herty-gertys, and minstrels everywhere. What a sight to see. As it was now nearly six and the evening December air blew cold, we huddled together deciding what rides Jen could ride. She most definitely wanted to ride the merry-go-round and clown around with the clowns. She played "hit the peg" game and became upset when she did not win a prize.

After her merry-go-round ride was over, we stopped at the McDonalds for cheeseburgers, fries, and large containers of hot chocolate to warm us before starting home. A truly enjoyable day.

The day before Christmas Eve, Nancy and I drove to Lakeside Mall to do some last minute shopping for Jen and Santa. I bought Jen a traditional British navy wool double-breasted coat with velvet lapels and matching hat. Nancy picked up some small toys she could easily pack in her suitcase for their return flight. I had told Nancy not to mail all Jen's gifts as the duty on them would double their cost. Nancy left Jen's major Christmas at home so Santa could put them out while they were in England.

Christmas Eve afternoon we attended the family Christmas service at church. I was dumbfounded and quite saddened to hear different melodies played to our traditional Christmas carols. I couldn't sing any of them. I reminded myself I was in England and not Michigan so things would be different.

About ten o'clock that night with Jen asleep, Nancy and Ron realized they were short some double A batteries for her toys. Remembering the Seven-Eleven in the village they said they would go there. I thought it would be closed but an hour later they returned from a romantic moonlit walk holding the needed batteries. I couldn't believe the store was open much less have the needed batteries. Quickly, they went about Santa's business.

Christmas morning was filled with shrieks of happiness. Santa actually had found Jennifer. The lounge never seemed so full as it did that day. Surrounding the Christmas tree were Barbie dolls, equipment, puzzles, coloring and reading books, clothes, and Christmas stockings. Everyone's stocking was filled to the brim with socks, toiletries, and fruit. Within minutes the room was filled with ripped paper and ribbon from opened presents. It was wonderful to see Christmas once again through the eyes of a child. We had not had that pleasure since our boys were little and Santa mesmerized.

Turkey, mashed potatoes, new peas, tossed salad, and hot rolls made the fare of the day. I was finally getting the hang of all those British flours. For the finale, pumpkin pie with real whipped cream. Early in December I was in Fortnum and Mason going through the American products and found a tin of pumpkin. I must have let out a shriek of excitement as people looked at me funny.

The day after Christmas was Boxing Day. NO, that doesn't mean people box each other. In manor houses and estates years ago the servants cooked and served sumptuous Christmas meals of ham, turkey, venison, roast beef, roasted potatoes, various vegetables, and desserts such as trifles, tortes, and maid of honor cakes. The following day (December 26) the servants came to the manor home and received a box filled with Christmas leftovers. Their masters also gave them the entire day off. Even today, Boxing Day is a legal holiday with shops being closed for business. Two days later we once again bundled up in our heaviest winter coats, trousers, and shoes and boarded the train for a day of sightseeing in London. It was frigid but the sun was radiating through the train's windows making us feel warmer than we actually did. After a half hour's ride we alighted from the train and began our walk to the underground.

Jennifer remembered the ticket procedure and demanded hers so she could do it again. We dealt with turnstiles, train transfers, and throngs of people until we reached St. James Station on the Circle Line. Once through the turnstiles and stairwells, we found ourselves outside in the bright sunlight. From the station we started down Birdcage Lane leading to Buckingham Palace. Along the way we spotted the Guards' Museum with its toy soldier shop. Nancy's father, a British Army buff, wanted one of the Royal regiments for Christmas. Realizing the Changing of the Guard ceremony started in less than ten minutes, we decided to return there after viewing Buckingham Palace and the ceremony. Hurrying along we passed the Wellington Barracks and the Guards Chapel, transformed into a memorial to the soldiers and medical personnel who were killed there during a German bombing run during the War.

Following along the high black iron fences we arrived at Buckingham Palace. Outside its front gates was a large roundabout with the Queen Victoria Memorial and floral garden in its center. We watched as cars and buses entered and exited it without a bobble of worry. When we saw a break in the traffic, we crossed the street. We wanted to get the usual tourist pictures of the Palace and the Guard ceremony. We pushed Jen in front of us so she could see everything taking place.

The horses' hooves could be heard clippity clopping down the Mall toward the Palace along with the taps from the foot soldiers' shiny black patent shoes. What an amazing sight to see The Queen's Guard dressed in their distinctive red and white jackets with gold epaulets, white trousers, black riding boots, and tall gold hats with tassels riding atop their well-groomed horses. Impressive to say the least! Each motion was made with great precision – no mistakes allowed here. Every tap of their black boots meant something as they demonstrated their military patterns. After the new guard (those going on duty) took their places, the old guard (those going off duty) marched ensemble back to their regiment quarters. At the close of the ceremony the horse guard would return their steeds to the Queen's Mews where they would be groomed, fed, exercised, and stabled by their masters. After all the pomp and circumstance finished everything returned to normal – silent and sterile.

We walked back to the toy soldier shop. Nancy looked through all the regiments of British, Irish, Scottish, Indian, and Australian armies. She finally decided to take a set of the Queen's Guard as well as one of the Horse Guard regiment.

We walked back through St. James Park to Westminster Abbey, St. Margaret's Church, and the Houses of Parliament. I took them into St. Margaret's Church; I love this little church with its rustic pews, front altar, and stained glass windows.

Westminster Abbey overwhelms its first time visitors – no different for Ron, Nancy, and Jen. The awe they showed at the war memorial in the Abbey's foyer area, the colorful stained glass windows, the sculptures, and the various tomb tableaus pleased us. We took them through the back chapel area pointing out the tombs of former royalty and religious heads along with side altars given in memory of various royals. Through this tour they received additional history of British life and royalty.

As Abbey's custom, the Dean of the Abbey announced the hourly prayer service. Everyone was to stop and bow his or her head while prayers were offered for the day, the monarchy, the war dead, and any special requests.

Afterward we pressed on to the Houses of Parliament and Big Ben. Passing along its tall black iron fence, we heard Big Ben announce bombastically – three o'clock. Anyone who stands near when Big Ben roars feels the reverberation of his power with each hour's strike. We had hoped since it was Christmas time we could get inside Parliament but because of the time the threat of an IRA bombing loomed even greater. Security watched every person passing by and no one went inside. Oh, well maybe on their next trip things would be different and we could tour.

We crossed over Westminster Bridge so they could take the touristy photos of Parliament, Big Ben, and the River Thames. With the cold breeze coming up our coats and under our collars, we took the Tube to the Hard Rock Cafe on Park Street instead of walking it. What a treat we found inside – memorabilia from the Beatles, guitars of American vocalists, stage costumes and programs from various entertainers along with old time jukeboxes blaring fifties tunes throughout the entire restaurant. After waiting twenty minutes for a table, we ordered beef hamburgers (imported from the States as the Mad Cow disease still loomed), fries, and good ole American beer. While waiting for our order to arrive, we strolled around looking at all the memorabilia displayed. What memories! Songs Ron and I had listened and danced to in the late 50's were heard in here. Our hamburgers arrived and tasted wonderful, especially since we didn't have to worry about any disease in them. We had become chicken and vegetable eaters since the epidemic hit here.

After lunch and a few purchases of Hard Rock items, we took a red double decker bus to Madame Tussaud's museum. Touring all the floors, we found real life wax figures of Henry VIII and his six wives, the Beatles, Frank Sinatra, Arnold Palmer, and all manner of notables. I flashed pictures of the guys standing beside muscle man Arnold Schwarzenegger and their favorite golfer, Arnold Palmer. After an exhausting tour of London we tubed to Liverpool Station then took British Rail home. A wonderful day!

The following day we drove to the White Cliffs of Dover, then to Rochester where Charles Dickens lived and wrote, and finally onto Canterbury Cathedral. I remember a mother saying to her young daughter, "Blyme 10p (pense) to use the loo; that's outrageous."

The background on Canterbury Cathedral began in 1070 when the first Norman bishop, Lanfranc, wished to create a major center for Christianity here and ordered this edifice to be built over the ruins of an Anglo-Saxon cathedral. Because of its reconstructions over the years, the Cathedral contains many examples of medieval architecture. What a magnificent building.

Its main entrance, the South-West Porch, was built in 1426 to commemorate the Victory of Agincourt. The 328 feet of the nave section made it Europe's longest medieval church. In a southwest transept window, a major stained glass window portrays a thousand year old Methuselah. Walking along a side hallway we found Trinity Chapel where Thomas Becket's remains reside. A Victorian painting of his canonization hangs just outside this chapel.

I always enjoy thinking about Chaucer and his wickedly humorous but pure Canterbury Tales. Chaucer wrote about a group of men and women (a cross-section of fourteenth century England) who met at a London inn the night before they began their pilgrimage to Canterbury. The innkeeper offered a prize to the one who could tell the best tale during their trip. Wanting to be a member of that journey and listening to their tales came second nature to me being an English teacher.

After the cathedral we decided we had had enough for one day. Jen was cranky from being pulled around from one site to another. Our drive home was quick and uneventful. Just being in the warm car added warmth to our feelings.

The following day we originally thought to rest but decided to go to Cambridge instead. With the students on Christmas hiatus we figured the town would be virtually ours. After parking our car we walked through the campus areas. We were delighted to find Trinity Chapel open. What a glorious place. Its elongated stained glass windows ran the full length down both sides of the chapel. The organ was encased in an overhead bridge between the sides of the nave. When the organist began practicing, the booming depth of the reeds and trebles reverberated through the length and breadth of the church. The choir area, just in beneath the altar area, was made of tall carved mahogany sections, desks, and chair benches. What a treat it would have been to hear the choir practicing along with the organist.

The altar area was blessed with a raised pulpit and lectern. I could only visualize the use of them: a bishop or minister expounding his weekly message to his congregation. Maybe some Sunday morning we would return for a service here.

After Trinity, we proceeded into the town to take in one of the stalwarts of British life, the pub, for a pint and a sandwich to tide us over until we returned home. The roast beef sandwiches, crisps, and ale fit the bill. Jen had milk with hers, of course.

As the day was waning, we hurried back to the car park and retrieved our car for the journey home. That evening we sat in front of the lit fireplace with beakers of hot tea or hot chocolate discussing the wonderful family time we were enjoying.

The day before New Year's Eve we were invited to lunch at the home of Tom and Mary Hite, a delightful British couple. They had invited the whole family so we could sample British cuisine and actual British life. When we arrived, Mary wasn't quite ready to serve lunch so Tom took Ron, Ron, and Nancy for a drink at their neighborhood pub, The Dirty Duck. Jen played with their children, Malcolm and Kerry. Malcolm and Jennifer were born two hours apart on opposite sides of the "pond". I talked with Mary, a gourmet cook, while she finished up her dinner. She served her wonderful hunter's stew, a mélange of steamed vegetables, hot rolls, butter, and topped it off with an exquisite English trifle. Afterwards, we retreated into their lounge for port and some cheese and crackers while the children continued to play. The day added a wonderful addition to Ron and Nancy's memory book.

New Year's Eve came. We all decided to stay up and welcome the New Year in. Ron and I had heard the British not only drink their bubbly but also set off myriads of fireworks. That evening I made my traditional menu of French onion soup and fresh salad. About ten Jen couldn't hold out any longer and fell asleep in her mother's arms.

At the strokc of midnight the sky filled with the glistening and booming of all kinds of fireworks welcoming in the New Year. I was surprised that the celebration went on for the better part of an hour. It was invigorating to really celebrate a new year this way.

The day before Ron, Nancy, and Jen were to leave, I took Ron into London, as he wanted to see the Tower of London and its buildings filled with armaments and weaponry from the days of knights to present day combat. While there, we toured the royal jewels display. Later, we had a ploughman's lunch and a pint at the Charles Dickens pub across from the Tower then we made our way back home. Nancy stayed home with Jen so she could pack for their return flight home.

The morning I had been dreading came. We took them to the airport, got them situated with their tickets, kissed them goodbye, and watched them go through the double doors toward immigration, customs, and their plane. When Nancy got to the security check, she was searched along with her carry-on bag as the guard thought she was carrying something suspicious. In her carry-on bag she had placed some lead vases and glasses she had purchased for Christmas gifts. Lead glass poses a problem for the x-ray machines, as they can't tell what the object is. Inspectors get nervous to find out what the blob or lump is so they check every piece of that luggage out to make sure nothing dangerous is inside. Nancy had to unwrap her gifts to show the inspectors what she was carrying then rewrap them. I learned a lesson: don't wrap anything before traveling. After the searches, they moved on to their plane.

Waving until they were out of sight, I let my pent-up tears flow. I hated seeing Jen leave, but knew I had to keep all the memories we had made together close to me until I could get myself back in sync with my life here.

25. My D Day Finally Arrives

What did D Day mean? To me, it wasn't the Normandy invasion but it felt like it to me. D Day, for me, was my driving examination day – thirty minutes of continuous driving and procedures along with twenty minutes of oral examination about traffic rules. As January 28 grew closer and closer, the more and more I felt like a teenager preparing for her first driving test. I couldn't believe the dive-bombing butterflies crashing into all sides of my stomach.

Having passed his test the week before, Ron said, "It's so easy anyone can pass that test and if they can't then they shouldn't be driving." What a thing to say to me. I was nervous enough about passing; this only added to my pressure. He thought telling me that would eliminate my concerns but it only aggravated the situation for me. Easy for him to say – he had passed.

As the days passed with more instruction and practice, I realized procedures I first had down pat now were creating problems for me – parallel parking was my nemesis while those I had initially had difficulty with reversing around the corner and the three point turn were magic in my hands. The more I practiced parking, the worse I became. I knew I had to perform the emergency stop and two of the other three procedures. All I could hope and pray for was the inspector wouldn't choose parallel parking.

The morning came. I couldn't get even a couple sips of my tea down much less eat some dry toast. Steve would pick me up an hour early so we could practice the parking maneuver again before I had to take the test. The more we practiced, the more I floundered. He and I both knew I was on the verge of failing – Steve's first failure.

At 9:15, I pulled up to the Inspection Building. Steve tried to reassure me while giving me last minute pointers about parking. He asked me to read the license plate on the car ahead of me hoping to take my mind off things. My jelly-filled legs made it difficult for me to put one foot in front of the other.

With Steve at my side, my driver's test form in my sweaty hands, and all the courage I could muster we walked into the foreboding gray stone and cement building. The room was devoid of any pictures on the wall or magazines on the tables, making it even more sterile. I sat down with three other applicants and their instructors. The first inspector came out naming his next candidate for the terror trip. I stood up but Steve pulled me down, as it wasn't my name. The name wasn't even a girl's. Embarrassment filled my face and body. Oh, how I wanted out of here. I was getting more nervous with each passing second. If the inspector didn't come out and call my name soon, I was afraid I would pass out when he did. How would that look especially with the frightened teenaged girl sitting across from me?

The second inspector came out. "Nancy Hurley," he said.

I stood up and left the room with him. As we were walking to Steve's car, he said he was Trevor Fairway. I said I thought he had given Ron his test last week and he had passed him. He couldn't remember but said it was possible. I just wanted to cut the ice between us.

As we approached Steve's car, the inspector asked me to read the license on the car in front of me. I rattled it off without a miss. I got the feeling this might not be so bad after all. I only had to do three procedures and drive well for a half hour with no touches or mistakes, answer about a dozen or so road questions, and it would be all over. Just think – in an hour it would be all over.

He asked me to pull away from the curb. Fastening my seat belt and watching my mirrors, I started the car and unlocked the emergency brake then pulled out into traffic. After a few minutes he had me drive down a lesser-used road and execute an emergency stop. No problem. I reminded myself when making a turn either way to always have two hands on the steering wheel – one to hold the wheel while the other pumped the wheel in the way of the turn. Crazy to me but to this day I still find myself using that technique in the States. I drove through Brentwood and negotiated the double roundabout without a hitch. Next, he asked me to turn into the next street left. The one Steve and I had practiced on many occasions. What would he ask me to do? He had three choices. He asked me to pull up past the corner behind the last car and reverse around the corner. Yippee! Smooth as glass! No touches and within the required measurement to the curb!

Now the real trauma and test began. Which would he have me do for my last required procedure – the three point turn or parallel parking. I kept driving around the town until he asked me to pull into the next right street. It was a dreary little lane. "Oh, God," I fervently prayed, "please, please let it be the three point turn." The answer came within seconds. He said, "Mrs. Hurley, I want you to go to the end of the lane, stop, then execute a three point turn." I could have kissed him but I didn't. I tried to keep a straight face – not one of utter relief. Everything went swimmingly. He asked me to traverse back down the lane. In order to get back to the inspection building I knew I had to go through the double roundabout I hadn't expected to do but did without a problem. Once at the station, he asked me a dozen road questions. I surprised him by knowing exactly how many meters it took to stop a car at 70 miles per hour.

While he ticked off my correct answers, I patiently waited for him to tell me if I had passed or not. He said the only thing I did wrong (a mistake all Americans make) was clutching going into a turn instead of changing gears before making the turn which gives the driver more control in the turn. He said, "Doing it your way will burn the clutch out faster." He wouldn't fail me for it but wanted me to be aware of it. Waiting on baited breath, he readied himself to leave then handed me my form. Shocked, I asked him, "Did I pass?" He said like I should have known, "Yes."

As I struggled to regain my composure after the test, I noticed Steve talking to Inspector Fairway. I guess Steve was concerned I had failed. When Steve got in, he said, "Congratulations, see you did do it and saved my record." All I could do was cry from relief and then smile my widest smile. I think he was a bit unsure whether I was calm enough to be driving. I assured him I was all right. Within a few streets I had regained my composure. Once home, I told Steve to wait. I ran into the house and returned with a bottle of champagne to thank him for all his perseverance and patience with me. He was quite pleased and said he would save it for a special day.

I telephoned Ron. Before I had time to tell him, he said, "You passed, didn't you?"

I said, "Yes!" Asking if I was going out, I said I was on my way to the weekly coffee hour.

He said, "If you don't mind, stick around the house for a bit, please." A little later I received a beautiful bouquet of cut flowers. The note read, "Way to go, Ron."

I was thrilled. Then I thought how I would have felt if I had failed. I didn't have to think about that anymore; I had passed and that was all there was to it. Now I could relax in my new country and not be overwhelmed by the fear of THE TEST.

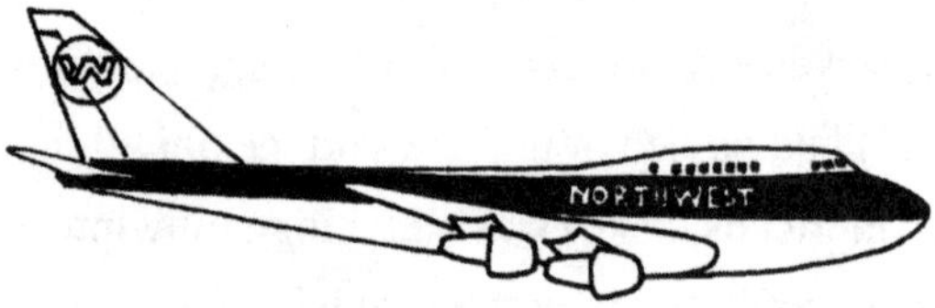

26. My First Solo Trip Home

February came upon us with its short days and long nights of darkness. I was having trouble dealing with the sun going down at half two in the afternoon and not rising until nine or so in the morning. Needing a rest from the gloom here, I used some of my frequent flyer miles and bought a ticket home.

On the morning of my departure I felt uneasy about traveling alone internationally, never having done that before. Since my flight was to leave at twelve thirty, we left home at eight giving us more than enough time to get to Gatwick for the two-hour requirement before international flights. The morning was cold and dreary which only added to my mood.

Once at Gatwick I retrieved a trolley, stowed my two bags on it, and pushed on to the Northwest counter with its already bulging passenger lines for both my flight as well as one to Frankfort. I looked at the departure board only to see that my flight had been delayed with something called technical. I wondered what that meant.

Behind me in the Northwest line were two lovely women, I asked them if they knew what the problem was. They hadn't even noticed the sign and were as much in the dark as I was. They were returning to Boston after a week's trip in London on one of Northwest's February ninety nine-dollar specials. What a wonderful week they had had. Not only were they teachers in the same school but best friends for over twenty years.

Giving my ticket and passport to the airport security before checking in, I was asked a battery of questions about my bag, whether I had packed it, who had access to it since packing it, had anyone asked me to carry a package on this flight, did I have any battery appliances such as a shaver – especially if it had been recently repaired or cleaned. Saying I had packed my cases which had remained in my possession all the time and no one had asked me to carry anything on, the inspector let me advance on to the ticket agent and check-in.

I presented my ticket and passport to the clerk who verified both then gave me the aisle seat I had requested. I asked about the delay. The woman said, "A navigational switch that needed to be replaced. Nothing to worry about." She handed me a lunch voucher since the delay would take us through the lunch hour. I wasn't hungry but knew Ron needed lunch before heading to work. I spied a Burger King on the upper floor.

He wasn't hungry either so we sat down in the lobby. Spotting a W. H. Smith bookshop, I decided to purchase some magazines for the flight. After making my purchases, I sat talking to Ron trying to ease the tension of the delay. All of a sudden I noticed a female constable approaching us. She said she and her partner were surveying passengers about their feelings about the police's anti-terrorist procedures within the airport. Within minutes she had ascertained that I was flying alone and she had my name, passport number, British and American addresses, flight number, and who would be picking me up in Detroit. What was going on here? Where are the survey questions? All of a sudden I noticed eight armed military and police guards with M-16 guns slowly and methodically cordoning off our area. I became quite nervous. After she left without a smile, I said under my breath to Ron, "Let's get out of here."

I tried to make sense about what had just happened. She had asked for all kinds of information but never any about the anti-terrorist survey. While trying to figure it all out, I looked back and noticed four armed guards surrounding a disheveled man who had been sitting behind me with a suspect package. The constable used me as a decoy until they could ascertain what the man might do if confronted. With Ron and I out of the way the police apprehended both the man and his package without a fault.

My legs went weak while my body shook from all the excitement. Wanting to get as far away from there as I could, Ron and I jumped on a nearby escalator for the Burger King on the upper floor. Ron ordered a hamburger, fries, and a coke and a strong cup of coffee for me with my voucher. After a few moments I had regained my composure.

Since international flights are not announced over a loudspeaker, I had to keep my eyes on the departure screen. About one o'clock I saw my flight's listing. Ron and I went to the Immigration area where we said goodbye and off I went for my first solo flight.

The closer I got to my Northwest gate, the more I sensed the problem hadn't been fixed. Arriving at the gate, I learned Northwest had delayed our departure another five hours. The problem wasn't technical after all. The plane had arrived at Gatwick late from the Middle East and its on-board crews were now over their regulated flying time for the day. Northwest had to pull together another crew from all over England and that might take another five hours.

I left a message on Ron's office telephone box as well as young Ron's telling them of the delay. Since I had already gone through Immigration and Customs, I could not leave this area. I was stuck. I was given a dinner voucher for fourteen pounds since dinner would now be missed as well. I teamed up with the two teachers, Carol Brown and Carol Haney who were also at loose ends. We decided to have a drink in the bar across the way as we could see any changes in our status from there.

We ordered glasses of Chardonnay. Within minutes a young man, Martin White, joined us. While he was a first year music teacher in the Chicago school system, we girls were seasoned teachers of twenty plus years under our belts. We discussed our families, trips, education, successful teaching techniques, and life itself.

Nothing was happening so we ordered another round of chardonnay since we knew we would be fed on the plane. Martin asked us for our remaining vouchers and said he would talk the bartender into selling us a bottle of champagne to celebrate our time together. We thought he was crazy to think he could accomplish this but he did. By the boarding time, all four of us felt toasty warm; the inconvenience of the plane's delay had dissolved. I felt happy I had made three new friends.

After boarding the plane and eating my airplane meal, I connected with my friends and spent another hour talking. By this time the wine, champagne, and dinner had made me drowsy so I said my goodbyes and walked to my seat hoping for a few hours of sleep. Even the dreams in my restless sleep were of the family.

About three hours later, I was awakened to the stewardess reviewing the procedures for entering the US. I needed to fill out the easy immigration and customs forms. The head steward explained that passengers with connecting flights needed to retrieve their luggage, go through customs, then hurry onto their next flights. Now, I was not happy. I would have to lug two suitcases plus my carry-on without a trolley.

The Carols and Martin knew the predicament I was in. The Carols pulled one of my suitcases while Martin took command of the other. As we were moving through customs, the thought hit me. What if they were asked about the contents of my bag, they would have no clue as to what was inside. We could be in serious trouble since no one was to carry through someone else's luggage. No problems occurred. They even placed my bags on the conveyor belt for my Detroit flight. I thanked them profusely and gave them hugs.

As I was about to call young Ron's home to tell him what was happening, the flight personnel said Northwest had held their last Detroit flight for our arrival. I must hurry to gate G-7 to catch the plane. Rushing, I just made it before its doors closed.

Two cokes and two bags of peanuts later, the plane descended onto Detroit Metro's runway. Since I had already gone through immigration and customs in Boston, I was free to find my family. It was now one thirty in the morning. Young Ron looked as tired as I was. A long winter's nap would do both of us good.

After two weeks of visiting, partying, and stocking up on certain foodstuffs unavailable in England, I returned home on an uneventful straight flight. My first solo encounter with international flight was over.

27. Old Friends – New Encounters

While I was home in February, our priest and his wife, The Reverend and Mrs. Books, told me of their plans to visit England during the last two weeks of March. I said if they had some time, we would love to have them visit and show them London.

Bob and Pat explained that they would be in the Midlands visiting clergy friends but would love to have a stopover with us before going to Canterbury. "That would be perfect," I said. They asked if Ron and I could meet them in Ironbridge in the Midlands for a day or two; they knew of a wonderful bed and breakfast there. I said I would check Ron's schedule. Bob asked if I could get him a country map showing all the roundabouts and roads throughout Britain. I said I would when I returned to England.

After Ron cleared his calendar for those two days, we called the Books to say we would join them. We were excited to see Ironbridge again, as the year before my Dad died, Ron and I had brought him there to see his family.

The drive up was miserable – fog, rain, and winds. By the time we got to the Ironbridge Lodge on the Severn (River), we were quite tired but happy to see our friends. Since Bob and Pat were great fans of Father Cadfield, a monk known for his solving medieval murder mysteries, they spent their first days touring the churches depicted in this series.

Benjamin and Mary Setters, our Lodge hosts, greeted us like old friends as Bob told the Setters we were close friends of theirs. We were escorted to our bedroom with a private bath on the upper level. It was lovely. Our double bed had a white lace canopy over it and a marvelous white feather duvet on it. Lace valances adorned the double pane window. A navy upholstered sitting chair sat on one side of the window with an armoire on the other. The bath was quite small but all we needed for our overnight.

After freshening up, we returned to their large lounge containing two overstuffed dusty rose sofas and three chairs, a side table holding all the accoutrements for an evening drink, and a roaring wood fire in the fireplace. The Setters showed us their large gourmet kitchen which any cook would love to create in. The kitchen's bake oven was made of adobe and had been here for years. Benjamin explained it took two hours of wood burning to heat up the oven enough to bake bread. This oven also served as a heat source for the house. The house had a comfortable feeling to it. During our house tour, another couple, Trevor and Mary Prindle, had arrived. When we finished our tour, the Books, the Prindles, and Ron and I sat around the fire talking while enjoying a glass of wine. A half hour later Benjamin and Mary placed serving tables (like our TV tables) in front of us then set a delicious chicken breast salad with hot rolls down on each of them. We ate heartly thinking this was our dinner, only to learn this was just our appetizer. Later, Benjamin placed steaks on a fireplace rack and turned the already baking jacket potatoes in the fire's embers. The meal was fabulous – meat so tender we could cut it with a fork, potatoes so full and fluffy that they tasted like floating clouds of air.

Benjamin told us the history of this Inn. Boats bearing needed coal, metals, food, and clothing for people along the river would tie up here for the night. Their pilots would spend the night enjoying the company of people since their trips kept them away from their families for many days. This inn was a comfort to them and thrived on those rentals for many years. After our history lesson, out came the desserts, an apple crumble and a fruit trifle to die for. Later, the men enjoyed a small glass of port to "help with the digestion" as our hosts said.

Ron and I fell into a restful sleep under the feather duvet. Before we knew, it was light. We showered, dressed, and went downstairs for breakfast. The menu included the traditional English breakfast of fresh juice, eggs, bacon, sausage, tomatoes, hard rolls, butter, orange marmalade and various homemade preserves along with pots of hot tea and coffee.

Discussion ensued about our room's history. Our room had been a brothel room used by some boaters for some private nightly entertainment. This room was chosen for that because it was the only one with a private bathroom. The remaining room guests had to share a bathroom down the hall. We must have looked red faced as everyone looked at us with smiles. They knew of the history and we didn't.

After breakfast we packed our suitcase and put it into our boot, then the four of us drove to a craft area. We drove to an old factory that had been gutted some years before then individual craft shops were put in to revitalize the old structure. A bookshop sold some best sellers, area pamphlets and maps as well as Ironbridge postcards. Another shop had all kinds of birdcages and feeding houses; the British love their birds. Bob and Pat wanted some but transporting them home presented a problem. The next shop consisted of a Victorian hat and costume shop. Pat and I spent what seemed like hours in there trying on hats and looking at the little girl dresses for our granddaughters. I didn't want to leave. The next shop taking our fancy was filled with all manner of shoes; nothing took our fancy enough to buy. Our final stop was the cook shop with all kinds of local pots, pans, and crockery. After our shopping trip we returned to the Inn and said our thank yous and goodbyes to everyone before returning home.

A few days later Bob and Pat arrived at our abode. I have always loved having friends visit. Since they wanted to spend time in Canterbury as well as drive through some coastal villages before returning home, we could only enjoy them overnight. We certainly were thrilled to have them for as much time as we could.

After Ron arrived home from work that night, he took Bob to a local pub, The Green Dragon, for a wee pint before dinner. Pat sat with me in my aroma filled kitchen while I finished baking a yummy shepherds' pie filled with lamb, spring onions, carrots, peas, seasonings, and topped with mashed potatoes then finished with the traditional shredded cheddar cheese. I created a large garden salad with romaine, endive, radicchio, tomatoes, spring onions, radishes, cucumbers, mushrooms, and sunflower seeds and sprinkled with a simple oil and vinegar dressing so not to overwhelm the greens. To sop up the pie's gravy, I had baked some rolls. For dessert I planned to serve an apple crumble I had made earlier in the day. Maybe even some ice cream with it.

By the time the two guys returned from their evening jaunt, dinner was piping hot and ready to be served. They had given me just enough time to finish my cooking. We sat and talked of the churches and clergy they had visited since coming here; some Bob only knew through correspondence.

The friendship we had for each other bubbled out. I felt like we were sitting in one of our kitchens or living rooms back in Michigan. We felt enveloped with all the good things friendship brings – companionship, support, caring, and involvement. We felt that even more that evening.

Sadly, the morning came. We said our goodbyes and sent them on their way so they could encounter their adventures in our new land. After spending a night in an old hotel behind the Canterbury Cathedral a priest friend had recommended, they would drive along the south coast. I envied their trip as I love the seaside. Being near water always revives me, giving me a sense of peace I don't feel anywhere else. One day Ron and I would do that, too.

28. The City of Romance

On St. Patrick's Day I drove into Brentwood to see Lisa, my trusty travel guide. I hoped she would have something available for a long weekend between then and the middle of April. She said, "What about Paris? Spring will be in full bloom then and love will be in the air." Sounded like a winner to me! She found a promotion through Paris Travel Service that was not only economical but inclusive: air fare, transfers from and to the Charles De Gaulle Airport, hotel room with breakfast included, and a five day pass for the Metro (the Paris underground) system. Since we did not know the restaurants, we chose to purchase dinner vouchers to show us some nice restaurants to try. We also decided to stay at the Hotel Brittany as it was in the Montmartre or artist section of Paris; I love that area.

On Saturday, March 27th, we arose at four forty-five to dress and find our way to Stansted Airport (about an hour northeast of us). Stansted, a small airport in comparison to the larger London ones, catered to domestic British airlines as well as some European ones. Until American Air Lines realized it was losing passengers to Heathrow and Gatwick Airports, it used this airport. Their customers liked to train or taxi into London but with Stansted they resented having to travel more miles losing commute time into London proper. Such a shame as Stansted was and is a superb airport.

It was a misty, cold morning with dew and frost everywhere. We set out with our optimism riding high. We were on our way to romantic

PARIS. I couldn't believe it. I had waited for Paris since we arrived in England. The drive seemed to take forever.

Once at the airport we found the long term parking area, put our car into its space, and hopped onto the airport bus. Gathering our bags from the bus we checked in with Air UK Airlines. The usual procedure ensued with passport control then customs. We always slowed down the process for everyone as we had to be checked into immigration records as going out of the country and then have our passports stamped. Once all the requirements had been taken care of, we walked through the international flights' doorway and onto a shuttle bound for our plane.

Our flight was full to the brim with other Paris travelers. To our complete surprise we were served a full English breakfast during our forty-five minute flight. We ate heartily on orange juice, scrambled eggs, bacon, link sausages, toast, marmalade, and our choice of coffee or tea. What a change from American flights serving only peanuts and cokes.

On arrival at De Gaulle Airport we scurried for the baggage return; then to immigration and customs so we could begin our romantic weekend. I remembered Lisa telling to me that a Paris Travel Service representative would meet us at the front of the terminal but none was in attendance. All of a sudden I felt a twinge of panic like a lost child in a huge, unfamiliar department store. In our hot little hands we held our transfer vouchers with no one in sight to tell us what to do with them or where to pick up the bus into town. I went to the Paris Tourist Information Center to get some transfer information but found it inundated with tourists needing room reservations, theatre tickets, and the like. After waiting in line for a representative, I explained our predicament. He told me to go to Exit 34 and get on the Air France bus which would take us to the Arch de Triomphe; from there we would need to get a taxi to our hotel.

Riding the bus into Paris only heightened our excitement and wonderment of all we would see and do. The bus left us off at the Arch. We stood for a few minutes watching all the cars, buses, and taxis whizzing around in every direction as if they were racing to a fire or a large clearance sale. We thought of using our Metro pass to get to our hotel but nixed that idea when we thought of lugging our bags into and out of the stations.

Ron whistled and put his arm out for a taxi. Within moments one came to a streaking halt in front of us. The taxi driver put our bags in the front with him. I told him the name of our hotel. He shook his head at my French pronunciation then took off like a NASCAR driver speeding for the finish line. What I thought would be a ten or fifteen minute ride took only five or six minutes. At times I just closed my eyes and prayed as he wove his way through traffic at top neck speed. I guess the more clients he serviced, the more money and tips he made so it was to his advantage to get his passengers to their destinations in a flash.

Oh, Paris. I was really in Paris. I had to pinch myself to make sure this wasn't just a dream. It wasn't. We arrived at the Brittany at half ten but couldn't get into our room until half two. We left our luggage in their secured holding room then decided to scout out the area to see what we could find. We found the old Opera House, a Galleria of many boutiques and stores, and a tour center selling tickets for day as well as nighttime tours of the city.

When we finally checked in, we learned the elevators didn't work as they were in the midst of a complete renovation. All the hotel wiring was being replaced and the walls were being repainted. In order to get to our room we had to walk up stairwells full of electrical wires, paint buckets, tarpaulins, ladders, and workmen everywhere. As soon as the electricians finished their work, the painters came to fill in, sand, and paint over all the holes in the walls and ceilings. This kind of renovation is true for most European hotels fifty years and older as they need updating just to keep up with all the city regulations.

Even with all this commotion going on, the Brittany was a wonderfully quaint and desirable place to stay. To top things off we were right in the midst of Montmartre and real French life.

Our next shock came when we opened the door to our room. It was the size of a matchbox. The room afforded us a bed, built-in closet, built-in desk, and a bathroom almost the size of the bedroom itself. Being so tired from the early wake-up alarm call, the flight, and the past four hours of walking, we did the unforgivable thing of holidays. We laid down for a quick nap; the next thing we knew it was dark. It was half six when we came to. We had missed an afternoon in Paris. Oh, well, we couldn't do anything about it but start anew.

We were starved so we asked the hotel desk to recommend a good place to eat. He said L'Intermede, across the street was nice. Looking at the name we realized it was listed in our voucher booklet.

Since European restaurants didn't open until seven, we took another stroll around the block to fully wake up. At seven the restaurant doors opened and the headwaiter motioned for us to come in. The place was charming. All the wait staff spoke French and some broken English. Looking at the menu then translating it for Ron, we chose steaming bowls of their bouillabaisse, hot rolls, and possibly an apple tarte for two for dessert. Since we were their only customers so far that evening, the staff catered to our needs. People say the French are aloof but we found them just the opposite. The problem I believe is Americans expect the French to speak English and the French are annoyed and offended we don't speak their language in their own country. I found out the French will go out of their way to help you if you attempt their language while those who don't try aren't given the time of day. What is the old saying? "When in Rome, do as the Romans do." No truer words. Don't expect them to be happy if you don't make the effort to be courteous with their language.

Sunday morning Ron and I got up early and went down to their tiny breakfast room. Inside this area we found twelve small tables filled to the brim with customers. As we waited our turn, we noticed the one and only waitress scurrying from table to table making sure everyone had the juice of their choice, hot rolls and croissants, and either coffee or tea. She was an elderly woman dressed in her prim black and white uniform, her grey hair pulled back in a tight French twist, and her cleaning-up towel was always in her hand or inside the trim of her waistband. Once a table was emptied she hurried to prepare it for the next breakfast guests. Neither Ron nor I envied her her job.

After breakfast we decided to attempt the Metro, Paris awaited us! The man at thc reception desk explained the nearest station was around the street and two blocks down. Excitement and nervousness came over us, as we were about to explore and encounter new, uncharted trails. Descending into the Metro I looked at my Paris book realizing all we had to know was the end stop on each subway line to know which train to take. I felt more reassured about the adventure we were undertaking.

Looking at the Metro map we found the lines and stops we needed in order to get to the Paris Travel Service. With our Metro passes in our hands we hopped onto the approaching train and off we went. Twenty minutes later we were standing in line at the Paris Travel office on Jardin des Tuileries purchasing tickets for their morning tour. We wanted to take that tour to get an overview of the city before deciding what we wanted to revisit at our leisure. The tour did precisely what we wanted.

Our tour bus took us to the Eiffel Tower where we got off to look around. Angelica, our guide, hoped to get us to the top but the elevator lines were too long for her time constraints. Our next stop was at the Arch de Triomphe where she told us about the bronze and silver wall plaques to fallen soldiers as well as the tomb of their unknown soldier with its eternal flame. Continuing on our tour we passed the Musee du Louvre, Notre Dame, the Hotel des Invalides (the military hospital established by Louis XIV for his men), the Ecole Militaire (a military school like West Point), Palais de Chaillot (palace of Chaillot), Grand Palais (grand palace), the Place de la Concorde (gigantic square where more than a thousand people were guillotined during the French Revolution and its counter revolution), and finally the Avenue des Champs Elysee (the long tree-lined street stretching from the Place de la Concorde to the Arch de Triomphe).

After our tour, we walked down the Jardin des Tuileries through the park area to Notre Dame Cathedral. The bright sunshine made the structure sparkle even more. Masses of picture-taking fanatics of all nationalities greeted us outside. An interesting tourist note: on Sundays the Police cordon off a portion of the street to the left of the Cathedral as well as the little footbridge to the right so skateboarders and roller skaters can race each other. Seemed so out of character for this kind of activity to go on the grounds of Notre Dame. Within moments of our arrival here and to our surprise, a real nip in the air caught both of us off guard. Also, at the cathedral's front courtyard vendors hawked anything from trinkets to post cards and booklets of Paris, Notre Dame, and other sites. One man sold berets, scarves, and T-shirts with various landmarks or themes on them. I talked Ron into buying a red beret to cover his head; the gentleman demonstrated different ways he could wear it for different effects. Positioning it on the side of his head, Ron looked like a real Frenchy kind of guy. Ooh, la la.

The inside of Notre Dame was as massive as it was exquisite with all the stained glass windows and candles. Notre Dame (Our Lady) has had religious significance for at least two thousand years. In Roman times a temple to Jupiter was erected on this very site then followed in the fourth century by the first Christian church, Saint Etineen.

A second church, dedicated to Our Lady, joined St. Etineen's two hundred years later. Both were left derelict by Norman invaders until Bishop Maurice de Sully commissioned the construction of this cathedral to replace both of them in 1163. The main part of Notre Dame took 167 years to construct. Its architectural design came from the Romanesque and Gothic movements. Notre Dame has been called the perfect expression of medieval architecture.

In 1430 Notre Dame was the site of England's Henry VI's coronation as King of France. In 1594, Henri IV attended mass here sealing his conversion to Catholicism and reinforcing his hold on the French throne. In 1804 the pope attended Napoleon's coronation. The pope arrived thinking he would crown Napoleon emperor of France but Napoleon crowned himself emperor. It was here Mary Queen of Scots celebrated her marriage to Francois II.

At one point the cathedral was almost torn down. but because of the influence of Victor Hugo's tale *The Hunchback of Notre Dame,* respect for this great church was revived. In recent years the cathedral has been the site of the military funerals for such French heroes as Foch, Leclerc, and de Gaulle.

The church's central and most renowned window, the Rose window, encircles the Madonna and Child depicting Redemption after the

Fall. Over the doorways the Galerie des Rois (gallery of the kings) reveals twenty-eight statues representing the kings of Judah and Israel. The South Tower contains the "bourdon", Notre Dame's only original bell. In 1953, the cathedral had installed an electric system to ring its great bells. It no longer uses people (hunchbacks in Victor Hugo's book) to ring them.

After taking in all the glorious cathedral sights, we felt hunger pangs. We walked across the Pont-Neuf (the oldest footbridge in Paris) to the Right Bank filled with its myriad of sidewalk cafes and "bouquinistes", salespeople selling everything from posters and postcards to literature and obscure academic pamphlets. We found a little cafe (Le Corona) to have a pizza and two cokes while taking in the atmosphere and people watch. The cost of this little leisure was thirty dollars. Their pizza and costs were nothing like what we had in the States. The area's great ambience more than made up for the cost.

After lunch we did the touristy thing and walked the quay (river). The Seine divides Paris into two sides or "banks": the left bank, the artsy side, from the right bank, the business and political center of the city. We bought some postcards then walked on to the Musee du Louvre only to it find closed. Looking at our watches, we couldn't believe it was almost five o'clock. We continued our walk along the River Seine then climbed the hillside to the Musee de Cinema (a museum entirely dedicated to reconstructed movie sets, historic posters, costumes from Greta Garbo, Catherine Deneuve, and others). When we arrived at the Musee, we gasped for air. As we stood on this pinnacle, we could view everything for a ten-mile radius. We could even see the Eiffel Tower in the distance. What a glorious sight!

Built for the 1889 World's Fair, the Eiffel Tower was then and still is today an astonishing engineering feat – fifteen thousand pieces of metal joined together by two and a half million rivets. She seems to stretch up into the sky using all her three hundred meter height (nine hundred eighty-four feet) and spreads out at its base one hundred thirty meters (fourteen hundred square feet). When the Tower was being built, residents were afraid it would fall down on their homes. After the Fair, Parisians wanted it torn down, but no one had the heart to do it so it still stands in all her majesty today. It truly was and is a wonder to behold. After some picture taking, Ron and I headed for the nearest Metro for our way back to the Brittany.

Most restaurants are closed on Sunday nights but we found a nice Chinese one open around the corner from our hotel. The egg rolls, the chicken and shrimp chop suey, and the large scoop of vanilla ice cream tasted good. The restaurant was clean and its service was applicable. What more could we ask for.

Monday morning was bright and cool. After our "le petit dejeuner" (breakfast), we boarded the Metro for the Louvre. Arriving at the Jardin des Tuileries stop we got off and walked to the Louvre. Walking through the Jardin we encountered several artists painting or sketching people or nearby buildings. One lone artist asked if I would let him sketch me. Since we didn't have the time then I said, "Maybe when we finish with the Louvre." I wish now I had let him, as a memento of our trip. Oh, well, maybe next time.

In the middle of the Louvre's courtyard was a disconcerting sight – a modernistic glass monolith in front of the museum entrance that seemed so out of place with the splendor of the baroque buildings surrounding it. Upon entering the museum, we rented cassette recorders which would give us our own personal guided tour of each period and nationality (Egyptian, Greek, Italian, Dutch, Flemish, German, Spanish, and English) of paintings. The museum was too much to take in a single day; even if we had a week we wouldn't have enough time to take in, digest, and savor each piece of art. Amazingly, tourists took pictures everywhere. We saw the *Winged Victory*, the *Venus de Milo* (Greek), as well as Leonardo de Vinci's *Mona Lisa* – now safely enclosed in heavy glass due to a recent slashing attack on her. Other significant paintings included *The Shipwreck of the Medusa* – shipwrecked men awaiting the arrival of a far-off rescue ship, *The Coronation of Napoleon* depicting his crowning of Josephine after he had already crowned himself. On display also were many beautiful religious paintings of Christ and the events in his life, medieval feudal events, royal paintings, various periods of furniture, as well as some "modernistic" paintings.

Throughout the Museum we watched aspiring artists standing at their wood easels mixing particular paint colors to get just the right color or studying a master's brush technique in order to reproduce it. Other students used sketchpads and charcoal pencils to recreate particular parts of a painting such as someone's eyes or hands in order to enhance their own expertise creating that particular body part. What amazed me was how near some came to the original artists' colors, lines, picture strengths, and emotions set within each work.

Before we knew it, it was four o'clock. We had spent our entire day there but knew it was worth every minute of it. We purchased two inexpensive Van Gogh prints, *The Haystack* and *Montematre at Night* which we planned to frame and put up in our TV room.

Leaving the Louvre we walked to the Hotel des Invalides. Directly under its golden dome rests Napoleon's tomb. Again, time was against us as we were too late to visit inside. We decided to return the following day, as Ron really wanted to see the interior and study its historical memorabilia.

We made our way to the Place du Concorde in order to walk the length of the Champs du Elysee from the Place to the Arch de Triomphe, a distance of about one mile. What an exhilarating walk! To walk down the most celebrated street in Paris, to buy a coke from one of the street vendors, to look in designer shops and dream of wearing one of those expensive creations, to see all of Paris hurrying to their cars or to the Metro going home after work, or to just be a part of the Paris scene was the best. When we finally arrived at the Arch, we were bone tired but we didn't care. We had done it all!!

That night we returned to the L'Intermed restaurant. We felt like we were coming back to a familiar place. We had an excellent white-fish dinner along with their apple tarte. The staff once again was great.

Tuesday – our last day in Paris! We knew we had to make the most of it. We packed our suitcase and went down for our breakfast. With our stomachs full we checked out of our room arranging to have our luggage stored in their secured luggage room. We walked to Montmartre, as I wanted Ron to see the artist area, as well as Sacre Coeur (Sacred Heart). On arrival I was disappointed to learn the artists only paint there on Sundays. With that we walked to the base of the hill where Sacre Coeur stood looking so stately and impressive. We rode the tram up to it.

The sun shone brightly on her white stone exterior. The interior demonstrated her smaller, more serene and regal qualities than Notre Dame. Her beautiful stained glass windows, purple curtains around the altar areas, mosaic tiling, and straight wooden pews allowed her to be more intimate and comfortable to all her viewers. Once outside again we stood on the ledge overlooking Paris. What an amazing sight to see all of Paris on this clear day for a radius of thirty miles in all directions.

As it was not half eleven, we took the Metro downtown to the

Tuileries to see if we could get the afternoon river tour with side trips to the Invalides and the Eiffel Tower. We reserved a seat on one then walked around the tourist shops in the area.

At one we boarded our bus and drove to the Bateaux-Mouches (open air and covered river boats) that would take us around the Paris sights. Since the day had turned much colder, we buttoned up our coats in order to sit on the upper open-air deck to see everything. We floated past Notre Dame on the Ile de la Cite (island of the city). Notre Dame was standing in all her splendor in the bright sunlight for all passersby walking or boating to admire her stained glass windows, flying buttresses, and stonewalls. Next came the Louvre, Trocadero Gardens, the Grand and Petit Palais, as well as the Eiffel Tower. We went under many of the Seine's bridges. Toward the end of the ninety-minute tour we chose to go downstairs and get into an enclosed area as we were getting quite chilled.

Once off the boat we reboarded our bus for the ride to the Invalides. Napoleon's body, dressed in the green uniform of the Chasseurs de la Garde, has rested under its dome since being brought here in 1840 from the island of Sainte Helena. His body is encased in six coffins, one inside another. The first was iron, then mahogany, two of lead, one of ebony, and the outer one formed from the Finnish red wood. His tomb rests on a green granite pedestal. His son, Napoleon II, was also buried here.

Before boarding the bus for the trip to the Eiffel Tower, we became aware of the time. We still wanted to visit it so continued on the tour. Once arriving there we realized from the long lines again, we wouldn't be able to get to the top. We told our guide we were leaving as we had to retrieve our luggage and get to the Arch before six for the Air France bus to the airport.

Leaving the tour we walked to the Musee de Cinema for the Metro. Upon returning to the hotel we retrieved our luggage then hopped back on the Metro for the Arch. We made the bus with time to spare. The bus ride seemed to take forever because of the evening commuter traffic.

We arrived at the airport ahead of our scheduled check-in time. We took the time to recheck the interior of our luggage as it had been out of our sight since morning and knew the airport security would ask about it. All was in excellent order just as we had left it – no added packages. We purchased some magazines and a *London Times* for the flight.

At seven o'clock our UK Air attendants and plane were ready for us. We went through immigration and customs with a breeze. The ride home was uneventful. Even the "dinner" was uneventful – finger sandwiches, an apple, a fruit tart of some kind, and a choice of tea, coffee, or soda.

Arriving safely at Stansted about nine o'clock, we got our car out of storage and zipped home along the M-25. Lovely dreams greeted us as we laid our heads down on our pillows. Paris was an impressive, bustling, cosmopolitan city to be in; I am sure living there would be even more exciting. This was a trip dreams were made of.

29. Shopping with a Big S

My friend, Loraine Meadows, said she, Nancy Mayer, and Jean Dorin were going to do some china and crystal shopping. Would I like to go with them? Leery but intrigued I said, "Yes." Loraine explained Stoke-On-Trent was the town for china outlets while Worcester was privy to the crystal outlets as well as the Worcester and the Royal Doulton chinas. It sounded like a shopping encounter not to be missed. Loraine told me to bring along a moist tea towel in a plastic bag. I would use the towel to remove the seconds' flaw markings on the various pieces. If the flaws underneath were too large or noticeable, I should not buy it. If the flaws making it a second were minute or almost non-existent, I could buy it. Good information.

The girls picked me up at half-six; it was still dark and cold. Each of us packed a lunch so we could eat and drive without missing a moment of shopping. We carried thermoses of hot coffee and tea to sustain us on the four-hour ride up the M-1, M-5, and M-6 motorways until we would arrive in Stoke. While we knitted or drove, we talked about our families and places to visit. Nancy and Jean were exquisite knitters. The sweaters they knitted could be sold in any London couturier at elite prices.

Headlights along the M-1 were obnoxious but reassured us others were also on the byways as well. By the time we found the M-5, the sun had awakened while cows were beginning to find their dormant pastures after milking. By the time we reached the M-6 the sun had come into full bloom making the day enticing for shoppers. All of us were ready to do battle.

We first stopped at the Spode outlet – two rather long sheds back to back containing long tables and shelves full of pieces from their most important china patterns. Loraine went for the bins of Christmas Tree plates and serving pieces. I loved the pattern but never thought I could afford it. When I saw the price of £1.99 ($4.00) on the dinner plates, I dove in with both hands. Working through the boxes I rubbed off black flaw marks with my trusty cloth finding a dozen dinner plates with minute flaws. I scooped up two vegetable bowls, a teapot, seven salad plates, and six cups and saucers. The total came to £76.94 or $115.50. I wanted to buy more but didn't know what I might find at other outlet shops. I decided to budget my money for the present time.

The next stop was the Portmerion outlet. Since I had never heard of it, I was curious to see what it was. This outlet contained two levels of rows and rows of large metal shelves filled with their main patterns. My friends were interested in their Botanical Garden (an unusual wildflower pattern) while my interest floated to the Pomona (a fruit pattern – the center of each piece had either an apple, peach, red currants, or purple plums). The pieces could be mixed or matched to suit the customer's taste. Each pattern contained dinner plates, cereal bowls, salad plates, cups and saucers, mugs, tea or coffee pots, and serving pieces. I loved the Pomona pattern but held onto my money. "Next time," I told myself.

Next was the creamwear outlet, I wasn't at all impressed with this grouping. All the delicate vases, potpourri dishes, and decorative bowls possessed beautifully raised and sculpted fruit, seashell, or other designs on them. The problem I had was all the pieces were a cream color, no other coloring or shading. Maybe in time creamwear would grow on me but for now it certainly wasn't on my priority list for British remembrances.

When we finished our tour of Stoke, we drove onto Worcester. Its majestic cream stone cathedral was locked so entrance was prohibited to us. Driving on we came to the huge Worcester China outlet. While the girls searched for their goodies, I took the guided factory tour learning the process of china making from design to final firing. After the process was completed, each piece was scrutinized for any imperfections. In keeping with their high standards of production, any minute bubble or flaw became an outlet second while a visible flaw became rubble in the dustbin. Only the flawless ones reached Harrods and Selfridges for sale. I loved the fruit and vegetable pattern, a trademark of theirs. Even the seconds, I considered too rich for my budget.

After Worcester, we moved on to the Royal Doulton outlet. None of us purchased anything there; their signature figurines and character mugs were absolutely divine. I hoped to get Ron interested in collecting the mugs.

The last outlet shop we visited was Stuart crystal. The shop was having a sale which we took advantage of. At £1.00 each I bought eight red wines, eight white wines, eight champagne flutes along with eight on the rocks glasses. I was so pleased I almost floated home on a cloud of happiness. The other girls purchased more as they entertained a lot more that I did.

With our boot, back seat, and window area full, Nancy reversed out of her parking space and right into a hidden wrought iron fence post. Wham!! Quite a jolt! We all got out to survey the damage – nothing of consequence other than that of being jostled around. The only problem of the day! Quite impressive, I thought.

About three we began our trek home. We wanted to be on the M-

25 before the evening London traffic made it a parking lot. A piece of advice for all driving visitors – stay off the M-25 during the morning and evening rush hours or I can promise you you'll regret it. It's a wicked drive.

30. John and Laura Come to Call

Excitement was again building in me. John and Laura were spending Easter with us. This was their first trip abroad and I wanted their week to be perfect for them. The Saturday before Easter Ron and I awoke early so we could meet their 6:05 plane. We hoped it would be on time, as Northwest had a habit of being late to quite late.

Dense fog filled the morning air making our commute a bit longer than we had expected. I couldn't see a "blooming" thing – no countryside, no grazing animals, no houses or barns, just our side of the M-25, even the oncoming traffic on the other side of this eight lane motorway was almost totally obscured. A bit eerie for traveling but that's part of driving here some days. The plane was only fifteen minutes late. John and Laura emerged from immigration and customs about a half hour later. Lots of hugs, kisses, and tears of joy flowed freely. Their faces belied their weariness from their nine-hour overnight flight.

On our drive home the sun was trying its best to break through the fog covering but wasn't having much luck. The kids attempted to focus on the English way of driving while surveying the awakening countryside. Arriving home we showed them our home and their bedroom. I put out some bagels, juice, and coffee before they had a catnap to recoup some of their lost sleep. Later, we walked into our village; busy with the hustle and bustle of shoppers getting ready for their festive Easter meals. I had bought a ham, some yams, fresh broccoli, and salad greens. I had made two apple pies, Ron and John's favorite. Getting them to wait until Easter to cut into it would be tough.

They, like Ron and Nancy, couldn't believe the quaintness of Shenfield, its small shops with meats hanging in Mr. Land's front window, the limited variety of tinned foods, the product names unknown to them, and the postal office being inside the newsagent's shop. Lots of new things for them to discover and explore! We introduced them to the train station and explained how we traveled to and from London. The things they learned in less than an hour amazed them.

Wanting to take them into Brentwood and some of the neighboring villages, we had a quick bite of lunch: sandwiches made from slices of Rose's French stick, ham and cheese, crisps, pickles, and cokes. We even got them to Lakeside Mall, another amazement for them.

After a dinner of pasta, green salad, garlic bread, and a bowl of fresh strawberries, grapes, nectarines, and bananas, they showed real signs of exhaustion and said "goodnight" to us. We told them we planned to go to the Easter sunrise service at St. Mary's in the morning. They begged off, as they knew they wouldn't be able to awake for the five o'clock service. We understood.

The sunrise service was wonderful. Upon arriving at the entrance door to the church, everyone attending received a lit candle as the service would be conducted in the dark. The candles allowed us to use our prayer books and hymnals. By the time the service began, our eyes had adjusted to the darkness. As the mass moved along to its conclusion, the sun began coming through the stained glass windows reminding us of Christ and His resurrection. Walking outside after the service, the dawning light enveloped everyone with the true meaning of Easter and its impact on each of us.

Once home Ron and I brewed a pot of coffee then filled our beakers to the brim with the energizing substance. For a bit of luxury we added a bit of cream and sugar or sweetener to each. Sitting at our kitchen table, we watched as the sun came into full brilliance with its rays of warmth and goodness surrounding us and the world with its splendor. What a marvelous time to be alive and together! About an hour later Laura came down saying John was sick. He had the same queasiness Jennifer did at Christmas – the residual motion sickness after the flight. Even though the flight was over, his body was still "in flight". His brain hadn't caught up yet. After some Dramamine and hot tea he felt better but still not his self.

The morning was so nice I decided to serve breakfast outside on the patio. Breakfast consisted of orange juice, scrambled eggs, and bacon, along with bran and oatmeal muffins. The luscious lemon curd melted right into the just-out-of-the oven muffins.

That afternoon Laura, Ron, and I toured the countryside while John rested. The day was wonderful with every element of a bright, green spring displayed before us. Ron couldn't wait to get John and Laura out to his Thorpe Hall golf course for a round or two.

By the time we returned home, John looked a whole sight better. We had a glass of port to celebrate his rejuvenation. I put the ham and the yams in the oven while sipping my port (another vice I learned here but, boy, was it nice and warming to the body). I cut up the broccoli into nice long spears while Laura made a big salad with baby leaf lettuce, endive, mushrooms, cucumbers, julienne carrots, and tomatoes. I had made a blue cheese as well as an Italian dressing for the salad.

About five o'clock I set the dining room table with my mother's white linen tablecloth and napkins, her gold and burgundy leafed Essex Maroon Lenox, and my own silverware. I proudly put out my new crystal flutes from my recent shopping spree with the girls. The table looked ready for royalty – which I felt my family was to me.

A half hour later the table was ladened with the ham and vegetables. We opened a bottle of champagne to celebrate the occasion. Such a fabulous and special time – having the family around to celebrate Easter with us.

By Monday John was back to normal. Ron took the afternoon off to play a round of golf with them. After a bite of lunch the three drove off to Thorpe Hall. Being in such a hurry to get there Ron didn't watch his speed. A South End constable (police officer) pulled him over for going 15 miles over the speed limit. How upset and embarrassed he was because it happened right in front of the kids. The fine of £50 ($80) was a little steep but had to be paid. Another lesson we learned – few speed limit signs define speeds, so beware of them when they are seen as they could lead into speed traps. An expensive afternoon but the golf was thoroughly enjoyed.

Tuesday, we took the train into London. They couldn't believe the maze of trains, exits, stairwells, and commuters present in Liverpool Street Station. I explained it is one of the largest railway stations within London; trains leave here for all parts of the country. As we proceeded down the stairwell toward the Circle Line (only line circling around London), Ron and I explained the turnstile procedure, how to read the line's directional maps, as well as the procedure for getting on and off the quick moving subway trains. Once at Westminster Station we got off and worked our way through the station and outside.

Coming out of the station their first sight was the magnificent Parliament building. Unfortunately due to the potential for IRA bombings it was still not open to the public. Security had things tightly bundled up. From there we walked around the corner to Westminster Abbey. Once again, the sun's rays beamed through the Abbey's stained glass windows filling the church with magnificence and edified the grandeur of this royal church. The windows' colors and designs intoxicated not only John and Laura but even repeat visitors such as Ron and I. We passed the crypts in Poets' Corner then followed along the taupe marble stones to see some of the royals' as well as military greats' resting places.

Afterward we began our walk down Birdcage Lane and St. James Park to Buckingham Palace. Along the way we had planned to visit the Guards' Museum within the Wellington Barracks grounds but it was closed so we continued on to the Palace. We spent time taking pictures of each other standing in front of the entrance gates implanted with the Windsor family crests. Within ten minutes the hourly non-ceremonial changing of the guard began. We stayed to watch this simple changing, as we had not gotten there early enough for the full ceremony.

Since it was lunchtime, we headed for Green Park and the Hard Rock Cafe. The hustle and bustle of the waitresses, orders being rattled off to the cook staff, 50's music blaring from every speaker, customers attempting to talk over the loud music, were all traditional fare here. Instead of moving to a quieter restaurant, we stayed as Ron and I wanted them to experience the ambiance of this eatery and check out all the memorabilia from the music greats – the Beatles, Buddy Holly, Elvis Presley, Elton John – just to name a few. Every visit Ron and I make here is a nostalgic music return to the fifties. Laura and I had chicken taco salads; John had one of their special hamburgers (US imported beef) with fries while Ron had their "Pig" sandwich with coleslaw. After finishing our lunches, we said goodbye to our waitress, Bess, and out the front doors we flew right into the bright sunshine of the early afternoon. John and Laura purchased some Hard Rock Cafe t-shirts and caps as souvenirs for the families.

We walked to the Green Park tube station where we hopped onto the Piccadilly Line for Knightsbridge. Coming out of the station we walked straight into the most wonderful store in London – Harrods. It is a must stop for all tourists. John and Laura couldn't believe not only the immense size of the store but everything they had for sale – first class clothing, handbags, scarves, suits, ties, shoes, meats, appliances and furniture of all description, inside and outdoor sports equipment, toys galore, meats, cheeses, produce, breads, pastries, sweets and chocolates, teas and coffees, and frozen foods along with takeaway sandwiches and salads for busy professionals and people on the run. After touring Harrods we began our trek home, as we needed to rest our feet before going to Cambridge the following morning.

We slept in until nine, had breakfast, piled ourselves into my little red Cabriolet with the top down, and headed for Cambridge. Leaving late, we missed the morning traffic rush making it a pleasant drive. The sun was shining, adding to our trip excitement. After finding a parking space, we walked briskly into town giving us so much energy we didn't even huff or puff from the excursion.

We strolled down Queen's Road until we came to King's College, everyone's favorite. Being almost lunchtime we found its large front courtyard full of students and tourists buying vendor's sandwiches and freshly made chips (French fries) then sitting and eating them on long wood benches outside its entrance doors. Some people lay on large blankets relaxing while others read, pulled pushchairs to and fro to keep little ones napping, or just sat and chatted between their classes or whatever.

Walking through the heavy wood doors of Trinity College's gothic gatehouse and breezeway, we found its courtyard, reported to be the largest in the world. In its center was the bronze statue of Henry VI, the college's founder. The imposing marble dormitories and classroom buildings on the encircling perimeter walls looked light yellow to golden depending on where the sunshine shown.

Its chapel, I would call church, was quite ornate in design with each of its four corners having its own large cathedral spire while eight lesser spires adorned the longer sides of the chapel roof. Two rectangular stained glass windows, one on top of the other, filled the interior walls. Carved between the windows were Tudor crests and various animals.

In the long center aisle was the organ. The organ and its pipes were encased in a fantastic wood-carved shell extending from one sidewall to the other. Awe-inspiring organ pipe sounds emanated from this instrument. Each time I heard the organist play I thought I was in a heavenly place where the wonderful sounds of God's instrument could be heard.

The choir area extended from the organ to the main altar; on its walls were wood carved backdrops with long, plain choir benches in front of them. The ceiling was arched and carved with intricate shell designs making an incredible sight. Various geometric designs and lines adorned the marble flooring.

The altar had a carved wooden overhang, similar to those in the choir and nave areas. The chapel was amazing. Again, I remarked to Ron one Sunday, we need to come for a service just to hear the organ and the choir. It must be a magical event.

After touring Trinity Chapel we toured its only other open area, The Hall, its formal dining room. The student tables were made of plain white Formica tops with supporting straight wood legs; the table's wood chairs looked uncomfortable with their straight lines and backs. Down the middle of each table was a line of tall, slender student lamps positioned in such a manner to give light to every other student sitting at them. On the room's four wood walls family crests and armor hung. The cathedral ceiling contained arched wood-carved buttresses to accentuate the formality of this room. Historians say that in the days before sanitation, rushes were placed on the floors to diminish the foul food smells emanating from the lack of cleaning after meals. Trinity professors ate on a dais away from the odors.

The dormitories and classrooms were closed to the public as classes were still in session. The Wren Library was also closed so students could prepare for their semester final examinations. Christopher Wren designed this library which was built between 1676 and 1690. Its interior is reported to contain exquisite lime wood carvings by Grimling Gibbons as well as a statue of Lord Byron whose academic career from 1805-07 was nothing to talk about. Hard to believe with his poetic works afterwards.

Finishing our tour of Trinity, we moved onto St. John's College. Its original use was that of a hospital by a religious group. During the early fifteen hundreds its use dwindled and subsequently was left to ruins. Later, St. John's College was built here. It became the chief center of Renaissance education in Cambridge. Its buildings were made of brown bricks with an arched turret on each of its gatehouse corners. The college's courtyard, built around sixteen hundred, was compact and simple. In its center was a statue of Lady Margaret Beaufort, one of the University's benefactors who helped found it in 1511. Victorians such as Wordsworth, the poet, and Wilberforce, the social reformer, were graduates from this college. Behind its main building the Bridge of Sighs crosses the River Cam; it reminded me of the Bridge of Sighs in Venice, Italy. Built in 1831, this bridge linked the nineteenth century New Court with the older part of this college. Bars were placed over the arched windows to keep the undergraduates or graduate students from throwing themselves into the Cam during test times.

Queen's College is the only college within the University to have its own president; all other colleges have masters. The point of interest here is the Mathematical Bridge so called as it was designed and built on geometric principles using no nails. From time to time it has to be refurbished but nails have to be used to hold the new parts together. No one seems to know how the first sections stayed together without nails.

Jesus College was originally a convent until the Bishop of Ely learned only two nuns were living here and promptly closed it. This college looks quite sparse in its ideas of comfort and studious endeavors.

We walked back into the town and Market Hill. Here pottery makers sell their vases, dishes, and mugs while others sell tie-dyed t-shirts, floral arrangements, stone necklaces, earrings, and paintings.

Since we were hungry and thirsty, we started down a narrow stone walkway leading to the town center in order to grab a bite to eat before returning home. In the center of Cambridge we found an inviting pub called the Cock and Horse. Entering this darkened pub with all its mahogany lined walls and dimmed lighting, we slowly made our way into the bar and pub area. The bar and its shelves were made of carved wood with bar glasses of all sizes and shapes hanging from its wood pegs. We ordered pints of bitter (light beer) and ploughman sandwiches with crisps. We sat in its eating area in the back talking about all we had seen and done since the "kids" had come. A good time together but I knew it was coming to an end soon as they had to return to their home and jobs. Later, we picked up our car and proceeded home; this time with the top up as the air had taken a cold, nasty turn.

While Ron and John played a couple rounds of golf at Ron's golf club the next day, Laura and I went shopping in the little neighboring town, Billericay. We toured the shops without finding anything we wanted but stopped in the local bakery and eatery for a bite of lunch; she had a chicken sandwich and greens (lettuce) while I tried their famous Shepherds Pie.

Saturday morning came too quick and we had to take them to Gatwick for their flight home. I couldn't believe how fast the time had flown. Tears and hugs flowed as we saw them go through the gates leading to Immigration and Customs then down the walkway on their way to their plane's gate.

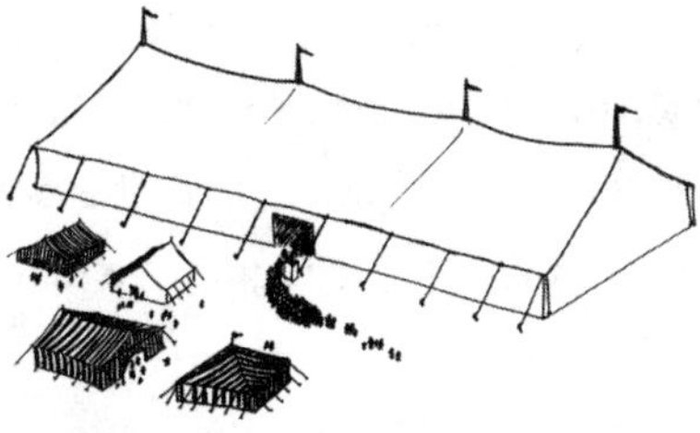

31. A Maze of Tents and Wares

On one April coffee morning, I heard the girls talking about Hatfield House, an aging manor house no longer lived in but kept up as a historical museum. The entrance fees from April through October each year were just enough to keep it from bankruptcy. The only weekend within those months the house was not open to the public was the first weekend in May when it hosted its annual craft fair. I asked, "What fair?"

The coffee klatchers looked and said to me in disbelief, "You don't know about the Hatfield House fair? It is absolutely marvelous. You can't miss it. There are probably fifty to a hundred crafters from all over the area bringing their wares to sell. There is just so much to see and buy."

Since shopping was my middle name, I couldn't resist the day or the temptation. I signed up for the coach (bus) trip and waited patiently for this special day to arrive.

At half eight I stood on Shenfield's High Street then merged into our coach with 44 other fair devotees. BBC weather reports said it was going to be only 20 degrees centigrade (about 72 degrees Fahrenheit) in the afternoon so I wore my levis, white turtleneck, walking shoes, and a light jacket which I could wear around my waist if it became too warm. I was ready for shopping.

As we jostled and bustled along the M-25 toward our destination, we girls talked about what we were interested in purchasing since this was the perfect place to pick up gifts for special occasions, Christmas, or even for ourselves. As I had never been before and didn't have a clue what to expect, I said I was just going to take it all in then make decisions.

The coach ride took an hour and fifteen minutes with all the morning caravans, lorries, and cars along our route. Finally, we turned off onto the road leading to Hatfield House only to be put into a queue with several hundred vehicles also going to this shopping extravaganza.

A half hour later we arrived at the entrance gate, our driver presented our tickets, and we were waved through. As our coach moved up the winding dirt road to the fair, I could see the tops of a number of long circus tents flapping in the morning breeze. I was glad I had brought my jacket, as I would need it. When our coach was parked, the driver said the bus would remain in this spot all day so as we accumulated packages we could bring them back to the bus and stow them in the overhead bins or our seats. This way our hands and arms would be free to buy more things. He would keep an eye on the bus for us.

After getting off, I got a map of all tents and their contents. I kept to myself so I could investigate on my own without being encumbered by others' ideas and whims. I love being a loner in these situations. The first tent dazzled me with rows of tables filled with all kinds of crafts and their creators. As I scanned the tent, I saw long dress racks filled with adult and children's sweatshirts in a myriad of colors, sketches, and sayings. Other tables displayed hand-painted tiles and paintings, stamp sets, and costume jewelry in every kind of design: metal and stone.

In another tent, dressmakers displayed little girl dresses and play outfits in all sizes, materials, and designs. I loved the ones with pinafores and knew Jen would look beautiful in them. I wished I could buy one of each but that was impossible. Each dress ran about £30 ($50). I did pick out a gorgeous taupe and navy checked dress with a large navy alphabet border around the hemline. Small red apples surrounded the short-cuffed sleeves. A plain white pinafore topped off the dress. I bought it two sizes too big so she could wear it when we gave it to her at Christmas. I also bought a pink overall with a kitten painted on the front of it along with a matching white and pink blouse with more kittens on it. Jen loved cats.

Another tent's crafters sold hand-painted stationery, handmade preserves and relishes, embroidered sheets and pillowcases, musical recorders, puppets, and more jewelry. In the next tent I found pottery wares: various sized vases, large coffee mugs, serving pieces for parties, and sets of hand-painted dinnerware sets for four and eight. I bought us two large taupe and cream coffee mugs.

In the center of the manor's courtyard crafters sold larger items such as picnic tables and benches of all sizes and large flowerpots or containers for use in front and back gardens. Also in this crowded area I began to smell the aromas of hamburgers, hot dogs, fish and chips, Indian chicken satays with peanut sauce that made me feel hungry. I told myself I wanted to see everything before I took time out to eat.

In back of the house was the stable area containing additional crafters – even a blacksmith selling anything from garden decorations to iron candle lamplights for patios, sailor's instruments, and iron house numbers. In another cubicle I found Hazel Boyle, the creator of the porcelain "A Nation of Shopkeepers" storefronts. Each store depicts an actual pub or shop (antique, bakery, china, clothiers, deli, florists, fish and chips, hardware, news agents, greengrocers, and butchers) along with restaurants and corner shops. She sketches each store then creates the porcelain mold for that establishment. After the mold was poured and dried, she hand paints each in all its glory. Collectors of these shops hang them on their walls or over windows in a straight line to recreate a street scene in keeping with her idea of Britain being a nation of shopkeepers. In an instant I fell in love with them knowing I would become one of her collectors. For now, her shops were relatively cheap at £15 ($25) a piece but I knew when people heard about her shops her prices would dramatically increase. What a winner this would be.

Another crafter had decoupaged and framed Dickensian pictures that were absolutely beautiful but pricey. Street scenes from *Oliver Twist, David Copperfield*, and *A Tale of Two Cities* sat prominently in holders on her table hoping to lure Dickens's readers in. Maybe next year I could succumb to them but not this year.

The day at the fair was coming to a close as the coach had to leave at three to avoid the evening traffic rush. Carrying my Hazels (a Victorian pub called the Dirty Duck, a greengrocer, and a fish and chip shop – all seconds) along with Jen's dress and play outfits, I headed for the bus to stow away my purchases. Leaving the bus I knew I had forty-five minutes to get a bite to eat before reboarding the bus. On my way to the food center I noticed another potter. Uh, oh! I thought I had seen everything. I was wrong. How could I have missed this one right in the center of the foreground?

I perused her work and found a large cheese plate with a chestnut colored rim on it. The potter had painted purple grape clusters and leaves around the plate's rim then toward the center of the plate she had painted names of favorite British cheeses like stilton, cheddar, and the like. A real prize for entertaining whether for after dinner cheese, crackers, and port or just for a simple wine and cheese party. I loved it and decided to use my plastic money to purchase it since my paper budget was used up. I knew it would pay for itself even before we would leave England.

At three, our chariot loaded to the brim with shoppers and purchases began its trek home. The coach was buzzing with chatter about what each of us had bought. Purchases ranged from picture frames and albums to knitted angora coats, two-piece dresses hand-painted with flowers and small animals to jogging suits I had missed to all kinds of pottery items. I was delighted with my purchases.

An hour later our coach pulled into our letting off place and we got off. Our exhausted and excited group, content with our day at the fair, said goodbye to each other then started walking home. We were already discussing next year's fair and how much more fun we would have shopping.

32. Our Anniversary in Stratford-Upon-Avon

Our thirty-first wedding anniversary was coming; it would be the first one away from family and friends to help us celebrate it. Ron and I decided to make it special. Stratford had been on our list of places to visit since we arrived in England so we decided to make that trip a reality.

Ron took off Friday afternoon and we meandered along the motorways and byways until we arrived in Stratford, home of the Bard, William Shakespeare. By the time we arrived there the sun was starting to wane in the distance. After checking into the Afton Hotel, we walked hand in hand along the River Avon into Stratford proper. As we passed the Royal Shakespeare Theatre, we stopped to see what was playing that weekend. Looking at its schedule we were deflated, the season didn't begin for another week. Nothing was playing. What a bummer!

With that we decided to have a wonderful dinner at our hotel, spend Saturday visiting Shakespeare's birthplace, Anne Hathaway's home, window shop, then return home as it was not worth the price of another night here if we couldn't take in a play.

We ordered a bottle of chardonnay, Dover sole muniere, boiled and parsleyed potatoes, asparagus, rolls, and a white chocolate mousse. It was lovely. Loving each other and just being together was enough to make our anniversary special.

The next morning we took another walkabout along the River

Avon with its tall, rotund, green-leafed trees surrounding us. We tried to visualize what living here would have been in the Bard's time. Probably horse drawn carriages, unpaved, dusty or muddy streets depending on the season of the year. I thought of women in their long bustled dresses and maybe broad brimmed hats while the men in their knickers, long stockings, waistcoats with watch fobs hanging so all could see, ruffled shirts or blouses, and some possibly in floppy hats.

In the Tartan Shop I found my paternal tartan, Hamilton, in both skirt and scarf but it was too pricey for my taste. Ron said, "But get it for an anniversary gift" and I said, "No, it's much too expensive. I don't know when or where I would wear it so it might be money thrown to the wind." The card and stationery store next door had all kinds of writing materials and implements along with some potpourris with either strong or light floral or fruity aromas to them.

Wanting to see Shakespeare's birthplace we walked to the far end of town. What a huge house – light yellow stucco with dark wood beams creating the traditional Tudor look. The rooms inside were small compared to the outside. The floors were stone tiles that must have been quite cold in wintertime. The living room had an immense fireplace and enough room for a sofa and probably two wingback chairs.

The kitchen was roomy with its own fireplace for cooking and a bricked oven for baking and roasting. The oven base must have been made out of a mortar mixture so it could retain the heat for the necessary baking or roasting. Actual cooking pans and utensils used by Shakespeare's mother still hung over the stove lending credence not only to her cooking abilities but the authenticity of the house. Shakespeare's original square, wood kitchen table with six wood chairs took their place in the center of this room. Next to the kitchen door sat the wood bench on which William courted Anne Hathaway when she came to visit.

The upstairs contained four rather small bedrooms – each having a dresser or chest and a bed, so small only a young child of today could sleep within its measurements. I remembered that people then were much smaller than today but I still could see problems for a middle or especially a tall person sleeping on that contraption. A couple of rooms had the luxury of a small chair or rocker for reading. An upstairs room became Shakespeare's writing room with his original desk, chair, schoolbooks, and some of his drafts still intact. Life then would have been hard but having the closeness of family and friends around during their jolly good days of celebrations would have been wonderful.

The traditional English garden in back glowed with yellow, red, and orange zinnias, red, yellow and white tulips, all colors of roses, along with blue delphinium. Along the walkway leading back to the street grew short cropped hedging and boxwood plants. What a picture of spring.

Finishing our house tour we walked back into the town's center then down a side street to see the school where the Bard boarded and attended. It was all Tudor design with ivory stucco and dark mahogany beams. Its entrance consisted of a porch with a wood overhang and iron fencing to enhance its look as well as to dissuade outsiders from coming in. Standing across the street from the school we approximated where his room was; the fifth window from the right on the top floor. Even today the school's reputation for excellence in education mandates its rules of corporal punishment on those who do not fit in socially or intellectually. We wanted to see the school's interior but school was in session negating that idea.

In this area pubs revealed their age; the peeling yellow and cream paints hung for dear life to the exterior walls while the dark wood beams were frayed and needed staining to regain their original color. If the ground shook too hard, I could picture these pubs unsteady from long lives crumble to their foundations. Walking back to town along the River Avon, we visited Holy Trinity Church where Shakespeare was baptized and attended when not in school. The light grey stone church with its towering spire was large for this area and beginning to show the effects of pollution on its exterior walls. Its spire seemed to be struggling with all its might to reach into the heavens. Narrow elongated stain glass windows of saints and other scenes dotted the church adding dimension and grace to all who entered her. On one sidewall was a bust of the Bard himself as well as a grey marble stone placed over his gravesite. Each year an unknown admirer places flowers there each April 23 to commemorate his birthday.

After our enjoyable walk through Shakespeare's village, we decided to return home. We had planned to visit Anne Hathaway's thatched cottage but by the time we had checked out of our hotel, rain was coming down like water running out of a boot. As we drove past her thatched roof and white exterior walls, we saw her front gardens full of blooming spring flowers and roses but looking a bit bedraggled in the rain. We had hoped the rain would lessen the lines of tourists making it easy for us to just walk in but to our surprise the line outside was long with visitors holding brawlees (umbrellas) to keep the rain off them. We would stop on our next trip to Stratford.

We had had a lovely anniversary celebration. Now we wanted to return again for another look-see and a play.

33. The Birthday Present

How vividly I remember May 27 just like it was yesterday. I had gone into London to do some shopping and see the chiropodist (podiatrist), Dr. Charlotte Hewett as my orthotics were giving me problems and needed to be checked. Dr. Richardson had highly recommended her to me.

I had buzzed into London on the 10:17 and made my way through the underground maze to get to Oxford Street. John Lewis was my first stop as I needed some knitting yarn for the new argyle sweater I was knitting, some DMC thread for the cross-stitch sampler I was making for my hairdresser, Karen Barden, who was getting married mid-June, and possibly a new hat.

I walked to the W. H. Smith Bookstore where I hoped to find a World War II book for Ron's birthday two days away. A trip to Ireland to celebrate his birthday was in the offing and a new book to read on the three-hour ferry crossing I thought would please him. Nothing looked interesting; most were too massive to cart around London all afternoon.

Since I did not know where Charlotte's office was on Harley Street, I decided to go early in order to find her so not to be late. After rounding the corner from John Lewis, I walked to Harrietta Square then onto Harley Street. Her office was in a three story renovated townhouse building. As I walked through its double doors, I felt I was in an exclusive doctors' building. What I didn't know at the time was Harley Street contained some of the most prestigious London physicians and surgeons.

I walked up to the Wall Street looking receptionist giving her my name and appointment time with Charlotte. She gave me some forms to fill out and said I could return them when she called me. I wandered into their lounge or reception area. In the center of the room on a large circular table was an oversized brass vase filled with colorful, freshly cut flowers. Underneath the table laid an enormous navy and gold Oriental rug probably measuring 20 by 30 feet. The bright yellow walls contrasted the long surgical white windowpanes. Three gold velvet loveseats were placed on either side of the large unused fireplace; six burgundy and navy stripped or floral overstuffed chairs filled in the remainder of the room.

Charlotte telephoned down to the receptionist to have me come up. Giving my forms to the receptionist, I climbed up the stairs to Charlotte's third floor office. She was a petite, slender, bubbly, Vogue woman of thirty or thirty-one. She had energy plus and greeted me warmly. I instantly felt at ease with her.

Her office contained an oversized leather topped mahogany desk with matching chair, two chestnut brown leather wingback chairs in front of her desk for patient consultations, an examining table, testing equipment, and a changing screen for those needing to remove their stockings or trousers for her exam. The office was devoid of window curtains or rugs on the wood floor. Within moments we talked about the problem bringing me to her. My new orthotics caused pain in my arches and plantar nerve.

After removing my stockings and hopping up on her examining table, she examined every inch of both my feet. She certainly knew what she was doing. She told me my left orthotic had not been made or fitted properly. I explained my Michigan podiatrist had ordered this new set of orthotics. When they came in, I was in the last throughs of our move here. Since I did not have time to have him check and fit them, I had created my own problem. The other sets he had made were always correct so I assumed this set would be correct as well. Wrong decision. The man who made her patients' inserts could fix my orthotics. I made an appointment to return the following week to pick them up. I was in seventh heaven. My aching feet would hurt no more.

After paying for my visit (on foreign assignment Comco employees and dependents pay for their doctor services then submit the bills to their insurance for reimbursement). Ouch, she didn't come cheap at £30 ($55) although I knew it would be worth it to be pain-free.

As I was floating along the street feeling great about my appointment, I realized it had begun to rain. I needed to hurry to the tube station so I wouldn't get drenched. Out of the corner of my eye I spotted a discount bookstore having a closing down sale. I thought maybe I could find a book in there for Ron.

Being in a hurry and not watching what I was doing, I did not see a five-inch step leading into the shop. Within seconds of turning to go in, I was flat on my face. Completely out of breath and totally shocked at what had happened, I tried to get up but my ankle hurt. I hoped I had only badly twisted it. One of the shop's customers and a passerby saw what happened and helped me up. They asked if I was all right. I said I didn't know. I stood there trying to clear my head and refocus my thoughts. I was surprised none of the shop staff came to my rescue. I went inside to get out of the rain for a moment before moving on. As I was limping out of the store, a cashier said, "You aren't the first one that has happened to," which I thought was an interesting thing to say.

As I hobbled along the street, I realized this was not a sprained ankle but a fracture. I had experienced two other foot breaks in previous years so I knew the signs. Fear began to overcome me as I realized I was in London and needed to get back to Shenfield to have Dr. Richardson check this out for me.

How I made it down the two flights of stairs into the underground then up the ones at Liverpool Station then onto the British Rail home plus another two flights of steps down in the Shenfield station I will never know. It took all my strength and courage to get home that afternoon.

Hobbling out of the Shenfield station, I took a taxi home as I knew I couldn't walk any further. When I called Dr. Richardson's office, I had found out he had left earlier in the afternoon for a long holiday weekend. I could see one of his nurses if I could be there by six.

I called Ron who said, "Could I call you back? I'm in a meeting." Forty-five minutes later he called. I explained what had happened and I needed to see the nurse. He said, "Call the nurse and see if she can stay an additional ten minutes as it's traffic time. I'll be home as fast as I can. Are you all right?" I said, "Just my ankle hurts."

Just before six Ron drove in and took me to Richardson's office. The nurse had waited for us. "I believe it's just a bad sprain." she said. I told her I had had fractured bones in my feet before; similar pain and swelling told me I had the same problem. She wrote a note to the Sister (head nurse) at the Harold Wood Hospital. Casualty (emergency service) would examine it then possibly take an x-ray if the doctors deemed it necessary. "You might want to take a lunch with you," she hinted, "as it could be six hours before they might be able to see you since it is a holiday weekend." I replied, "Thank you for the suggestion."

Ron drove me directly there. Once inside I explained to the receiving nurse my situation and gave her Dr. Richardson's nurse's request for examination. I filled out forms until I was blue in the face. Within thirty minutes I was called into the examining room. The Sister called the on-call orthopedic doctor who wanted x-rays as he agreed with me it looked like a fracture.

Fifteen minutes and four pictures later the doctor said I had diagnosed my problem correctly; I had a clean fracture of the fibula. His nurse would cast me with a boot cast. I needed to stay off it for at least two days to give the boot's interior time to fully harden before walking on it. Probably only four to six weeks in a cast, he predicted. There went our trip to Ireland.

After learning the results, Ron and I went into the casting cubicle. A young father was being recast after his x-rays determined his arm hadn't healed completely. She asked him what color he wanted. Confused, I looked at her then him. "Oh, yes. You can have the standard white or one of our fluorescent colors," she said. The man chose a florescent yellow color so his young sons could find him in the dark. I chose the hot pink as it would go with my wardrobe. "Wouldn't I look perfect for the vogue's bazaar?" I thought. "Me in my pink cast modeling the latest fashion on the front of Vogue or Elle. Wouldn't I be hot stuff then?"

When she finished, she asked me how the cast felt. I said it was tight. Checking she agreed, removed it, and then replaced it with a new one. This one within moments was also too tight. My foot was swelling so fast she couldn't keep up with it; her solution was to slit it up the middle to let it expand as I did. After a weekend of keeping it raised and not walking on it, the swelling would go down and she could recast it the following Tuesday. She put a sock over my toes so I wouldn't get any gravel or dirt into the cast. The Sister reminded me to make an appointment at reception for the refitting on the following Tuesday.

She ordered, “Keep that foot propped up all weekend so the swelling goes down then your leg can be properly refitted.” I stumbled trying to learn how to use crutches again. At times I felt like Tarzan swinging in mid-air with only two wood sticks under my arms to balance me. I noticed people amused with my gyrations while I hoped to get it right. After some successful attempts, my thoughts ran to how much is all this going to cost us – the x-rays, the orthopedic surgeon, the castings, and the crutches I needed until my proper cast hardened.

Leaving the casting area, I saw the receptionist’s desk and made tracks for it. After making the Tuesday appointment, I nervously asked how much the bill was and where I paid it. She told me since the fracture was the result of an accident the British Health Service paid for all the costs. I looked at her dumbfounded. I couldn’t believe I heard her right. I asked her again. She explained all accidents and casualties were taken care of by the government health service. I was dumbfounded but thrilled.

Once home I inched my way up the stairs and placed myself on the study sofa where I spent the weekend. I was so ashamed of myself as Sunday was Ron’s birthday; he had to take care of me and not the reverse. After the cast was off, I would have to make it up to him for his birthday as well as Ireland. No easy task.

On the next Tuesday I went back to the casting clinic and had my pink cast replaced and checked. This time the cast fit just as it should. Now to wait out the four to six weeks! An appointment for next month’s orthopedic check was made. Hopefully, I wouldn’t have to wear it any longer than that.

Once the cast was dry inside, I was able to function again but I couldn’t drive. Fellow members of my various activities took turns picking me up and dropping me off so I could attend the meetings.

They loved my new hot pink boot color. Everyone could see me coming for "miles". Before my cast, I was the "Hat Lady" as I wore a hat everywhere. Now, I would be known as the boot lady as well.

Four weeks later I returned to the hospital for more x-rays. The orthopedic surgeon declared my fracture was healed and the cast came off. What a relief! I had to learn to use that leg again as I didn't have the cast weight on it anymore and the leg muscles had weakened during the month's non-use. Within days, I was beginning to walk like my old self again.

34. New People – New Events

The week after my cast came off, Ron and I went with some of the Comco and Comat people for the second day of Wimbledon. We had been given a parking pass close to the entrance so walking would be shorter and easier for me.

The overwhelming excitement of being at WIMBLEDON ran through our veins. This was THE place to be and see the world's tennis greats play. We met Colin Hanley at Center Court and he took us to Comat's tent where lunch was being served.

Lunch!?! Dinner was more like it. First drinks were served then a prawn (shrimp) cocktail with seafood sauce, roast beef with potatoes and steamed vegetables and then red or white wine to wash it all down. For dessert we had a choice of rich chocolate torte or lemon mousse. Ron had the torte while I picked the mousse.

Colin gave us tickets to see the Navratilova and Vacarrio match, a real slugfest, until the rain stopped play. We ran for shelter in Comat's tent since it looked like an afternoon filled with rain. Inside we spent an hour talking with Comco and Comat attendees. When the announcement play had been suspended, we decided to return home. What a lovely visit with new friends and tennis greats.

A month later we were asked to join some Comat and Comco couples going to the British Open being held in Sandwich, Kent County. We were delighted not only to be asked but to say yes.

On Friday morning, July 16, Ron and I drove to Sandwich along the English Channel. What a sight. We had made reservations at a pub/ hotel, the Horse and Saddle, owned and operated by friends of Paul and Diane Betters. They greeted us warmly upon our arrival. We had a ploughman lunch of ham and cheese along with bowls of Scotch broth, and a pint of coke that fit our taste buds and stomachs to a T.

Later that afternoon Ron and I drove over to Royal St. George Golf Course where the Open was taking place. The British Open rotates between courses within the United Kingdom: one year at Royal St. George in England, one year at St. Andrews or Turnberry in Scotland, one year at one of the courses in Wales.

Driving through the winding roads to the course, we followed the coastline with its fishing marinas and boats. Fishermen sat mending their fishing nets, cleaning decks, and selling their day's catch. The white stucco and mahogany beams of their homes only added to the fishing flavor of the area. Sandwich contained the usual newsagents, both Sainsbury and Tesco markets, fish and chip shops, greengrocers, butcheries, and a bakery. One shop had little girls' lace and frilly dresses as well as a needlework shop; both I wanted to venture into. "Maybe before the weekend was over," I said to myself. I would love one of the cute dresses for Jennifer and maybe a new cross-stitch for myself.

Finally we came to the crowds and parking areas for the Royal. The course was a links one versus the traditional American course. A links course maintains manicured greens but its roughs contain tall brush, grass and reeds presenting even the most accomplished golfers with dangers they would rather not have to face. American courses possess short manicured grass tee areas, fairways, roughs, and holes. We noticed another major problem for these golfers would face – the wind gusting in off the Channel would create havoc with any ball on its way to the greens.

That evening's dinner was fantastic. Jon, the pub owner/ manager, had brought in one of his favorite cooks. She was wonderful. Our dinner group started with a rich seafood bisque yet it was remarkably light to the palate and stomach. Her beef stew was filled with potatoes, carrots, celery, parsnips, cauliflower, and peas and served with freshly baked white and whole-wheat rolls. For dessert she created a divine hazelnut and chocolate torte.

Following dinner our group moved into the lounge where we sat around a blazing fire in the fireplace while having a small snifter of port or drambuie. The camaraderie felt more like friends rather than business acquaintances. We said early good nights as we needed to be up and fed by seven o'clock in order to get good parking places at the course. Being our first Open, we wanted to fully take in everything.

Waking at half six we quickly showered and dressed then went downstairs for breakfast. We enjoyed fresh orange juice, oatmeal, toast, and tea and were ready for our ride to the course. The group would carpool since the parking space was quite limited. Ron and I drove with Rob and Mary Summers and Jack and Betty Woods. Since the winds were gusting, we dressed warmly. We could always take our jackets off if we got too warm.

After parking, we walked to the entrance showing our Open badges. We all decided we wanted to follow a different golfer. The Summers would follow Nick Faldo and Fanny, his ponytail caddie, the Woods wanted to follow the Shark, Greg Norman, and we wanted our favorite, Tom Kite.

I was glad we had worn our golf shoes. Walking through the tall, grassy knolls along with the slippery, undulating fairways wet from the morning dew made walking tricky. Without golf shoes we would have slid and slipped all over the place making a nuisance of ourselves to other spectators. This way we walked everywhere without incident.

We watched Jack Nicklaus in his Golden Bear clothes, Curtis Strange, Paine Stewart in his NFL outfit, Colin Montgomerie, and Greg Norman in his black shark straw hat until we finally caught sight of Tom Kite wearing his big smile, red shirt, khaki trousers, and traditional straw hat. He waved to the cheering crowd. Number 10 hole was great for him as he birdied it with no problem. We followed him for the next three holes then followed Jack Nicklaus and Nick Faldo. What a charge Ron got from seeing two of his idols playing together. They seemed to have an unspoken contest between themselves to prove who was the best golfer.

Our group was invited to have lunch at the Comat tent. Lunch was hamburgers, hot dogs, crisps, cokes or whatever to drink. Everyone debated who each thought would be the leader at the end of the day's play as well at the end of the final round. It would be a real horse race to the winner's cup. Who would it, we all asked? Some had very definite choices even if their man wasn't in the lead at the moment.

In the afternoon wc just sat in a grassy, dusty knoll along the eighteenth hole watching the advancing gladiators play their hearts out hoping for a place in the next day's major action. Position, position is the only thing in golf other than winning. After play finished for the day we found our carpool group and drove back to the Horse and Saddle.

When we returned, Paul and Diane told us Jon had a real treat in store for us. He and his fiancée, Carol, had invited us to dinner at the home they were building along the Channel. Diane said their house, even unfinished, was spectacular; I had my doubts as to this English house splendor.

We dressed for the occasion. I wore a black all-occasion short-sleeved dress and a double strand of pearls and earrings. I thought I looked chic. Ron put on his blue oxford shirt and navy double-breasted pinstriped suit. He looked spiffy.

Carpooling again we followed Paul and Diane's car to Jon's home. "What to my wondering eyes did I see" but the most spectacular white stucco Western ranch house with a pebbled circular drive. The house was built on a ridge overlooking the Channel. Gracing either side of the large wood carved entrance door and stoop stood four majestic palm trees. Seeing this, I couldn't wait to tour it.

Once inside I thought I had walked into a Hollywood home. This unfinished home must have been a minimum of 4000 square feet. The living room was about twenty by thirty feet. The kitchen was a chef's heaven. It must have been twenty by twenty feet with wood cabinets on all sides, an eight-burner hob, four aluminum built-in ovens, a sink with a triple window above it, and a restaurant-sized aluminum refrigerator as well as full-size freezer. This house was meant for entertaining in the grandest style. Four fairly large bedrooms with baths resided on this floor as well.

Moving downstairs we found an enormous "family room" with its own wood dance floor, a built-in stereo sound system as well as a bar covering most of the back wall. The shelving behind the bar contained every possible libation known to man. From the overhead brass grid hung every type of drinking glass in which to create any imaginable concoction. Wood paneling surrounded the walls lending to the special ambience of this room.

The piece de resistance was yet to come. Going out the family room's triple patio doors we found a three-layer flagstone patio with tables and chairs. What a breathtaking place for entertaining on starry nights. Topping off this magnificence was the view of the Channel with the lights of Calais, France twinkling in the distance. How overwhelming this place was. All twenty-four of us couldn't believe what we were seeing. I couldn't believe that something this fantastic could be built here. I would have loved living here. It was fabulous.

The evening was a blur to me. The music, stargazing, and eating the most delectable shelled shrimp and crab legs, barbecued steaks, jacket potatoes, garden salad, and a montage of steamed fresh vegetables were unbelievable. Jon served a coconut cake as well as a trifle for dessert. Being too excited and too full from dinner I couldn't even begin to touch either of the desserts.

As Ron and I sat under the clear starlit sky and looked over to the lights of Calais, we talked of our future. We wondered what life held for us not only while on assignment but more especially when we returned to the States. We didn't have a clue. We both hated to leave this fairytale place for reality but we had to do.

After a good night's sleep at the Horse and Saddle, Jon and his staff served a full English breakfast. Again, we ate too much. I felt I had gained at least five pounds just since coming here just a day and half before. It was worth it. All I would have to do is work it off again.

This had been a marvelous two days of golf and being entertained to the height. I didn't want this magical time to end but, as with all things, they have to come to an end. After the last golf ball entered the eighteenth hole and Nick Faldo had won the Open, we said our farewells, returned to our car, and headed home. Ron and I spent the entire drive home thinking and talking about all we had seen and experienced. It was glorious.

35. Unwanted Pressure

As the end of our second year on assignment came so did my anticipation of our return home scheduled for August. Our eighteen months had been extended to the full two years. As the days passed, I felt pressure mounting both from England as well as the States for us to accept another year's assignment. I decided Ron and I had to sit and talk this out.

Even before I asked, I knew what Ron wanted to do. He enjoyed his assignment here. He had made strides in his catalyst work and definitely wanted to renew. I, on the other hand, was ready to return home. Traveling in England and Europe had been wonderful but I missed Jennifer, my family and friends terrifically and needed to get back to my life again. This time of having nothing of consequence to do had to be over. My contract with Ron was for eighteen to twenty-four months; I had kept my part of the bargain. Now it was time to go home. Knowing the company's reputation for pressuring employees to extend their assignments, I definitely wanted to make it clear I was finished here. I didn't want any part of this extension bit.

When we began talking about this thorny issue, Ron said, "It is your decision what we do." What conflict and pressure I felt. I could leave and return home but what would that do to our marriage? There was no happy medium. Not wanting him to fault me later, I said, "All right, one more year and that's it."

My heart broke into a thousand glass pieces, each cutting me inside even more. I kept saying to myself, "Next year, we'll go home" as I denied to myself the reality that this could happen again next year. I prayed, "Lord help me get through this next year without being bitter about what just happened."

36. Visitors from Afar

What a wonderful gift Ron and I were about to receive. Five of our closest friends were coming for a visit. Ron and I couldn't believe they were coming, as Pat was deathly afraid of flying anywhere, but to fly across the Atlantic would be even more so for her. A few years before she and her husband, Lyn, had flown to Germany to visit some relatives there. By the time they got off the plane her knuckles and hands were as white as new fallen snow, while Lyn's arm showed a terrific coloring of black and blue. She had clutched his arm from the time they took off for Frankfort till their arrival and the same on their return trip home. I couldn't believe she would do this for us. She knew how upset I was about spending another year (our third) on assignment and wanted to give me moral support. To do this was a real demonstration of our friendship.

For days Ron and I planned what we would do with them and where we would take them while they were with us. Since we did not have enough room for all of them to stay with us, I needed to find a bed and breakfast that would accommodate our little group. Through a European supplier of Ron's, we got the name of a marvelous Austrian bed and breakfast in Stock, only ten miles from us. He always stayed there on his trips to our area and highly recommended it. He told Ron to have me call for a tour of the place soon, as it was usually booked months in advance. I would do that.

After making an appointment to see the place, I drove to Stock.

The two story detached house (single dwelling abode) was lovely. Its back garden was in full bloom with a wide variety of colors and flowers. The Austrian lady, Hazel Brindle, had operated this bed and breakfast for fifteen years. Truly a delight, she exuded warmth as well as a dedication to those who came into her immaculate home.

The ivory walls and raised flagstone flooring in her entry lent a warm, cozy feeling to her home. The sunshine shone through all her front rooms making the home even more inviting. Her large lounge contained two rust velvet sofas sitting perpendicular to the fireplace with a round coffee table between them. On the wall opposite the fireplace a large bay window with lace curtains looked out on her front garden. A folding leaf dining table decorated with a lace runner and fresh flowers graced the far wall between two other windows. A spinet piano took up most of the room's far right corner. To the side of the lounge I found a breakfast-dining area containing two long serving tables covered with white Austrian lace cloths along with four square tables and chairs for eating; each was topped with a white linen table cloth and a vase of freshly cut flowers from her garden.

The upstairs contained four bedrooms: one with an en-suite (private bathroom) while the other three bedrooms shared a communal bathroom at the end of the hall. The en-suite bedroom was papered in pink stripes with rose buds. The bed had a beautiful hand crocheted bedspread on it, a dresser, as well as a wood chair and table for reading. Another bedroom had bright yellow flowered paper. This room contained a bed with a yellow and white lace coverlet, a dresser, and a small rocker. The third room was a pale purple. Its bed had on it a beautiful duvet with a purple floral design on it, a wood dresser, and a small wood stand with an antique pitcher and bowl. The fourth was being refurbished so she didn't show it to me. She said my company could see it when they arrived and could choose it for one of their bedrooms if they liked.

After the tour I knew our friends would not only be well taken care of, but be quite comfortable here as well. I asked to engage three bedrooms for the nights they would need them. I told her that they would be here for a week, be gone a week and a half, then be back for a final night before returning to the States. She had no problem with that at all. She said she would block those dates out and not take anyone else. They would be her only clients while with her. Before leaving, I left her a deposit for all the rooms. I knew my group would be thrilled to be here. I know I would love to stay here.

Their itinerary included Lyn, Pat, and her sister, Sandy, spending a week in our area, then they would drive on to York to collect some family history about Pat and Sandy's grandparents who had been born and lived their entire lives there. In addition, Pat wanted to take a few days and visit her pen pal of more than twenty years in Horley, near Gatwick Airport. The final part of their trip would be Canterbury, then back to us. During the time they were away, Jim and Marge wanted to stay with us. Our TV room would become their bedroom. When the others returned, all would return to the bed and breakfast for their final night in Britain before flying home.

Anticipation abounded as their arrival date approached. When the day came, Ron and I drove to Gatwick to "collect" them. What a greeting! Long hugs and kisses for all. Although Pat had fared the plane ride well, she was thrilled to be back on terra firma. Our next stop was Hertz to pick up their hire (rental) car. Being concerned about Lyn's navigating the British roads and roundabouts on their first day here, Ron and I were relieved to know they had ordered an automatic car.

Once their car was out of the "barn", Ron suggested driving their car in order to show Lyn needed driving techniques and regulations on the way home. Lyn, Pat, and Sandy rode with Ron while Jim and Marge rode with me. We drove them to Stock where they checked into their bed and breakfast.

Once they saw it, they agreed how wonderful it was and settled in. Ron and I told them they needed to stay awake all day in order to rid themselves of their jet lag then go to sleep at their regular bedtime here. We explained we could drive them around some of the nearby villages and have a pub lunch or we could take the real plunge and go into London. Since it was only half nine in the morning, we needed something extended to keep them going. The consensus was to go into London.

After driving to our place, the group and I walked to the train station while Ron drove off to his office. Because it was after ten, we could purchase the cheaper day pass. While standing on the Shenfield platform waiting for our train to come in from Chelmsford and points east, I told them we needed to stay together so no one got lost, especially in the underground mazes. Next, I explained the use of the day tickets, the turnstiles, the escalators to and from the train stops, and the underground maps.

Once on the train all five of them were glued to their windows taking in all the passing countryside and small villages. Even now, when I remember my trips in and out of London, I still remember the loveliness of all I saw. Oh, yes, I know the trains went through some poor or slum areas on our way into London but I took them as part of the landscape along the way.

After arriving in Liverpool Station we walked to the Central Line's entrance, walked down two flights of stairs, through the turnstiles, down the escalator to the last flight of steps to the west platform to await the next train. They couldn't believe the blackness of the air pollution in the stairwells and tunnels, the screeching of the train's brakes, and the quickness of the trains' uptake.

We changed trains at Holborn for the Piccadilly Line to get to Piccadilly Circus. To get the lay of the City I suggested we take the purple double-decker city tour. We walked to the Hippodrome where we got our tickets and bus. The bus driver drove us up Shaftesbury and the theatre district on to Holborn to view the magnificent St. Paul's Cathedral. Oh, the oohs and aahs I heard. Then we passed the Bank of England, the Stock Exchange (FTSE), and Mansion House, residence of the Lord Mayor of London. Moving on to Leadenhall and Mansel we took sight of the Royal Mint, the massive walled Tower of London and the Tower Bridge. Following Lower Thames we passed Customs House then on to the once newspaper district of Fleet Street. The next sight was Trafalgar Square with all its lion statues guarding the area, the Lord Nelson Column, the pigeon feeding tourists, and the National Gallery as well as the beloved little church of St. Martin in the Fields. Continuing the tour we circled to enter the Pall Mall leading to St. James Palace and Clarence House then on to Buckingham Palace decked in all its opulence. We drove around it twice in order for tourists to take whatever pictures of the palace. Next on our docket was the Queen's Mews where her horses are stabled as well as her royal carriages, then we drove up Victoria past the New Scotland Yard and on to the Houses of Parliament, Big Ben, St. Margaret's Church, and Westminster Abbey. From there we moved along Whitehall passing Downing Street and the Royal Treasury then back to Trafalgar, Haymarket, and the tour's conclusion at the Hippodrome. While four fifths of my group was glued to the tour, I lost one to the oblivion of sleep. No snoring, just sleep. Poor Jim. He had been done in by his night of flying.

By the time we finished our tour, we were hungry, so a stop at my favorite Ponti's for sandwiches, crisps, and cokes was in order. Finding a couple of empty tables, we pushed them together so we could eat and discuss all we had seen and what they wanted to revisit. I knew Harrods would be on the list as well as the Tower of London, Tower Bridge, Westminster Abbey, the Changing of the Guard, and St. Paul's.

After renewing our energy with sandwiches and cokes, I walked them down Piccadilly to Fortnum and Mason to show them another world of shopping, then we took off to the world famous Harrods. What a shock for them as they took in its size and their myriad of products on each floor! They couldn't get over the number of tourists bustling around with their purchases or about-to-be purchases.

By three they were spent, so we found our way back to Liverpool Street Station – then home. The train was packed with commuters on their way home for tea (dinner) and a good night's sleep before beginning the rat race all over the next morning.

Arriving home at four, they wanted to go to their place and freshen up. I said, "Do that and return here as I have dinner planned and almost ready for us tonight." They were reluctant but I said please do come, otherwise Ron and I will have to eat it for the next couple of days. They agreed. I led them back to their place to make sure they knew how to get back.

By half seven we had eaten our fill of chicken, potatoes, green beans, and trifle. Being totally exhausted, they took their leave of us before they fell asleep in our lounge. Ron and I said by the time they made it home would be the right time for them to get a good night's sleep before touring again.

By morning they were rested for another day of travel. Pat and Sandy wanted to drive to Luton, south of London, to find an elderly cousin who owned and operated a crystal shop there. We mapped out our drive then armed ourselves with coffee and tea for the trip. Since there were six of us and we had no caravan (van) for all of us, Lyn, Pat, and Sandy followed me in their car while I drove Marge and Jim. We kept in sight of each other along the London Ring road then through the pastoral countryside to Luton.

Arriving in the little village, we made our way through the streets to their cousin's shop only to find it closed. We learned he had sold it; leaving no forwarding address. Finding a telephone directory hoping to find him in it, we learned he no longer existed in the town. I felt badly for Pat and Sandy as they were looking forward to meeting him. We decided since we were close to Windsor we would press on and tour Windsor Castle, the Queen's favorite residence.

Working our way back to the Ring Road then down the A-308 we drove into Windsor proper. What a glorious day! The sun shone brightly as the temperature rose to a hot eighty-five degrees, quite unusual for England. Summer temperatures run in the low to mid-seventies but this week, heat was definitely on the agenda. Weather readers (forecasters) said a heat wave was upon us. Driving along the River Thames, we saw swans and mallards swimming to their hearts content. Picnickers enjoyed their repasts on blankets or at wooden picnic tables, while others strolled by us licking their lollies (ice cream treats). What a lovely picture of life this presented us.

On the other side of Windsor we finally found the Castle sitting on the hillside overlooking the surrounding territory. We wove our cars around until we found a car park beneath the Castle. We parked and took a shuttle bus to the Castle. The sunshine bore its rays into the castle bringing forth all the brilliance of her grey stone walls, turrets, as well as her own private church.

Being the oldest continually inhabited royal residence in England, her history goes back to 1070. At that time, William the Conqueror built this castle on this hillside for two reasons: first, it afforded him a high vantage point from which to see oncoming marauders hoping to attack him or London and second, its close proximity to London, only a day's journey to and from his Tower of London headquarters and home. Over the years each monarch has altered the castle to fit his or her own needs or tastes. In 1917, King George V loved this castle so much he named it after his Windsor family. It's here that the present royal family spends many weekends, as it is the Queen's favorite even though she spends her annual August holiday at her Balmoral Castle in Scotland.

Getting off the shuttle we walked up the steep incline past the village shops until we reached the castle. The design for this castle and its grounds was rectangular in form with three distinct parts. Entering its grounds through its iron fence and stone turrets, we found ourselves in the middle part with its massive, well-manicured courtyard (known as the Middle Ward). Standing in its center was a statue of Charles II as well as the Round Tower, originally built in wood but rebuilt in stone by Henry II. The tower contains the Royal Archives and Photographic Collection. To the left of the Middle Ward is the Lower Ward, home to the gothic St. George's Chapel (where ten monarchs are buried) as well as the Albert Memorial Chapel, built in tribute to Queen Victoria's Prince Albert.

Walking from the Lower Ward through the Middle Ward, we passed into the Upper Ward. This area contains apartments rented to distinguished governmental workers and military men for a pittance of the public rent outside these walls. Rooms on display in the castle included the State Apartments containing many art treasures, Queen

Mary's dollhouse, The Queen's Ballroom, The Queen's Audience Chamber, and the Waterloo Chamber or Banquet Hall. This room was so named because along its walls are portraits of the men who helped defeat Napoleon at Waterloo.

Next to the Queen's chambers was the Royal Art Collection displaying paintings on loan from various art galleries. These paintings are constantly changed, not only for the Queen's pleasure, but for the visiting public as well. During the Fire of 1992 the media and the country watched a devastated Queen in her tartan headscarf, raincoat, and wellies (tall rubber gardening boots) along with the Duke of York in his raincoat and wellies work feverously to help the fire brigade and the palace workers remove all manner of art works before they could be damaged or destroyed either by fire or from the fire brigade's hoses. Watching these scenes made the fire's destruction even more real. People driving on the M-2 could see the flames and smoke miles away.

After viewing the castle and its East Terrace Garden filled with flowering shrubs and plants, we walked back into Windsor proper, surveying the village shops selling wool sweaters, tartan skirts, blouses, books, camera supplies, bone china cups and saucers, beakers, teapots, Hazel's porcelain store fronts, and teas of any conceivable variety or combination. My group was enamored with all the collectibles to behold and purchase. They loved watching the shop cats sunning themselves in their owner's front windows.

The Nell Grymm's House, operating since 1640 or so their front sign said, became their favorite. Pat and Marge purchased bone china beakers to take home and would have bought a teapot or two if they had a way of getting them home unbroken. With two weeks yet of vacation remaining, they decided to wait and check out other villages in case they found something they liked better. They knew I could come back after they left and purchase and mail to them what they really wanted.

Lunchtime found us frequenting the Barry Tea and Sweet Shop that touted their cream teas, sandwiches, and sweets. After looking at their fare (menu), our order included homemade beef vegetable soup, cheese sandwiches, and shepherd's pie. Large beakers of tea were in the offing as well. The homemade bread came straight from the oven. Oh, how scrumptious and wonderful to our hungry palates.

After reviving ourselves, the girls continued their hunts while Lyn and Jim took residence on a wood bench nearby. An hour later, when the shopping was complete, we decided to start home in order to beat the evening rush traffic. To our surprise we quickly found the shuttle bus, our cars, and the road home. Our timing couldn't have been more perfect as the traffic on the Ring road was only beginning to pick up. Exiting the Ring onto the A-12, we noticed the increase in traffic but that wouldn't bother us now.

We arrived at our house about six. Lyn drove his group home to clean up and return as we had decided to have dinner at the Artichoke, our friendly pub. Most selected to go to the carvery for roast turkey, chicken, or beef, along with roasted potatoes, roasted onions, steamed carrots, cauliflower, broccoli, cooked peas, cabbage, and parsnips while Sandy and I ordered their famous fish and chips dinner. After dinner we had a choice from their desserts: fruit trifles, butterscotch pudding, a selection of ice cream sundaes as well as apple crumble (apple crisp). When we left, we were stuffed to the brim.

The following day we trekked into London to tour the Tower of London and St. Paul's Cathedral. After boarding the 10:17 train to London, my group wanted some way of knowing where I was if they became dislodged from me. Since I had my trusty small pink Totes brawlee with me, I said I would hold it up like all the other "tour" guides did so they would know in an instant where I was. This pleased them to no end; they wouldn't get lost. From Liverpool Street station we moved on to the Central Line for St. Paul's station. With my brawlee in the air I led them to St. Peter's Cathedral around the corner where we found her standing in all her glory. She dominates the middle of her own city block. A statue of Queen Anne stands in the forecourt surrounded by iron fencing to keep visitors from sitting on her steps.

Coming up its West Portico, we spied under the center roof, the pediment carvings depicting the Conversion of St. Paul. Twin towers were added later in order to house twin clocks. Only the right clock is in place; the left one is vacant. After walking up two flights of stairs to the front entry, I pointed out the matching columns along its full-length cathedral front.

As we entered the church proper, the church's magnificence came to life. Using Baroque architectural ideas, Wren designed the cathedral's interior (the nave, transepts, and choir area) in the shape of a cross to enhance and show off this area. Walking up the north aisle leading to the main altar we looked up and saw the flying buttresses that support the nave walls and great dome. The Inner and Outer Dome (360 feet high, second only to St. Peter's in Rome) contains the Whispering Gallery, where even the slightest sound (the drop of a pin) reverberates within the dome. The Stone gallery along the dome's exterior offers a spectacular view of London. The dome's oculus or opening allows the lantern weighing 850 tons and supported by a brick cone to be seen.

The area just prior to the Main Altar contains two ascending rows of the wood choir desks, each having its own pillared lamp and chair. The first row is designated for the boys' choir while the second contains the adult male voices. Surrounding this area are beautifully carved overhangs, gold and white block friezes, and wrought iron screens to block the congregation from invading this area. Mosaic paintings decorate the overhead ceiling.

After the High Altar and Reredos of 1888 were damaged by bombs in 1940, the present altar was consecrated in May 1958 and serves as a memorial to the war dead for both World Wars. White Italian marble creates the altar itself while its tall gilded cross and candlesticks adorn and magnify this important area. Mounted in the center of the cross are polished amethyst and rock crystal. A beautiful English oak canopy hangs over the altar. Christ Triumphant hangs from overhead.

On our way down the south aisle we passed John Donne's tomb, the only monument to survive the Great Fire. In the center of this side aisle is the entrance to the Whispering Gallery. In order to get to this gallery, the visitor must climb 259 steps; only the hearty should try this feat. There are no elevators here for the faint of hearted. Lyn took on the challenge and said just hearing his whisper come back to him made the climb worth it.

As we finished our tour, we looked back at all the beauty we had seen. How impressive she was. Each visit only makes me love her more. Once outside with my umbrella in full view, we made our way back to the tube and off we traveled to the Tower of London and its bridge. As we arrived there, we felt the pangs of hunger in us and decided to stop at the nearby Dickens pub for various ploughman sandwiches, crisps, and pints of coke before touring the Tower.

The Tower Bridge was completed in 1894 and quickly became a London landmark with its twin towers and catwalk giving all visitors willing to climb its 300 steps a beautiful view of the Thames. When the center of the bridge is raised, she is 135 feet high and 200 feet wide.

William the Conqueror built the Tower of London in the eleventh century so he could contain and protect the city from foreign attacks. By the thirteenth century the walls had to be expanded as the city had grown so much. Today, the Tower perimeter walls enclose eighteen acres. This entire area is guarded by a group of retired military men called the Beefeaters who live on its grounds in their own apartments. Not only do these highly selected men guard the Tower but they also lead tours of it. Their extensive knowledge of the Tower's history along with their dramatic and vocal ability at times make their tours a must on anyone's list of things to do.

Over the years The Tower has served as a fortress as well as housing the royal jewels, the Royal Mint, the Royal Menagerie, the Public Records, and at one time the Royal Observatory. It also has served as a palace for all kings and queens since James I. By tradition, or maybe for old wives tales to create good luck in his or her reign, each monarch lodges in the royal suite here the night before his or her coronation.

We moved from the Tower's prison to the building housing the crown jewels. The guard around them is strict and strong in number. The magnificent crown jewels include a regalia of crowns, rings, scepters, orbs, and swords used at coronations and special occasions. While inside we watched a short documentary on the history of the major pieces of jewelry along with the crowns, state orb, and sword.

The Tower's armories house the mail body armor and the weaponry of William the Conqueror as well as that of Richard I and his Crusaders. Here the history of gunpowder and muskets is documented. The English Civil War is depicted through its helmets and half armors. Also, an assortment of crossbows, jousting lances, elegant silver hunting swords, and various firearms are displayed as well.

We visited the Chapel of St. John containing a nave and aisles as well as an apse, a projected part of the chapel. Its heavy columns carry carved initials of an early date. Double windows sit above the chapel's plain arches. The altar hangings are made from the cloth used to decorate Westminster Abbey for the coronation of George VI, Queen Elizabeth's father.

As we finished our tour, our Beefeater explained the Ceremony of the Keys to us. This takes place every evening just after the public has left. The Beefeaters check the grounds making sure no stragglers still remain within the wall's confines. Once it has been ascertained no public individual remains, the sergeant and three of his men close the three gates. Through ritual coded messages between the men, each gate is locked and secured. When the procedure is completed, the keys are carried to the Chief Warder in the Queen's House where they are secured for the night.

After my friends had seen all they wanted, we returned to the trains for our journey home before the commuter traffic would play havoc with our time schedule. We were home by four. They drove to their bed and breakfast before returning for a barbecue in our back garden.

The next morning we boarded an early morning commuter train for London in order to see the Changing of the Guard. At Liverpool Street station I used my pink umbrella to make sure my brood changed correctly to the Circle line for Westminster Station. They certainly loved this idea and kept in line so no one got lost. After arriving at Westminster station we moved from the depths of the underground to the outside where we saw the Houses of Parliament in the glow of the morning sun. The air was cool but the sun began to warm us. About the same time we heard Big Ben sounding off its ten strikes telling everyone who could hear it was ten o'clock; which made the moment even more gripping. As we strolled past Parliament we noticed people already taking pictures of it from every angle possible. Strict closure rules were still in effect because of IRA bomb concerns.

We decided to press on to the Palace and return later to Westminster Abbey. The walk down Birdcage Lane was exhilarating and woke up my little group. We passed the Wellington Barracks and Hospital. We finally approached Buckingham Palace with its black wrought iron fencing surrounding it. Lyn, Pat, Jim and Marge gazed at the royal crests on the main wrought iron gates then the cement pillars displaying the royal crown and other royal symbols. The Royal Standard, Queen's flag, hung from its flagpole, meaning the Queen was in residence. Wonder if we could go in for tea? Oh, back to reality. A few people had already begun positioning themselves along the fencing in order to get the best view of this special ceremony; others had taken residence around the Queen Victoria memorial to see the approaching Queen's guard pass in front of them on their way into the Palace grounds. Again, we snapped pictures to remember this moment. Since we had come early enough to get a "seat" on the right side cement sill, we would be able to freely see the ceremony without being obstructed by two or three people ahead of us.

We sat for about a half hour then heard the marching of her Majesty's guards' boots coming toward us. Their musical instruments shone in the sunshine and their music made us onlookers stop and take notice while our feet tapped to the lively beat. Marching in their regal uniforms of black trousers with their red side stripes, their shiny leather shoes, their vibrant crimson tunics, and their tall, furry black bearskin hats only added to this event's pomp and circumstance. After this group moved around Queen Victoria memorial and into the palace's forecourt, the horse delegation with their black trousers, boots, sabers, and various regiment tunics and fur headgear took their place in the ceremony.

Once all her guard was inside, the ceremony proceeded with the old guard leaving their posts while handing over to the new palace guards the palace keys and all the responsibility that goes with them – keeping the Queen and nation safe. The procedure took about a half hour but it seemed to be over in minutes. Afterward, we walked back up Birdcage Lane to Great George Street to first visit St. Margaret's Church then across the street to the Abbey. It amazed all of us that it took about 600 years to complete this building (1245 to the 1800's).

Would we Americans or American architects and builders stick to a project that long? I don't think so. This church has not only been the burial site of monarchs since the thirteenth century but also the setting for many coronations, the most recent was Queen Elizabeth II's in 1953, as well as royal weddings including the Queen and Prince Philip's and that of Prince Charles and Princess Diana. The nave demonstrates the austere French Gothic architecture. Its height is one hundred and two feet making it the tallest in England. The ratio of height to width is three to one.

Walking around we took note of the sanctuary built by Henry III where thirty-eight coronations have taken place. Poets' Corner honors many great British poets such as Shakespeare, Chaucer, and T. S. Eliot. The Pyx Chamber, in medieval times, was the place where coinage was tested. We found St. Edward's Chapel which contains the Coronation Chair, then Edward the Confessor's shrine, and the tombs of many medieval monarchs.

Having toured the complete Abbey, we needed some lunch to sustain us for the rest of the day's touring. I walked them around the corner to Parliament Street and The Red Lion pub. A rather small, stuffy pub but a worthy place to stop. We ordered various meat and cheese sandwiches, crisps, and pints of coke.

After lunch, with my trusty tour guide stick, I marched my little group further down Parliament Street to see Number 10 Downing Street, the home of the British Prime Minister since 1732. His residence contains a Cabinet Room where government policy is discussed, an impressive State Dining Room, and a private apartment for guests. Number 11 is the official residence of the Chancellor of the Exchequer, the overseer of the nation's financial affairs. In 1959 I remember my parents and I walked down past number 10 Downing Street when tourists could actually do that, but now, with the IRA threats the government has iron fenced the street and put in its own security police force. No one is allowed down this street unless they can identify themselves with particular passes and those driving in must have dogs and metal detectors check every inch of their cars inside, outside, and underneath.

Further down Parliament Street is the Cenotaph built in 1920 to honor the war dead. Each Remembrance Day, like our Veteran's Day, the royal family, parliament members, and military units come to this spot to hold a memorial ceremony to their fallen heroes. Many red poppy wreathes are laid at the foot of the memorial while the Queen herself places a large poppy wreath on the top front step. Strolling further down the street we passed the building containing the Cabinet War Rooms where Winston Churchill created the war plans for World War II. His desk, communications equipment, and maps used for plotting war strategy still remain in place. During times of conflict or war this building houses strategic ministers and military leaders. The Cabinet Room itself is soundproofed so major decisions can be made here. Thick, three-foot walls protect all rooms. Although this building was open to the public, my group didn't want to spend time here. Harrods mightily beckoned them.

Even though bone-tired, my fledglings wanted to stop at Harrods before heading to our house. The amazement on their faces to see what could be seen and bought here was one to be behold. Shocked not only by the size of it but the variety of merchandise on sale, they headed for the china department for teapots and Dunnon beaker sets. After seeing all the choices of beakers, teapots, and everyday china, they made their selections.

After our tour of Harrods we headed home with my pink umbrella leading the way. I put one of my frozen lasagnas in the oven, tossed a salad, then poured glasses of merlot for my fatigued group while waiting for Ron to come home. I waited to put my loaves of garlic bread into the oven until Ron walked into the house and the lasagna was done and needed a few minutes of resting time before serving. Another reason I waited – my lasagna took up all the space in my little oven so the bread had to wait its turn.

That Sunday, Ron and I took our group to St. Mary's for the Sunday service. They loved our little white Tudor church but especially Roderick and Allison. As a surprise to them I had asked Roderick and Allison to come for lunch after the service and they had graciously accepted. Ron barbecued steaks (via Costco and the USDA beef) on our outside grill while I baked jacket potatoes and tossed a huge garden salad. For dessert I had made Pat a chocolate cake as it was her birthday. We had a wonderful afternoon talking about the States, traveling, and just being together.

The next day our group split up. Pat, Lyn, and Sandy left for York in search of family roots, then on to Canterbury and Horley. When they returned we would have just one night with them before they would fly home. Jim and Marge came to stay with us. I got them settled into their room then we sat around the kitchen table planning what they wanted to see and do: Canterbury Cathedral, Dover, Margate (Jim was stationed there during the War), Butterfly Village (butterflies were Marge's passion) in King's Lynn, and Harrods for another look-see.

Since Marge was feeling tired and not up to par, we decided to stay home and visit. Early the following day I suggested we drive to Canterbury to see the Cathedral then drive along the coast past Sandwich then the White Cliffs of Dover, and finally onto Margate before returning home. "That sounds like a good plan of action," they said. I reminded them to bring their windbreakers as the winds around the Dover Cliffs tended to be cool. With their apparel in hand, they stepped into my little red chariot and off we went.

We first stopped in Rochester, a quaint little village along the River Medway where Charles Dickens summered and gathered ideas for his coastal settings for *David Copperfield* and other books. Dickens' house has been turned into a museum.

From there we stopped at Canterbury Cathedral. Much to our chagrin a college graduation service was in process, closing the church to the public for at least three hours. Marge decided to get some booklets about the Cathedral. We walked through the tightly knit streets of this town peering into shop windows to see what was available. In a little while she found just the right beakers for friends at home. After her purchases we retrieved my car and off we went again.

By the time we arrived in Dover, the Cliffs shone brilliantly in the sun's rays. Despite the bitter winds we got out and took pictures of the area then drove on to St. Margaret's at Cliffe, Deal, Sandwich, Broadstairs, and into Margate. Jim was so excited to revisit his old haunt; he looked like he had just won a million dollars in the lottery. He wanted to find the arcade, Dreamland, where he and other off-duty soldiers had spent their Friday and Saturday nights.

Since the War, Margate had become a summer resort town. Tourists sunned themselves along the beach while others sat on seaside benches enjoying their variegated ice cream cones. Others just took in the sights – like us. Jim walked until he found Dreamland but the pinball machines and video games for today's young clientele had taken over. What a delight I had watching Jim relive those days of yore. His eyes twinkled remembering those past times. After he treated his "girls" to ice cream cones, we left for home so we could get ahead of the evening traffic problems.

The following day we took it easy again going to Audley End, a wonderful old manor home with beautiful flower gardens, another of Marge's loves. On weekends the home allows concerts by the London Symphony as well as other known groups to take place. On those evenings makeshift stages are pulled out, then the group's sound systems are placed on scaffolding to bring out their best sounds. Many a night Ron and I treated ourselves to an romantic evening under the stars bringing a picnic dinner, bottle of wine, and a blanket to sit on while we listened to the melodious music emanating from their instruments.

Before returning home, Marge wanted to see Scotland with its heather and sheep filled hillsides. By a stroke of luck we purchased walking tickets to the British Open being held that year in Turnberry, Scotland. We decided to make a weekend of it. Marge devoured the hillsides full of flowers, grazing sheep, and heathers in varying shades of purple and pink. She had the wonderment look Jim did at Margate.

After a full day of driving we arrived at the Kirroughtree Hotel in Newton Stewart about four in the afternoon. We rested, then met for dinner in the hotel's dining room. That evening the hotel put on a Kalie, an evening of Scottish dancing, and provided instructors for all attendees wanting to learn the Scottish dances. What fun we had.

The British Open featured Jack Nicklaus, Tom Kite, Greg Norman,

Steve Ballesteros, Nick Faldo, and Colin Montgomerie. We spent the weekend walking along with various players scrutinizing each technique and stroke. That Sunday morning Ron ordered kippers (smoked herring) and scrambled eggs for breakfast. My mother made that breakfast for my Scottish Dad and us on many occasions. Over the years I had kept up this tradition, since Ron loved kippers. When the kippers came, it was a whole fish with its head still intact according to Scottish tradition. Marge, bless her, couldn't get used to the idea of serving the whole fish head and all or Ron's ordering or liking them. Ron enjoyed his meal thoroughly. She fell in love with their wonderfully rich homemade yogurt.

About ten we began our long trek back home, as Ron had to fly to Germany early the next morning for meetings there. Even though we did not get to see who won, we listened to it on our radio. The weekend had been fabulous – being with friends, seeing new territory, and watching some spectacular golf.

We returned home early enough to do a barbeque in the back garden. While we sat on the patio, a helicopter kept circling around our street and downtown Shenfield. We didn't understand why until we heard that Clare's had been burgled and the police were searching for those responsible. This unnerved all of us as we didn't know whether they were armed or not. We stayed inside where we knew we were safe until the police captured the thieves.

Later that night Ron packed his travel bag and put it in the car so he wouldn't have to do that in his rush to Heathrow in the morning. He retired early while the rest of us watched a bit of television before turning in. Just as I was getting ready for bed, I heard Jim yell for Ron. He had noticed our front door was ajar and thought Ron was outside. I told him Ron was sound asleep in bed. Ron thought he had completely shut and locked the door but the lock hadn't caught so the door opened itself. Since Marge was already unnerved, this didn't help the situation as she was afraid the robbers might get in and take her passport and money. Going downstairs, I made sure the house was secure and the door locked. Unfortunately, Marge had a fitful night of sleep worrying about the uncaptured robbers getting into our house for her passport.

Unfortunately, the unnerving didn't stop there. At four in the morning, Ron was taking his shower when the smoke detector went off. In recent weeks the alarm had taken to the idea of going off when the bathroom door opened up and the hot steamy air from within hit it. Poor Marge! She sat straight up in her bed assured someone was in the house stealing her purse and passport. Adding to this confusion, Ron tried to fan the steam away from the alarm with his towel when Jim came out and saw a nude man waving a towel beneath the alarm. What a shock that must have been for Jim until he realized the nude man was Ron and not a burglar. I felt so badly but there was nothing I could do to alleviate Marge's fears and shock. She rested the remainder of the day.

The following day we ventured into London to do some last minute shopping before the other group returned. Marge, Jim, and I revisited Fortnum and Mason for some tea, Ponti's for lunch, then Harrods for a final look.

That evening the whole group got together for our final dinner together at the Artichoke. Well, Lyn wanted to play a joke on us. Lyn, a teacher for a number of years, left the table on a fake men's room trip. While gone he conned our waitress into playing the part of one of his former students in the States. When she came to take our order, she said, "Didn't I have you for high school math a few years ago." A couple of us, myself included, took it hook, line, and sinker while Jim realized the con immediately. Within minutes we knew Lyn was up to his old tricks once again and we laughed at ourselves for being so gullible. Even today, when we remember the incident, we still chuckle. It reminds us of the wonderful time we had together.

Once dinner was over, the group went back to their bed and breakfast to repack for their flight home. The following morning I guided them back to Gatwick then Hertz rental to drop off their car. Saying goodbye was hard. I will never forget my friend who put aside her flying phobia to come and see me. What a true friend. At 11:45 their Delta flight 29 took off for the States and I drove home to Shenfield with tears of joy and sadness in my eyes remembering our wonderful time together.

37. Trolley Number Five

Ron and his colleague, Derek Eade, needed to go to Hannover, Germany to inspect some new catalysts that Artec had coated with a new compound. Ron said to Derek, "Why don't we take the girls with us and make it a real trip?" Derek agreed to talk to his wife, Susan, as Ron knew I would say yes. Susan also said she would love to go.

About four in the afternoon two days later, the four of us climbed into Derek's car and headed for Dover and the ferry to Calais. We hoped to catch the six o'clock ferry so we would be in Hannover about half-past nine, or so. During the drive, Derek and Ron discussed their upcoming meetings with Artec. Susan and I sat in the backseat talking about our granddaughters – her Shannon was two years younger than our Jennifer. Both girls were the apple of their grandmothers' eyes and hearts. And, we threw around ideas of what we could do with a whole morning at our disposal.

The Channel crossing was pleasant. Ron and I had never been to Hannover, while Susan and Derek had been there twice on business, as well as pleasure. They offered to take us on a tour after the meetings. Since Derek knew where he was going and all the shortcuts, we arrived at the Dorint Hotel ahead of schedule.

While waiting for Derek to park the car, we checked into our rooms. Although we were tired from the trip, we were famished. We had decided to save our calories for a great meal when we got to the hotel. We learned the dining room would be open for another forty-five minutes. If we hurried, the staff would serve us.

Quickly, dropping our bags off in our rooms, we proceeded to the dining room. What a place. Linen covered the dining tables, mauve tapestry covered the high back chairs, and the staff was dressed in formal black and white uniforms. It was elegant.

The menu had everything from steaks to chicken to quail to pasta and vegetable dishes. Derek selected the roasted duck with roasted potatoes and vegetables. Susan wanted the grilled chicken with scalloped potatoes and a green salad. Ron ordered Dover sole with jacket potato and green salad, and I ordered fresh pasta, shrimp, and vegetables in an Alfredo-like sauce. Being in a festive mood, we bought a bottle of German Riesling to go with our meals. We passed on dessert, as it was late and we didn't want to go to sleep on a full stomach.

Susan and I delayed our morning itinerary until we could talk to Terry Martin who lived here and knew things we could or should do and see. I remembered him from my first Brussels' trip, and Ron's first Artec visit. When Terry came to pick up our guys, we asked his sight seeing advice. He told us to take the Number 5 trolley to the Herrenhausen Garten, a manor house being renovated for governmental functions and state dinners, and had a fabulous garden. As the house was closed to the public, he recommended we tour the gardens, then get back on the Number 5 trolley, which would take us into Hannover's shopping Centrum, where we could shop to our hearts' content. We thanked him for his advice.

For breakfast, Susan and I splurged on fresh cantaloupe, strawberries, blueberries, bananas, croissants and sweet rolls, and pots of hot tea. After our taste fest, we set out to find this Number 5 trolley. Walking from our hotel, we found streets filled with flower stalls, newsagent stores, small meat and produce markets, and outdoor cafes which were just beginning to open. We strolled past stoic, pastel apartment buildings – darkening due to the pollution from gas fumes. I wondered what that same pollution did to people's noses and chests; it made it quite clear Ron's catalysts were desperately needed to clear this menace away. As I walked, I also wondered what secrets these buildings held about their occupants. In my mind, I created some of my own ideas. Maybe a princess once lived here in one of these large complexes, or two or three families living together to conserve their money, or maybe there was someone's love nest hidden in one of these buildings. Who knows what secrets lurked inside?

After walking another two streets, we found the covered bus stop. Looking at the schedule, we found the next Number 5 would arrive in 15 minutes. We sat on the waiting bench and discussed whether we wanted to risk going into the city after seeing the gardens. Since we were both adventurers, we decided to give it a whirl.

The trolley, powered by overhead electrical wires, moved swiftly on its chosen rails to its various destinations. Watching our trolley map, and having made the fourth stop, we realized the Garten was next. Stepping off the trolley, we walked through its exterior black iron fencing. Along with its light yellow exterior, the manor house had a long cement porch traveling the length of the house. On both sides of the porch were two equally positioned white columns – one at each porch and roof corner, and the other two positioned on either side of the main entrance. Being curious, we peeked into the portico windows, hoping to get a glimpse of what renovations were being made, but all we saw was furniture covered with white tarps. The walls, crown moldings, and chair railings had been sanded and ready for their new coat of paint. The frescos on the ceilings were being hand painted in order to get the proper color, brush strokes, and emotion originally painted into them. I tried to imagine what the house would look like, once the rejuvenation was complete. I wondered who would be invited to one of its gala state affairs. If Ron and I returned here after the renovation, I wanted to come back and see the newness. I was sure this would be a real treasure.

Buying a brochure from one of the kiosks (street vendors), I learned information about this residence. Through many years, this home has been the residence for rulers and aristocrats, but now it is under the government's domain and used as a museum to tell the house's history. Herrenhausen Garten was the old Palace of the Hannoverian kings – George I ruled Hannover for many years. Later, he became King George I of the British Isles, and ruled both the British Isles and Hannover (Lower Saxony), until Queen Victoria took over the reigns in 1827.

Realizing we could not go inside, Susan and I walked into the back gardens. Some original buildings were still standing, although not used. Since it was October, gardeners were manicuring the shrubs and trees and pruning away thorny dead rose branches for winter, as well as planting some new rose bushes and spring bulbs (tulips, hyacinths, crocuses, and dahlias) in mass within the sculpted low hedge areas, so each would accentuate the other. This would be a spectacular view for next year's tourists.

We walked through the garden's winding pathways, dotted with military and mythical statues – a wonderland even if nothing was in bloom. In a corner section of the garden was a small swimming pool with a nymph fountain to one side. A small stone amphitheater circled the pool area; here people could meditate or commune with nature. Many people did not know the real reason for the fountain's existence. Underneath the stones lay a water purifying system used to clean the house's water supply. Anyone not knowing this, would see this area only as a pool with a place to sit down and relax and not realize its true function. Extraordinary.

After our visit, Sue and I went back to the trolley stop and boarded our eastbound Number 5 trolley going into the city. We watched all the passing buildings, boutiques, and market areas along the way. Finally, in Hannover's shopping area, we stepped off the trolley and proceeded along the pedestrian walkway under a viaduct carrying rapidly moving traffic overhead. This pathway led us into a large open-air shopping mall – large even by American standards. Walking around its center, we heard musicians playing everything from Chopin and Bach to the Beatles and hoping for a few coins to help them survive the day. We entered a large department store where Susan and I looked for outfits for our granddaughters. Susan found a pretty pink and white speckled dress with a matching pink sweater. I found Jennifer a cute two-piece dress with a plain navy under dress with long sleeves and an overdress with colorful flowers and butterflies on it. I was so excited, as it would be a great Christmas gift for her.

Outside again, we moved from shop window to shop window looking for other family Christmas gifts. All of a sudden, I saw a shop with all kinds of hand-painted steins. I was thrilled, as I wanted some authentic ones for my three "guys" – Ron, and our two sons, Ron and John. I was in seventh heaven. As we entered, we saw two long rows of shelves filled with steins of all sizes, shapes, paintings, and prices. I knew my budget wouldn't extend to more than thirty dollars for each one. I explained to the pleasant shopkeeper ,in his red, yellow, and navy plaid flannel shirt and brown trousers, what my price range was. He seemed pleased and asked his English-speaking assistant to help us. She was pleasant, but wanted me to spend more than I was willing to pay.

She told us where each stein had come from. Each German city had its own way of making, baking, and painting its steins. She also explained the significance of each scene painted on them. I found two different medium sized celebration scene steins for Ron and John, and a larger one with Bavarian people sitting around a table drinking liters of German beer for my Ron. Each one had its own sculptured silver engraved, cone lid. They were beautiful and I was pleased with them. The storeowner wrapped them in heavy newspaper, then gingerly placed them in boxes so I could get them safely back to England. I could send them on to the boys in time for Christmas. What a sense of accomplishment I had. Since Susan only wanted the dress for her granddaughter, and I had my purchases, we decided to return to our hotel in time to meet our guys.

Retracing our steps, we found a westbound Number 5 trolley. I was aglow with my purchases, but wished I had found something for Laura and Nancy. While waiting for our trolley, Susan noticed a car hanging upside down under a nearby viaduct; I guess it was an art statement. We could tell an accident wouldn't have left it there. It was a real mystery for both of us. One we would ponder, but never learn the truth about.

We arrived at our hotel in good time to meet the guys and check out of our rooms. Derek wanted us to see Hannover's town hall. After packing the car with our luggage and goodies, we drove to the town hall and parked in their large car park. As the four of us walked up to the hall, we were amazed by this large, dark-tan, stone building with rounded black, wrought-iron, dual stairwells on either side of the entrance doors.

As we mounted the stairs, Derek told us much of the city's history was displayed inside. We bought our entrance tickets and waited for the next guided tour. The upstairs area contained various governmental offices. Upon returning to the ground floor, the guide showed us four large squares, each depicting the buildings, land formations, and housing of four historical times. The first square depicted Hannover from its beginnings as a civilization; the second was 1939, just before the beginning of World War II, showing how the town had grown and prospered; the third was 1944, revealing the devastation from the war; and the fourth square showed the rebuilt and thriving city of today. The maps gave us a greater understanding and feel for Hannover. Realizing it was getting late and wanting to stop in Bruges before heading home, we left the town hall. Susan and Derek had never visited there and we wanted to show them what a wonderful place it was.

The drive though the countryside was enjoyable. We pulled into Bruges about three o'clock. The temperature had dropped considerably and rain had started to fall. Fortunately, we had brought wool sweaters to wear under our jackets and coats. Finding a lone parking space along a side street, we began our walk into the town centrum, five blocks away. Almost into town, we spotted a lovely, little teashop with all kinds of pastries in its front window enticing us to come in. Since we were beginning to feel a bit cold and wet, we decided to stop. Each of us ordered a pot of hot tea and a different pastry, so we could sample each other's delicacy. We ordered an apple tart, an éclair with chocolate sauce and topped with sifted confectioner's sugar, a piece of carrot cake, which turned out to be passion cake, and a blackberry turnover. Our taste buds tingled from the flavors and textures they came in contact with. We couldn't select one as the best, as they were all excellent.

Finishing our treats, we left the shop and moved toward the center of town. Even in the cold and heavy drizzle, we could see the enthusiasm and excitement on peoples' faces. Being here reminded us just how full of love and happiness Bruges was. We took Susan and Derek on a tour of the square's shops, the town hall, as well as the St. Michael's Hospital.

On exiting the hospital's lower level, we noticed a stone patio adjoining a newly opened restaurant. We decided to try it as we needed to eat before beginning our trip home. The charming dining room contained a dozen or so tables, covered with white linen and clear hurricane candle lamps, and a large roaring fire in their fireplace. Brass railings dividing table areas, and silk greenery and trees strategically placed, gave off a homey feeling to all who entered. Since we were their first customers of the night, we were afforded special treatment. The menu was filled with marvelous fish entrees, including fish soup, Dover sole and salmon steaks. Also served, were steaks and chicken grilled in a white wine sauce. Decisions, decisions! Ron and Derek decided on Dover sole, Susan had the chicken with streamed vegetables, and I had the fish soup with a green salad. Again, we splurged on another bottle of German Riesling. How decadent.

As we sat enjoying our glasses of wine, we became aware the restaurant was slowly filling up with other couples, families, and tourists. Waiters busied themselves attending their patrons and tables. Our meals were superb. We took tastes of each other's delicacy. I don't know how, but at one point I got up the courage to ask our waiter if he could ask the chef for his secret to the creamy white sauce in my soup. He said he would ask. Returning, he said the chef would give me the recipe as it was a widely used French fish sauce. Expecting him to write it out for me, I was shocked when the chef himself came out and told me exactly how to make it. I was to take two cups of white wine and reduce it to half, then add two cups of cream and reduce the mixture to half. So simple but so fabulous! We all told him how wonderful our meals were, and I thanked him for coming out and talking to us. I felt so special and regal. I could hardly wait to get home to make this wonderful sauce myself. It reminded me of the fish stew I enjoyed at the little restaurant in Pont L'Eveque in Normandy, France. Since we had eaten our desserts earlier, we turned down their tray of luscious looking tarts, cake slices, and white and chocolate mousses, and opted for cups of coffee.

We had a smooth crossing, as well as drive home in the pouring rain. We arrived home at half past midnight. We fell wearily into our bed, content with all we had seen and done.

What a pleasure to get to know Susan and Derek better.

38. Our Shenfield Church Family Accepts Us

Since arriving here two years ago, Ron and I had been a part of St. Mary the Virgin Church. The British gruffness or demeanor towards us Americans was softening, and we felt welcome and at home in this lovely eleventh century church.

Each Sunday, after parking our car in their car park, we walked through their flowering rose covered, double-latch gate. The fragrances emanating here would gladdened any heart and nose, even on the saddest day. Once, we walked through the latch gate and their parish cemetery, we entered the church through it dark wood portico.

Inside, the upper portions of the walls were painted a cream whitewash, while the lower halves displayed wood siding. Mahogany carved beams, placed strategically throughout the nave, held up the church's roof and ceiling. Left of the entrance was an alcove filled with eight full-length pews. Here, the bell ringer pulled repeatedly on the bell's dangling rope to announce to the outside world the church's readiness for morning or evening services. To the right of the doors was the nave. Each sidewall contained stained glass windows depicting various biblical scenes and religious personages in vibrant primary colors. Over the nave, carved wood arches gave me a sense of St. Paul's Cathedral in this tiny parish church. Perpendicularly to the altar stood two rows of choir stalls where each Sunday the choir combined their voices in hymns and anthems. The wood-carved altar was impressive and accentuated the ceiling beams. Behind the altar itself was a Reredos in three separate arched and gilded frames depicting *The Last Supper* in vibrant cranberry, royal blue, white, and gold colors. What a special congregation and place to worship.

On Roderick's first visit to our home, we had told him we wanted to take an active role in our church. He was aware of our licensing as lay readers and chalice bearers in own diocese in Michigan. He had petitioned Bishop Boswell of the Diocese of Chelmsford to license us here as well. Since we had our licenses with us, he saw no problem in conferring similar British licenses on us.

One Saturday night while reading in the lounge, Ron and I heard the telephone ring. It was Roderick who told Ron our licenses had been conferred with pleasure by the Bishop. Roderick wanted to plan a dedication service for us one Sunday soon.

The following Sunday, Roderick invited us to come before the congregation to be installed as chalice bearers and readers. We walked proudly up the main aisle to Roderick who explained to the assembled members that the Bishop had licensed us to serve this parish. After some prayers and vows to diligently serve our new parish family, Roderick conferred our licenses upon us.

My heart was pounding so hard and my knees were shaking so much I thought everyone would know how nervous I was. I worried how this congregation would receive us. I felt all their eyes on us thinking – "Oh, there go those bloody Americans pushing their way into everything including our church services. Who do they think they are, anyway?"

At the end of the service, I was astounded as people told us how happy they were that we wanted to be a part of their church family. Now, I really felt at home in my little church away from home.

39. A Shocking Homecoming

In October, Ron and I spent a week in Germany on business. Entering our home on November 3rd, we did not notice anything wrong. Ron gathered up the accumulated mail the postal carrier had dropped through our door mail-slot, then put it on our kitchen table. As he laid the mail down, he saw the ominous police notice. The Brentwood Police had been called about a burglary to both sides of our semi-detached. Constables Hanes and Withrow had investigated the interior of our place and had assessed we had been "seriously burgled" on October 31st.

Ron called me into the kitchen and showed me the notice. It was hard for me to believe, since nothing seemed out of place. Then, I remembered that my two cleaning ladies, Jill and Susan, would have come to clean two days before our return. They must have been the ones to report the burglary to the police. The police came, fingerprinted them, then dusted for prints. We would also have be fingerprinted so other prints could be checked out as suspects. We were to call the police immediately upon our return.

Looking around the kitchen, we found the broken window and its smashed lock where the perpetrator had gained entrance. While Ron called the police, I walked around the house finding it in apple pie order. Jill and Susan must have cleaned up whatever mess they had found. Since it was near midnight, I decided to call Jill in the morning to get the details.

Getting into bed, I was shaken trying to understand how this could happen to us. I was upset, as the homes rented to Comco's top management families had been fitted with alarm systems,while the rest of us weren't afforded that luxury. Unnerved enough, I asked Ron to request an alarm system for us. With Ron traveling so much, I now felt quite unsafe.

In the morning after Ron left for work, I called Jill. She was still shaken as she and Susan had walked into the burglary aftermath. She said the dining room drawers had been pulled out with silverware being everywhere. The books in the lounge had been ripped out of their bookcase places and thrown helter-skelter in the room. Jewelry, clothes, shoes, and underwear had been thrown out of our bedroom dresser, chest of drawers, and closets. I figured young kids were looking for drug money. Jill said instead of working their regular two hours, they had stayed all day putting everything back, so we wouldn't walk into that mess. I thanked her and told her I would pay both of them for the additional work to save us from that mess. I don't know what I would have done if I had walked into that.

The police came that evening to fingerprint us and to relate what information they had about the theft. They needed an itemized list and cost of everything taken. They believed the robbery had taken place on October 31, as our neighbor's neighbor had heard a crash of window glass about 7:30 that night, but didn't find anything wrong, so he didn't report anything. Even though Halloween wasn't really celebrated in England, a large group of children and parents had been out that night. The perpetrator had been able to burgle both sides of our unit, then blend into the crowd unnoticed.

I phoned our neighbors' daughter in Liverpool to tell her of the burglary at their place as well. Niamh, a medical student at the University of Liverpool, said she would call her parents in Hong Kong, as they were on a Barclay Bank assignment there. She would drive down later that afternoon to see what needed to be done. She was quite shaken and I worried about her driving so far alone. Since her parents had left, Niamh, Ron, and I had become quite close; she became our surrogate daughter and we became her surrogate parents. We made a wonderful trio. Her parents, Mary and Trevor Martin, were absolutely fantastic to us and we loved them dearly. I still remember the night we met Mary – she came knocking at our door. Ron answered it. Mary said, "I want to introduce myself. I am your neighbor on the other side. I am Mary Martin, but I don't sing or dance." What a lovely woman and such a wonderful sense of humor. We took to her immediately; soon after we met Trevor, who we also took to immediately.

As I went through the bedroom closets, drawers, jewelry box, and dining room chest, I took note of missing items. First, I realized all Jennifer's Christmas gifts were gone. My heart sank. I tried to rationalize that young people took the clothes as they needed them for their youngster. Then I realized all the person would have to do was return the clothes in their store bags along with my cash receipts and get a cash refund for everything they took. I had paid cash for everything since we would be stateside when the British Visa bill would arrive and become due, so I paid for everything so not to have any finance charges on our bill. In this case, having finance charges would have been less than losing Jennifer's Christmas presents. Adding to my heartbreak, I found two of mother's broaches were missing. No monetary price could be placed on them as they were mementos of her. Since I knew the police needed a clear description of them, I sat down and drew pictures of each broach.

Finally, I realized our wheeled carry-on bag was missing. We surmised the thief had put our things in the bag then walked leisurely down to the train station pulling our bag in tow, just like any other traveler, purchased a train ticket and took off for parts unknown, as if nothing had happened.

That afternoon I drove to the Brentwood Police Station and gave my information, drawings, and list to the young constable at the reception desk who said she would give it to our constables, forthwith. They would call if they needed anything additional or had news for us. Later they called and thanked me for my drawings and help. They said, "If anything else turns up missing, call us straightaway."

Even though we had been burgled, Comco denied our alarm request. We decided to put one in ourselves. Ron nor I felt comfortable about my being alone while he traveled. Jill's elder son, Ian, sold alarm systems and would give us a good price for it, as well as the installation. In fact, he and his father would install it for us making the price even cheaper. Within a week they came and installed the system, making both Ron and me feel more secure.

I thought I had put the incident behind me until I realized my special Christmas gift for Ron was missing. Being an avid golfer, I had bought him a Nick Faldo Pringle sweater. I was crushed and just sat on our bed sobbing. The whole incident terrorized me once again.

Some weeks later Constable Withrow called and wanted me to come in and view some jewelry taken in their "Operation Bumblebee". I hoped I would find mother's broaches since one had special significance to me. The trip was for naught; lots of jewelry and things but nothing even remotely resembled my pieces. He said, "Maybe in the next sweep." I knew the broaches were gone and I just had to accept that. They never turned up, not even in London pawnshops. Well, c'est la vie – such is life.

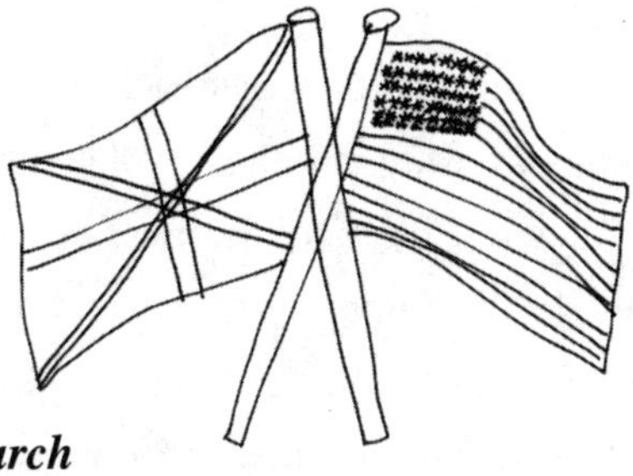

40. The Grand March

Thanksgiving was approaching for my fourth year in England, and the girls wanted to do something special for it. Each Thanksgiving, St. Paul's Cathedral holds a special Thanksgiving service for all the Americans living in the London area. Both the Lord Mayor of London and the U. S. Ambassador to the United Kingdom take part in the service. The service includes American hymns and a full American honor guard from Europe.

At a mid-October coffee, Linda Grand asked people to sign up if they wanted to go to the service. If there were enough of us, she would attempt to make lunch arrangements at Simpson's on the Strand for a Thanksgiving dinner. To get good seats at the Cathedral, we needed to be there no later than half past nine, meaning we needed to take a very early commuter train. I signed Ron and me up, hoping he would take the day off to enjoy this celebration.

Two weeks later Linda said that she had twenty people signed up for the lunch and she had arranged with Simpsons to create a turkey dinner with all the trimmings. Ron said it sounded like a real treat and would arrange his schedule so he could go.

Thanksgiving morning Ron and I met thirty other Americans for the half past seven train into London. Part of our group had to return after the service, as they had to be home for their school aged children in the afternoon. Remember, England doesn't celebrate Thanksgiving, just as Americans don't celebrate Boxing Day.

Being an early train, we stopped at each small village picking up every commuter along the way into the city. I never thought we would get there in time. Once in Liverpool Station, we migrated to the Central Line and St. Paul's. The underground was full of commuters and we were just a piece of its fabric. As we boarded our train, we were crushed in like sardines in the can. I do not think any of us could breathe. Finally, at St. Paul's we disembarked and for the first time in five minutes were able to breathe, even if it was sooty underground air.

We walked as a group around the corner passing the yet unopened tourist shops with their London T-shirts, mugs, flags, and other trinkets just waiting for someone to buy them. The sun was coming up and the dome of the Cathedral was beginning to show its golden glow. We stood outside taking group pictures as a remembrance of this day.

About a quarter past nine we decided to go inside to find some good seats. We thought we were the first group to enter and thereby have the pick of the seating. As we walked down the center aisle in mass, we realized we were not the first group inside. Other spectators along with their purses and coats had reserved seats in the front four and five rows on either side of the center aisle for potential friend attendees. Our group took the sixth through tenth rows on the left side. Not what we wanted, but we could see from there.

As we looked around, we saw the columns on either side of the choir area holding unfurled British and American flags proudly representing both nations in all their color and strength As we waited for the service, I read the service program which was full of American hymns: *America the Beautiful, The Battle Hymn of the Republic*, and both the American and British national anthems. I knew these would bring tears to my eyes when I thought of family and home during this service.

At precisely half past ten, a trumpet flourish could be heard from the street entrance. As the congregation began singing *America the Beautiful*, we watched as the American honor guard processed up the center aisle in their dress uniforms, trooping the flags. Behind them walked the Lord Mayor of London with his official medallion of office hanging around his neck, as well as his traditional hat and cape, while the U.S. Ambassador wore his navy pinstripe suit with white oxford shirt and cranberry tie.

After taking their seats of honor on either side of the altar, the Dean of the Cathedral began the Thanksgiving service complete with the Holy Eucharist. For their speeches, both the Lord Mayor and the Ambassador spoke about the closeness of our two countries and the hope of expanding those bonds. They talked about how each nation had worked individually, as well as collectively, for world peace and the hope of continuing those efforts.

The service was beautiful and moving. During the singing of *Come ye, Thankful People Come, My Country Tis of Thee, God of Our Fathers in Ages Past*, and the American national anthem, I felt the tears of joy coming from the meaning behind the words I was singing. We Americans live in a wonderful land of freedom and prosperity like no other country in the world and how fortunate we are because of that. Americans who don't see that, don't deserve all they have. I have said many times: before every student graduates from high school, I feel they should be required to spend some time in an Eastern Block country, newly emancipated nations from Communism, or a third world country so they see the reality of the problems and poverty other countries have in comparison to all the luxuries we take for granted. Students can't fathom what people outside of the United States have to do just to survive daily life. Even seeing it on the movie or television screen, they think it is a movie about unreal conditions. They have never been a part of what people in Russia, Africa, India, Hungary, or China have had to live. To see Czechs or Hungarians working sixteen to eighteen hours a day in order to have a morsel of food or a roof over their one room apartment, housing three or more people or families, might make our young people appreciate what they have here. Even today, when I remember looking into those eyes as they live in horrible circumstances, still brings tears to my eyes. We have so much and they have so little or nothing but their lives.

After another flourish of the Honor Guard, the dignitaries and the Dean walked down the aisle and outside. We waited our turn to exit. Once outside, our group walked down the Strand to Simpson's. There the maitre d' escorted us into the main dining room. While finishing their lunches, some businessmen looked up as we walked in. I am sure they wondered why we were there. Simpson's finest white linen tablecloth, napkins with sterling napkin holders, sterling silverware and candlesticks, crystal glasses, and bone china dishes dressed each table. How elegant.

Since Linda had already planned the menu, we did not need to concern ourselves with ordering. Our two waiters began bringing in the prawn salads consisting of a bed of shredded lettuce covered with prawns (shrimp) and topped with a Louie sauce.

After removing the plates, the waiters rolled in a wooden cart containing a large silver serving platter. Under the dome were two roasted turkeys and sage stuffing. The chef carved the turkeys and spooned out the stuffing. Once that was accomplished, he placed turkey and stuffing on each of our plates which were served to us. Next, came the mashed potatoes, gravy, steamed broccoli, carrots, and onions and a substitute cranberry sauce the chef's assistant had created for us. Within moments, hot rolls and butter were served. As we sat savoring our meals, we all reminisced about our family Thanksgiving traditions at home. Although it made us sad as well as glad remembering those times, we knew we were making new memories with those surrounding us on that Thanksgiving Day.

After finishing our turkey, we wondered what the pumpkin pie would taste like. Our taste buds were waiting to find out. The chef had gone all out to create it for us. He had used some kind of squash since the consistency was a bit stringy and stark in taste but he had really tried to make it authentic for us, even topping each slice with real whipped cream. We all applauded his efforts when he came in to ask how everything was. He beamed as he knew we appreciated his work.

It was about three when we finished our "Thanksgiving fare". As we walked outside, we were aware of the sunset glow encapsulating London. With the winter months coming, our days were shortening and the nights were lengthening. After saying goodbye to our lunch companions, we decided to walk to Piccadilly Circus, about ten blocks away. As we walked hand in hand into the city, the setting sun and a slight haze (smog) hovered over everything giving us the eerie feeling of being in Victorian London. We fell right into the magic surrounding us. We realized how lucky we were to be in this great city and a part of its experience. The more we walked, the more romantic we felt. It was glorious.

After stopping at Fortnum and Mason for some breakfast teas, we began our trek back home, filled with more memories to write home about.

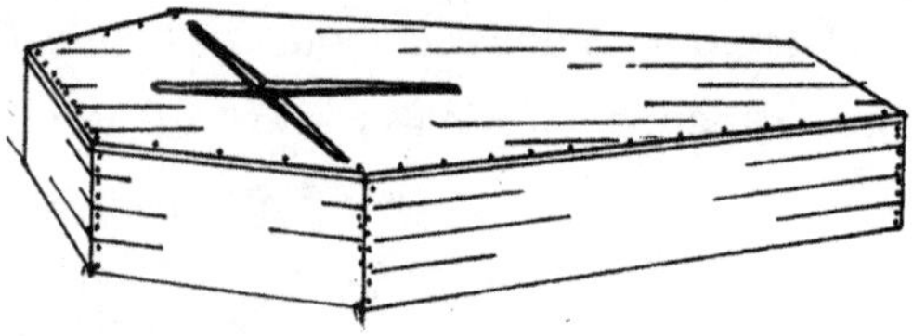

41. Sadness Within Our Community

One of our own had been diagnosed with melanoma cancer. Since the diagnosis, Gavin Meadows, Loraine's husband, had been working with Dr. Richardson and also with London's finest cancer specialist. Even while undergoing experimental treatments, he continued to work full time for the company. Ron and I wondered why he did not return home for treatment, but he and Loraine felt the treatment he was receiving in London was superior to that Stateside. Loraine's brother was fighting similar cancer and Loraine and Gavin weren't pleased with his medical treatment, so they remained here.

By mid-December, Gavin's disease was so advanced that no one knew if he would make it through the Christmas season. Ron and I left England with heavy hearts as we trekked Stateside for the Christmas holidays. While we were away, he was to try a new experimental treatment.

When we returned, I called Loraine only to find out Gavin had been too ill to have the treatment. He was now home and in bed most of the time. Dr. Richardson visited him at home at least once a day and sometimes twice, depending on his condition.

As January moved forward, Gavin was getting much worse. I ran errands for them and gave support whenever I could. Since we had been in England, Ron and I had become quite close to the Meadows. Loraine was first on the scene to welcome me to England and take me to my first Thursday coffee. She told me where to shop, even taking me, so I knew how to get there. She had been there for me when I needed an ear or shoulder to lean on. During these days, I only wished there was more I could do for her. Their precious time together was quickly running out.

When the doctors knew the end was near, their family flew in immediately. People within the company surrounded them in any way they could. I talked to Loraine daily, although I knew some days it was an effort for her to talk to me about what was happening in her life. Sometimes, with all the calls she received, she was quite drained emotionally as well as physically. With all she was dealing with, her emotions were raw.

On the morning of January 24th, I called to check on her. She said that Dr. Richardson had prescribed some new medication for Gavin and would I be able to go to Mr. Rees, the chemist, to pick it up, as he knew me. I quickly drove to the chemist shop, then dropped off Gavin's medicine. I knew things were really bad as she took the medicine and shut the door quickly, so I didn't have time to ask questions. She said she would call me later as Gavin wasn't doing at all well.

When the telephone rang about three that afternoon, I knew it was about Gavin. It took all she had to tell me, "Gavin is gone." Even though I suspected it in the morning and stayed close home to be of any help, it was a shock when the reality became truth.

In England, there are no visitations other than for immediate family. Bodies are placed in wooden caskets in cold storage areas of the funeral homes then cremated because of the lack of cemetery space. Loraine planned a beautiful cremation service then a memorial service for him. Ron and I felt honored to be asked to come to the funeral home to say goodbye to Gavin along with two other very close couples.

Looking at him, I couldn't believe how much the disease had taken out of him in just one week. I had seen him the week before he died, when I had taken him some medicines and a few of his favorite magazines. He looked thin and very frail. As that week progressed, he didn't want anyone to see him in his condition. Seeing him at the funeral home, I saw how thin, haggard, and fragile he had become. The disease had taken all the life and marrow out of his body

Lorraine asked Ron and I and a few of their closest friends to attend the private cremation ceremony at the Chelmsford crematory; two hours later the memorial service was held at the overflowing Brentwood Cathedral. People they knew through business on both sides of the "pond" and those they knew socially, were in attendance. The choir and congregation sang his favorite hymns; his son, Eric, gave a glowing eulogy to the man who was not only his father but also his mentor. Gavin would have been proud of Eric's words.

After the service, Loraine had arranged a luncheon for the assembled. We needed to get together as a group to remember Gavin and how much he meant to us. Loraine was so composed; I couldn't believe how well she did.

During the next six months, she worked through all the legal, as well as company papers pertaining to his death and pension. She flew to the States, bought a home near her son and daughter-in-law, and obtained the papers to allow her to take Gavin's ashes and urn home with her. A lot to do, but she needed to keep busy now.

Before getting ready to move home, she and I went out for lunch, then antiquing together. We took time to get her house ready for the move as well. She worked day and night, packing special breakable items. As moving day approached, all her close friends pitched in as well. Her grief was evident, but very much under wraps. I knew when she moved into her new home, her grief would begin to emerge. I wished I could be there for her, as she was for me when I arrived on assignment.

The day I said goodbye to her, I felt part of me was missing. She and I would remain friends, even with the three thousand miles between us. I knew I would miss running over for a cuppa or going antiquing with her.

Gavin's death unnerved both Ron and me, making us realize how short life is and that we must make the most of each day. Thank you, Gavin, for the lesson about life and time.

42. Fields of Tulips

Easter time was upon us again. This year we had a long holiday weekend to enjoy it, as well. Ron and I had talked about taking a trip somewhere. We decided upon Amsterdam to see the tulip festival there. What a marvelous idea. The burst of all that color would make us think spring was just around the corner.

I went to our trusty Lisa and booked passage on the overnight ferry from Harwich on the English coast to Heck Van Holland on the Holland coast. She reserved us a room at the Europa Hotel, along one of Amsterdam's canals. Amsterdam was one of the cities on our 'to visit' list.

Ron would be in Germany on business for the four days prior to our trip. He knew he had to be home with enough time to catch the ferry that evening. When he arrived home, we took his Germany bags out of the boot, then put our travel bags and cameras in, then we drove to Harwich to catch the 5 o'clock ferry to Amsterdam.

Driving fast, but not racing, we made the ferry with a few minutes to spare. Checking in with immigration and the ferry personnel, we were given our cabin number and told to board the ship. We chose the overnight ferry, so Ron could make up some of the sleep he had missed due to his hectic business schedule.

We drove aboard, parked our car, and went upstairs to find our room, number 115. Upon entering our matchbox room, we found bunk beds, the top with a wood railing, a small turn-a-bout bathroom with minute shower, and a desk and chair, which I presumed lorry drivers used to fill out their transportation forms and travel time cards.

After stowing our things, we ventured upstairs for the dinner buffet which included all kinds of herring, soups, salads, and sliced hot and cold meats for sandwiches, sliced cheeses, breads, roasted potatoes, cooked vegetables, and a tray of different tarts and puddings. Ron and I had the vegetable-barley soup, roast chicken, roasted potatoes, vegetables, and apple tarts. Sitting at a window table, we were able to watch the water go by and dream of the vacation ahead of us.

The crossing was smooth, but family groups and lorry drivers in cabins around us became noisy making sleep almost impossible. By morning, we were ready to have breakfast and leave this boisterous situation.

As we exited the ship, high winds and rain greeted us. Not a good beginning for our trip, but we could deal with them. The winds at times pushed our little navy Sierra from one side of the road to the other causing Ron to keep a tight grip on the wheel to keep us on the road. I was glad he was driving and not me.

About an hour later we arrived in Amsterdam. Keeping close tabs on the city map and watching all the roads and canals, I finally found the street we needed for our hotel only to realize it was a one way street coming toward us. We turned at the next left, followed it until we found a canal bridge, crossing to our hotel's street.

The Europa Hotel was a small townhouse hotel. Its large reception room and inviting desk personnel made us feel right at home. Arriving at past two, we found our room ready for us. We took the elevator to the third floor. Our room overlooked the canal. We unpacked a few things, freshened up, and then went outside to investigate our surroundings.

The wind and rain was still whipping us around. I was glad I had packed our rain gear, we were somewhat protected from the elements. Walking down our canal to the main thoroughfare we found the streets filled with bicycles, cars, motorbikes, electric trolleys, and bicycles pulling flatbed wagons full of goods. What an amazing sight this maze of traffic was. On the corner, we saw The Westerkerk, with its blackening bell tower. Built in 1638, it was the largest Dutch resistance church in all of The Netherlands.

Since we had not converted our money into theirs, we needed to find two things: bank or exchanger and the current rate of exchange so we could figure the actual prices of food and goods. Walking into Dam Square, the heart of Amsterdam, we not only found what we needed, but the beautiful dark brown, ornate Royal Palace, as well as, the Monument of the Liberation, depicting events and people involved in their World War II liberation. On top of everything else we discovered, would you guess what Ron found? If you guessed his favorite McDonalds – you'd be correct.

Having all our cash and "dietary" needs taken care of, we walked around the square to see the Royal Palace; we found it closed to the public that day. We inspected surrounding shops and boutiques touting camera equipment, chocolates, tobaccos, and laces. All of a sudden, I noticed all the pigeons in the square. I remember one woman covered with pigeons sitting on a bench, hand feeding them seeds and corn. Hoping to earn a day's wage, a photographer commissioned a mime to pose covered with the pigeons, to entice onlookers to have him take their pictures in the same way. I couldn't and wouldn't do that for anything.

After returning to our hotel, we took a short nap before dinner. When leaving the hotel for dinner, we asked the receptionist to recommend a restaurant with good seafood or Italian cuisine. She told us Marco's, then explained how to get there. We followed her directions to a marvelous little Italian restaurant filled with red and white-checkered tablecloth tables, and candled wine bottles in the center of each. The aromas were indescribable. We ordered a small carafe of their house red wine, the house salad with their own dressing, and pasta. With the wine, we received a breadbasket filled with hot rolls and breadsticks. The salad contained various greens, cherry tomatoes, anchovies, and fresh-slivered mozzarella cheese along with their vinaigrette dressing. The pasta was fabulous – Ron had the lasagna while I had the ravioli. We tasted each other's and couldn't decide which was better.

Upon leaving Marco's, we realized how dark it had become. On our way back to the hotel, we noticed the canal was aglow with hundreds of clear twinkling miniature strands of Christmas lights strung on wires above the pedestrian walkways and canal bridges. It was a winter wonderland of lights; all we needed was Bing Crosby to sing *White Christmas* to culminate this utterly beautiful scene. Walking hand in hand, I felt one with life.

After breakfast we set out with our map for Prinsengracht Street and the house where Anne Frank and her family had resided. Arriving before opening time and realizing how the brisk wind had chilled us to the bone, we sought refuge in a small basement coffee and sandwich shop two doors away from our destination. We sat down at one of the wood booths and ordered mugs of hot chocolate. We lulled over our chocolate while waiting out the half hour until the Frank house would open. Being Friday morning most people were at work, so we only had a small line to contend with.

The office building that served as their home from 1942 until 1944, was crushed between two other office buildings. The large sign hanging outside the Frank's company and house, let everyone in passing distance know, this was a historical place. Upon entering this townhouse-sized building, we felt its narrowness and height. If three people lay down on the floor foot to head, they would just about make the width of the house.

The Franks converted their tea warehouse into two parts – the office areas on the ground floor and their living area upstairs. The front part of the ground floor contained the main or front office and a small storeroom, while the back had the private office and small kitchen with its own gas stove and toilet room. Our tour guide showed us the bookcase that concealed the secret staircase leading to the Secret Annex. We walked up that steep, narrow staircase which led to the Frank and the Van Daan residences where they hid until the Gestapo found them in 1944. The Franks occupied two rooms. The first was a bedroom for Anne and her older sister, Margot, their cots still in place on either side of the rectangular room. Here Anne wrote her famous diary during her seclusion. Along the wall next to her bed, Anne pinned posters of entertainers she loved; her father had smuggled them into her on various special occasions. The other room served as an all-purpose room for the Franks, as well as their bedroom.

Another stairwell led to the Van Daan's quarters on the third floor. The major room here served not only as the living room but the kitchen as well. The dreary room contained a washboard, a makeshift gas stove, and a table; the walls were yellow with large squares of green and yellow linoleum on the floor. Very sparse! Also in this room was a folding bed and the entrance to Peter's, their son's, apartment.

Since the Frank tea warehouse, usually quite busy with people from all over the world who came to buy their famous teas, they helped conceal the family's existence for almost two years. During the day the

Frank and Van Daan families could move about without any concern of being detected since the business noise concealed their footsteps. At night everyone had to remain in virtual darkness and silence so as not to be found out. No one knows how the Franks were found; one rumor says the Van Daans turned them in.

To think of all this spirited young girl and her family endured during their time here was overwhelming. I felt a great sense of sadness and loss as their lives had been tortured and taken by the War and the concentration camps where they were sent. Thinking of the terror and pain they must have endured, sent chills through my body.

After finishing our tour and returning outside we found the sun had come out, but the wind was still quite crisp. We walked back along the canal, noticing all the houseboats moored there. They were painted bright colors with contrasting windowpanes. Wood tables and chairs were placed on the deck so the occupants could eat outside or just have a bottle of wine with friends and watch the sun go down or possibly rise. Many houseboaters grew gardens of flowers and herbs in large pots and window boxes on their decks; some even hung flower baskets from the eaves.

All the buildings along this canal contained ground floor shops with apartments above. These buildings seemed glued together to save every ounce of space, as real estate taxes were based on their footages. For some aging buildings, being glued together was the only way they could remain standing, as they were beginning to sag in many places. Many of the homes still displayed ornate heraldic emblems of Amsterdam's glory days of trade and travel. An interesting tidbit we learned – under rooftop overhangs were pulleys used to hoist furniture up from the ground floor. When arriving at the correct floor and window, the furniture was swung and pulled into the apartment. I could just imagine a large overstuffed sofa or grand piano being hoisted up the side of one of these buildings. When a family decided to move, once again the pulley was used to remove the furniture. An interesting way to move!

That afternoon we booked a boat tour of Amsterdam. What a spectacular city this was with all its old churches, temples, industries, hotels, townhouses, and its myriad of bicycles and riders going everywhere.

When we learned we were near to the Van Gogh Museum, we decided to get off and visit the "great master". The waiting line to get in was short so we were inside within a few minutes. As with the Louvre, we invested in two taped tour headphones and began our tour of the Van Goghs and other masters, sculpturers, and architects. To see the variety of styles, colors, brush techniques and view all the wonder these masters had painted for our perusal was amazing. We often paused and sat on a nearby bench to take in all a painting was saying to us. Three hours later we heard the museum was closing in fifteen minutes. Time had flown away. What a marvelous time we had had.

Back outside, we walked to the tour stop-off to wait for the next tour boat to pick us up. We had about a thirty-minute wait so we treated ourselves to a hot coffee from a nearby street vendor.

Reboarding our boat, we finished our tour then got off and strolled back to our hotel. The air was cold and night was beginning to close in on us. We decided to walk to the seafood restaurant our receptionist had recommended to us. It was packed to the hilt. As waiters moved quickly passed us, we saw dishes filled with wonderful foods. The smells coming from the kitchen made the decision to stay and wait for a table an easy one. We ordered a bottle of chardonnay. For dinner we dined on shrimp and scallop pasta that was well worth our wait. We even split a luscious apple tart. Stuffed to the brim, we started our walk back to the hotel through the twinkling lit canal. After our continental breakfast the following morning, we pointed our car in the direction of Delft and its factory. Its white and blue plates always intrigued me. Rains and blustery cold winds greeted us. Not a day for fish, ducks or us.

We arrived at the factory at nine forty-five, then fought the strong wind gusts and rain to find the entrance. Finally, pounding on the door we hoped to be let in only to find out we were fifteen minutes too early. The proprietors seeing what we had to do to get to their entrance, allowed us to come in and sit in their reception room.

Ron and I sat there about a half hour while the staff hoped more tourists would arrive before starting their tours. When that didn't happen, we got our own royal tour. We saw the crafters working the green pottery, cutting any uneven or rough edges then damp sponges smoothed out any remaining abrasions or flaws. Each completed piece of the greenware was placed on racks to allow it to dry completely before being immersed in a vat filled with a base enamel paint. From there the pieces were placed in large hot kilns to bake before the blue designs were painted on. Once painted, the pieces were refired and cooled before going on sale either in their own shop or shipped to their markets all over the world.

Being the only ones on this particular tour, we had free access to the crafters, asking any questions we had about the various procedures used to create this distinctive world-renowned pottery. What startled and intrigued me was they not only created their traditional blue and white designs but now dabbled in multicolored designs as well.

At the end of our tour we realized we were in their shop. The staff told us that a tour bus had just stopped with passengers wanting to tour the factory as well. I was pleased for them but eager to check out the new colored plates and vases. The factory not only sold the traditional blue and white designed plates, vases, and pitchers, they also sold the beautiful new colored ones. I purchased a small traditional blue and white plate and one of the new ones: a white, scalloped, blue edged plate with a leaning pink tulip bud and green stem, and two narrow willowy leaves in its center. Both were lovely and I was happy to add them to my collectibles.

As we left, we thanked them for our royal tour and said goodbye to Martha, our guide. Even though the weather had not changed, we decided to drive on to the Keukenhof Gardens. Our friends from Wiesbaden, Carol and Max, implored us to see these spectacular garden – they were not to be missed at any cost. When we arrived, the rain was coming down so hard, we decided to return to Amsterdam hoping the next day the weather would be better.

We returned to Amsterdam by way of The Hague, Eiden, and Aarlem. Because of the weather, the towns were deserted of people. Only the brave ventured outside on their bicycles or walked beside buildings, using them as shields against the elements.

That night we returned to Marco's where we were remembered and seated without any ado. Ron and I ordered green salads then I ordered their spaghetti and Ron the lasagna. Again, our palates were inundated with marvelous tastes. Oh, how I wished we could transport Marco's to Shenfield or Brentwood. But on the other hand, I was glad we couldn't, as my waistline would be a hundred inches around and that would never do. So I contented myself with my dinner and said if we ever returned to Amsterdam, we would visit again.

The following day was Sunday, Easter Sunday to be exact. Our last day of holiday! We were greeted by full sunshine; no wind or rain. The streets were still damp, but we didn't care. After breakfast we checked out of our hotel, packed the boot, then headed for Lisse and the Keukenhof Gardens called the "Greatest Flower Show on Earth". I was concerned Ron would be so bored with the gardens that he would not enjoy any of it.

When we arrived, we paid for both the car park and entrance fees. The attendants directed us to a spot in the car park. After days of rain, the ground was so saturated that we put on our "Wellies", tall gardening boots, which I fortunately had thrown in for some unknown reason. What a stroke of luck for us.

We trudged through their muddy lot and entered the gardens. What a feast for our eyes. The sun shone brightly giving all the blooming flowers a spring glow. Built on the site of a 17th century castle, Keukenhof Gardens covered seventy acres. Each year the garden's board of directors selected one hundred forty-one nursery and floral establishments to design, propagate, and plant their own portion of the grounds; each vying for the prize of being named the best floral designer and nursery. More than seven million tulips, hyacinths, amaryllis, orchids, forsythias, chrysanthemums, lilies, and narcissus of all colors, sizes, and dimensions are used. Some include flowering shrubs, splendid pond and fountain displays, trees of all shapes and sizes along with their myriad of flowers. Along the brick pathways, statues of nymphs, saints, and animals stand along with coffee and sandwich shops with brick patios filled with tables and chairs so patrons can sit, talk, or just admire the surrounding setting. One coffee shop had a children's playground so parents could sit and enjoy a cup of tea while watching their children at play. Children, you know, need to run off excess energy so after their play they can sit quietly in their strollers so their parents can enjoy the gardens and floral arrangements.

Only open during the spring bulb flowering season, this garden season is only four to six weeks. As we strolled through the areas, both Ron and I became aware why Max and Carol emphatically told us to visit here. We were so grateful. Spectacular it was and much more. We wandered along the brick walkways past gardens of tall yellow, red, and white single and double tulips – even some unusual purples and oranges, white and purple hyacinths in both miniature and regular heights, as well as single and double yellow and white narcissus with centers of varying degrees of orange. The flowering shrubs exhibited their white, pink, mauve, cream, and cranberry petals along with their green leaves. Man-made ponds defined and enhanced the flowers surrounding them. On some knolls, floral designs made trees and shrubbery unforgettable pictures or scenes. Unbelievably, Ron was as enthused as I was about Keukenhof; he took video film of the splended gardens while I snapped away with my camera so we could never forget this.

We spent the better part of three hours before we knew we had to leave to return to Heck Van Holland and our return ship home. As we walked out of the gardens we stopped at the gatehouse souvenir shop and purchased Jennifer a pair of wooden shoes. I wanted to purchase some bulbs but they were a bit too expensive for my taste even though I knew they would be beautiful.

We made our way back to our ferry in plenty of time for easy boarding. This time we found it not only quiet but we also had a smooth ride. Traveling midweek instead of the weekend, we missed the tourist trade. We read, took in a movie, slept, and just walked about the ferry at our leisure giving us a fitting close to our wonderful time in Amsterdam.

43. A Trip to Long Ago

The day had come. Ron and I were going to Rome. ROME!! The Eternal City, the Trevi Fountain, St. Peter's, the Coliseum, the Pantheon, PASTA, Chianti, and Italian gelato (ice cream)!! I couldn't believe we were actually going, a dream come true for me. I had longed to see Rome ever since I studied ancient history in school a long time ago.

Ron and I got up at 6:45 AM to finish our last minute packing and zip our bags shut. We had a cup of coffee and a bite of cantaloupe before jumping into our car for Gatwick Airport. Outside it was warm and sunny. A good omen our trip would be wonderful. After the lingering winter, feeling the warm sun, seeing the trees putting on their finest leaves, and watching all the new lambs and calves in the pastures made our spirits even higher. The M-25 was free of road works making the trip of forty-five minutes easy.

We arrived at Gatwick's car park at 10:45, unloaded our two small bags, and caught the shuttle bus for the airport proper. We checked in and asked for two adjoining aisle seats. The ticket agent obliged saying "I knew without your passports you were Americans as you always ask for the aisle seats. The Germans ask for the window seats."

To avoid adding to the usual hectic airport necessities in Rome, we exchanged £75 for 170,000 lira. It seemed like a cache of money until we figured out that 10,000 lira equaled about $6.65. With that, we knew the lira would go fast.

While waiting for our departure, we decided to have a cup of coffee and maybe a Danish at one of the upper level sidewalk cafes. We watched the departure board for our flight. When Monarch flight 906 (a charter flight) came on the screen, we went through passport control as early as possible, not wanting to hold up any Brits. Sometimes, they get agitated and impatient waiting for us to complete our passport procedure while they only have to show or wave theirs at the immigration officers. After passing through customs, we headed for gate 35.

We boarded and took our seats. The window and middle seat next to me were unfilled so when the airplane doors were closed I moved into the window seat and Ron took my aisle seat. We laid our books and magazines on the seat between us. I love sitting with him. The plane took off on time. The exhilaration I felt as the wheels left the runway was overwhelming. We were on our way to ROME.

Amazingly, our meal consisted of seafood cocktail, filet of beef tips with potatoes, carrots, and green beans, roll, and apple tart with Devon cream all served with a glass of wine and a beverage. Just as I finished my dinner, I spied the snow capped Alps – what a sight. They were breathtaking to say the least. I could even see the little villages nestled along the mountain range. What a life to live within sight of the Alps. To the residents this probably meant nothing out of the ordinary, but to me it reminded me of skiing, yodeling, and wonderful family times accentuated by these majestic mountains and streams. A touch of *Heidi* and *The Sound of Music* caught my thinking.

Descending into Rome filled me with even more anticipation. ROME! We departed our Boeing 757 via a metal 1950's exit ladder instead of today's computerized ramp attaching directly into the plane's side door. Reminded me of my travels as a teenager.

We walked the prescribed path as the Polizzi (Police) were in force to see no one deviated from his or her path. Waiting to walk through the immigration doors, I felt warmed by the sunshine although the breeze was cool.

We retrieved our two small bags. I was so proud of myself; I had finally learned how to pack light for trips. We worked our way through passport control and customs without any difficulty. We checked in with the waiting Thomson bus to take us to our hotel – about a fifty-minute drive. The countryside was green with farming and vineyards. The architecture was definitely Italian – terra-cotta tiled roofs and pastel or white stucco exteriors on homes and buildings; some even had laundry hanging out their windows on pulley clothes lines.

I had suspected the city of Rome would have modernized itself more but the true Rome was still its ancient self. What was sad to see was how pollution had taken its toll on things. Robbie, our Thomson guide, gave us information about how to obtain subway and bus tickets at the tobacco shops or in the Metro (subway) itself. Each ticket was good for a single ride along a particular subway line, not like London where a day pass was good all day for the subway as well as the city bus service. Each time we used the Metro we would need to purchase a new ticket (L1000); a bus ticket (L1100) was only valid for ninety minutes. Robbie repeatedly warned us about the numerous pickpockets, beggars, and gypsies working the streets. I was glad I had purchased two undergarment money pouches during a recent trip to Brussels. With our money and passports stashed in the pouches under our clothes, no one could take our valuables from us. We decided we would put our valuables in our room safe, if we had one, when we would be out of our room for tours, meals, or just communing with Rome itself.

We arrived at the Morgana Hotel tired, but anticipating the adventure that lay ahead of us. The hotel was quaint but nice; the receptionist was quite friendly and informative. The elevator was a cage large enough for two people to use at one time. Our room was small but came with a private bath. We didn't care about its size as we didn't intend to spend much time in it. Outside our window we could see a maze of apartment tenements with newly washed clothes hanging from their pulley ropes.

We spent the remainder of the late afternoon marking our map with places we wanted to visit – the Spanish Steps, the Trevi Fountain, the Pantheon, the Roman Forum, the Coliseum, St. Peter's Basilica and its square. Thomson Tours had scheduled a meeting with all their clients for the next morning; they would discuss their available tours and sign us up for them. However, I had already booked ours through our trusty Lisa, and unless we found something extraordinary, we were all ready for Rome. I had scheduled first a tour of ancient Rome which would give us an overview of the city, then the following day was to be filled with Vatican City, its Museum, and St. Peter's Basilica. The following morning we would leave for Venice. We knew how limited our days were so we had to make the most of them.

By evening, feeling hungry, we went downstairs and asked the night receptionist where to go for a good restaurant. "Giuseppe's. Just down the street on the hotel's side," he suggested. We found it in the basement of an apartment building. It was a charming place. The whole family worked in the restaurant – father was the maitre'd, mother, grandfather, and grandmother were cooks, and two nephews were waiters. Concerned about not knowing Italian, the maitre'd placed us at a table with another couple and their daughter who spoke both Italian and English. After we sat down, the maitre'd asked our preference – red or white wine; then brought us a carafe of his own home brewed white. We asked him what we should have; he suggested the lasagna, veal chops, and salad. We said, "We'd like that." Italians frown on people

(Americans) who only order pasta and nothing else. To Italians, pasta is considered an appetizer – not an entrée.

Seated right in front of the kitchen, I could watch all the food preparation as there were no doors leading in or out of the area. I learned some Italian techniques I could use at home. While we ate our dinner and drank our wine, we watched as the little restaurant started filling up with customers. When we left an hour later, the place was full and more people waited for tables. That said a lot about their food and service. To see Italians coming here to eat Italian food, we definitely knew this was a good place to eat. After returning to our room and getting into bed, we dreamt about things we would see the next day, our first full day here.

The next morning we were up at 7:30 full of energy and enthusiasm. We had the usual continental breakfast in their "Breakfast Room". Afterwards, we walked in the dismal rain to the Universo Hotel for our Thomson "informational talk and tour packages". We did add two tours – one for the papal blessing in St. Peter's Square and an illumination tour with a four-course dinner. Oh well, we rationalized that this might be our only trip here so we should enjoy all of it.

After the meeting we found a little stand-up cafe on a side street where we bought two slices of pizza and two cokes (L6100). The pizza wasn't like the standard American or British fare. The crust was baked on an olive oil skillet with the toppings, similar to those in the States and England, put on later. Robbie had told us to always get a receipt for everything you buy even food so you can prove you paid for it if someone asks. After lunch we walked to the Appian Way tour office for our afternoon tour. Being early, we had some time to catch our breath and take in all the sunshine Rome was now bestowing on us.

We boarded our tour bus and drove along the streets past the Baths of Dioceleziano (Roman history reported that Roman women could only use the baths in the morning while the men had the access in the afternoon and evening). We moved up the Via Nazionale to the Piazza Venezia, the traffic nerve center. Here, four major thorofares (Via del Corso, Via del Fori Imperiali, Via Nazionale, and Via del Teatro de Marcello) converge in front of the massive Vittorio Emanuele Monument designed by Guiseppe Sacconi. This white marble monument with its colonnade celebrates the first king of the unified Italy as well as making sure people know Rome is the capital of Italy. When the colonnade was placed between the foundation and the upper level, it was greeted with jeers and given the name of the "Wedding Cake" or "Rome's False Teeth". I could see how it could have been given each name but in the sunshine this impressive monument glistened for everyone to see all its beauty.

From there we drove to the base of the hillside where the Church of San Pietro in Vincoli, (St. Peter in Chains) stood. Leaving the bus, we made our way up a windy, narrow street leading to it. The sights looking down the hillside to the Coliseum and the Roman Form were breathtaking. When we entered this little church, we learned the difference between a church (no columns) and a basilica (church with columns). This beautiful small church consisted of cream and white marble statues, monuments, flooring, and cream painted walls with white paned windows. At ceiling height on its interior walls were friezes (portraits painted into the plaster) of all the popes. Legend says when the remaining thirteen friezes are filled the world will come to an end. I hope each lives a long life, if that is true. I remember a few years back when there were three popes in a matter of a few months.

Two momentous pieces reside here. The first was Michelangelo's finest sculpture – the formidable and inspiring Moses. On either side of him were figures of Jacob's wives – a powerful Leah and a melancholy Rachel – his last completed sculptures. The other one was encased in unbreakable glass. It was mesmerizing – the marble statue of St. Peter bound in his actual chains. These chains make all viewers take time to think about Peter's life and death and to do some soul searching of their own.

From there we walked down the embankment to another relic of ancient Rome – "the gladiators' bloody circus" – the Coliseum. This has remained the symbol of Rome's eternity. Built in 80 AD by 20,000 slaves and prisoners, this four-tiered amphitheater seated up to 50,000 spectators on its stone benches. Over each entrance or opening was a Roman numeral signifying the section inside just as our sports arenas do today. Over the years churches, princes, and popes have ravaged the Coliseum for its precious marble, travertine, and other metals; leaving it a ruined maze of cells and corridors. An Anglo-Saxon prophesy states that "while stands the Coliseum, Rome shall stand; when the Coliseum falls, so will the world fall with it" therefore the government makes sure it is well taken care of. It is open to the public on alternate days; this was not one of them so we could not go in. Not being able to go inside, I had to be satisfied to just look through the "entrance doors" and imagine what the interior looked like.

From there our group walked to four carved marble maps depicting the stages of the Roman Empire – before the Roman Empire was an empire, the Roman Empire in its entirety, after its fall, and after World War II. What a history was chiseled out on those charcoal and ivory stones for all the world to see.

From there we walked to the Roman Forum with its columns, arches, and porticoes. This had once been the hub of imperial Roman life. Also, contained here – the underground channel, the Cloaca

Maxima. Three of Rome's seven hills – the Palatine (cradle of the city once covered with palaces especially those of the Caesars), the Capitoline (ancient citadel of government), and the Esquiline (site of Nero's Golden House) surround the Forum. Under the watchful eyes of the emperors, the Forum attained its splendor with its gilded rooftops and white marble temples dedicated to various Roman gods (Vesta, Saturn, and Caster), its law courts, and its market halls all glittering in the sun before us. After barbarian invasions, earthquakes, fires, and floods, this area was abandoned and became a cow pasture until excavations in the nineteenth century brought it back to life.

Grass now surrounds the cracked stones of the Sacra Via (Sacred Way). This walkway begins at the Coliseum then moves through Hadrian's Wall and the Triumphal Arch into the Campidoglio or Capitol Hill. Followed by their legions of men, returning victorious generals rode their mighty steeds up the Sacra Via to Campidoglio where they brought their captured prisoners and also laid their spoils of war (chests of gold, silver, and jewelry) at the feet of their emperor or the governor of Rome and the Roman Senate. In return, the governor bestowed some special title or distinction on the general in full view of the citizens of Rome. With that ceremony over, tumultuous cheers came from the onlookers and the general and other officials waved and smiled at the assembled mass in recognition of Rome's continued success in the world.

As Ron and I stood at the peak of Capitoline Hill looking down on the Forum, I let my mind float back to ancient Rome and envisioned the whole area complete with all its citizens and military processions. What Rome must have looked like in all its splendor. Boarding the bus, we drove outside the original walls of Rome to the Basilica of St. Paul's, the largest basilica after St. Peter's. Built by Constantine in 314 AD, it survived in its entirety until it was destroyed in a tragic fire in 1823. Later, it was rebuilt. At one time the Benedictine monks used it for their cloister.

Formed in a square shape, the basilica's pastel yellow walls accentuated the brightly colored mosaic murals on them and the slender white-spiraled columns enunciated the overhanging roofs as well. Completing this picture of loveliness, rows of roses lined the courtyard's walkways adding additional color and beauty to the scene projected here. In the center of the front courtyard was a statue of St. Paul. Walking the grounds, we felt its peacefulness, quietness, and serenity as if we were surrounded in a world of oneness with nature and the Lord. Almost the same feeling we had at Mont Saint Michel in France a few years before.

After completing our tour, we knew we had some free time before dinner so we purchased Metro tickets to Piazza Spagna hoping to find the Spanish Steps, the Trevi Fountain, and the Pantheon. We almost took the Metro in the wrong direction but Ron caught our mistake in time. After getting on the correct train and passing three stops, we exited the train. As we came out into Piazza Spagna, we found the square filled with artists, musicians, some hippies, lovers, families, and many other tourists. Amazingly, to the left we found the Spanish Steps. At one time the Spanish ambassador to the Holy See (the Pope) lived in an apartment at the top of these stairs and therefore the steps were named in his honor. On either side of the three tiered Steps, retaining walls with shepherd's hooks jutting out of them held up hanging baskets full of massive ferns and blooming flowers. At its top we found the lovely but aging French church named Trinita del Monti. As usual, tourists were everywhere snapping their memory or scrapbook pictures while vendors sold their "trinkets" and ice creams.

After viewing the little church and walking back down the steps, we moved onto Via Condotti, Rome's most exclusive and expensive shopping street bearing such names as Cartier, Gucci, Valentino, and Armani. No one can enter these shops unless you have a letter of reference from someone the proprietor knows or he knows you personally. These proprietors welcome these customers as they can lay down some serious money for their fashions and accessories. Since we definitely didn't know any one of them, we just window-shopped and dreamed.

Continuing our walk along the side streets we looked for the Trevi Fountain and the Pantheon. No such luck. We decided to ask the Thomson guide in the morning for directions. What we didn't know – at one point on our walk we were just a street away from both of them. Just think – so close but yet so far.

We returned to Piazza Spago and saw the venerable Babington Tea Room. The story purports that two British sisters came to Rome. When they could not find a good cup of tea, they stayed and opened this tea shop. As people became aware of their wonderful teas and sweets, their business grew and grew and so did their prices. Their food and service rank as impeccable.

Tired, we returned to our hotel without any hitches. We rested listening to the Italian evening news which we could not understand but it was nice to hear.

Guiseppe's served as our port in the storm for dinner. Our maitre'd saw us coming in, motioned us to a table, then brought us a carafe of his white wine. I couldn't believe he remembered our taste from the previous night. He suggested the spinach and ricotta ravioli, beefsteak, salad, and some ice cream. His choices were fabulous. After dinner we walked around the area hand in hand for about an hour hoping to walk off a few of his wonderful calories. This night was so special; Ron and

Rome to boot! What more could I ask for.

Our days here were quickly going. We had breakfast and headed for our tour of the Sistine Chapel and Vatican Museum. Roberto, our guide, from the day before led this tour; we were so pleased as he had a vast knowledge of Roman history as well as art. What a wonderful combination for us. Once on the bus we traversed through tree lined streets filled with people and traffic. Roberto had hoped to get us there before the other tour busses arrived but, pulling up to the Museum, we realized we were only a parcel of the hundreds – maybe thousands – waiting entrance as well.

Finally, making our way inside, our group walked up the Spiral Staircase leading to the Museum's four miles of galleries. Each gallery contained different exhibits such as Egyptian mummies, Etruscan jewelry, Greek and Roman sculptures, medieval to Renaissance masterpieces, as well as modern religious art. We were awestruck by the paintings, tapestries, and friezes on the rounded ceilings above the hallways. Many friezes dated to the Raphael and Michelangelo periods. The gilded and cream frames only brought out the brilliance of the portrait colors. We hoped our camera shots would do them justice. Each pope had his own gallery devoted just to his style and collection.

After the galleries we walked to the Scala Regina – the stairway the Pope uses to go from his Vatican office or apartment to the Sistine Chapel or St. Peter's Basilica. We hoped we would see him on one of his walks but he didn't accommodate us.

The Sistine Chapel (Capella Sistina) itself was built in the fifteenth century. Before entering, Roberto told us to refrain from talking or whispering so people could enjoy the magnificence of this place. The Chapel's art narrated the biblical history of man in three parts: from Adam to Noah, the giving of the law to Moses, and the birth of

Jesus to the Last Judgment. Michelangelo's *Judgment Day* had just been fully restored. What an overwhelming, magnificent painting. The ceiling painting revealed an almost naked Jesus dispensing justice more like a stern, even fierce judge rather than a gentle shepherd. Michelangelo even imprinted his own face on that of St. Bartholomew to the right of Jesus. Historians say at one time, Pope Pius VI asked Michelangelo about his work – "Your sculpture is wonderful but don't you have any paintings?" To that he replied, "I don't paint." The Pope said, "Then I think you should begin now" with that the Pope commissioned Michelangelo to paint this fabulous painting called *Judgment Day.*

From the Chapel we walked outside into the blinding sunshine of St. Peter's Square. The Square's length and breadth overwhelmed us. On television it had always looked so much smaller. Roberto pointed out the 141 statues of various saints on the roof ledges surrounding the Basilica, the Vatican palace, and the Pope's official residence and office areas. Once again, I hoped to get a glimpse of The Holy See waving out one of his windows, but no such luck.

Having a half-hour stop here, Ron and I went into some of the tourist shops around the area. In one we found a beautiful pink rosary for Nancy and I purchased Jennifer a letter which the Pope was to sign, stamp, and send to her. I am not sure she even got it. Another tourist bait. I do know Nancy got hers, as we took it with us.

After the tour was over, we took the Metro back to Piazza Spagna hoping to find the Trevi Fountain and the Pantheon. Getting out of the subway, Ron was famished. He remembered seeing a particular sign. You got it – McDonalds. Walking down a few streets we found it. The place was packed. The sandwiches and cokes tasted good but I would have preferred a large gelato cone instead. That's my passion, but we were able to take care of his quarter pounder attack.

As we began our search for the Trevi Fountain and the Pantheon, we noticed an Italian woman giving a couple ahead of us directions. We hoped to impose on her to tell us how to get our two sights. We used our map to explain where we wanted to go and she in turn pointed the way we needed to go. We had been all around the Fountain the day before but never found the correct alley to it. It was just as I had pictured it, although a bit smaller. I remembered seeing it in the movie *Three Coins in the Fountain*. I didn't remember seeing all the apartments and businesses surrounding it in the film either. But there it was in all its splendor. Neptune was standing on his clam shell being pulled through the water by a pair of mighty steeds – each representing a part of the ocean: its calmness and its turbulence. People tossed their coins into the fountain hoping their wish to return would be honored. Neither Ron nor I could resist that hope either.

A few minutes later Ron spotted an ice cream or gelato shop and suggested a little "nourishment" after all our walking. Italian ice cream is the best! So smooth and rich and it goes down ever soooo easy.

From there we followed the map to the best-preserved monument of ancient Rome. Built by Emperor Hadrian around 120 AD, the Pantheon stands one hundred forty-two feet wide as well as tall. Although it was built as a temple to the gods, it contains the tombs of the artist Raphael and two modern kings: Vittorio Emanuele II and Umberto I. In the seventh century it was transformed into a church. I was disappointed with its dismal, dark interior.

When we returned to our hotel, we rested before our illumination tour of Rome and dinner. As with every city, night changes everything. As our bus drove through Rome it sparkled under the twinkling of its city lights. One of our stops along our tour was the Trevi Fountain. Ron and I both tossed two more pennies into it in hopes of one day returning here.

On our way again we passed many of the major tourist stops before arriving at the restaurant where the tour group had scheduled our dinner and an evening of entertainment. The welcoming and jovial proprietor, his wife, and sons served us a fantastic antipasto, three different pastas, veal chops, salad, and for dessert sponge cake. They had us join in singing some Italian songs like *O Sole Amio* with the owner's cousin playing the accordion. When we returned to our hotel, we fell into bed exhausted but full of memories.

Our last day in Rome took us to St. Peter's Square for the Papal blessing ceremony. About ten thousand others and us congregated there to see him. Our tickets afforded us a folding chair in the center of the Square where we waited for his arrival in his popemobile. When he arrived, he looked so frail and delicate but he waved and smiled for all the assembled crowd to see. After many international groups were introduced to him, he conducted a mass sans communion through his aides.

Afterward Ron and I left the tour to investigate St. Peter's Basilica. Many artists and sculptors collaborated on this edifice sometimes to its detriment as each had his own idea of what it should look like. Designed by Michelangelo, the Basilica holds the record for being the world's largest church – 695 feet long, 613 feet wide, and 435 feet to the tip of its dome.

To the right of the entrance doors in its own side alcove Michelangelo's Pieta – Mary holding the crucified Jesus in her lap – was displayed and humbled many of us. This true-to-life sculpture shows with utmost simplicity Mary's grief and deep love for her son. This was the only sculpture Michelangelo signed; his name was clearly visible on Mary's sash. Since an attack on it, the Pieta has been encased in bulletproof glass to protect it. Also housed inside this building, is the thirteenth century bronze statue by Arnolfo di Cambio of a seated Peter. Because countless pilgrims kiss his feet, Peter's toes are wearing away.

Beneath the dome, Bernini's great baldachin (canopy) soars above the high altar; only the pope celebrates mass here. Behind the altar the bronze and marble Cathedra of St. Peter, the throne of the Apostle's successor is encapsulated in the wooden chair of St. Peter.

We spent the remainder of the day revisiting certain memorable sights: the Coliseum, the Roman Forum, and the Spanish Steps. I really hated to leave, as I wanted to spend more time here, but Venice called to us. I hoped I would like it as well as I did Rome.

That night we repacked for our train trip to Venice. We planned to have our final meal at Guiseppe's. When we arrived, one of the sons told us the restaurant was closed for a private party but our delightful maitre'd spotted us and motioned for us to come ahead. We felt so privileged, almost like part of his family. He brought us our carafe of white wine along with antipasto, lasagna, beef chops, salad, and ice cream. After taking pictures with him, we gave him big hugs and thank yous for being so good to us.

After breakfast the next morning we checked out of the Morgana and walked to the train station with our wheeled bags trailing behind us. We met Robbie, Thomson's Rome representative, who made sure we had our proper seats. He asked if we would mind taking a bundle of mail to their Venice representative who would be meeting us. He said, "The mail costs too much and sometimes takes weeks to get to its destination." "Sure," we said.

The countryside alternated from level ground to rolling hills. Traveling along I noticed all the farming, particularly the vineyards, showed varying stages of maturity. Most land was dry and dusty, making farming difficult and in places virtually impossible. In the farming areas people lived in simple, plain one-floor houses while in the towns multiple level tenements displayed newly washed laundry blowing in the breeze on pulley lines. On the way to Venice, we noticed distinct changes in environment. No television antennas emanated from rooftops along the way, whereas in Rome every apartment building, home, and office building had one wherever an inch was found for them to be installed. Homes had little in the way of flower gardens except in places where water was plentiful. Poverty was as evident here as it was in certain sections of Rome. Remembering the French farming families, I knew the Italian pasta, home brewed wines, and family life kept them going in this present day of unemployment, changes in world and national affairs, and their lack of monetary wealth.

Upon arriving in Venice, Suzie, Thomson's Venice attendant, met us at the train station. We handed over the mail pouch Roberto had entrusted us with. As we boarded a water taxi with five other couples headed for the hotel area and St. Mark's Square, she gave us a packet full of information about our hotel and Venice's points of interest. The travel brochures and postcards of Venice with all its gondolas and water transportation were accurate. Apartments and shops surrounded the waterways or canals. Gondoliers serenaded us hoping to lure us into their gondolas. The summer temperature had not become hot enough to bring out the "renowned and unappetizing" smells of Venice.

Leaving the taxi, Susie gave us final hotel instructions. Being tired from five hours on the train, all we wanted was a hot shower and a minute or two to lie down. Entering our room we found it unique to say the least, as it was on two levels and had three twin beds. We asked that one bed be removed. The most unusual thing was the bathroom. The shower and toilet were almost one and the same. One could take a shower and do all of nature's business at the same time. What an odd situation!

The hotel recommended a restaurant three viaducts up. It wasn't Guiseppe's but had to do. We ordered spaghetti, fish, salad, and ice cream and were disappointed. After dinner we walked in the moonlight into St. Mark's Square which was aglow from the hundreds of tiny twinkling lights strung around it as well as a myriad of sidewalk cafes. Enclosed on three sides of the Square, an actual square, were ground floor shops with apartments above. The fourth side was filled with St. Mark's Basilica. Many floodlights illuminated it from many different angles in order to bring out its massive front and the artwork situated above its heavy wood entrance doors.

In the background we could hear different cafe bands playing anything from classical greats to Broadway show music. In the center of the square, artists displayed their paintings, hoping to entice us into letting them sketch us or realizing we were just looking continued to work on their painting in progress. Other vendors sold trinkets, Venice prints, and leather products. We just stood there in the middle of this Square, soaking in all it had to offer us. What a shame. We were too tired to sit and have a cappuccino or listen to the music all around us.

On our first true day in Venice we slept until nine o'clock, had breakfast, and then ventured out on our own. The sunshine was ablaze making everything picturesque. We took a stroll around. We found the prices of leather and jewelry dear (expensive) in the Square proper. so we ventured down side streets and alleys where prices were more to our liking. The Venetians knew they had a captured audience and priced accordingly.

St. Mark's Square was and is the very heart of Venice; its former grandeur is still evident today. During the time of the Republic, all the most important civil and religious events were celebrated here. Napoleon said it was the most beautiful drawing room in Europe. The Square's dimensions were 175 meters long, 81 meters wide at the Basilica end while the opposite end was only 57 meters. The creation of this area began in 832AD when the first basilica was built on the site of a garden belonging to San Zaccaria nuns. The present square was founded by order of the Doge (chief magistrate) Sebastian Ziani in the 12th Century. Later a crevice in the Vatario canal divided the square in two. When this crevice was filled with new ground, the square's area grew, becoming what it is today.

St. Mark's Basillica, begun in 888AD under the Doge Pietro Tribuno, was built on a similar Greek cross plan as that of St. Peter's in Rome and St. Paul's in London. After the Doge Guistinian Partecipazio stole the body of St. Mark the Evangelist from Alexandria, Egypt, he commissioned a larger edifice as the resting place for St. Mark's body. St. Mark's was completed in 1073 and consecrated in 1094. For the next four centuries thc Venetians enriched their basilica with beautiful mosaic paintings both inside and out.

The exterior of St. Mark's is a combination of many architectural styles – Romanesque, Byzantine, Flowering Gothic, and Renaissance. Arches and cupolas dominate its facade with sparkling mosaic portraits over its doorways adding to its finery. On a terrace above the main doors is the bronze quad Riga (four horses), the only one preserved to this day, a masterpiece of Alexandrian workmanship from the fourth century BC. During the Fourth Crusade in 1204 the Riga was transported here to decorate the Hippodrome.

Depicted atop the front exterior wall was a magnificent mosaic painting of the Last Supper. On either side of the lower doorways were mosaics depicting the months, the virtues, and the Beatitudes while the center lower doorway demonstrated the trades of that time.

Inside, the solemn majesty of its architecture, along with the richness and the brilliance of the marble and gilded decorations, make this unique basilica unforgettable to anyone entering it; be it visitor or worshipper. The ceilings were adorned with mosaic religious scenes and personages. Due to flooding and years of people walking over them, the marble floor slabs are quite uneven; even for an avid walker.

Placed beneath the chancel itself is the crypt of St. Mark. The most spectacular item within these church walls is the gold altar screen, a masterpiece created by fourteenth century Venetian goldsmiths and patrons who embedded it with many precious stones so the basilica's treasury would never go bankrupt. The beauty of its jewels, gold, and carvings is overwhelming.

Outside, across from St. Mark's is its bell tower standing 99 meters high. The lower portion was Romanesque while the upper part was Renaissance. Its pyramid-shaped cusp top ends with a golden angel.

Hungry for a bite of lunch, we ventured into the byways and alleys before stopping at an outdoor cafe. We enjoyed our pepperoni and mushroom pizza and cokes. You know when on vacation one has to keep up his or her strength for more walking and shopping. We toured all the shops looking and pricing Italian gold, leather shoes and bags, and Merino glass. Ron wanted a pair of Italian shoes; he found a pair of loafers at our last shop. I bought a small Merino multi-striped bud vase for myself at a reasonable price. These were our Venetian remembrances.

After almost exhausting our shopping budget, we walked the "boardwalk" along the Grand Canal and perused the souvenir vendors. Nothing interested us. We returned to our room for a rest before dinner at the neighborhood cafe. Dinner was more tolerable but we decided to look for something better for the next night.

We slept in again, then just milled around as we had done all we wanted. This time when we entered the Square we became aware we both were sneezing and our eyes were watering. Before entering this area we were fine, then we began our sneezing and eye rubbing. With this we realized we must be allergic to the pigeons and their down.

We planned to see the art in the Doge's Palace but every time we came near the lines circled around the side of the building. After several attempts to no avail, we decided to return the next morning when everyone would be at church and the lines would be minimal.

That evening walking down some alleyways we found a little outdoor café where we ate some wonderful spaghetti, ravioli, and garlic bread, and finished off our meal with a bottle of Chianti. We wished we had found this place our first night here.

Later when the pigeons had gone to their nighttime retreats, we were able to go into St. Mark's Square. We found a street vendor selling the fabulous Italian ice cream, so Ron got a strawberry cone while I had the raspberry sorbet. Oh, what a delight. We sat close together on a vacant bench and listened to the café orchestra music in the moonlight. What a magical, romantic ending to our vacation.

Sunday, our final day, we slept in again, repacked our bags, and checked out by 11 AM as required, leaving our bags in their storage area. After breakfast we walked to the Doge's Palace only to find it wasn't open on Sundays. Now what do we do? We just walked some more around the shop areas; great exercise to work off some of the Italian pasta, wine, and ice cream we'd eaten during the past week.

About 11 o'clock we decided to treat ourselves to a cup of cappuccino at one of the three open cafes. It was wonderful to sit in the sun's warmth and people watch while listening to the nearby cafe bands.

The cappuccino tasted so delicious we splurged on a second one. When the bill came, we realized our four cappuccinos had cost us thirty dollars but it was truly worth sitting around a café table and taking in all the exuding joy and atmosphere there.

With time still on our hands before we had to leave for the airport, we walked the length of the boardwalk then watched the Merit Yachting Race going on in the Grand Canal. It amazed me how easily each boat weaved through the gondoliers, water taxis and busses (overgrown ferries). Polizzi boats patrolled keeping everyone in line so no one got sideswiped.

After our walk we decided to go back to our little cafe from the previous night and have a pizza and a small bottle of Chianti. Our maitre'd asked where in the States we came from. When we told him Detroit, he said he had a brother living there. From then on he catered to us, even honoring us with a special house aperitif. We discussed our time in Europe and said we would mention his place to friends visiting Venice.

At five we met Susie for our water taxi to the bus station and on to the airport. After checking in with all the customary airport personnel, we sat waiting for our plane to be listed. Becoming aware of no air-conditioning in the airport and the increase of the air temperature in the waiting room, we knew we needed something cold to drink. We walked around the airport shops until we found one selling sold bottles of mineral water. Oh, how wonderful that tasted and how it helped cool our hot bodies. I also spied bottles of Chianti and purchased four of them in my favorite shop – the duty-free. You know me, I can't miss a duty-free.

Our plane arrived. After refueling with food and gas, we boarded our fully packed Monarch flight for home. We didn't even eat dinner as we were still full of pizza and were too tired from all we had done in the past week. All we wanted was to rest and possibly sleep on our flight. After arriving at Gatwick, we retrieved our car and drove home.

What a dream come true. Rome was all I had expected and more. Both Ron and I wished that we had spent our entire week in Rome as Venice did nothing for us except for the beautiful St. Mark's Basilica and for the allergy the pigeons gave us. I knew I wanted to go back and spend much more time in Rome but that had to be another trip. I hoped my pennies and wishes at the Trevi Fountain would bring us back before we returned to the States. I loved Rome.

44. The Octoberfest Nuptials

Summer had been good to us: mild weather, beautiful gardens, and plentiful golf for Ron with his friends. We were looking forward to all the fall colors. Adding to our excitement, Laura's sister, Kelly, who had been our first Thanksgiving guest, was getting married in the Nuremberg Castle chapel in Germany. Oh, how romantic.

Ron and I planned to meet John and Laura in Amsterdam and drive with them to Nuremberg for the wedding. How wonderful it would be to spend some time with them. Gretchen, Laura's youngest sister, her husband, Joe, Adam, the girls' brother and Anita and Dick, the girls' parents were to fly into Nuremberg the day before we were to arrive. Since both Kelly and Gerhard, her fiance, were in the Army there, they made arrangements for all the family to stay at the American-Bavarian Hotel run for U. S. Army personnel and their families.

On the Monday before the wedding, Ron and I took the ferry to Calais. From there we drove through France and Belgium arriving in Amsterdam amid gale-like rain and winds. After checking into our hotel, we found John and Laura. John was down with reverse motion sickness again after their long overseas flight. Laura was fine even after ten hours in air and being six months pregnant with their first child. Since she, Ron, and I were hungry, we went to lunch at a nearby hotel restaurant, as ours was closed. We brought John back some hot tea and soup.

By the next day everyone was ready to tour: we took them on a tour of Amsterdam Centrum as well as Anne Frank's home, before driving along the Rhine to Koblenz and the German wine areas. The next day we drove into Heidelberg and checked into the Zum Rutter Hotel where Ron and I had stayed on a previous trip. After checking in, we took the tram up to the castle, as we knew it was too strenuous for Laura to walk up the hillside. The castle, sitting amidst the fall coloring of the hillside surrounding it, was fantastic.

After our tour of the castle, we sat at one of the little outdoor cafes near our hotel. Laura and I had cups of hot tea while the guys had pints of beer. We had dinner in a German restaurant around the corner. I overdid myself ordering a plate of ricotta and spinach ravioli topped with cream sauce; the sauce was too rich for me. The next morning I didn't feel well. Coming into Nuremberg, waves of nausea hit me. Just as John drove around a corner I smelt a street vendor's fried onions. The nausea overcame me. I told John to pull off the road; I had to get out. He pulled into a side street next to a car dealership. Before he came to a complete stop and I could open my door, I lost everything I had in my stomach. The most embarrassing part was I had to change my clothes outside the car giving everyone a free peek show. I felt sorry for John as he stood there helpless while Ron and Laura cleaned up the inside of the car. I couldn't remember being that sick except on our trip home from Normandy a few years earlier.

Once at our hotel, I slept; Ron found a pharmacist who gave him anti-vomit and Kaopectate medicines to settle me down. While the family had dinner together, I slept between bathroom sessions. The following day I felt better but was weak from the ordeal. That night we went to a wonderful German restaurant for the rehearsal dinner. Kelly's landlords, Carl and Dragoon, sponsored this dinner as they were so attached to both Kelly and Gerhard. The proprietors were so pleased with themselves, as they had been able to purchase freshly slaughtered meat from that morning. Everyone said the beef and the sausages, the sauerkraut, mashed potatoes, and beans tasted the best they had ever had. I stayed with the potatoes as I knew I could handle them.

When we awoke the following morning we knew the day would be perfect for the wedding. Thankfully, I was back to my old self again. We dressed in our wedding finery and walked to the wedding site. Somehow Kelly and Gerhard had gotten permission to be married in the Nuremberg Castle's chapel. The castle was on a knoll above the buildings where the famous post-World War II Nuremberg Trials had been held. John, Laura, Ron, and I walked up the cobble-stone path to the chapel. Adorning both of the heavy wood entrance doors were grapevine wreathes with white and purple flowers befitting the wedding color theme. The interior of the small chapel was stark white and had simple mahogany pews, beams, and altar.

When Kelly arrived, she looked lovely in Laura's wedding gown; each of the girls had worn the gown on their wedding days. Gerhard wore the traditional Bavarian wedding costume. He had been born near here but his family had immigrated to the States many years ago and all had become naturalized.

The service and hymns were spoken and sung in both German and English – English by the minister and German by Gerhard's mother – so all in attendance could understand and participate in the ceremony.

After the service, the entire wedding party walked down the knoll to the restaurant where the luncheon was being served. People along our way smiled and peered at us like we were celebrities, making us feel special as well as a little embarrassed by all their attention. When we arrived at the restaurant, Kelly and Gerhard, according to tradition had to begin their married life working together before they could have their wedding celebration. They had to saw a log in two with a rather large "lumbering" saw. This was to teach them they had to work together in a give and take manner to make their marriage work. Laura's gown was so tight and straight I worried that Kelly would tug or pull too hard on one of the sawing motions and the dress would rip. I didn't need to worry, as it held together. After the log was divided, the entire retinue proceeded inside for the celebration.

The lunch consisted of sliced beef, potatoes, vegetables, and a wedding cake. After lots of toasts and champagne, the couple left. Anita, Dick, Ron, and I walked around the *Octoberfest*. Kelly and Gerhard had picked this particular weekend for their wedding so their guests could take in the festivities as well. After sitting at one of the little outdoor café tables, having some beer, and renewing our friendship, we headed back to the subway for our hotel.

After boarding our train, Ron noticed a rather intoxicated man entering our car just after us. He sat down on the aisle across from us. I noticed how nervous Ron became and kept asking him what was wrong. "Was he sick? No. What is the matter?" I kept asking. He said, "Nothing", but I knew something was bothering him since I never had seen him act this way before. Suddenly, Ron grabbed our camera making me even more nervous. Ron kept looking around for something or someone. After the man got off the train at the next stop, Ron relaxed a bit but still was looking for something or somebody when the train pulled out of the station. What Ron had noticed and the rest of us had not was the man had a gun. While he was sitting in his seat, he was filling it bullet by bullet. Ron had watched for a policeman who could disarm and detain the man before he would hurt someone or himself. To this day we never found out what happened to him.

After returning to our hotel we all went to the hotel bar for a drink.

We tried to pay for them with German marks only to be told the hotel only dealt with American money. Since the hotel catered to American military personnel and their families, only American cash was accepted. Dick and Ron went to an exchanger for some dollars for our marks.

Our last day before returning home was full of sunshine and warm breezes. We walked around the old part of Nuremberg; most of which had been destroyed in World War II bombings and subsequently restored. Old Town had regained its original charm while the rest of the city had become modern buildings. Because of the *Octoberfest*, Old Town was full of tourists shopping at outdoor craft stalls all over the castle area. At outdoor cafes people ate and drank tankards of good German beer. I bought some German pottery for Christmas gifts and some newfangled cooking gadgets for myself.

After saying goodbye to the families, we began our trek home. We drove to Wiesbaden where we stayed overnight with Carol and Max, our friends whom we hadn't seen in almost a year. The following day they drove us through the Mosel Valley and its vineyards. Being fall, we stopped and watched men harvest the ripened grapes, place them into their cone-shaped back packs, then pour them out into large wagons which would take them to the vineyard presses to begin the wine process. Max drove us to a lovely medieval village called Bernkasel Kush, a vestige of Roman inhabitation. Max didn't do much walking as his back was quite testy from a pulled muscle, so the rest of us walked around. A little later we found a wonderful upper room coffee shop where we treated ourselves to a pastry and a cup of coffee before we had to leave to catch our ferry home. What a wonderful trip to see family, attend a castle wedding, and renew friendships. I had many more memories to put into my diary.

45. Spring Reprieve

Well, it happened again! The pressure was put on me to extend our assignment for another year – our fourth. Both sides of the "Pond" said they needed Ron to stay and continue his work. Once more I felt I had to put the company before everything else. My thought of returning Stateside and living 3000 miles away from my husband was not my idea of marriage. After believing this year would be our year to go home, my heart broke into a million pieces. I knew I was only seeing this extension from my own perspective, but both Ron and I were missing out on our little ones formative years: Jennifer was now seven and a half and Christopher (Laura and John's son born in December) was six months old. I was also missing my students and classroom. This blow was almost more than I could bear. I knew I had to reconcile myself to it but the lingering question was HOW?

I still remember that previous November when John and Laura called to ask if I could come home early for Christmas, as Laura needed a caesarean section and would need my help when she got home from the hospital. Elation came over me like a warm blanket. I was needed and wanted in a very special way. Since Ron would be in Austria on business when Laura would go into the hospital, I said, "Certainly, just tell me when and I'll be there." I flew home alone.

On the day of the surgery, Ron made it clear to everyone he was to be called the instant my call came in. He was in a dinner meeting when he got the call. He was over the moon with delight. He ordered two bottles of champagne, so everyone there could help him celebrate this occasion. All I knew was, I thrilled to be a part of Christopher's big day, as well as John and Laura's. To be a part of their lives was so special to me.

Now with the extension I had to put all that on hold again. I tried to rationalize the company's need for Ron's expertise over my need to be home. It didn't work; as I felt I had already given my dues to the company and they didn't care about me at all. I was angry at the company and Ron for the pressure they put on me to extend, then making me feel guilty for wanting my life and family back.

Ron decided a little time away might help me over the hump of this. I went to see Lisa and asked where could we go for a week of sun, sand, and warm temperatures. She said, "What about Tenerife?" I had never heard of it but she told me it was in the Canary Islands off the west side of Africa. Lisa said, "This time of year it's warm, sunny, and just right for a holiday." I said, "Book us."

The morning we began our holiday, we drove to Luton Airport for our flight to Tenerife. The inside of our charter plane looked like a cattle car filled with 244 other holiday makers. Besides cramped seating, no movies were shown during the four hour flight. Thank goodness, I had brought my new Maeve Binchy book. Lunch consisted of pressed turkey slices, sage dressing, Duchess potatoes, green beans, potato salad, and a lemon mousse cake along with the usual cheese and crackers.

While flying into Tenerife we saw a beautiful, rolling golf course Ron wanted to play. He had cleaned and brought his clubs along, just in case there was a course nearby. The island itself consisted of volcanic hills and soil, palm trees, cacti, and other plants giving a green richness to everything.

Sunshine and warm breezes greeted us as we exited the plane.

Walking to the non-EC immigration station, we found it unattended. A gentleman behind us in line said all we needed to do was fill out the immigration cards he had pulled out from inside the station's window opening. We started filling in all the required information when the man said don't worry about what you are putting down as they can't read English anyway. When the inspector finally came, he pretended to understand everything on the form, but we knew he couldn't. After retrieving our baggage, we hopped onto the awaiting Thomson bus for the ride to our hotel.

Traveling along their modern four lane motorways I watched the landscape. The ground looked similar to that in New Mexico but didn't have the volcanic element in it. The bus made a leisurely drive into the city. After stopping at other customer's hotels, the bus stopped at ours – the Guayarmina Princess, a light salmon colored hotel with lots of palm trees, grass, and a volcanic sand beach backing up to the Atlantic. We thought what a restful place this was. After finding our room, we went onto the patio where we felt the sun's warmth enlivening our bodies. Our patio overlooked the tennis courts and the ocean. After checking out the room, Ron realized he had two major problems. The first was no television in our room. The second one, he had forgotten to program our VCR to tape the Masters' Golf Tournament. Oh, well, he would just have to spend that time with me. We walked around the hotel to get our bearings. The pool's two interconnected circles looked delicious. The patio accommodated many beach and lawn chairs for reading and sunning purposes or one could just sit and relax in the breeze and watch the ocean's movement. It was breathtaking. Later, we ate dinner in the hotel's dining room. The buffet food and service were adequate but not spectacular. After dinner we noticed a poster board listing nightly disco entertainment in the bar area, but we didn't go in as we were tired from the flight and all the excitement of not having any television.

We almost overslept the next morning. Knowing we had a meeting with the Thomson representative at ten, we quickly dressed and had a bite of breakfast before meeting Melanie. She said the weather had been rainy but weather forecasters were predicting this month to be better. We decided to take three tours: a catamaran trip to see the dolphins and whales, a trip up the volcanic mountains, and a round of golf for Ron. Melanie warned us to use lots of sunscreen as the sun became quite intense and sunstroke was a possibility for those not using sun protection. She also recommended always using bottled water for everything from brushing our teeth to meals.

After our discussion with Melanie, we strolled around the neighborhood to see what the shops were selling. To no surprise, vendors were hawking lots of trinkets, postcards, straw hats, skimpy bathing suits, and seashells. We bought six bottles each of mineral and tonic water. You know gin and tonics go well in hot weather.

After our walk, we changed for a lay in the sun. As we stopped at the reception desk to ask about sun chairs and umbrellas, Ron noticed a sign saying, "No bare chests in the lobby." Ron commented that men should wear shirts in the lobby. Reaching the pool area, I realized what the sign meant. Topless women lay everywhere. At that moment I told Ron to give me his glasses and look straight ahead, he immediately knew what the sign meant. After a half hour of #35 sunscreen, reading, and snoozing, we returned to our room for a nap before dinner.

After dinner, we went for a moonlight walk. In the distance we heard a mariachi band and started to investigate, but the evening's cold breeze caught us by surprise, so we didn't venture any further.

Breakfast was a feast, with everything from three kinds of sausages, bacon, eggs of all descriptions, rolls, toast, juices, cereals, fresh fruits, and beverages, we didn't know where to begin. Europeans fill up on breakfast so they can skip a costly lunch, then have a hearty dinner.

We took the Geranium Walk – a three-mile walk into the center of town and back. What we didn't realize before our walk was along the way were throngs of pushy timeshare salespeople trying to sell tourists their apartments. They spoke every language in order to get us to talk to them. "You speak English, French, German? I have free gift for you." With one I said, "Nine" but he corrected my German pronunciation to which I said, "You won't get my business with that kind of attitude." The more bombarded we were, the more belligerent we became. Adding to my frustration was the vendor who became indignant when I began filing through his piles of T-shirts for the correct sizes and the perfect saying on them. I told him, "I am not buying anything I cannot check out for imperfections or sizing. Thank you but I will go somewhere else where I can look for what I want without being harassed" and walked off to another vendor. He couldn't believe I would do that to him, but I didn't like his attitude or treatment.

Melanie warned us about purchasing videos here. "Vendors play tapes in their VCR for tourists then sell them unopened tapes containing blank or unusable tapes. The buyer doesn't know it until he arrives home and tries to use them. If you want a particular tape, make the shop open and play that tape before purchasing it."

Beginning our walk back to our hotel, we were once again pestered by the obnoxious salespeople trying to sell their timeshares, tour excursions, and fake watches. At one place we noticed a man running a bogus shell game. Children watching him knew he was cheating and pointed that out to his customers, infuriating him. He would drive the children away so he could con more unsuspecting people.

We followed the ocean path back, passing other hotels, pools, sandy beaches filled with sunbathers and swimmers, and the usual sidewalk cafes selling sandwiches, cokes, and stronger libations. After changing into our swim gear, we ordered hamburgers, fries, and cokes at the hotel's pool barbeque. For the next hour, we sat under an umbrella to shade us from the sun's intense rays and read. The gentle ocean breeze kept us cool and invigorated our senses. Later we bought some additional sunscreen, water, and two straw hats to protect us from the sun's rays on the following day's catamaran trip. After dinner we took another walk around the patio and listened to the delightful mariachi music.

After breakfast we decided to sit under our umbrella and read until it was time for our trip. Oh, the ocean breezes, the sun, and a good book – it was heaven. With the onset of school holidays, more families were arriving. The pool area had become crowded with unruly children and bare chested women. I couldn't believe one German woman being bare chested before her two pre-teen boys. But I guess that's Europe.

The "Freebird" bus (tour bus) picked us up promptly at ten for our catamaran tour. By half ten we walked up to the gangplank where we removed our shoes and placed them into a basket before boarding the "cat". Since the sail launcher was broken, the crew had to hoist the sail manually. Our crew consisted of Arelio, the captain/navigator, John, the knowledgeable guide, and Jamie, the gopher/trainee. They offered us refreshments from coke to beer or mineral water. "Just a coke and a mineral water," we stated. John told everyone on the trip to refrain from going below deck, as that quickly disorients people, making them nauseous, so it was best to stay topside unless absolutely necessary. He explained motion sickness comes from the sun dehydrating the body and not, as many people believe, from the boat's motion. We needed to continually drink non-alcoholic drinks to replace the water loss in our bodies from the sun's rays and to keep us nausea free. Alcohol only adds to the dehydration process. Information I never knew before.

About an hour later we came upon a small school of whales playing. John explained the females lived to be 65 years old while the males only lived 45 to 50 years. The reason being, the males must dive to depths of three thousand feet in order to get squid and other sea urchins to feed themselves and their families. Some young females do this as well. As the males die off, the reproduction system of their mates shuts down in response. The new job of these non-producing females is to become the "grandmothers" or "caretakers" of the young while the parents searched for food.

Dolphins can live 75 to 80 years in the "wild", but in captivity, such as Sea World, their life span is cut to about five years. Dolphins are quite intelligent animals with brains larger than a human's, making them quick learners of circus tricks and naval assignments. This captivity creates serious problems for them. As sound waves bounce off the walls of their small caged pool lanes, the circus dolphins lose their sense of hearing as well as their sense of balance. After losing these two senses, they become lonely and die. About 650 dolphins have been captured and trained as couriers for military operations. Noises bouncing off ships and other sounding devices create the same sensory loss in them. In time, they also die in captivity.

The whales are beautiful creatures. From time to time, John goes into the water to swim with them. He said the only reported problem with a whale was a woman in Hawaii who tried to ride one by hanging onto its dorsal fin. The whale only nipped her then dove seventy feet down in the water before releasing her unharmed. The whale was supposed to be an Orca. Wrong one to try to ride.

As we watched the schools of whales in various places, we took photographs of them. At one point, John spotted a school of dolphins but another hotshot "cat" pilot saw them as well and cut us off so his passengers could get the best look. In doing so, he frightened the dolphins away so no one saw them. Drat and double drat.

Lunch consisted of cheese and tomato baguettes, crisps, and cokes. On our way back to port we made a fifteen-minute stop at Spaghetti Island for those wanting a dip in the ocean. Reportedly, a nudist colony lived here but none were seen. That was just fine with me.

Upon returning to the marina, we picked up our shoes and boarded the bus for our hotel. Thank goodness we had booked the morning tour as the sun bore down on us; I could only imagine what it would be like in the afternoon. We would have fried, even with 30 plus sunscreen! Back at the hotel, we found some chaise lounges and umbrellas, then read in the light afternoon breeze.

A Spanish meal greeted us in the evening with an excellent navy bean and potato soup, Spanish ribs, chicken, and sausages, saffron rice and peppers, as well as corn, brussels sprouts, and scalloped potatoes. Toward the end of our meal, a Spanish troubadour signaled the arrival of a huge rum banana cake carried in by the waiters on a gigantic tray then they flambéed it in the center of the dining room. Applause reigned, then everyone was served a piece of this luscious dessert.

After the dinner festivities concluded, we took another moonlit walk, listening to the mariachi music. All of a sudden we saw fireworks emanating from some nearby hotels. We never did find out why.

Friday came quickly. Ron was picked up by a nearby golf club for eighteen holes of golf. While he golfed, I decided to shop, since I could not find a vacant chaise anywhere. Although guests were not to "save" chaises, some had tied towels through the arms of chaises to hold them until their towel owners came to retrieve them. This upset not only us but other guests looking for chairs as well.

At a small shop almost in town, I purchased a little clay wind chime made of small twinkling porcelain white bells. The woman shopkeeper urged me to purchase a good luck charm – a miniature clay vase filled with all kinds of beans. I gave into her request. At a street vendor's shop, I bought T-shirts for the grandchildren and our boys and tropical smocks for our girls.

Finishing my shopping, I remembered Melanie telling us on the day we were to leave, we had to check out by eight o'clock in the morning. The hotel made available to its Thomson clients a complimentary changing room so those who wanted to swim or sun until time to leave for the airport. Here clients could take a quick shower and change into their traveling clothes. I decided to pack us up so we didn't have to miss anything we might want to do on our last night here. I thought we might go to the disco as a treat.

About an hour later, Ron came in looking and acting completely dehydrated. I quickly pumped two large bottles of water into him. Fortunately, he had remembered his sunscreen, so he had not gotten sunburned. While he rested and rejuvenated himself, I finished reading my book. He said he had played with a wonderful Irish man and his son. The boy was fourteen and quite good.

Later we bought and mailed some postcards home to the family and our friends, then took our last stroll along the Geranium Walk. On our way back, we stopped at a British cafe for some fish and chips. Tasted wonderful. The remainder of the afternoon and early evening we spent sunning, reading, and taking in the last bit of warmth and ocean breezes available to us.

After a tough roast beef dinner with all the trimmings, we had a cappuccino at the hotel's outdoor cafe. We sat there until the breezes became too cool for us. What a lovely ending to our holiday. As we reentered the hotel, we heard the disco music and sat down. We ordered a drink and watched a full Las Vegas show complete with boas, sparkly costumes, and show tunes we knew and loved. After the show we watched hotel guests of all ages gyrate to dances that would put most people's backs out.

Sunday we arose at half seven, dressed, finished our packing, and checked out, putting our luggage in the hotel's secure storage area. After breakfasting on orange juice, scrambled eggs, link sausages, bacon, toast, muffins, and fresh fruit cup, we went to the pool. The sun hadn't blown off the morning's coolness so we wrapped up in beach towels, drank hot coffee, and read the *Sunday London Times* until it became warm enough to enjoy the morning.

About half past two we ordered cheeseburgers, chips, and cokes, then walked the volcanic sand beach hoping to find some seashells to take home. No such luck. Before getting ready for our bus to the airport, I made my last shopping run; I bought a two-piece purple bathing suit, skimpy but ooh la la. I got back just in time to shower and dress before our airport bus came. At five we stood outside the hotel waiting to be picked up, when we struck up a conversation with a lovely British couple from Manchester. We wished we had met when our holiday began so we could have enjoyed activities together. We would have gotten along famously. At the airport I made my usual duty free run – nothing I wanted. I surprised myself as well as Ron. We boarded our plane at seven and had a lovely chicken potpie dinner. After arriving at the Luton Airport about eleven fifteen, we picked up our car and were home by half past midnight – tired but happy. What a wonderful respite away from the pressures of Comco.

46. Searching for Ron's Irish Ancestry

From the time we arrived in England, Ron and I had wanted to visit Ireland and search out his ancestry. Since we hadn't taken a summer holiday, we decided to make our pilgrimage the end of August. We had been told how green it was, how friendly its people were, and how filled with Guinness it was.

When we walked out into our driveway on our way to the ferry to Ireland that September morning, wind, rain, and cold greeted us. We drove through hills and valleys of middle England and then into the rough terrain of North Wales. It's amazing how each portion of the United Kingdom has its own flavor of countryside and architecture. England has rolling and open farmland and pastures while Wales has its rolling stony hillsides and Scotland has steep hillsides full of heather and sheep. Rain is always part and parcel with all three provinces.

After a six-hour drive, we arrived at the Port of Holyhead about two forty-five. I had hoped we could catch the earlier ferry, but it had already left so we needed to wait for our booked time of half seven. The earlier ferry was a regular ferry making the crossing in three hours while ours was a hydrofoil that would make it in half that time.

We puttered around the tiny seaside village of Holyhead until about 4 o'clock when we returned to the port to await our ship. By six I began to wonder why our ship hadn't arrived, but she pulled in at seven. Within minutes Stena Sealink announced our ship had experienced technical problems on her voyage from Ireland and it would take two hours to repair it. When we saw divers in full gear diving under her, I became a bit concerned and nervous. The line gave each passenger a £5 voucher to use on the ship to ease our delay discomfort.

We finally berthed our car at ten fifteen and used our vouchers to buy a jacket potato and two baguettes filled with bacon, cheese, and tomato for our dinner. Once at sea the captain came over the loudspeaker telling us one of the ferry's motors was still inoperable, so, instead of a fast trip to Ireland we would move at 20 knots; making our trip the usual three-hour trip. Further, he told us to be prepared for a rough ride. Since he had just piloted this ferry in from Dun Laoghaire, Ireland, he knew how turbulent the sea would be. He promised to keep the ride as smooth as possible.

The captain couldn't keep his promise, as the sea was as rough as he had told us. Eighty-five percent of the passengers became quite sick. Fortunately, we were not among that number. A mother sitting near us had her hands full with her two youngest daughters while her two teen-aged daughters held their own. At one point she asked a steward to bring her a glass of water for one of her little girls. We suggested she give her defizzed coke, not water as water generally comes right back up. The defizzed coke helped settle the little girl's stomach.

During the voyage we had Stena Sealink alert our hotel of our late arrival time hoping someone would be there to let us in. Joyfully, we disembarked the ship about one o'clock. We were mighty glad to be back on solid ground after our bucking bronco ride. When we knocked on the hotel entrance door, the night receptionist opened it for us. We were never so glad to see anyone in our lives.

The next morning we woke up to clouds and rain, although the sun was trying its best to come through. Being quite cool outside, we wore our heavy sweaters under our windbreakers. We asked reception how to use DART (Dublin Area Railway Transit) to get into and out of Dublin.

After our fifteen minute train ride, we began to scour the shopping areas of Grafton, Nassau, and Kildare Streets. Along these streets tourists purchase Celtic jewelry, Erin (Irish) woolen sweaters, skirts, and jackets as well as Waterford Crystal, Wedgwood China, picture postcards, newspapers from all over the world, books and pamphlets on finding family roots and leprechauns of all description. Inside this area also flourished pubs and even some American food establishments.

We walked through St. Stephen's Green, a lovely park with ponds full of mallards, ducks, and even a swan. Along the pond's walkways were scattered benches. These served as a relaxing place to come and meditate or eat one's lunch, feed the ducks, or just sit and talk with friends.

We stopped by The Duke, a pub frequented in the mid to late eighteen hundreds by such literary greats as James Joyce (who actually made the Davey Byrne pub famous with his novel, *Ulysees*), George Bernard Shaw, W. B. Yeats, even Charles Dickens visited here. We decided to stay for lunch, consuming steaming bowls of their homemade soup – Ron had turkey vegetable while I had tomato-basil. Their breads – wheat, soda, and whole grain – were distinctive, delicious, and wholesome. I wanted to get the recipes to try at home.

In order to get a first hand idea of Dublin, we got on one of Gray Line's double decker buses. Walking up the interior steps to the top of the bus, we knew we would have a ringside seat for all that was to be seen and learned about. Also, I knew I wanted to take as many pictures as possible for our Irish memories book, so again I knew we needed to be topside. That was the place to be.

Our tour began on O'Connell Street opposite the GPO (General Post Office) that occupies a special place in Irish history. From its steps,

Padraig Perse read the *Proclamation of the Republic* on Easter Monday in 1916. Bullet scars from that uprising are still imbedded in its pillars. Even today, the GPO serves as the focal point for political rallies and demonstrations as well as the place where all VIP dignitaries stand for the annual St. Patrick's Day parade.

Crossing the O'Connell Bridge, we found Parliament House that at one time housed the Irish Parliament but today it is no more than a branch office for the Bank of Ireland. The government sold Parliament House to the bank on the condition it never be used again for governmental offices or affairs. An interesting tidbit – Paddy, our guide, told us Dublin's St. Andrew's Church was being renovated for future public offices.

Around the corner we passed Trinity College, Dublin (TCD), founded in 1591 by Elizabeth I as an all-Protestant college. Catholic students were not allowed to study there until 1978. Newman College was built for Catholic students. Today, seventy percent of Trinity students are Catholic. Two of Trinity's illustrious alumni include statesman Edward Burke and poet Oliver Goldsmith. Others included philosopher George Berkeley who later gave his name to the University of California, Berkeley, and writers Jonathan Swift, Oscar Wilde, and John Millington Synge to name a few.

Driving down Parnel Square, one of Dublin's earliest Georgian squares, Paddy told us when architects designed this area, they wanted to create the illusion of height and perfect proportions in their building facades. To do this they made the ground floor windows quite large and each consecutive floor the windows became progressively smaller to attain the result they wanted. Another reason was the architects wanted the large ground floor windows to provide passers-by a look inside at all the festive celebrations and distinguished guests. Still another interesting touch, each entrance door was designed and painted a different color so they didn't look identical. The reason for this, inebriated owners and guests walking home from a night of imbibing or pub-crawling needed to know which door or house was theirs.

On the corner of Merrion Square, one of the most appealing residential squares in all of Dublin, stood the residence of Oscar Wilde's parents. Oscar was an anti-war playwright who hoped the messages of his plays would stop wars. Theatregoers not appreciating his ideas would walk out during intermission and sometimes during the play itself. The government also did not like his anti-war ideas and sentenced him to prison for twenty years. Within months of his prison release, he died.

On the west side of Merrion Square stands the National Gallery housing over two thousand works of Irish, French, Italian, Spanish, and Dutch painters. This is the only museum in the world that doesn't charge an admission fee. Next door to it was Leinster House, the seat of the Irish Parliament – an imposing eighteenth century building.

At one time, Iremand Cunningham, the leader of the Irish government and a true egotist, wanted architects to build a city as well as a country house for him on the same piece of property so he could have the best of both worlds without ever having to leave Dublin. His architects rejected the idea as the land he wanted to use was marshland, but he retorted, "I am the trend setter and those who want to be fashionable will follow me." In 1890, builders built two identical buildings on Cunningham's land: one now houses the National Museum and the other the National Library.

Following the roads and getting close to St. Stephen's Green we saw the Archbishop Marsh Library built in 1701. It is the oldest library in Ireland and contains 250,000 volumes on a wide range of subjects. The library had to install "cages" inside the rare book section in order to keep researching scholars from stealing their books. Rumor has it that the Archbishop's ghost still roams the building on occasions.

Standing on the site of many of St. Patrick's fifth century conversions is St. Patrick's Cathedral which was built in 450. In 1191 the original church was replaced by the present one, the largest cathedral in Ireland. Over the years it has served as the first University of Ireland (1320 - 1520). In the seventeenth century Oliver Cromwell stabled his army's horses inside it. Today, St. Patrick's is the national cathedral for the Protestant Church in Ireland. One of its most famous deans was Jonathan Swift, the author of Gulliver's Travels, and he is buried here. Nearby Christ Church Cathedral, founded in 1038, is the oldest building in Dublin and at one time belonged to the Holy See of Dublin.

We drove past the new headquarters of the Bank of Ireland. Paddy told us an interesting story about this building. It seems that the architect decided to add an additional floor to the building without telling anyone. When the building inspector realized what the architect had done he made him remove the entire floor. The price tag for this removal was as much as the building cost of the rest of the building.

Our tour continued into Phoenix Park on the city's outskirts where many sporting events take place. Of utmost interest to Ron and me was the house of Jean Kennedy, the U.S. Ambassador to Ireland. She is well respected in Ireland. He further told us that for many years a candle was lit and placed in the front downstairs window of the Irish Preside nt's home. It was to welcome home all Irish soldiers. The new President, after her inauguration, placed an eternal flame outside on the front portico to welcome all soldiers, citizens, and visitors to Ireland.

As we were returning to the city center, we saw the famous University Maternity Hospital that has a nine-month waiting period to get in. Down the street was the University chapel. If a couple wants to be married there, one of them must be a graduate from one of the five Irish colleges/universities. The interior is said to be impressive. We couldn't go inside and visit. Oh, shucks.

During an especially long period of poverty and homelessness, the Guinness brewing family built a hostel for the homeless. Over the years, as it expanded, it added its own recreation center. Today, it contains a rehabilitation center for alcoholics – the irony is, the hostel was built around the corner from the Guinness Brewery making people wonder if there was a correlation between the two. Another interesting tidbit for me as an English teacher was the fact that towards the end of James Joyce's life, he thought he was going insane and bequeathed £7,000 to the city to build a mental hospital. Only after his death was it learned that he had suffered from a brain tumor, not mental illness. His hospital still stands today and has become one of the finest and largest in Ireland.

Back on O'Connell Street we passed an obelisk erected to the Duke of Wellington who defeated Napoleon at Waterloo. Interesting fact – he did not want anyone to know of his Irish ancestry. He once said, "Just because someone is born in a stable doesn't make him a horse."

Paddy told us about a period of time when the government needed additional monies, so to get the finances it needed the government decided to tax its citizens for the amount of sunlight that came into their homes daily. It was called the Sunshine Tax. In order to avoid this tax, the people bricked up their windows so no sunshine could get inside. Another interesting thing Paddy told us was about the halfpenny toll the city decided to charge to cross the Metal Bridge. Dubliners, including W. B. Yeats, thought this toll was outrageous and rebelled by walking further down the street crossing the river at the O'Connell Bridge where there was no toll. To this day the O'Connell Bridge is known as the Half Penny Bridge.

After returning to our hotel and needing dinner, we walked across the street to a wonderful seafood restaurant known as the Na Mara which overlooked the harbor. The seafood platter was fantastic. If I could have, I would have snatched the chef, as meal and the raspberry soufflé dessert were fabulous.

The following day the sun poked its head through the clouds as we awoke. At breakfast in the hotel dining room, we noticed an American gentleman wearing – of all things – a Penn State T-shirt. Since Ron received his advanced degrees there, we struck up a conversation. The man said his nephew had sent it to him, saying this year's football team was supposed to be great. The man's wife, an Ohio State graduate, looked forward to her almamater beating Penn State in the fall. Ron jokingly said to her, "We'll see about that."

Before leaving the hotel we had reception call ahead to the Aberdeen Arms in Lahinch and tell them we might arrive after the six o'clock check-in time. Without any time schedule, we could meander there at a leisurely pace, stopping to see anything of importance or interest to us.

Once out of Dublin proper and its traffic, lush green farmlands welcomed us. We drove through the county of Limerick and its namesake town – a market town for some years. Coming into County Clare and the village of Newcastle, we noticed the blue and yellow streamers and flags everywhere on shops, houses, and buildings. It looked like a real celebration in the making.

We continued on to our hotel in Lahinch, arriving about half past three. It was a lovely, little seaside village. Their homes, built solidly to withstand the winter winds and snows, reflected the bleached whiteness of the summer sun. Many looked like simple seafarer's homes on the outside but I suspected on the inside they were full of family love and celebrations. Since the summer tourist season was over, the residents had started returning to their normal routines and lives.

Our room in the Alberdeen Hotel was on the second floor and overlooked the main street with a lake in the distance. Its yellow walls accentuated the white and yellow bedspread and pillows on our bed. A mahogany table and two chairs for writing or reading sat in the window corner while a chest of drawers was situated on the adjacent wall. The bathroom was small, but all we needed.

After unpacking a bit we decided to tour the village and maybe find a bite of lunch. We passed a couple of antique shops and woolen sweater shops. Most restaurants were closed for the season but Mrs. O'Brien's was open. When we walked in, delightful soup smells waffed up to us. We ordered large bowls of homemade vegetable soup and hot-crusted rolls. The soup warmed us while filling the emptiness in our stomachs.

After lunch we walked the length of the boardwalk, watching children as they played with their sand shovels and pails while their parents and some young couples swam close by. A cold shudder surrounded me as I thought of the cold water covering them but they didn't seem to mind it.

On our walk back to the hotel we passed Kenny's, the Irish Woolen Shop carrying everything from sweaters and scarves to Irish cookbooks in the front of the store, to Waterford Crystal in the rear. We were dismayed to learn Ireland had no family tartans like Scotland so neither of us would be able to wear the Hurley colors.

Our timing couldn't have been more perfect, as Kenny's was holding their annual Waterford Crystal sale. Attending this event was one of Waterford's master cutters who would engrave any pieces purchased during this event. The crystal was spectacular. Steve, the young man seemingly in charge, noticed our interest in the Waterford and introduced us to the cutter who gave us all kinds of information about the processes for designing, blowing, and cutting each piece. He described the crystal maker's lengthy and rigorous apprenticeship program and the history behind many of their famous designs. Ron splurged and bought me an Irish designed vase as a memento of his heritage and our trip here. We had the cutter engrave the base with our names and the date. While he was engraving, I bought my usual postcards.

As we left the shop with our purchases, I asked Steve the significance of the blue and yellow flags in Newcastle. He said the flags celebrated County Clare's hurling team's victories over both County Limerick and County Cork, advancing them to the finals in the All-County Hurling contest on Sunday in Dublin. If they won, it would be the first time since 1914. Recently, they had won the County Monster contest for the first time in 64 years, so the flags represented the people of Newcastle's wish for their continued victories as well as congratulations for their recent ones. From the excitement in Steve's voice it was clear he was an avid County Clare fan.

It was early afternoon when we left the shop. Ron wanted to find the Lahinch golf course and find out why everyone called it the St. Andrew's of Ireland. As we walked along the coast road, we found it. What a monster it was with its valleys, link course fairways, and the winds coming off the water! Across the main road was its sister course which looked more lenient and more like a US PGA course. After the first course, this one looked like milktoast.

Walking back to the hotel we remembered Niamh, our surrogate daughter, telling us if we saw nothing else in Ireland we had to see the Cliffs of Moher. We had no idea where they were or why she was so adamant. After deciding to take a drive around the area to see if we could find this special place, we came upon a road sign saying the Cliffs were only seven kilometers ahead.

Fortunately, we had not taken our cameras out of the car so off we sped. Seeing them, we understood her enthusiasm. The Cliffs were spectacular. Seeing the scalloped cliffs hugging the water in such a stately fashion while jutting out for about a half kilometer on both sides of its lagoon was more than worth the trouble to find them. Watching over the Cliffs and the surrounding area stood an old tower deserted years before but still protecting everything in its sights. We walked to the cliff's summit where we could see for miles around. Although it wasn't a blustery day, the breezes coming off the water were strong and cold. I am sure on a windy day visitors would have difficulty keeping their balance and their hats on.

About an hour later sunset was upon us so we returned to our hotel for a hot shower and something to eat before bed. At dinner we met a lovely couple and their infant son; the husband had come to golf in the annual Lahinch Golf Club tournament. Although he and his family lived near Wimbledon, he had retained his membership; his father, who lived here, also retained his membership. The two made it an annual affair to play this tournament together. We said we had seen the course earlier and said how tough it looked. He agreed it was a monster but it was exhilarating to play and compete on. He could hardly wait for the beginning of the morning's competition. We said we might come out and cheer him and his dad on. He seemed pleased by that. Ron said he would love to play the course; the young man said if Ron got there before seven, the course might let him play a round before the tournament began.

Unfortunately, our alarm clock didn't wake us in time so Ron missed the possibility of playing a round there. We decided to do a full day of touring and investigating. We first stopped at the tournament to watch for our dinner companion but couldn't find him. We rationalized he and his Dad must already be out on the course somewhere or had a later tee time. We decided to press on.

Our day began with a drive along the rambling River Shannon to Tralee. Since the morning was overcast, we could not see her in her true glory. We traversed through hills and farmlands full of grazing cattle and sheep (some bleating to welcome us). We finally came into the tiny market village of Tralee. We wanted to see where the song *The Rose of Tralee* originated. It was an unassuming village with nothing unusual to see or do. It wasn't until the following morning that we learned we had missed the crowning of the "Rose of Sharon" the night before. There were no banners or flags announcing the event; I guess the town wanted to keep the festivities and contest exclusively for the town's residents.

After Tralee we drove on to Killarney, a bigger and busier town. As we passed through we saw the women doing their daily marketing, men drinking their pints of Guinness and mulling over the news of the day or just enjoying being together while the children just enjoyed being on summer holiday.

Driving back to Lahinch we passed through Newcastle, once again filled with their blue and yellow flags, while other villages had raised black and white flags. I wanted to find out what those flags and banners meant.

We returned to the hotel for an early dinner and an authentic Irish coffee in their bar area. Ron hoped he could get in a round of golf in the morning. Not seeing the young couple from the night before, we figured they were having dinner with his parents. Again we overslept.

Ron was too late for golf but he bought some of the club's golf balls for himself and the boys. We stopped by Kenny's before leaving town. We wanted to find out about the flags. Steve said they were for Newcastle's local, not county, team (the Newcastle Magpies) who hoped to win tonight in order to be in the weekend finals. I succumbed and purchased another piece of Waterford, a footed Irish fruit bowl that could only be sold in Ireland. The sale price on both pieces was too good to pass up. We had the master cutter once more engrave it with our names and the date. In years to come, each of the boys will get one. Steve gave Ron some free Irish golf balls as a memento. Ron was as pleased as I was with both Waterford pieces. With our purchases in the boot, we drove through Limerick on our way to Emly. In the fields, cylindrical bundles of harvested hay lay. So strange to see cylinders instead of bundles. So peaceful. God's time of the year!

Almost as we entered County Cork, we arrived in the sleepy village of Emly. No one seemed to inhabit it, although there were women outside conversing with each other; maybe about the day's menu or their children. We found the little church of Emly on a small knoll about half way through the village. Majestically, it stood in the sunshine for all to see and admire. The bricking contained an intricate design and the stained glass windows just gave added depth to its existence.

Before coming to Ireland, an aunt of Ron's had sent some family history and personages to look for. She had told us about a David Hurley, Bishop of Emly in 1547 and a Dermot Hurley, Archbishop of Cashel, a nearby village. We walked through the church cemetery, hoping to find one of their graves or a grave marker with the name Hurley on it. The first of three Hurleys we found was Patrick who died on March 3, 1877 at the age of 76, another named Daniel Hurley with an illegible date, and M. Hurley who "died in August... age 58". The sun-bleached stones looked incredibly old; two had moss growing on them. Ron spoke to a groundskeeper. He told us the church historian who could have given us the information we wanted had died three months earlier. He suggested we go on into town and see Jackie Lonercan, the town victualler (butcher). He might be able to help us.

Wanting to see the inside of the church, we walked in to see if there was any information on either man. One of the stained glass altar windows bore the name of Archbishop Dermot Hurley. Displayed on a side altar was a marble plaque stating that Pope John Paul II had beatified him in 1992. An altar guild member said we should talk to the parish priest as he might be able to give us additional information. We hated bothering him at home but should have.

We drove into the town hoping to meet Jackie Lonercan. His shop was a real trip. No meat visible in his shop window although there were several dozen free range eggs sitting in his meat case. The shop looked closed for the day. We rang the bell and his wife answered the door. After telling her of our query, she went into the back to get her husband. He looked skeptical until we told him who we were and what we wanted, then he lit up like a Christmas tree on Christmas morning. His eyes sparkled and he had a grin that spread from ear to ear. He was like Santa Claus to us – he couldn't do enough for us. He didn't know much about the Hurleys but showed us a booklet he had put together about his own family that contained a listing of two dozen or so Hurley birth records from the eighteen hundreds. He allowed us to take his only copy to the neighboring town of Tipperary so we could photocopy the information. He then suggested we go to the county's Heritage Center where its staff might be able to steer us in the right direction to find out more about Ron's ancestry.

After photocopying the pages, we attempted to find the Center but only succeeded in getting ourselves lost. We stopped a woman on the street who was only too happy to help us with directions. Ron and I just looked at the glow and pleasure she seemed to get from helping us. We said what a wonderful place this was, as its people were so warm and friendly. The Center unfortunately could not help us because I had not been able to make the American-Irish connection needed to do a thorough search. I had followed the American Hurley line back to 1775, when a Samuel Robinson Hurley came to North Carolina from Ireland; no town or county listed. I needed to search further to see if I could find more information about him in order to make the Irish connection.

We returned to Emly and Jackie. We told him how much we appreciated all his help and that he was one of a kind to lend us his only copy of his family heritage so we, total strangers, could get a handle on our family history. Few people were that trustworthy. He was overwhelmed by our admiration. He said he wrote a column for the weekly newspaper and would put Ron's name and address in it hoping someone would be able to help us. He knew of a woman in Tipperary whose name he couldn't remember and hoped she would contact us. We asked if we could take a picture of him as a memento; he smiled and agreed to our request.

After thanking him again, we began our trek to Knocklong, another area inhabited by the Hurleys over the years. Unable to find the castle, we stopped at a petrol station for directions. We found the castle on a hillside just outside of town. We had to drive up a single lane dirt road to get to it. I was afraid we might get stuck and have no way to get back down the hill. We decided to risk it. As we drove up the hillside, householders sitting on their porches wondered why we were going up the road. I guess they were concerned what we planned to do there.

When we were about half way to the castle, the road ended forcing us to park. We walked the rest of the way until we came upon a roaming boar. After jumping a nearby wood fence we felt safe but he just stuck his nose up into the air and moved further down the road in deference to us. What relief!

The only remains of the castle were two eroded perimeter stone walls. Its cemetery was so old that none of the gravestone inscriptions could be read. What a fabulous feeling we got from being in this spot of family history. An additional gift was the unobstructed view we got from being on top of this treeless plot of hillside. We could see for miles around and take in all the little towns beneath us. As we were leaving, we kept an eagle eye out for our wandering boar who was nowhere in sight. Returning to the bottom of the hill, the residents looked relieved as we drove away leaving the castle and cemetery area in tact.

As it was becoming late in the afternoon, we decided to move on to Cork City leaving Cashel and other Hurley family areas for the next day. Cork City was much larger than I had expected. It seemed like a small version of Dublin. We were able to find our hotel without any problem even though it was on a narrow side street. What a treat we were in for. What I didn't realize, this hotel contained only suites. Since we had prepaid for all our accommodations, this was a luxury we hadn't planned on.

Overlooking the canal, our room was rather large with a lounge area along with our bedroom and a full bathroom. Tired, we sat down on the large overstuffed sofa, put up our feet then poured ourselves a glass of wine to celebrate Jackie Lonercan and the information he had so graciously given us.

We had heard the hotel had a fabulous young award-winning chef whose specialties were laid mainly in an area we loved – seafood. He definitely did not disappoint us. The Dover sole was topped with a magnificent shrimp sauce. We even splurged on lemon mousse parfaits to culminate this wonderful meal.

The next morning we ordered breakfast in our room as it was part of our room fee. How decadent we felt. It was great to feel the luxury of it. The sad part, we realized was our holiday was coming to a close and didn't like that. We both loved Ireland and especially its people.

We walked around the city looking for postcards and historical points of interest. The only monument we found in the immediate area was quite ornate by Irish standards; it was a Memorial to the Irish patriots (1798-1867). Continuing on we passed the statue of Father Matthew, the Irish temperance apostle.

What astounded me was finding the building called the English Market. On one of the BBC food shows, *Gourmet Ireland*, Northern Ireland expert chefs and restaurateurs Paul and Jean Rankin toured this market discussing with fishmongers their various fresh fish catches of the day and how they would use them in their program meal. Since I had seen that particular show, I felt like I knew this place which sold everything from freshly baked breads and pastries to freshly butchered meats, to freshly caught fish, to freshly harvested vegetables. I wished Shenfield or Brentwood had a similar market area, but I knew that would never happen in a million years. Each Rankin creates his or her own specialties; Paul's expertise is in the entree area while Jean's is in the desserts. They both have apprenticed under well-known chefs all over Europe as well as the States. A few years ago they bought up a bankrupt restaurant in Belfast, named it Roscoffs, and made it the world-renowned restaurant it is today. Someday I want to have a meal there and meet the Rankins.

After our walk and postcard mailings, we drove to Blarney Castle that stood inside a quaint little village full of buses, tourists, and narrow roads. We walked from the central car park with our camera and video camera in tow, paid our entrance and camera fees, and made our way into the castle. The castle contained the most interesting features of a medieval fortress with its sentry box, dungeon, protected well, courtyard, tower, "murder hold", chapel, great banquet hall, and battlements. We walked up the square tower's winding, well-worn stairwell to the top of its 83 feet. Even with all the huffing and puffing, I was glad we made the steps, as the view from there of the wooded hills of Muskberry, the Baronial House, and of the town below was breathtaking. We learned the Blarney Stone was inside a top battlement wall and not in the courtyard below where we thought. Well, were we surprised.

The procedure for kissing the stone was hair raising but worth the effort and the scare. As the "kisser", in this case, I sat on a stone floor ledge with my back to the outer wall where the stone was imbedded. A guide sat next to me helping me lean back so I could work my hands to pull myself down the rock to the place where I was to kiss the rock. Mind you, this area is open to the outside with only a grate below the stone to catch me if I went too far. Once I kissed the stone I quickly worked myself back up the wall. What exhilaration I felt after completing my task! With that Ron did his own Blarney stone kissing. The person kissing the stone is supposed to be given the gift of gab. Once we finished, we received a ticket to purchase a certificate stating that we had kissed the Blarney stone. We were to frame and display the certificate in our lounge for all to see. Right?? Once on the ground outside the walls we looked up to the stone and couldn't believe how far up we had been. I wouldn't have missed it for the world though.

We drove back to Cork and our room where we each took a hot bath, put our feet up, and enjoyed a glass of chardonnay before dinner.

The seafood casserole and the house salad were outstanding. Yum, Yum. Oh, to have a restaurant like this nearby would be heavenly. The only problem would be it would become routine and not special any more, which would be a shame.

After dinner, hearing the sounds of a synthesizer, we were drawn into the hotel's bar/lounge. We listened to a young man who I would have sworn was an American singing some American oldies but he didn't know any Sinatra or Bennett songs. Growl. Drat. He said he had lived in Cork all his life. After a half hour we left him for the comfort of our bed.

Saturday, our last full day in Ireland, we dressed, breakfasted, and checked out by ten fifteen as we had a lot to do. On our way to Kilkea Castle where we would spend the night, we stopped at the Jameson Heritage Centre. It was one of the founding distilleries for Irish whiskey; the others being Powers, Bushmill, and Middleton. The Jameson Distillery had been founded in the eighteen hundreds. Our guide, Paddy O'Shannessey, started by telling us how, from the distillery's beginning, the farmers brought in and sold their grains to them. He explained the procedures for baking the grains, creating the grist, and purifying the whiskey. The initial and main copper kettle used to purify the whiskey held 32,000 gallons of the liquid. He continued our tour by showing us other machines, vats, and kegs used in those early days.

Jameson continued to use those original processing methods until a few years ago when it opened its new distillery down the road. There, the distillery uses computer technology to create its elixir. The only thing that did not change was the five plus years it takes to age and harvest their finest liquids from their huge kegs. It was a fascinating tour.

Afterwards, Paddy asked for three volunteers to taste and select the best of three different whiskey groupings. Two men and a woman took part. First, they sipped five different Irish whiskeys picking their favorite. Once each favorite was chosen, each contestant was asked to test it against five Scotch whiskies choosing the one they liked best. Finally, they took that choice and put it up against an American as well as their Irish one. The tasters all picked the Powers Irish whiskey not the Jameson, as he had hoped. Some days you win and some days you don't.

Driving out of town, I saw a little news agent shop along the street with the name of R. Hurley painted on its front window. I thought I was just dreaming and had Ron turn around so we could check it out. Ron parked in front and went inside. The R wasn't Ronald but Richard who wasn't in the shop at that time. I got out my well-worked camera and took a picture just for posterity.

Afterwards, we drove on to Cashel. Archbishop Dermot Hurley was born in Emly in 1530, graduated MA in Louvain in 1551, then was ordained a priest. In 1581, Pope Gregory XIII elevated him to Archbishop of Cashel. It was here we learned Dermot had refused to accept Elizabeth I as his queen and for this his feet were burned in oil at Dublin Castle. He continued to refuse to pledge allegiance to her, and on June 20, 1584, he was hanged in College Green, Dublin. He was buried at St. Kevin's, Dublin. Pope John Paul beatified him in 1992.

Driving around we found the Rock of Cashel (castle) but no cemetery. Finally, stopping at a little tourist shop, the shopkeeper gave me directions to the church. He also gave me directions to the church clerk and the church priest; neither was at home. The church was deserted and the cemetery had an electric fence around it to keep their grazing sheep in and everyone else out. I assume people had desecrated or done something to the cemetery so they didn't want anyone in there. Oh, well, maybe on another trip we can get more information.

We drove to the Cashel Heritage Center. When the young lady who worked in family heritage learned we had not made the Irish-American connection, she repeated what we had been told in Tipperary – until we made that connection, she couldn't help us.

Dejected, we drove to Kilkea in the misting rain for our last night in Ireland. Lisa had been able to make it a special night for us as she had booked us into a room in the old part of Kilkea Castle. What a place! As we drove up the long winding road to it, we felt we were returning to the eleven hundreds.

Although the castle was ancient, it had been renovated into this wonderful hotel thirty years ago. The outside buildings were still in use for various farm activities; the grounds were immaculate, with flower and vegetable gardens intermingled into unusual designs. Four years ago, wanting to lure more clients here, the hotel/castle had built an eighteen-hole golf course on the grounds; the course had just opened that spring.

When we checked in, the desk clerk suggested we make dinner reservations as the hotel had a large wedding dinner going on as well as the other guests of the hotel. We chose 8:45 for dinner as that would give us time to find our room and relax before dinner or even take a walk in their gardens.

Our room overlooked the back gardens still full of blooms. We watched the wedding party festivities going on on the flagstone patio beneath our room. What a lovely way to end our holiday. Ron and I discussed changing our ferry time to a later sailing time so we could sleep in and leisurely drive to Rossalare before boarding our ferry for home. Ron called Stena Lines; they changed our tickets without a problem or a penalty.

Before dinner we walked in a slight misting rain through their gardens full of vegetables, roses, zinnias, and wisteria. We talked about our holiday and all we had seen and been able to do. Both of us wanted to return to Ireland and spend much more time searching for Ron's ancestral roots and spending time with the loving Irish people.

After dressing for dinner, we walked from our bedroom down a long winding red carpeted staircase. Being a half hour early for our assigned dinnertime, we walked to the bar for a drink before dinner. I ordered a glass of chardonnay while Ron wanted a pint of Guinness that he had become fond of on our trip here. The bar itself was right out of the middle ages – wood paneled walls filled with family armor, crests, banners, as well as long sabers. On one side of the large room was a cozy fireplace filled with blazing logs. The room was inundated with overstuffed, rust-colored leather chairs surrounded by heavy wood tables. The elongated wood pub bar contained hand carved insignias. From overhanging racks, glassware of all sizes and shapes hung. Behind the bar itself was a delightful bartender full of jovial stories and humor.

While we waited for our dinner call, an older couple came in and sat down at the table across from us. They were driving from their home in Dublin to their children's home, a two hour drive. Being tired they had stopped here for the night as it was halfway between the two homes. I couldn't believe they had only driven an hour and were fatigued enough to stop. They would drive to their son's home the following morning. It never ceased to amaze me how people in Ireland and Britain see an hour or two drive as exhausting while we Americans drive for six or more hours without giving it a thought. We had driven and walked for nine hours before stopping here. Then I thought maybe in thirty years Ron and I might feel the same way. Not a pleasant thought.

A honeymoon couple came in to have a drink. The elderly couple asked them to join them for a drink so they could apologize for their dog frightening the young bride. The older couple had left their huge dog in their automobile, since dogs were persona non-gratas with the castle. The couple didn't think the dog would cause a problem. The young woman must have gotten too close to the car and the dog started barking or growling at her, upsetting her to no end. The young couple accepted their invitation and their apology.

Dinner was fantastic, from the shrimp cocktail to the chateaubriand to the apple tart. We slept soundly although Ron swore the castle ghost had visited us during the night. I thought his imagination must have been working overtime. Ron said he had woken in the middle of the night to what he believed was some kind of smoky apparition walking around our room. It didn't touch anything or come close to us – just walked around.

We took our time getting dressed for breakfast and actually were one of the last breakfast couples. Sitting next to us were some guests from yesterday's wedding who had stayed and partied into the wee hours of the morning. We had heard the bartender and servers finally had to "toss them out" at half past three. After a full day of working the wedding, reception, then these revelers, the wait staff were exhausted. A lady at the table made sure everyone at her table knew she had not had a drink last night and was totally sober before she went to bed. She said she remembered placing her glasses on her nightstand before going to sleep. She said a ghost had visited her and placed her spectacles on the nightstand on the other side of the bed. I thought maybe Ron's imagination wasn't working overtime after all.

About eleven we checked out and made out way to Rossalare for our ferry home. The rain didn't brighten our mood about leaving here. At half past one we boarded our ferry. The ship pulled out of port without a hitch or time problem. At times we experienced a slight chop but the sea was virtually smooth for our ninety-nine minute crossing from Rossalare, Ireland to Fishguard, Wales.

While in my favorite place – the duty-free – a customer asked a cashier if the crossing was always this rough. Standing next to her I said, "This is nothing. You should have been on the crossing from Holyhead to Dun Laoghaire last Sunday night; it was a roller coaster." The steward said to me, "I heard about that one, that ship should never have left the port." I said, "I wish it hadn't, it was awful."

Disembarking the ferry in Fishguard, we noticed road signs posted in Welsh and English so all drivers and backseat drivers would know where to go. Returning home five hours later, we were tired but had many wonderful holiday memories to savor. The truest one was meeting Jackie Lonercan, a truly wonderful man, a real Irish diamond. We hoped to visit him on our next trip there.

47. Christmas Markets

This was the final Christmas we would spend in England. During our four years here, I had heard about the wonderful German Christmas markets held in the little villages as well as towns during November and the first part of December. I hoped Ron could take a few vacation days so we could go.

Well, my prayers were answered. Ron had meetings in Aachen, Cologne, and Berlin the first week in December so I decided to tag along. I suggested taking the car so we could combine business with a little time for us. He agreed.

We left on a Sunday morning, taking the Calais ferry and driving on to Aachen, Germany. We had been there before so I knew my way around this enchanting little town and enjoyed its company. It was about six that night when we checked into our usual hotel on the corner. Since all we had eaten on our drive were the sandwiches and snacks I had put in our cooler, we felt hungry. Our Red Rooster restaurant was still open, so we dropped in for a pizza and coke.

Since Ron had very early meetings the following morning, he said I should sleep in. Upon waking, the sun was out but the temperature was frigid, so I put on my heavy winter trousers, boots, coat, hat, and leather gloves. The stores were just opening when I walked into the town center about two blocks away. I searched the shop windows for unusual Christmas gifts. The only items that interested me were two hurricane glass candleholders, one taller and wider than the other.

I pictured putting a candle in each holder, then potpouri around the candle creating a distinctive look all my own. I decided to investigate the Christmas market stalls before making my decision.

It was a wonderland of wood-front Swiss store-stalls selling anything from hot grog to filled cheese or fruit crepes, to porcelain dolls with handmade dresses, to mantillas, to Christmas ornaments, to chocolates, to crafters' jewelry, to puppets. So many enticing things to buy, but I remembered I still had the Berlin and Cologne markets to visit, so I just browsed. On my way back to the hotel, I spotted a little boutique with a lovely window display of silver wire Christmas tree balls for sale. Continuing my Christmas tradition I started when our boys were born, I have always bought a new Christmas ornament each year for each family member. These unique silver balls would do the trick. I bought a box of six silver ornaments. I had already bought the grandchildren their personalized teddy bear ornaments in London, so these silver balls were for Ron, Nancy, John, Laura and Ron and myself.

After my ornament purchase, I stopped at the candle shop and bought the two holders. I knew they would be gorgeous on our living room table or mantle in our new home in the States.

Ron finished his meetings about noon and we were off to Berlin. The day was now cold and rainy; driving visibility was limited. After arriving in Berlin about nine, we spent another hour looking for our hotel, as it was in the renovation area. Berlin was creating a renaissance for the new millennium, a facelift from the World War II remembrances. Sitting between scaffolding and road hazards was our hotel. It was lovely and quite German in architecture and interior design. The staff was stiff and unyielding; much more so than we had ever encountered before.

We ordered some sandwiches from room service, then went to

bed quickly as Ron had early meetings scheduled. We were so tired and welcomed our duvets enveloping us with their softness and warmth.

Ron was off early and I ate a late breakfast before going out to explore the area. I knew I had to be careful where I walked, as Americans were generally not greeted well here in the heart of the old Nazi and Gestapo city. As usual, I made myself find a main artery. Uter Den Linden radiated with the most magnificent boulevard boutiques and fine clothes stores. I looked at the window prices and said, "There's no need going in there as I can't spend that kind of money." Back to the hotel I went. I found the hotel's travel agency and booked a city tour for the next day. This way I knew I would see Berlin.

Dinner that night was at a family German restaurant with other Comco people who had flown in for meetings. The restaurant served German meats, noodles, sauerkraut, red cabbage, breads, and tankards of good German beers. I felt good, surrounded by some familiar people I knew from the States.

After dinner our group walked two blocks to the Berlin Christmas market that took up a full city block. As we walked around the small Swiss craft stalls, I found the same variety of goods I had seen in Aachen but with more choices, colors, and shapes. Almost too much for my head to take in. After saying goodnight to our companions, Ron and I walked back to our hotel. We got lost but I spotted some familiar places that helped me get my bearings and get us back to our hotel.

The morning presented itself well. The tour bus picked me up at the hotel and whisked me off to their office. As the bus filled with more people, a young girl of about twenty asked if she could sit with me. I said, "certainly." Our guide spoke German, French, English, and Italian so all could understand her.

Beginning our tour, the bus driver drove us past the former

Friedrich-Wilhelm-Universtat, renamed Humboldt Universtat as the Germans wanted to erase the memory of the Prussian kings and the German Reich. We toured the magnificent grey stone Berlin Cathedral that was built between 1893 and 1905. Its size was 117 by 73 meters and sitting over its central structure was a large dome. The Cathedral has served as the court church and the burial grounds of the Hohenzolleren family whose palace was only a few streets away.

Across the way was the Gothic Marienkirche, one of Berlin's oldest churches. Its conception was noted in the 1249 city records. After a fire in 1380, it was rebuilt. Its exterior was unusual with its orange tile roof accentuating its brown brick exterior walls. Its tower was a greenish blue color even up its spire which had a gilded ball and cross on its top. We drove past the German State Opera, built in 1743 during the reign of Frederick the Great. Fire encased it in 1843 and it had to be rebuilt. It was destroyed again in 1945, but this time it was due to Allied bombing. In 1955, the Opera was rebuilt almost identical to the original one. We motored past the Theater des Westens (Theater of the West) which originally opened in 1896, for staged light entertainment. Today, it has become one of the leading German musical theaters.

Later we exited the bus for a picture taking session at the Brandenburg Gate, symbol of the East and West divisions of Germany. On November 9th, 1989, when the Berlin Wall was torn down, Berliners from both sides of the Gate converged here, rejoicing and shedding tears of happiness in sight of the Chariot of Victory to celebrate their newfound freedom. After reboarding the bus, we drove through the areas Berlin was renovating before the Millennium. I wondered if it would be complete by that deadline.

With our tour over, the bus returned to the tour office, not our hotels as I had been told. Our guide was indignant when I told her we were to be let off at our hotels. To which she said, "This is end of trip. You find way home." My young Italian companion and I had no idea how to get back to our hotels. We decided to head for the underground, hoping to find a way back to our hotels, as we realized we didn't have enough money for a taxi, even if we shared one. We asked the subway agent for directions to our respective hotels. He was gracious enough to plot out our subway route. Fortunately both of us were on the same train. We stuck together until she got off at her stop; I held tight to my courage until my turn came three stops later. Once off the subway I took out my map to get my bearings then began to search for my hotel. After a few nervous and lost moments I found it still encased in scaffolding and hazard cones.

Later that afternoon, after collecting my thoughts and my trusty city map, I set out to find the Berlin Wall and Checkpoint Charlie. After walking for about an hour I finally came upon the wall. Even though most of the wall was torn down on November 9, 1989, pieces still remained to remind onlookers of all the suffering, death, and sadness families had incurred because of the separation of that wall. On those wall pieces still standing artists have painted symbols representing the emotions people endured during this period of time.

Checkpoint Charlie filled me with all kinds of emotions thinking of those who had died trying to escape persecution but only found death at the hands of the German guards and their guns. One such person, was Peter Fechter, who was shot, wounded, and left to bleed to death when he tried to escape on August 17, 1962.

I returned to the hotel exhausted but proud of my findings. I ate in the hotel restaurant as Ron had a business dinner. The food was overcooked and mediocre. The wait staff's snippiness didn't help the meal other than irritating me more.

The following morning I walked back to the square where the Marienkirche and the Berlin Cathedral were. I spotted a bank where I could exchange some traveler's checks for Deutsch Marks. After deciding to window shop for some Christmas gifts, I found a store displaying German steins in its front window. I found three steins I wanted, only to find out that she wanted 168 marks cash, no credit cards. I had 200 but that only left me with 32 marks. I wanted the steins for the boys and thought I wouldn't need any cash until we got home, so I bought them. I had her wrap them well and returned to the hotel with my purchases.

Late that morning Ron returned from his completed meetings. After packing the car, I asked him if he wanted to see Checkpoint Charlie. He did. While driving around I took him on a tour of all I had seen, then guided him to Checkpoint Charlie. We got out and walked around the area, even taking time to tour its museum. At one display we saw a green, bullet-riddled car which had contained six people attempting to escape; it sent chills up my spine thinking of what people had to do to escape and live. We learned Checkpoint Charlie would be torn down as part of the German renovation plan to diffuse anti-German sentiment still widely felt in Europe and America.

After saying goodbye to Berlin, we drove on to Cologne, still the capital of the Rhineland, situated on the River Rhine. The Roman influence and heritage remains everywhere from the stone city walls to the ruins of some ancient churches to the city plan of streets. We planned to spend the evening with one of Ron's former supervisors who was overseeing the creation of a new company laboratory at the technological university there. Neil and Claire Johnson had always been wonderful hosts; this time was no exception. We shared stories about the people we had met as well as the places we had visited.

They took us to a nearby beergarten they frequented for their famous German boiled meal and steins of beer. The place was packed. Once Frederick, Neil and Claire's usual waiter, spotted them he quickly took us to one of his tables. He rushed around his tables plying his customers with never ending steins of beer.

After dinner the four of us walked into the city Centrum where the Dom, Cologne's Cathedral, sat center stage. Its initial construction began in 1248, at the instigation of Rainald von Dassel so he could provide a resting place for relics of the Magi he had brought with him from Milan. It took nearly six hundred years to complete this edifice, as there were periods when construction stopped due to lack of interest or money.

Walking up to it, the Dom was engulfed in floodlights to bring out all its magnificent light and dark grey Gothic stones, buttresses, twin lower front spires and a taller center roof spire. Years of pollution had darkened her exterior and she was undergoing a major cleaning. Scaffolding was everywhere and I tried to imagine how striking she would be cleaned and without her scaffolding.

Cologne's Christmas market surrounded the square alongside the Dom. Myriads of twinkling clear minilights sparkled everywhere, lending magic and a specialness to the evening and this event. Clowns, puppeteers, and musicians added mirth as they wove in and out of the throngs of people wandering around in search of trinkets for Christmas. The stalls, like those in Aachen and Berlin, were very Bavarian in paint and decorations. Cologne's stall keepers created their own distinctive designs out of bright primal paints and accentuated them with swirls of ribbon and bows. Part of their plan was to create original stall designs so shoppers could easily identify them if they wanted to return to their shop after milling around other ones.

A crisp breeze blew through the square but no one seemed to care, as people kept warm with the hot grog and filled their stomachs with hot bratwurst sandwiches or huge pretzels with or without mustard. People were willing to buy all kinds of puppets, ornaments, handmade toys, and candies.

As we were finishing our tour of the market, I spotted a traditional German Christmas wood tower with levels of candles, little boys, and topped with a wood spined fan that moved when warmed by the candle heat from below. I wanted it but knew I didn't have enough cash to buy the one I wanted. He didn't take credit cards. I thought maybe next Christmas I might find one in the States for our new home. I contented myself with the steins I had bought in Berlin; that was enough for me.

The next morning after breakfast we said our goodbyes to Neil and Claire then headed for Calais and our ferry home. What a wonderful trip we had. We had done and seen a lot, as well as spending some time with special friends.

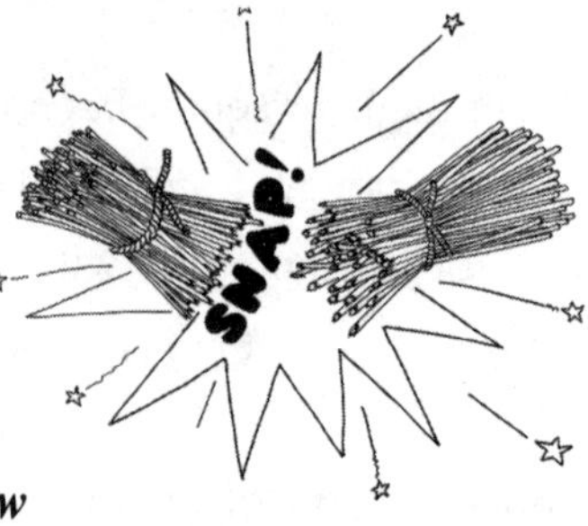

48. The Final Straw

When we came Stateside for our last Christmas on assignment, Ron and I started looking for a new home to return to the following August. Each year we had expected to return, but we never did. This particular Christmas we felt we would be returning home and needed to talk to some builders about housing plans. One of the builders had an excellent reputation and the floor plan I wanted.

We had a problem. The builder wasn't opening up the new housing subdivision until late January. He wouldn't take any deposit until then. Since we would be back in England at that time, John said he would do it for us. The lots were on a first come, first buy basis. He even got up at five in the morning to be first in line as we wanted one of three particular lots. He was able to get the one we wanted.

The builder poured the foundation the first week of April with a completion date of August 27. The timing couldn't be more perfect as we expected to return home the last of August.

Spring was coming and I began smelling the company's air of extension again. I knew the smell like my favorite perfume; it hadn't changed since the two previous extensions. This time the odor was oppressive. Pressure was being brought to bear for us to commit to another year. Ron desperately wanted to stay while I was diametrically opposed. This time I decided I was not breaking down. I was emotionally spent and would take no more. This time I would be heard. If Ron wanted to stay, he could, but I was going home. I had endured enough.

I had done my duty to him and his company.

Ron and I spent a week compiling lists of pros and cons of remaining on assignment and returning Stateside. When we had finished, we sat down one evening in the lounge in front of the fireplace and tried to discuss our lists calmly and rationally.

There was no doubt Ron wanted to stay as he loved his job here. I told him I knew what he had been able to accomplish and what he could yet accomplish. I told him I was emotionally spent and would not take another extension. Our travels were fantastic but the daily routine and boredom of having nothing to do was more than I could handle any more. He said he saw that. I told him he could stay but I was going home. We would commute although that wasn't good for our marriage but I had done all I was going to do for him and this assignment. I had to think about myself now. Emotionally, another year was not in my best interest.

He reported to his boss I was returning home and that he would be also. He was not a happy man. His boss said he could not get his replacement in place until October; Ron would need to stay and train him to do his job. The earliest he could return was December. Ron said he would do that, but no longer. The agreement was made.

49. The City of Gold

The true purpose of this trip was the Isata Conference (a world environmental conference) where Ron had been asked to present two important papers. I tagged along so I could see another part of Italy.

The electricity of anticipation filled the air as I waited for my new encounter with Europe to begin. I had heard Florence was one of the most beautiful cities in all of Europe. I looked forward to its art museums, countryside, as well as its pasta and wonderful bottles of Chianti. Oh, the magical images of Florence I had. It sounded too good to be true so I was going to find out for myself. Was it hype or truth? I would soon know.

After finishing our last minute packing for our trip, Ron and I settled in for a full night's sleep. Before moving here, I would stay up until the wee hours of the morning figuring out what to pack for a trip. Now my packing skills had become impeccable. No more burning the midnight oil trying to figure out what or how much to take. I was spot on.

The morning we left we showered, shaved, dressed, and then had a glass of orange juice and a cup of coffee to fortify us before setting off for Heathrow. At 7:30 AM, motorists had no way of knowing what traffic jams or road works would instantaneously lurk on their way to the airport. The sun shone brightly but the air was cool. Typical of England's springtime! The drive took us along the usual southern part of the M-25.

As we drove along, Ron and I commented on how green the countryside was and how filled it was with new lambs and calves. I felt sorry for the new calves because with the BSE declaration, many herds were being killed off in order to thwart the spread of the ever-growing mad cow disease – meaning some of these calves could or would become orphans in the near future.

Our drive was quick and uneventful. After arriving at Heathrow, we found a place in the business car park and took the Pink Elephant bus to Terminal 1 for check-in. "It's really going to happen!." I thought. With our boarding passes in hand we went through passport control, past duty-free and into the British Airways lounge for another glass of orange juice and a cup of tea. Brian Hanley, a colleague of Ron's, joined us there as he was also going to the conference. The men huddled over their talks then decided to work each other's film carousel during the presentations. About an hour later our flight was noted and we moved to the embarkation area. After our boarding cards and passports were checked for a second time, we were allowed to board our flight.

After pulling away from our gate and waiting for our turn on the runway, our jumbo jet poised itself in readiness to speed down the runway on its way to Pisa. British Airways doesn't fly into Florence as its airport cannot accommodate a jumbo jet like ours. Looking out our window I knew sightseeing along our route would be impossible as the clouds covered everything. Fortunately, Ron and I had both bought new books so we were set for our two-hour flight. Lunch was served - a casserole of pasta, chicken and vegetables, a fresh green salad, and a white mousse tart. Lovely.

As we descended into the Pisa airport, I became a little nervous; taking note of what I thought was their only runway. After landing I realized we had used a much longer second runway. Pulling up to the terminal, I saw a number of old olive camouflaged aircraft. Ron said the Italian Air Force base still functioned with 1950's planes. I guess if the need ever arose, they would be ready. It was like a look back into time.

After disembarking the plane by a metal stairway, the sun and heat hit us like a hot, wet blanket taking our breath away while turning our clothes into wet sheets of cotton. Polizzi ropes cordoned us along the way into their immigration area. After the usual immigration and custom duties, Brian, Ron, and I made our way outside. Turning the corner, we found the railway terminal and our train to Florence. After purchasing our tickets, we tried to make sense of the confusing train timetable as it was all in Italian. We just hoped we would get on the correct train. The train was packed, making the heat inside the coach even more unbearable than outside. Once the train started, a nice breeze cooled us. As we moved out of the station, I noticed old train cars which looked like some the Nazis used to transport the Jews, as well as their German troops and supplies to their destinations. What an eerie feeling – like time revisited, especially since we had just watched *Schindler's List* a few weeks prior. I almost felt like I was reliving that scene. One I really did not want to be a part of.

The countryside was rolling, dry clay. Most people in the Tuscany region were poor farmers – using old methods of plowing, irrigating, and harvesting their meager crops; as they had little or no money to update their equipment. Each house or abode had its own vegetable garden, as well as 2 - 5 rows of grapes in order to make their own wines. Cultivated olive trees would soon be harvested for the olive oil producers.

The dwellings were as poor and meager as the land on which they stood. Some homes barely stood upright. Newly washed clothes flapped in the breeze as they dried on makeshift clotheslines. To avoid the daily hubbub of the city and its noise, wealthy people built luxurious homes along the hillsides among cypress trees and shrubs. The houses' cream or tan stucco exterior walls were topped with clay terracotta tiles. The contrast of colors between the houses and the green foliage surrounding them was outstanding. As I watched from my window, the train passed pristine white village churches with their bell towers or campaniles and terracotta roofs. It must be lovely to hear these ancient church bells summon their parishioners to daily and Sunday masses. The Italian mainstays or lifelines are the church and the family.

About 45 minutes later we stopped at the first of Florence's two train stations. The first didn't seem busy enough to be the correct one so we remained on for the second. Thank goodness, we stayed on. Brian got specific directions to our hotel which was only a 5 plus minute walk away. Pulling our bags behind us, we trudged on to find our "home" for the next few days. Carefully following his directions we arrived at our hotel. Before going to our rooms, we decided to meet in an hour for a walkabout and dinner; this would give each of us time for a shower and a change of clothes, if we wanted.

About six o'clock the three of us met in the lobby and walked to the Arno River, about two blocks away. What a sight. The water was so clean compared to some we had seen. We walked all the way up to the Ponte Vecchio (Bridge Vecchio) where craftsmen in the 13th century came to sell their goods. They soon set up shops on the bridge. When they began dumping their refuse into the river, the government revoked their licenses and cleared the bridge of all shops. In the 16th century, goldsmiths set up shops on the bridge and have been there ever since. Here they create their beautiful 18-carat gold jewelry; their workmanship is the world's finest. During World War II the land areas on both sides of the Ponte were heavily bombed and damaged, but for some unknown reason the bridge was spared.

Florentine architecture is a combination of various styles and times. Romanesque (5th to 13th century) is displayed through its marble banding on exterior walls, rounded arches, Roman columns, massive walls, gables, central portals, and separate campaniles (bell towers). Pointed arches, narrow pillars, high vaults, miniature spires, and gabled niches for statues characterize the 13th–15th century Gothic design while the 15th–16th century Renaissance design is exemplified through its elegant lines, keystone arches, classical Roman cornices over windows giving the feeling of strength and stability. Whereas, the Baroque, 16th–17th century, demonstrates itself through the angular space between the roof and the porticoes, doors, and windows; below some of these spaces are intricate moldings which bring about a delicate balance between curved and straight lines. Everywhere these styles were portrayed, even on the most simple apartment house, government building, or church. What a maze of delights. As I was taking it all in, I knew I wanted more.

Florence is divided into segments – each with its own distinctive flavor and square. We walked up the Via Por Santa Maria with all its pottery, leather, and gold shops. The Piazza Della Signoria contained the Plazzio Vecchio ("Old Palace"), the heart of politics for many centuries. Its bell tower called the townspeople to public meetings (parlamento) or warned the citizenry of impending floods, attacks or even fires. Along its roof hung the coats of arms of reigning Medicis. Two shields denoted the two Medici popes. The square itself was full of statues commemorating major events in Florence's history. Some depicted Florentine heroes while others were mythological in origin – Neptune's Fountain (he was surrounded by water and nymphs), Perseus holding the head of Medusa, the statues of Hercules and Cacus, plus a reproduction of the *Rape of the Sabine Women*. A copy of Michelangelo's

David stood in front of the Plazzio. This statue not only symbolized David's defeat of Goliath but the Republic's victories over its enemies, thus combining political and religious themes. Even today, buildings in this area as well as others still bear the water stain lines of the 1988 flood which devastated Florence's library, art galleries, and many businesses.

While we strolled around the piazza, we saw a cozy little outdoor Italian restaurant. The menu looked varied and well balanced. We sat down, taking in all the ambience of the moment and the passersby. What a wonderful place to be on Sunday evening. Ron and I ordered spaghetti first then I had veal Marsala while Ron had a steak – his first in a long time. Brian followed Ron's lead. The meal, as well as our waiter, was a delight. Needing to walk off some of our calories, Brian suggested looking for the Duomo (cathedral). With our trusty Florence travel book we moved through the pathways until we found the Duomo. I always thought the Dom (cathedral) in Cologne, Germany was the most magnificent but Cologne's Dom didn't hold a candle to this one. I was dazzled by its intricate shades of grey marble work on the outside, its cubicles filled with statues of popes and saints, its massive terracotta dome, and its peeling bell tower telling passersby what hour it was. Its size alone took up the better part of a city block. As I was trying to find the right place to take its picture, Brian said, "No camera could do this justice." I just stood there in awe of its towering effect and its massive expanse. Just in front of the Duomo was a small building called the Baptistery where all baptisms take place: then the newly baptized are carried into the Duomo for their first mass or ceremony. I was anxious for my tours the next day so I could see the interiors of both buildings.

The three of us ambled past Italians eating, drinking, or just talking at sidewalk cafes. We examined all the latest Italian fashion styles, shoes, and jewelry displayed in shop windows. I wanted to take in all of Florence's sights, sounds, and smells. There was so much to see and digest here.

Before we knew it, we had walked back to the Arno River and our hotel. Hot from the heat and tired from all the walking, all the three of us wanted was a shower and a good night's sleep. After showering, Ron opened our two shuttered windows hoping for a gentle breeze to lull us to sleep. On the Continent, especially in Italy, few hotels have air-conditioning. As we dropped off to sleep, we listened to the street noises below: of scurrying scooters and motorcycles taking their riders to their destinations and walking groups of young people talking and laughing together.

We arose early the next day as both Ron and I needed to be at the Conference Center before 8:30 – Ron to check-in for the conference and I for my tours. Since I had not received written confirmation of the wives' tours I had signed up for, I had to find out if I was on the tour lists. Once that was taken care of, Ron left for his meetings and I went to the meeting place for my first tour – *The Latter Years of Michelangelo*. Our guide was a young female Italian artist and art scholar who had studied Michelangelo extensively and talked expertly of him, his works, and Florence.

As our group walked down side streets, she pointed out the various architectural styles and designs on the buildings we passed. Our first stop was at the Museo del'Opera. Numerous Duomo artifacts had been moved here when it became evident thieves had targeted them. The outside of the museum was plain so not to attract attention. As we entered its outer courtyard, the atmosphere changed. Tall, unused marble sculptured crypts stood beside each of the two entrance doors. On either side of the crypts hung angel sculptures.

Upon entering the building we saw, on opposite walls, two white marble sculptured choir lofts – one created by Donatello, the other by Luca della Robbia. Della Robbia depicted happy children playing musical instruments while Dontello, on the opposite wall, displayed a frenzied tribal scene. Both scenes could be appropriate today.

Just outside one of the interior rooms *La Maddalena* (Mary Magdalene) by Donatello took residence. Donatello depicted her as she took onto herself all her sins before being cleansed by her affirmation of Jesus and her new life. The weight and agony she felt before she became new overwhelmed me with feelings for her.

The room behind Mary Magdalene contained sculptures of the apostles: Matthew, Luke, and John. I never found out why there wasn't one of Mark. Additional sculptures within the room included various Florentine dignitaries, Pope Bonfitius VIII, and two unnamed popes. One other sculpture was of Mary sitting with baby Jesus.

Moving into the next room we found Ghiberti's majestic gold carved panels of early Old Testament stories. These panels or plates were made into two door panels and called *The Gate of Paradise*. Our guide told us Ghiberti spent 29 years creating the original doors then spent an additional 24 reproducing them so the originals would be safe from thieves. The copies now hang on the Baptistery's north entrance doors.

From here we moved up the stairwell to the second level. On a pedestal in the stairwell's center was Michelangelo's *The Pieta* (The Peter) – Peter being held by Nicodemus while Mary Magdalene looked on. Many believe Michelangelo placed his own face upon Nicodemus. Critics say an apprentice must have created Mary, as the quality of the work was inferior to the master's. The first room off this stairway contained a copy of Donatello's *St. John* that Michelangelo used to create his famous *Moses*.

Leaving this museum, we walked past the flat (apartment) where Michelangelo lived while in residence here. I got a picture of the plaque but not the residence, as my group walked too fast for me to take an additional picture. What a shame. "Oh, well, maybe next time if I can find it again." We moved quickly, as our guide wanted to get us through The Galleria Della Academia (The Academy of Fine Arts) before other tour groups came. The Galleria, founded in 1563, was the first school to teach the techniques of drawing, painting, and sculpting as well as allowing art students to come and sketch works of the great masters. In various rooms here, I observed three different art classes working.

In another room I noticed a professional woman using her lunch hour to sketch intricate hand portions from one of the paintings. The next room centerpiece contained *The Rape of the Sabine Women* sculpture. The intensity of the emotions, as well as the act itself, was quite powerful. Surrounding rooms displayed Italian Renaissance paintings. The Renaissance gave religious rebirth to all arts. Paintings of that era, usually quite large, portrayed biblical themes and personages. Artists used royal blues and deep pinks in people's clothing while putting golden halos over their heads. Oversized gilded frames made the paintings even more intense and at times overpowering. Fantastic became the word of the day for me.

Back on the ground floor we walked into the main gallery. On either side of its walkway stood four unfinished Michelangelo works: *The Young Slave, The Awakening Slave, The Bearded Slave,* and *Atlas*. We learned that Michelangelo would work on one sculpture until he grew tired of it then moved onto another, but never completed any of the four. Further down the walkway was *The Pieta Di Palestrina*, a different version of Michelangelo's *Pieta*, an expertly carved sculpture of Peter, Nicodemus, and Mary Magdalene.

Across from the *Pieta*, encased in glass, was Michelangelo's *David* in all his glory, youth, vitality, virility, and physique. He was magnificent, the epitome of the body beautiful, a Renaissance characteristic. Michelangelo wanted to show not only David's body but also his concentration, determination, and readiness to take on any task handed to him. Portraying these attributes only intensified David's stance and movement.

Overwhelmed by all the things I had seen, I tried to absorb as much as I could. I knew it would take days, weeks, and maybe months to do it. I photographed as much as I could so I could document and assimilate all the bits and pieces in my journal when I returned first to the hotel then at home. What an enormous undertaking.

Our tour ended here. I had lunch with a Welsh woman I met while waiting for my second tour to start. She thought her husband knew Ron only to find out he was another Ron Hurley who worked for Lucas Industries in the UK. Small world. I met another woman from Ann Arbor, Michigan whose University of Michigan professor husband did know my Ron quite well.

At half past one, I walked back to the Convention Center for my afternoon tour. Our bus drove through the outlying streets and residential areas of Florence while Gina, our guide, told us all about the architecture. A half hour into my tour she asked our driver to go to the top of a nearby hill so we could see the panorama of Florence. It was a steep, winding road that the driver didn't like but the view was magnificent. How picture perfect it was. The intertwining of the green shrubbery and trees, the little white parish churches with their stunning bell towers or spires, and the sun drenched pale yellow and cream homes with terracotta tile roofing just accentuated the fabulous *Duomo* in the center of the picture. It was breathtaking! After a fifteen-minute stop needed for picture taking, cokes or bottles of water, ice cream bars or cones, rolls of film, or trinket purchases, the bus worked its way back down the hillside and to the *Duomo* and the *Baptistery*.

The *Duomo* was as massive as it was impressive; the *Baptistery* was small but equally beautiful. As we neared the cathedral, we learned we had to disembark the bus as no vehicles could enter the Piazza San Giovanni where our buildings were. The *Duomo's* actual name is *Santa Maria del Fiore, St. Mary of the Flower* (Florence being the flower). Dating back to the 4th century, it is Florence's oldest and tallest edifice. It has the capacity to hold 20,000 people. Gina said next year many parishioners and non-parishioners would vie for seats for the services to commemorate its 400th year anniversary since its last major renovation. Its exterior is full of Neo-Gothic marble designs in varying colors of grey and interspersed with terracotta panels to give it more dimension and design contrast. In 1871, Giotto created and added the Campanile (276 feet tall - 20 feet shorter than the dome) he used white, green, and pink Tuscan marble. The overwhelming dome itself, designed by Brunelleschi, is a miracle not only because it was the largest dome of its time but even more amazing, it was built without any scaffolding whatsoever. Visitors can climb the 463 steps to its top. The reward for their determination and effort is the magnificent panorama of Florence as well as its surrounding mountaintop villages such as Sienna. The main altar sits on a dais within an octagonal marble sanctuary area. Beautiful frescos, most notably Vasari's *Last Judgment,* fill the ceiling. Interlocking grey marble squares create the *Duomo's* floors. I marveled at the cathedral's magnificence, majesty, and presence.

Once outside we walked about 35 feet to the *Baptistery*. Its exterior is similar to the *Duomo*. As I approached it, its *Gate of Paradise* doors glistened in the bright sunlight. Each door exhibited a long rectangular gold tabloid containing four inlays placed lengthwise on the tabloid; each inlay told a different biblical story beginning with *Creation*.

Covering the *Baptistery's* interior dome was the *Last Judgment* painted in colorful 13th century mosaics. The font itself takes center stage, as it is the reason for this building.

After viewing the *Baptistery,* our tour ended. Our guide gave us directions to our respective hotels. I stayed in the area for awhile reviewing all I had seen. A bit later I made my way back to our hotel. Ron and Brian hadn't returned so I showered hoping to take off all the clamminess I felt after my hot day of touring.

When the guys returned, they had an invitation from one of Comco's suppliers for dinner. We walked to a small family restaurant where the family plied us with a beautiful antipasto, then mounds of pasta, veal parmigiana, steamed vegetables, homemade Chianti, and fresh fruit. It was a lovely evening. We walked back to our hotel hoping to work off some of the calories we had just eaten. Back in our room we again opened our windows hoping for a cross draft to cool us but the night temperature was still a sweltering 80° plus.

In the morning we awoke, showered, and then met Brian for breakfast at seven o'clock. I stayed around the hotel waiting to meet up with Carol, my friend from Wiesbaden, Germany; she had come with her husband for the conference. Max and Ron had been friends for over 20 years. Max was chairing one of the sessions. Since Carol had been here before, she was to give me her tour of this wonderful city. She knew a lot about art and artists, as Max was an artist in his own right.

At ten o'clock I met Carol at her hotel then we walked to the San Marco Convent where a lengthy line had already formed in front of it.

As we stood outside on the sidewalk, vendors tempted us with prints of Florence, Florentine countryside, and religious sketches. We said no. The Police frequent tourist areas in an attempt to rid them of any unlicensed street vendors and gypsies working the tourists. While standing there, two gypsy women carrying their "babies" (usually large dolls) came down the street ready to beg until the Police quickly escorted them away. The painting vendors used a lookout to alert them of approaching police so they can quickly put their prints into their portfolios and move away before being caught.

After waiting forty-five minutes, we entered the building. Founded in the 13th century by Dominican monks, this convent contains 39 cloistered rooms. In the center floral courtyard people sit on marble benches to admire and assimilate the beautiful frescos known as *The Deposition, The Entombment, The Annunciation,* and *The Mocking of Jesus* which filled the encircling walls. The greatest of the frescoes was Fra Angelico's *The Crucifixion*. In one interior section, the convent stored pieces of old Roman columns made in various designs and materials. Carol loved looking and sketching them.

After spending an hour, we decided to find the cafe where she and Max had lunch the day before. She chose a large salad but I love my pasta and ordered the lasagna. The sauce was different from the usual tomato – it was a creamy béchamel one. I didn't appreciate the change. Later we walked to the Ponte Vecchio where she hoped to find a gold chain as a birthday gift from Max. We talked to the proprietors of a half dozen shops before finding one she liked. I knew Max would be pleased.

About one thirty I realized I had to hurry back to the conference center for my afternoon tour on the early life of Michelangelo. Walking back I realized how hot and tired I was and decided against another three hour walking tour. I slowed my pace and window-shopped instead. Later, I regretted my decision, as I should have learned more about the master.

About half three I returned to the room and had a quick lie down before Ron came back. I hoped to entice him into staying an additional day so he could see Florence. When he returned, I talked to him. He said if he could get our flight changed and an additional night in our room, he would. He was able to accomplish both feats. Yea!!

At half past seven we met Carol and Max for dinner at another wonderful family restaurant. Carol was wearing her new gold chain – Max was beaming with pleasure. The food was great. I loved the antipasto, the pasta, and the veal and fish dishes they served. I tasted Ron's fish to see if it was as good as my veal. It was. I wanted to recreate these dishes at home or at least give them a whirl. I hated saying goodnight and goodbye to them, but they had to return to Germany in the morning.

The moment we woke up the next morning we knew it was going to be another scorcher of a day so we dressed as cool as possible. After breakfast we made our usual run to the Arno River then up to the Ponte Vecchio, our usual starting point. We walked the bridge to view the gold shops with all their necklaces, bracelets, and earrings. Then, I proceeded to take him on my own-guided tour of Florence.

First was the *Duomo*, then the *Galleria* where we took each other's pictures with *David*. We wandered through the rooms full of the beautifully intense Renaissance paintings. Ron couldn't get over the deep blue, pink, and white Renaissance colors along with the gilded frames which he felt gave deeper meaning to the paintings.

Afterward we walked to the *Uffizi* where the Medici family housed many of their Renaissance paintings – a must see on a trip to Florence. The line outside let us know the wait to get inside would be at least an hour. With the sun beating down hard on us, we opted for the *Pitti Palace*. In my estimation, although I hadn't toured the *Uffizi,* I thought the *Pitti Palace* was magnificent. The *Pitti Palace* was built for the banker Luca Pitti but within little more than a hundred years the Medicis took command of it. All the future Florentine rulers resided here.

The *Pitti Palace* contains many of the Medici art treasures. Since there are four distinct sections, a tourist could spend days here and not be able to absorb all that is inside the palace or the outside gardens. The first section we viewed was the Palatine Gallery exhibiting both Renaissance and Baroque paintings. Many paintings were encased in massive gilded frames. Again, we noticed the artist's use of the intense Renaissance colors giving depth of field to their work while attempting to invoke a particular emotional response from its beholder.

The second section encompassed the Palace's state apartments filled with the regality through its use of red velvet walls and furniture, gilded tables, sconces and chandeliers, large Medici family portraits, and white stucco ceilings. We did not have time to venture into the third and fourth sections or the garden areas as we had run out of time. The third section was devoted to the Modern Art Gallery containing paintings from 1784 to 1924, many of them collected by the Dukes of Lorraine. The Gallery of Costume, the fourth area, displayed fashions from the 1750's to the 1920's. In the back of the Palace were the *Boboli Gardens* that I was told would take an entire day to see properly.

We left the Palace happy but our poor bone-tired feet needed to rest for a bit. As we walked back into the city proper, we found a little cafe where we ordered ham and cheese sandwiches and a coke for Ron and mineral water for me. I needed water to revive me. I could not believe how dehydrated we both were. Refreshed, we decided to look for the market area where good Italian leather handbags were sold. If the price was right, I might buy one for myself and maybe one for each of my girls. I had also heard that the silk scarves were spectacular as well. What interested me was the thought of haggling with the market vendors on their merchandise prices. Ron worked with one until the price was just right for the navy and brown bag I wanted.

We returned to our room about five o'clock, had a lie down, then decided to find the outdoor restaurant where we ate our first night. The temperature was still hot but a gentle breeze helped cool our walk into inner Florence. We were early enough (half past seven) to get a table outside. We ate spaghetti, veal marsala, and enjoyed a bottle of Chianti from a nearby winery to celebrate our time here. We didn't have any of their desserts, as we wanted to stop at an ice cream shop Ron had spotted along our way. Finding it, we agonized over which flavor or flavors to choose. Ron ordered a large cone with strawberry and blackberry ice creams. WELL!! You should have seen it. The cone and the ice cream to fill it must have measured about 12 inches. I kid you not – I have the picture to prove it. I got a single scoop of blackberry. It was heavenly! Worth all its calories! Who cares?!? We're on holiday. I said to myself, "I will take it off when I get home."

As this was our last night in this fascinating city, we roamed the streets full of twinkling mini lights, wonderful food, beautiful clothes – too expensive to buy – and tourists. What magic! We got back to our room about midnight and decided to repack in the morning.

After packing and having breakfast, we decided to take one last walk around Florence. Just a leisurely stroll! Ron saw a pair of hand painted plates, one of a Florentine man and the other of his wife. Ron purchased them as our memento of Florence. The shopkeeper wrapped them securely in bubble wrap so they wouldn't break on our flight home.

About eleven we returned to the hotel, checked out, and walked to the train station. We checked the times and learned our train to Pisa didn't leave until 1: 20. Fortunately, we spied a British Airways check-in area at the train station so we investigated. After learning we could check ourselves and our luggage in, we gladly paid the service charge of an English pound for each bag. We wouldn't have to lug our bags onto the train then in the Pisa airport. We were relieved of them until London. Great news!

We made the Pisa airport with 30 minutes to spare. We checked the gate number as our flight had already been noted. Sadly, we boarded our flight; as we were leaving this glorious city. What a wonderful time we had had. Ron's technical papers had been well received and we were able to take time to explore a city we probably would never have visited otherwise.

We got to Heathrow without any problem, got our car, then headed home. As the old saying goes "It's great to holiday, but it's great to get home."

Florence was wonderful and I knew I wanted to return someday!

50. Table Decorations

Three other couples, Kathy and Ted Sanbury, Alice and Mike Walling, and Mary and Mike Martin had invited us to go with them for a concert at Audley End, the old manor home I had taken Marge and Jim to when they visited us two years before. The London Symphony Orchestra was performing there on the Fourth of July. The concert had nothing to do with the idea of the U. S. Fourth of July celebrations but we decided to go and celebrate the day. Mary said she would bring their folding table and chairs and I needed to bring two chairs for us to sit on. She also suggested bringing blankets just in case the temperature dropped that night.

Kathy, a floral designer, said she'd make the table decorations and wondered who could bring some silver candlesticks and serving bowls. I asked, "Why?" Kathy said, "There will be a contest for the best table decorations."

Each couple was to bring an appetizer or casserole to pass for dinner before the concert. Since everyone loved my special meatballs, I said I would bring them and some baguettes in order to make meatball sandwiches. Along with that I would make my special chocolate trifle for the dessert. The others were bringing fried chicken, potato salad, a mandarin spinach salad, cheese and crackers, and some bottles of wine.

When the night came, we packed our car with our food basket filled with goodies, two blankets, and two patio chairs. It took us about thirty minutes to drive to our destination but the trick would be to find our group. About ten minutes later I spotted the American flags, banners, and red, white, and blue streamers Kathy had lined the tablecloth with and knew we had found our group.

The evening was cool, but not cold. We added our provisions to the others along with our silver candlesticks and serving dishes. My trifle bowl overflowed with layers of chocolate cake, Jack Daniels and apricot jam, custard, and whipped cream topped off with chocolate and almond shavings.

As we sat there enjoying our meal, we watched for the judges to come and evaluate our table. We feared the Brits might take offense to our American theme. No one gave us a problem, although some were intrigued enough to ask the reason behind the decorations. When Kathy sensed the judging was over, she gave some of the streamers and flags to one group who expressed an interest in them.

As the sun went down, stage lights illuminated the orchestra for us as well as the sheet music for the musicians. The concert began with bravado when it played one of John Phillip Souza's marches. It became melodious and awe-filled as the orchestra, working together as one group gave even more life and depth to each classic played. By intermission the sun was down and the air had turned quite cold. We wrapped up in our blankets but after another half hour Ron and I excused ourselves and made for home. The next morning I learned the other couples had packed up and left within fifteen minutes of us because it had become too cold for them.

It was a lovely evening to spend with friends and at the same time listen to some great music played by one of the finest orchestras in Europe. More memories for my book of remembrances.

51. Our Final Trip into Europe

Our last encounter with Europe was a trip I never thought we would or could make to the Eastern Bloc. Our trusty Lisa arranged plane reservations for us to Prague, Czech Republic, train reservations to Vienna, Austria two days later, then hydrofoil cruise tickets to Budapest, Hungary two days later, then our return flight to London.

Our adventure began when our alarm clock awakened us at half past six. We showered, drank a glass of orange juice for energy, and then jumped into our little blue Escort for our trip to Heathrow's Terminal 1. The drive was slow as we were traveling with the London commuters – our usual sixty-minute trip extended into two hours due to clumps of traffic stoppages.

After arriving at Heathrow at half past nine, we parked the car and pressed on to the spot for the Pink Elephant transfer van to our terminal. Checking in with British Airways, we learned Lisa had not booked us non-smoking seats. I had forgotten to remind Lisa to book non-smoking seats; I assumed she would remember and she hadn't.

After a bit of haggling and the use of Ron's silver British Airways card, we were given two adjoining non-smoking seats. I wished we could have been bumped up into business but I couldn't expect such a coup. We attempted to get some clarification on the proposed British Airways pilots' strike that was to begin the day we were to fly home. No such luck. Although we realized we could be stranded in Budapest, we made the decision to take the chance and go, as we really had been looking forward to this trip. Their best suggestion was to wait it out; the strike wasn't a sure thing and a settlement could come at any time, even before our return date. Ron was my main concern, as he had to be at a three-day meeting the day after our return. We'd just have to wait and see.

At 10:45, we boarded our flight. With the doors locked, emergency information given, runway taxi complete, and a final check of the engines' energy levels, we raced down the runway toward our liftoff. Prague here we come. I felt a bit nervous going into Eastern Europe. After reading all those spy stories and seeing James Bond battle the evils there, I didn't want to be the next tourist taken hostage by some dangerous person. I decided to put those thoughts on the back burner and remember that those things only happen in movies and books. Right?!?!

After a chicken pasta salad and two hours in the air, the captain told us we were arriving in Prague. The gentleman seated next to Ron recognized Helen Sukorav, the Wimbledon Tennis Women's double's match winner. She was discussing, with the business class stewardess, how to quickly exit the plane so not to attract attention to herself. The stewardess whisked her off so quickly and invisibly that no one other than the stewardess and the three of us even knew she had been on this flight.

Before deplaning, I noticed security forces surrounding the plane with their M-16 rifles so no one could exit the plane without going through immigration and customs. We walked down the metal stair ramp and into their awaiting busses. After standing in line for about 25 minutes to have our passports examined, accepted, and stamped, we retrieved our suitcase. Before leaving the airport we exchanged some money then grabbed a taxi to our hotel, the Maxmillian, about 15 minutes away.

For centuries Prague has been the crossroad for European trade and travel. As we drove through it, we saw the two flavors of Prague: the palaces of old and the modern buildings of today. At hotel reception we used our first hotel voucher then checked our room. It contained twin beds, a desk and chair, an entertainment center filled with a television and its own toilet facilities. Our window overlooked the mid-fourteenth century Gothic Church of St. Castillus whose exterior was a yellow-brown color with blackened spires.

After resting for an hour, we took our traditional search of the area to see what it held for us. Our hotel was located on the edge of the Old Town area. Prague encompasses four distinct city districts – the Castle District, the Lesser Quarter, the Jewish Quarter, and the Old Town.

From our hotel we walked through a maze of souvenir shops, outdoor cafes, and restaurants on the little side streets leading into Old Town Square. Historians first spoke of the Staromestske (the Old Town Square) in 1091, with houses and churches soon surrounding it. In 1338, the townspeople erected the Town Hall giving this area even more prominence and importance.

As we entered the Staromestske itself, two large churches greeted us along with numerous cream, pale yellow, light grey buildings with various shades of blue, brown, tan, and white accent shutters glowing in the setting sun. The buildings displayed not only interesting colors but also varied architectural styles including Baroque, Rococo, Renaissance, and Gothic; the influences of Dutch and German architects were also evident here. It was a wonderland of contrasts.

The further we moved into the square, the more we saw and were intrigued by. In the center of the square stood the Monument to Jan Hus – the symbol of integrity. Initially a Czech religious reformer and hero, he later was declared a heretic and burned at the stake. Other statues of men who played significant roles in the triumphs and failures in the republic took a lesser stage to Jan Hus.

On the square's northeast corner rose the impressive baroque church of St. Nicholas. No one could miss its glory – its white exterior walls contrasted its gilded accents, its intricately framed windows, and its lofty ornate and open spires topped with what I like to call gilded Hershey kisses, an Eastern Orthodox phenomenon. The dome's interior contained frescos of St. Nicholas and St. Benedict. The history of this church began in the twelfth century when it became Prague's parish church, then the Benedictines took it over and used it for their monastery. During war times, it became a garrison church for the Czech troops. Today, it is once again a parish church, although during the summer, it is also used as a concert hall.

Leaving the church and moving back into the square proper, we came upon an open market area similar to the German Christmas markets where vendors sold everything from hand puppets and wood toys to freshly baked huge wafer thin cookies to medieval jousting helmets just like those of King Arthur and his Crusaders. While perusing the vendors' wares, we heard St. Nicholas' mighty bell tower chime five o'clock.

Originally, the Town Hall was built as a private home for Volfin of Kamen who later added its bell tower in 1364. Tourists can climb its steps to the open gallery where a wonderful panorama of Prague and the surrounding area awaits those who make the trek.

Below the tower's bell a large clock with Arabian numerals and golden hour and minute hands was attached to the exterior brick wall. Affixed underneath this clock was the most intricate and unique astronomical clock. The clock incorporated two different timepieces each telling time by a different method. The larger clock's center represented the earth with time being told relative to the position of the sun and moon revolving around it. The smaller clock told time relative to the zodiac elements which were important in sixteenth century Prague. Just above these clocks was another focal point. As the tower bell struck the hours, figures of the Apostles revolved around the outside of the tower's doors just as a glockenspiel does. On the nearby wall, the images of Death, Vanity, and Greed were placed to remind people of their significance in their lives. In Death's left hand he supported an hourglass while his right held the cord to the death bell. When the tower bell rings, Death pulls his own bell reminding us to think of the time we have left before the cock crows. Below him Vanity posed before a mirror to admire himself while Greed was depicted as a Jewish money collector.

The adjoining building to the left held the entrance to the Town Hall. Over this entrance a hand carved plaque recorded the Old Town coat of arms and its inscription: *Prague: The Head of the Kingdom* (adopted in 1784).

In the open area in front of the Town Hall street vendors played with bright colored spinning tops hoping to entice children or their parents to purchase one of the little toys. Sitting under umbrellas at outside cafes, people enjoyed a glass of Pivi (beer) or a slice of apple strudel and cup of coffee or just a cappuccino itself. What a pleasant way to sit and rest, talk with friends or family, or just people watch. It was a magical time and place to be.

We ventured a little further into some side streets to window shop. The hand-blown Bohemian crystal was fabulous. Glassblowers created various intricate colors and designs into plates, vases, or bowls. Other traditional pieces included hand-painted clay figures depicting peasants doing their daily chores; whether at work or in the home.

Once we realized we were hungry, we started back through the town square to our hotel. Along the way and to our surprise we spotted five Chinese Mongols dressed in their colorful native costumes studying the astronomical clock. Two local gendarmes escorted them so they wouldn't be interfered with. Because I didn't want to forget them and their costumes, I snuck a couple candid pictures.

On our way back to our hotel, a couple of violinists serenaded us with classical music. I thought I would see this in Vienna, not here. We passed Our Lady of Tyn Church, founded in 1365; which later became part of the Bohemian reform movement. Even in the dimming sunlight its Gothic exterior glistened in its magnificence. On its north entrance scenes of Christ's passion were painted and above them was the gilded statue of the Virgin Mary. Continuing on, we felt good about all we had seen and done.

About 6:15 we dropped off our cameras in our room and headed for Chez Marcel for dinner. Earlier in the afternoon an American hotel guest had recommended it to us. He told us it was only a few doors down the street; their food was good and prices were reasonable. Chez Marcel was a combination of an open-air cafe, wine bar, and French restaurant. The waiter/maitre'd took us to a table near the bar. After giving us menus, he explained he couldn't take our dinner order until seven o'clock, the usual time in Europe but we could order a drink from the bar while we waited. He suggested we try some of the Czech beer, Pivi. We took him up on his offer.

While sitting there, we saw other people coming in waiting for tables while other couples or groups sat outside in the late afternoon breeze drinking their glasses of Pivi or wine, talking or laughing about some funny experience they had had or remembered. We sat reflecting on all we had seen and done since leaving London just hours before.

As the clock stroked seven, our waiter, the sole waiter in the establishment, returned to take our steak and frites (fries) order. He was kept quite busy trying to please all his customers at the various tables inside. Our dinner was superb. The steaks topped with a wine and cream sauce were thick, moist, and just pink enough to tickle our palate while the frites were just that and no more. To our surprise our total bill was only £12 ($18). We bid our waiter good night and left.

We strolled arm in arm back to our hotel. Once in our room we practically fell into bed – tired but happy. Twelve hours earlier we were in London and now we were in Prague – a fabulously magical and romantic city of the past.

What we didn't know when we awoke the next day was that this day would hold an unusual, frightening experience for us. After checking CNN for updates on the impending British Air strike, we learned that no resolution was in the works. I peeked out our window to see what sort of day we could expect. The cool breeze coming in our windows told us it would be a cool day. My running suit would do just fine while Ron would need his windbreaker. From our window I watched the city come alive with jackhammer sounds emanating from the sidewalk outside our hotel to cars taking their passengers to work.

By 7:45 we were in the hotel's breakfast cafe indulging in orange juice, scrambled eggs, hard rolls, and cups of coffee. At 9:20 we were picked up outside our hotel by a Cityrama van that would take us to their tour bus depot. Boarding the bus, our tour tickets were taken; later a head count was taken to see if the numbers matched. With that done, our guide introduced herself as Linca. After accomplishing all that, our bus started toward its first site. While pointing out the places of interest along the way, she told us Prague's existence dated back to the ninth century. Not until the fourteenth century and the influence of Charles IV did its urban development begin to flourish. The Charles Bridge, named in his honor, is a pedestrian bridge allowing commuters to cross the Vltava River. Statues of saints and historical persons adorn each side of the bridge.

Over the centuries Prague has stood majestically against marauders, sieges, and battles. For some reason while World War II bombings took place in central European cities, this city was left untouched. The effect of the War left Prague's rich architectural heritage intact. Today, not only do tourists flock to see its distinctive images, but also artists, photographers, and architectural students come to study and sketch its edifices. Many of Prague's buildings exhibit German and Dutch influences in their Baroque spires, Gothic arcades, Renaissance windows, Rococo angels, as well as the nouveau art designs which Europeans do not accept.

Continuing our drive along the Vltava River, I understood why Prague was called "the city of a hundred spires". Many churches had spires jutting out of them for all the world to see and admire. We passed cubistic buildings where sculptured atlas men held up window shelves beneath crystal window inserts. Along the way we saw *The Palace of Culture* used for concerts and other cultural purposes. Having mythological and historical significance for the Czech people is *Vysehrad Park* (a city stronghold) which was chosen in 1870 to be the national cemetery. Linca also said the Czech Republic fell apart three years ago but today its population numbers approximately 10 million Moravians, Silesians, and Slovaks.

We passed St. Ignatius Church founded by Jesuits. Next came the statue of St. Wenceslas, the ninth century patron and Bohemian duke whose brother killed him. A little further on we drove by the old Wilson train station named after one of our own presidents.

The Prague Castle is a mighty fortress overlooking the Vltava River and a number of magnificent ambassadorial homes surround it. Unnecessary cars and tour busses are forbidden into this area. After being dropped off five blocks from the castle, our group walked through the cobbled streets to it. Just before the castle itself we stopped for a moment to view the exterior of the impressive *Shrine of Loretto* with its soaring clock tower. Its carillon of twenty-seven bells plays an hourly hymn. The story behind this shrine reports that in 1626 angels from the *Loretto Shrine* in Italy carried a representation of the Nazarene home where the Virgin Mary was born. The Bohemians built a replica of the home and placed it in this shrine hoping to use it to rally the country's peasants to the Counter-Reformation. In the eighteenth century, 120 sculpted angels lavishly decorated the interior of this small shrine. Its treasury room contains jeweled miters and monstrances (radiating crosses); one monstrance in particular, dating to 1699, is encrusted with thousands of diamonds and precious stones. Linca said we would visit the interior of this shrine on our way back to the bus.

Walking into Hradcany Square which led to the castle, we passed by the castle guards' barracks. As our group approached the castle, we were serenaded by a group of excellent Czech musicians playing anything from classical music to American jazz. To the square's west side was the Tuscan Palace while on the right was the Renaissance styled Martinic Palace.

Finally, we came to Matthias Gate, the black wrought iron fence with double gates, which begins the first of three courtyards. All along the fence sections were stone columns topped with massive mythological statues. Instilled in the center iron fence section was the gilded family coat of arms giving onlookers a sense of royalty and regality.

Moving on we came into the second of three courtyards. In this area were *The Church of the Holy Rood, the Czech President's Office,* the seventeenth century Baroque *Archiepiscopal Palace* (open to the public only one day a year – Maundy Thursday), *The National Gallery* (formerly the Sternberg Palace), and the *Scwarzenberg Palace* (now the Military History Museum covering five centuries of military history). This courtyard opens into the third courtyard containing the *St. Vitas Cathedral,* the *Royal Palace, St George's Convent, Labkowicz Palace,* the *Dalibor Tower* (named for its first prisoner inmate), and the *White Tower.*

In 1344, Charles IV commissioned Matthew of Arras (France) to design and build this massive edifice known as *St. Vitas Cathedral*. After Matthew's death Swabian Peter Parler accepted the commission to complete but it wasn't completed until the late nineteenth or early twentieth century.

In the heavy west entrance doors carved metal panels illustrated many different themes. Once inside the church dimensions overwhelmed me as did its vaulted ceilings. Fanned wood ribbing supported the Gothic arches of the Golden Portal which until the eighteen hundreds was the main cathedral entrance; today it is only used for special occasions. Over the portal was the mosaic portrait of the *Last Judgment*. Many precious stones decorated the tomb of St Wenceslas, secluded in a small side alcove. It took Ron and me forever to maneuver our way through the throngs of other groups to see this room.

In the meantime, Linca kept her pace up without knowing part of her group was left behind (two Italian couples, a single woman, and us). The seven of us attempted to find her throughout the church but to no success. While searching we viewed a number of side altars each with its own Renaissance painting over them. At one point I happened to look up and saw their Rose window, designed in 1925 by Frantisik Kysela, and depicted scenes of creation. The deep colors of the glass and the intricate designs overpowered the viewer. The church also had its own repository for crown jewels.

Outside I noticed the twin Gothic spires and the Renaissance bell tower with its Baroque ornamentation. On the roof corners stood gargoyles; their open mouths disguising their real intent to be the church's rainspouts.

After walking back to where our bus was to pick us up, Ron and I noticed the bus was nowhere in sight. It had left without us or the other five. We returned with the other five people to the cathedral but could not find Linca anywhere. Remembering a #22 bus stopped at the bus area, we hoped it would take us back into town. Ron purchased 2 tram tickets (75 cents each) and off we went. Once on the tram we realized in our frenzy to find Linca and being left we had not taken the time to visit the *Loretto* shrine that we had wanted to visit. Oh well, it would give us something to see on our next visit here. Hopefully, we would have another trip here some day.

As our bus neared the city, we realized that we didn't know where to get off. By luck a young American girl sat next to Ron. We learned she took creative writing classes here at the Charles University. I was dumfounded, as there are so many excellent universities in the States. My unasked question was why did she choose to come here. I didn't ask because she might think I was impertinent. She told us where to get off the bus and how to get back into the Centrum (center of Prague).

By now Ron was hungry and hoping to find the golden arches. I couldn't believe he thought there would be such a thing in an Eastern Bloc country. When we found the Margaret Bridge, we knew the Charles Bridge was near as it ran parallel to the Margaret Bridge. After another ten minutes, we came upon the Charles Bridge stretching for all its worth across Vltava River. The sandstone block bridge was 1706 feet long. The story says that the cementing mortar for her was mixed with eggs to give it strength. Who knows if that is true or not?

A tower entrance stood at each end of the bridge, just like Heidelberg. Moving through the pedestrian entrance we started our trek across the bridge to Prague's Lesser Quarter. As we crossed, we noticed the statues of saints and other biblical characters, replicates of Bernini's sculptures in Rome's Ponte San Angelo, were placed evenly along the bridge. Two major statues depicted the seventeenth century recreation of the Crucifixion and the reproduction of the Pieta. Along the walkway vendors sought customers for their crafts: artists selling and commissioning paintings, sketches, and photographs, and jewelry makers selling earrings and necklaces of wire, stones, and clay pieces. We rejected them all. After our years of traveling we knew tourist trinkets from better merchandise.

Once across the bridge, Ron spied his friend the double arches. We gravitated inside along with many other tourists for Ron's quarter pounder with cheese and my fish filet along with fries and cokes. We didn't know how famished we were until we began eating. It was now three o'clock.

After lunch, we toured the shops in this district for a while then decided to find our way back to the hotel. Following our trusty little map we made the trek in about 30 minutes without incident.

Ron lodged a complaint with the manager of Cityrama about Linca leaving us but he was indifferent, saying that they lose a few each tour. Ron said seven out of twenty-five was a rather large percentage. He said this tour had forty and left the discussion there with a promise to call after talking to Linca. Sadly, we received no call. He had our money and that's all he cared about! What a shame. With that kind of attitude I was concerned about the treatment we would receive on the three other Cityrama tours we had booked – two in Vienna and one in Budapest. Hopefully they wouldn't have the same cavalier attitude. We decided to be real careful if that was their attitude.

We rested for about an hour then decided to go into the Old Town for one last tour around. Again, the sun shone brightly. The tourists were out in force as were the street vendors promoting their wares. We decided to venture down some side streets to look for our remembrance of Prague. We found everything from authentic Czech costumes to their famous hand-painted porcelain glazed eggs of all sizes to the beautiful Bohemian crystal. A medium sized egg displaying a Prague landscape caught my eye but the price was out of our shopping budget so we continued meandering around but found nothing that took our fancy.

An hour later we found we had made a full outside circle tour of the square. Ron suggested having a cappuccino at one of the sidewalk cafes in front of the town clock. Sitting there we just relaxed and enjoyed our cappuccino and people watching. At times we try to match people up as couples or families then attempt to figure out where they came from and what kind of life story they had lived. An interesting and enjoyable occupation when relaxing and enjoying people.

An hour later we left to go to our "favorite" restaurant for dinner. When we arrived at Chez Marcel, it had only one table open and we took it. We ordered the steak dinner again knowing it would be good and inexpensive. We wanted to conserve as much money as possible after hearing how terribly expensive Vienna was and we had three days there. Walking back to the hotel we decided to repack so we wouldn't have to do it in the morning.

The following morning we were up early, showered, and had breakfast by 8 AM. Lots to do before our taxi would pick us up at 11:30. Again hearing nothing about the proposed British Airways strike, we walked to their office in Old Town. The girl gave us the company line that an agreement was possible. We needed to stay tuned to the radio or television for additional news. She didn't know any more than we did. She wrote down the British Airway's Budapest address and telephone numbers so we could keep in touch with them. We thanked her and off we went.

Since we had not purchased our Prague memento, we thought to take one last look around and decided if we didn't find any we liked, we would leave without one. In one shop window I saw a beautiful crystal decanter, about a third the price of the egg I had wanted. The squatted decanter was created out of various bright Bohemian glass stripes encircling it vertically. It was exquisite. We decided it would be our memento. The only problem was transporting it. Oh well, I wanted it so I couldn't grouch about having to carry it the rest of our trip. It was a treasure.

At eleven we returned to the hotel, checked out, and hopped into our awaiting taxi for the train station. Although our train didn't leave until 1:39, we needed to confirm our seat assignments. We had been told there might be long lines; many travelers (usually students) wait until the last minute to purchase their tickets. It took us only 30 minutes to confirm our seats in about a fourth the time we had planned on. I regretted having come so soon as we could have spent an additional hour in Old Town, our favorite place, but I knew it was best to have our seats locked in.

Walking into the station's waiting room we found a cement bench where we could sit and watch all the goings on. At one point an old, disheveled homeless man crawled up on the large square cement table in front of us and fell asleep. A little later Police roused him then warned him not to be there when they returned. He moseyed on his way still looking tired and nondescript. A half hour later we realized we were surrounded by groups of Japanese students touring Europe. It amazed Ron and me how young people and students travel all over Europe without a single fear. The Japanese are noted for taking pictures of everything in sight and this was no exception. No arthritis in their camera trigger fingers.

About 1:10 we began our walk to Platform #2. After going through the terminal and climbing two flights of stairs we reached the upstairs outside platform. The tracks and trains were old and well used. Although there were no Nazis, guns, Gestapo, or supply trains, I had another flashback to the days of Schindler and his Jews.

At 1:45 our train arrived. Our first priority required us to find car 262. It was the last car on the train. The next assignment was to find our compartment and seat numbers 59 and 60. Each compartment contained six seats. What luck – we had window seats until we found a businessman sitting in Ron's seat and a Japanese student in mine. We checked our tickets making sure we were in the right compartment. Once that was established, we showed them our tickets and they moved to their seats in the compartment. The train pulled out of the station around 2:00. Fifteen minutes later the conductor asked to see and stamp our tickets. I watched as our train took us through some beautiful countryside between Prague and Vienna, the former imperial capital of the Austro-Hungarian Empire and said to be one of the most cultured cities in all of Europe. Our six hour train trip allowed us time to rest up before our three day stay in Vienna – home to Beethoven, Mozart, Haydn, and Schubert, along with the famed Boys Choir and the Lippanzer stallions.

An hour into our trip we realized we were hungry and headed for their dining car for lunch. I pictured us eating on the Orient Express like I had seen in films. We started with a lovely garden salad followed by a chicken breast and steamed vegetables. No dessert, as we wanted to wait for some delicious Viennese desserts we had read about. We returned to our car and read for a while.

At our seventh stop we noticed uniformed and armed border guards boarding our train. At first I was concerned about why they were coming aboard. After looking at the train map I realized at the next stop we would enter Austria and our passports would need to be checked before we could enter their country. Within moments one guard entered our compartment requesting our passports. He looked at them, smiled, and then returned them to us.

About 8 o'clock we arrived in Vienna, went through the usual entering procedures then walked down a long flight of stairs where we exchanged some money into Austrian shillings for our taxi to the Hotel Tigra, a completely remodeled, modern hotel just minutes off the Stephansdom Quarter.

After checking into our room, we asked reception where we could get something light to eat. The young woman recommended a little restaurant around the corner and two streets over where we ordered two bowls of freshly made chicken and vegetable soup which filled us with warmth and nourishment.

As we strolled back to the hotel in the moonlight, we watched the horse drawn carriages taking couples through the streets, restaurants filled with customers, and people walking everywhere. Back in the room we watched a bit of CNN, the only English speaking channel available, then we turned in for some needed sleep.

Morning again and we were up at 7:45, breakfast at 8:15, and ready for the Cityrama van to pick us up at 9 AM. We resolved to keep up with our guide no matter what. We were not going to be left behind again. Already on the van was a couple from Phoenix, Arizona, who had come to get away from their abominable heat but were freezing here in the low 70-degree temperatures. They had bought some sweat shirts just to keep warm. They had two daughters – one was on holiday in the Lake District of Scotland while the other remained at home. The older one had been to Prague with her school band several years before and had told her parents Prague was the best city in Europe. Prague was their next stop. We told them Prague was definitely a #10 in our book.

Our group arrived at the large tour-assembling place. We gave our tickets to our guide then boarded our bus. She introduced herself as Kathi and her driver was Freddie. She gave us a tour itinerary which included a pass-by of *Charles Square*, the *Ringstrasse* (Ring Road), a 30 minute stop at *Belvedere Palace*, a 20 minute or so stop at *Schonbrunn Palace*, and other important sights to see along the way.

The *State Opera House*, the most famous in all of Europe, had large front columns, light creamy grey marble exterior walls, and the roof edges filled with statues of composers and musicians. The Vienna Opera season ran from September to June; during July and August its musicians competed in the Salisburg Festival and Competition. During the season a concert is held every evening.

We drove past the Museums of Fine Arts and National History, The Imperial Palace, the Parliament with the *Goddess of Wisdom* statue standing in front of it, the People's Garden, the City Hall (now home to film festivals and classical concerts throughout the year), the University of Vienna, and the Wattif Church, created in the historist style (a mix of Gothic, Baroque, Renaissance styles), the River Danube canal (constructed to regulate the river's water levels), the Ministry of War, and the City Garden which contained the golden Strauss statue and monument.

Before arriving at Belvedere Palace, Kathi gave us some background information. The Habsburgs had been so pleased with their brilliant commander, Prince Eugene of Savoy, and his battle successes against the Turks that they had paid him handsomely. He used a small portion of this money to have Johann Lukas von Hildebrant design and build this palace on a sloping knoll. Interestingly enough he wanted to have two separate residences or palaces on the same property. The palace at the bottom of the knoll the Prince used for his residence while the one at the top of the knoll was used primarily for entertaining foreign and domestic dignitaries as well as to showcase his vast array of art treasures. Halfway between the two palaces grew a magnificent garden area full of well-manicured flowers, shrubs, and short hedges that defined the theme of each season.

With his death and the end of the Habsburg dynasty these palaces fell under the auspices of the Austrian government. The government turned the upper palace into a museum for nineteenth and twentieth century paintings while the lower palace was filled with Baroque and Renaissance paintings. To pay for the upkeep of these palaces, the government instituted an admission charge.

The upper palace's roof was adorned with a number of copper cupolas or Turkish tents to signify the number of victories he had over the Turks. The foreign coats of arms over the top floor windows signified specific battles he won. Ron and I had just enough time to peruse the lobby of the upper museum. The lobby' s walls were cream marble while black and cream marble tiles adorned the floor and cream marble steps created a long flowing staircase. The decorators placed a long cranberry runner over the staircase steps to add contrast and elegance to the whole area. Quite impressive!

Looking at our watches we realized the time had come to reboard our bus so we hurried down the long driveway. We looked back for one last look at the splendor we had just seen. With everyone accounted for, our driver moved on to our next stop – the Schonbrunn Palace – the summer residence of the Imperial Family. Translated, Schonbrunn means beautiful mountain. This palace was small in comparison to those of the ruling Habsburgs since they were the only ones allowed to have the most impressive palaces – the only exception to this was the Belvedere.

Schonbrunn contains 1141 rooms and a magnificent back garden. Kathi told us there were two tours of the palace and we needed to make a decision which one. We could either view the gardens or the house. Even if only 20 rooms were open to the public, we wanted to see them. The gardens didn't interest us. Family portraits decorated each room; one important one contained Maria Theresa and her 16 children (Marie Antoinette being one of them). Each room exhibited Rococo and Baroque furniture – some replicas were so good even experts couldn't tell them from the genuine pieces. Religious themes and victorious leaders frescos lined many of the ceilings. Most rooms displayed red velvet furniture inlaid with gilded arms and legs. Monstrous, overwhelming Austrian crystal chandeliers graced many of the rooms. The house tour pleased us and we were glad we chose it.

With everyone accounted for, our bus made its way back to the Opera House where our tour ended. Since it was closed to the public at the time, we attempted to peek through its windows to see its interior but couldn't for the darkening curtains. Lunch break. We decided to make our way to St. Stephen's Cathedral. Along the way we met some wigged musicians, Beethoven and Mozart look-alikes, hoping to sell us tickets for that evening's performance. The price of the Mozart concert was 490 Austrian shillings ($90) apiece. Although we would have loved to go, the price was much too expensive for our tastes.

We kept walking until we saw the impressive gothic St. Stephen's Cathedral. Most of it was under scaffolding due to the cleaning and sandblasting going on to rid it of the ages of pollution. A real shame, as we would have loved to see its entirety. The interior was a joy to see. Filled with white walls accentuating its wood paneling, vaulted ceilings, numerous side altars with Renaissance paintings over them, and enormous crystal chandeliers, it was a wonder to behold. Over its main altar was a beautiful gilded cross of Jesus. Since it was confession time, the center nave portion was closed.

As we came out, we noticed the sky had really clouded over. Almost at the same moment it began to rain forcing us to seek cover in of all places, you guessed it – a golden arches shop. Ron had looked forward to his quarter pounder with cheese but when he bit into it he tasted mayonnaise breaking his taste and appetite for it.

We couldn't believe how expensive Vienna was and had to exchange some more money. We continued our own tour for the next three hours – window-shopping, watching tourists, and just taking in all the sights and sounds of violinists and other musicians. On our walk back to the hotel, we found in the middle of one major arcade area, a very ornate white marble memorial to the Trinity (Father, Son, and Holy Spirit). It was lovely and received much attention by passers-by.

Knowing restaurant prices were high but not wanting another sandwich for dinner, we asked the hotel for a restaurant recommendation. The lady told us of a good restaurant serving Austrian food just 3 blocks away. We found it without any problem. Walking in we saw its distinct

German flare with timbered ceilings, white walls with wood paneling, and long wood tables and chairs. The waiter took us into a back room where three of the six tables were already filled. At one table three couples sat celebrating something. One couple had brought their year old son with them. He certainly reminded both of us of Christopher in looks; he was so good all evening, even fell asleep in his car seat before they left. Our waiter recommended the traditional Austrian boiled beef, Viennese potato rolls, baby carrots, brown sauce, mayonnaise, and horseradish sauce. For dessert we splurged on strudels with ice cream – Ron's was apple while mine was apricot. Since our waiter had made us feel so welcome, we decided we would return the following evening. The price of dinner there was reasonable considering other establishments. Feeling full and content, we knew we needed to walk off some strudel calories so we walked back into Stephansdom Quarter. The area was full of people just sauntering around enjoying each other's company. After returning to our hotel, we jumped into bed for some much needed shut-eye.

We slept-in the following morning, as our tour to the Vienna Woods didn't leave until two o'clock. We breakfasted on orange juice, halved hard-boiled eggs, halved tomatoes, hard rolls, and coffee. We wore clothes that would let our skin breathe, as forecasters predicted sunny and hot (80°) weather.

At reception we posted our Vienna postcards, ordered a taxi to the hydrofoil terminal for the next morning, then asked if we could have breakfast in the lounge at 6 AM since we had to be at the terminal before 7 AM. After asking for directions to the Russian soldier monument Ron wanted to see, we walked the Ring Road to the area. In front of the monument was a massive variegated floral garden with spraying fountain. The soldier was impressive. Under his statue was a plaque telling his history, but since we couldn't read Russian, it was all Greek to us. I am glad we went. We just sat on a nearby bench for a bit taking in all the colors and flavors of the garden flowers.

Leaving the monument area and about to cross the street, we noticed in the center of a large nearby roundabout a crop of corn growing, which astounded us. The corn symbolized birth, growth, and the harvest yet to come for everyone.

We continued walking the Ring Road, stopping at the Peoples' Park. Upon entering it we saw a floral clock made of multiple roses and other flowers in all shades of the rainbow. In the park we discovered the renown, golden Strauss monument. Surrounding it stood a white marble archway into which etchings of various musicians had been carved lending to the theme of Viennese music and waltzes.

We continued our walk back to St. Stephandom Square and our hotel. Arriving back at our hotel about 12:45 we felt we needed some nourishment before our four-hour tour. We walked to a little cafe we had seen that had takeaway (carry-out) chicken. We bought some chicken and salad then ate it in a nearby park under the shade of some imposing trees. While there, some interesting young people walked by complete with florescent yellow, hot pink, and green hair. Living in the London area we had become accustomed to young people coloring their hair in shocking colors to make a statement about themselves. I don't know or understand what they were trying to say, but they thought they did.

Revived, we returned to the hotel to await our Cityrama bus or van. At two o'clock the van picked us up and off we went for our tour of the Vienna Woods. Our guide introduced himself as Carl and his driver was Wolfgang. Our itinerary included The Seagrotte, the largest subterranean lake in Europe, the Monastery of the Holy Cross, and the

Maylering Convent.

On our way out of Vienna, Wolfgang put on some Viennese music I thought added a lovely touch. As we headed for the motor-way, Carl pointed out the cemetery where Mozart is buried. Working our way up hilly roads and tall tree forests we arrived at our first stop of the afternoon, The Seagrotte. We divided into language groupings; our group had an English and French guide. Carl told all the groups the temperature inside was a constant 9°C (52°F). If we thought that was too cold, we should put a blanket around us from the wooden box next to the entrance then return it after the tour.

We descended approximately 1600 meters into the bowels of this limestone cavern. The walls were damp with trickling water in places while above us lit lamps guided us further into our encounter here. At one point we saw the place where in 1944-45 the Germans developed parts for their Heinkel He 162 fighter. Some fuselage pieces remained in place for show.

After turning another corner, I saw a new set of descending, well-worn steps that looked quite slippery from the walls' condensation. These would take us further into the lake area below. At that point feeling quite queasy and wishing I could go back out but not wanting to get lost in the maze of tunnels down here, I pressed on with a reassuring smile and arm from Ron. At the bottom of the steps we had to wait a few minutes for the next boat to come and take us through the lake area. I became more uneasy when I saw the old wood flat-bottomed boat we were to take pitch sideways as each new passenger boarded. After thirty of us climbed in, we floated along. The underwater lights guided our boatman through the lake caverns. The water was so crystal clear I could see the graphite seabed. Our guide explained each niche and cranny of this underground world.

Once we disembarked the boat and returned outside, I felt safe again. While waiting for all the groups to reunite, we could buy a refreshment or souvenir and use their facilities for 2 shillings a person.

About 10 minutes later we were all aboard and heading for the Cistercian Abbey of the Holy Cross. We passed the inn where Franz Schubert wrote love songs to the village miller's daughter. Her father didn't approve of him and forbid any contact with him. In1133, the Babenberg family founded the Abbey; it had to be rebuilt twice due to battles waged here against the Turks in 1529 and 1683. Today, approximately 50 monks reside here in virtual silence and communion with God. It was just about the most serene place I had been to in a long time. It reminded me of the peacefulness of Mont St. Michael in Normandy and once again I felt at home.

The abbey and chapel entrance walls were a mixture of Romanesque and Baroque. The exterior walls were pale yellow with off-white accents. The interior was filled with extraordinary focal points. The first was the absolutely magnificent wood carved choir area used by the monks for Sunday mass. The second, taking up most of the sidewall, was the main organ encased in carved wood paneling. The third was the main altar that was home to the cross of St. Francis of Assisi. On the right wall overlooking the altar was a smaller gilded organ used by the monks for their Gregorian chants and compline services. This chapel, which I would call a small church, was absolutely breathtaking.

Leaving the chapel area we made our way to the gothic *Fountain House*, a room containing a three tier fountain culminating with a cross. Underground water flowed through this fountain and was used by the monks in their daily life. Surrounding this fountain were three walls full of tall rectangular stained glass windows. The afternoon shone through them, increasing their intensity and beauty.

The Chapter Hall stored the tomb of Frederick II who was killed in 1246 during a battle with the Hungarians. Other focal points of this room included its nineteenth century rose window and its vaulted ceiling full of biblical frescos.

After finishing our tour of this monastery, we came upon the tomb of Mary Vetsera, the seventeen-year-old mistress of Crown Prince Rudolph, heir to the Austro-Hungarian Empire. Before driving to the nearby Carmelite Convent, Carl told us the story of its founding. The Prince had visited the Pope seeking an annulment from his loveless marriage to Stephanie of Belgium so he could marry his love, Mary. The Pope refused. With this rebuff and his unhappiness with the political views of his father, Emperor Franz Joseph, he decided to end it all.

On January 29, 1889 he took Mary to his hunting lodge where he killed her, afterwards covering her with flowers. He sat with her until dawn when he committed suicide next to her. His parents (the Emperor and his wife Elizabeth) were completely distraught and tried to make sense of this tragedy. The Emperor wanted to keep everything that happened here a secret so he had the lodge torn down. Elizabeth pleaded with him to establish some memorial for their son. In place of the lodge, they built a convent and chapel. In a side room off the chapel, Elizabeth had a statue of the Madonna constructed in her likeness. She also asked that a sword be placed through the heart to tell her son what pain he had created in her. The parents gave the convent and chapel to the Carmelite order with the proviso that they live, worship, and pray every day for their son's soul. To this day the order still honors their commitment. Our tour allowed us a short tour of this small, simple convent and its memorial chapel; what pain and anguish was portrayed on the Madonna's face.

After reboarding our bus, we began our return to Vienna, surrounded once again with lovely Viennese music. The bus dropped us off at the Forum Hotel a few blocks from our hotel. As we walked back, we strolled through the Pedestrian Shopping Mart. Merchandise prices here were steep. I wondered where in Europe are prices reasonable for the working person.

After a fifteen-minute walk back to the hotel, a shower to revitalize our bodies, and a change of clothes, we were off for dinner. At 8:30 we stopped at our restaurant. Our waiter said if we could wait 5 minutes he could get us a table outside which we thought would be delightful. There we could take in all the sights and sounds of the tourists and city folk as they meandered through the alleyway returning to their homes after work or looking for places to eat. Our waiter recommended the beef stroganoff. Tasting it, we realized it contained slivered beef, julienne dill pickles, and was topped with a tomato cream sauce. A side plate of spraekle (small twisted dumplings) came with it. The meal was unusual but tasty. We splurged on a banana split for dessert.

When we finished, we said goodbye to our waiter. We knew we had to take another walk to work off the fullness and calories before retiring to bed. We walked until midnight in the Stephansdom Quarter aglow with its lit globe candles and its many other tourists.

Returning to our hotel room we packed, as we had to be up no later than half past five to have breakfast and catch our taxi to the hydrofoil for our cruise to Budapest on the Danube. We fell asleep about one o'clock, tired and happy.

We woke up at five fifteen. We dressed and came down for breakfast at 6 AM. The hotel had made us lovely cold plates of sliced meats, Swiss cheese, sliced cucumbers and tomatoes, halved hard-boiled eggs, hard rolls, and coffee and tea. Another couple came down for their breakfast, then three New Jersey elementary school teachers traveling together joined us. The women were on holiday and had just visited Budapest. Today, they were taking a day cruise to Bratislava, then would go to Prague tomorrow for a few days before returning home.

After checking out, our taxi picked us up at 6:30. The driver drove us to the hydrofoil terminal where three couples were already in line ahead of us. We could check-in our luggage but had to wait for the passport control personnel to come. While waiting, Ron ordered a medium strength coffee. I said I didn't want any, as I wanted to give my camera finger some exercise taking last minute shots of Vienna. After tasting his, he said it was like strong Turkish coffee.

At 7:45 the passport control officers came and stamped our passports. After boarding the ship, I sat down at a table near a window. Investigating the ship, Ron found a small front section he thought would give us a better view of the river sights.

At 8:15 we pulled away from the dock and embarked on our five-hour journey down the Danube. Musicians say it was the rhythm of the Danube that influenced Johann Strauss to compose his Blue Danube Waltz. Coming to the first of three locks we had to pass through, the pilot told us each lock would take 30 minutes for the water to lower to the level we needed to proceed. The stewardess pointed out sights along the way in Austrian, English, and Hungarian. It amazed me how multilingual guides and shopkeepers had to be in order to service the language diversities of their clients. Our five-hour trip stretched into almost eight making it a long haul. Since the windows in our section could not be opened, we became quite hot under the sun's unrelenting rays. Since a hydrofoil has no deck, we could not get any fresh air or stretch our legs. We read and even attempted to sleep to cut the hours of the cruise.

What really surprised and upset me was the Danube was not a beautiful blue river but a muddy brown one with logs or other debris in it. What a shame. Ron and I said almost simultaneously "Next time we'll take the train to Budapest." We loved our scenic train ride from Prague to Vienna enjoying the sights along the way and our compartment windows could be opened if needed. Before arriving in Budapest, the stewardess told us to purchase our taxi tickets on board, as taxi drivers took unscrupulous advantage of tourists by charging exorbitant rates. Ron purchased ours to our hotel.

At four we docked and went through passport control. The Hungarian official stamped it although he couldn't read English. An interesting law here – people cannot exchange any money into Hungarian *forints* until they entered the country, and must be exchanged into other monies before leaving. Their money doesn't leave their country. After completing our business, we took our taxi to our hotel, Hotel K+K Opera.

Our hotel was modern and elegant. The lobby walls were red, the floor was inlaid cream and black speckled marble, as was the reception desk, and gold velvet drapes and cornice boards accentuated the large picture windows. The lobby chairs themselves were made of the same cream marble and decorated with large red velvet seats and pillows. Brass railings separated the various sections of the lobby from the rest of the hotel.

Our hotel room had been recently remodeled with modern furniture and a marble bathroom. Our bellboy spoke little English. We asked him for directions to the nearest McDonalds or Burger King as well as the nearest British Airways office. He left us and came back in a few minutes with a telephone book showing the addresses and telephone numbers we needed. Quite a nice young man!

Being hot and bone-tired, we didn't want to leave our air-conditioned room. We checked the hotel directory and found they had room service. When we realized two club sandwiches with chips and two cokes cost no more than a fast food restaurant, we decided to give them a call. My, did we feel elegant.

After a shower, our food, and a rest to revive us, we went scouting the area. Our hotel was on the Buda side (the old world area) while across the river was the Pest side (the modern or new era area). The buildings and shops on the Buda side had kept their old world flavor and traditions. We could see the residents in Budapest, especially on the Buda side were struggling with the realities of the modern economy (capitalism) and a government, no longer Communist, that didn't take care of them.

An hour later we asked reception where to go for dinner. The woman told us their restaurant was on the corner. To her embarrassment we found it closed. She recommended a nice Hungarian restaurant about six streets away and even booked us a table there. After getting explicit directions, we found *Muveszinas* quite easily. The walk made us even hungrier. The corner restaurant came with a rather large, imposing bouncer-type maitre'd outside, checking out would-be customers. Some tourists and even Hungarians had tried to skip out without paying their bill and he was here to see that didn't happen. The interior was quite dark. In the center of each table was a thin wrought iron candlestick and candle, the only true light for the table, as the restaurant lighting was subdued. Linen tablecloths, napkins, china tableware, and crystal stemware immaculately dressed each table. Ron ordered a green garden salad for a starter then Paprika Chicken with noodles in a cottage cheese sauce (our waiter's recommendation) for his entrée, while I had a Greek salad, then Wiener Schnitzel with vegetables steamed in a touch of paprika, Hungary's red gold. No dessert, as we were full to the brim. We walked back to the hotel arriving about half past eleven, then it was off to dream land.

The next day we were up at 7:45. Breakfast was wonderful – fresh fruits (first since Prague), cereals, fresh sliced cucumbers and tomatoes, cheeses, sliced meats, scrambled eggs, stewed tomatoes, bacon, and a variety of homemade breads and rolls (white, whole meal, and seeded). Their raisin bread was fabulous. At a table across the dining room I noticed an English couple that had been at our Prague hotel. At a table near us I was impressed to see two sons (probably our age) taking their elderly, disabled mother on holiday. What a wonderful gift they were giving her of themselves as well as their time.

At 9:20 we were ready for our tour bus to pick us up but were surprised to be picked up by a taxi instead. We got to the tour bus about 30 minutes early so we were able to commandeer the choice front seats. We would be able to see everything.

Buda and Pest have their own individual flavors. The total city is lovely with its gothic churches, spires, domes, and tall corporate buildings along with its old world charm, culture, and people.

Erneco Kobliczek, our guide, introduced herself and our driver as Yanish Smedyovi. Once on our way we passed the massive Parliament building built at the turn of the century in neo-gothic style. She said many architects had bid for the right to design and build the building. The judges couldn't choose from the top three designs so they decided to incorporate all three into one large building. The first design became the Ministry of Agriculture wing, the second wing became the State Museum, while the third became the actual Parliament section. This was the largest and most expensive building in Budapest – 268 million *forints*. She said the interior was luxuriously decorated.

Driving over the Margaret Bridge, Erneco shared the history behind Margaret Island. In the thirteenth century, King Bela IV had two daughters murdered by the Mongols. He resolved that if he ever had another daughter, he would dedicate her to God. He was blessed with another daughter, Margaret, who at the age of nine entered the convent on the island. She lived there until she died of tuberculosis at age 29. The island became Margaret Island in memory of her.

St. Matthias Church and the Fisherman Bastion were the next stops on our tour. We journeyed up the winding steep streets leading to Castle Hill (150 meters above Budapest) and St. Matthias Church. This church was named for Hungary's favorite medieval king who had married twice in the fifteenth century. The original baroque styled church was built about 1250, converted into a mosque during the Turkish occupation (150 years) then seriously damaged during the Hungarian recapture in 1686. Its final neo-gothic redesign came between the seventeenth and eighteenth centuries. Its unique roof was designed by the use of multi-colored black and gray tiles in diamond patterns. Inside we saw breath-taking frescos, an intricately carved wood pulpit, a dramatic Jesus cross over the altar, four wood carved side altars, a jeweled anteroom containing a Madonna statue, and the Imperial family balcony where they sat during services. History reported that when the Turks captured Budapest, they decreed all religious and Hungarian military statues were to be destroyed. As it happened, the Turk soldiers were about to discover the statue of the Madonna when the roof caved in; covering her so the soldiers didn't find her. She was the only statue to survive.

Leaving the church, we walked along a sandstone wall leading to the Fisherman's Bastion. Eighteenth century fishermen defended the castle area from this hillside bastion. Walking along this wall, filled with an array of turrets and arches, we were greeted by fantastic views of the city, the Danube, and especially the Parliament below. Our guide also told us in the thirteenth century Jesuits founded a college on the hillside behind us and that recently it was bought up by the Hilton chain and transformed into a luxurious hotel overlooking Budapest. What a view one could get from a window room facing the river.

Built in the 13th century, the Royal Palace housed the Roman-German kings through the Turks. The palace, along with sixty-two percent of Budapest, was bombed in World War II, then had to be reconstructed. Artist sketches drawn before the bombings gave architects the image of what Budapest looked like before the war.

After the Berlin Wall was dismantled, the East Germans gave Budapest two large wall sections in appreciation for the Hungarians allowing Germans to escape to the West through Hungary. Another legend and memorial here was that of St. C, a Venetian missionary who brought Christianity to this area. When paganism reasserted itself, an angry mob kidnapped him then threw him off the top of the hill which now bears his name. At that very spot a statue was erected over a waterfall symbolizing his last day of life. He was canonized in 1083.

The Pest or modern part of the city began at the end of the last century. We drove around its new, modern multi-purpose sports center – fifteen percent of the funding money came from fan donations. Today, it is open to sport events, as well as concerts.

Heroes' Square, our last stop, was a sight Ron wanted to see but had not been able to find. The square was a massive open area filled with the monument of the Archangel Gabriel who, according to legend, offered King Stephen the first Hungarian crown. Figures of Hungarian heroes were carved into the monument's base. In front of the Archangel, their Tomb of the Unknown Soldier rested. Surrounding the monument were two large columns that held statues of additional national heroes. On parallel streets on either side of the square stood two fine art museums.

As we were returning to our drop off point, Enreco told us to take time to see St. Stephen's Basilica, the largest Catholic church in Hungary. After departing our bus and thanking both Enreco and Yanish, we walked along the river until we ran right into a large craft fair selling anything from hand embroidered tablecloths, doilies, and blouses to hand painted dishes and steins to leather goods, hand crafted knives, hand carved toys and puzzles.

After purchasing T-shirts for the grandchildren, we started looking for a money exchange to add to our emptied pockets. While searching for a bank, we saw a thermometer saying it was 31C or 93F. It was definitely hot. We returned to our hotel quickly to get some water and a bite of lunch.

Later after it had cooled some, we strolled along the river taking in the entire atmosphere and revisiting with our eyes the sights we had seen during our tour. We decided to sit down and relax at one of the river's outdoor cafes. After ordering glasses of Hungarian beer, they served us Heineken instead, as they had completely sold out of their beer due to the heat. As we sat there relaxing under the shade of our table's umbrella, we watched the trains or trams fill up with workers going home for the evening, tourists taking leisurely walks, as well as enjoying the sight of the Royal Palace and St. Matthias on the hillside across the Danube from us.

Returning to our hotel, we had the hotel book a table again at "Muveszinas" for half past eight. As we approached the restaurant, we saw on the sidewalk before us a group of grubby, entranced men listening to a very vocal political activist or unionist talking to them in very animated terms. Since we didn't want to become involved in any way especially if the Police came, we crossed the street ahead of them.

We had new waiters. I had a chilled fruit soup (quite rich with cream and berries) and a traditional Hungarian stew (spicy with a paprika and chili sauce). Ron had a tomato salad and the Wiener Schnitzel with potato croquet. Again, we did not have dessert because our huge portions left no room in our stomachs. We couldn't have even split one. Dinner for both of us cost around twenty-five dollars.

We walked slowly back to our hotel talking about our wonderful trip. Ron showered while I wrote the last of my postcards then I took a long hot bath to get the walking soreness out of my legs and shoulders. You realize carrying a camera, rolls of film, and a handbag is hard work!

Turning on CNN for the eleven o'clock news, we learned the British Airways strike had been averted. What a relief! Now we could head for home without a problem. Thank goodness.

Our final holiday morning started at 7:45. Completing our repacking, I put all the purchase receipts together for customs so if they asked I had everything in order. With that done, we were free to enjoy the rest of the morning as we wished.

A couple of hours before we had to vacate our room, we booked a taxi to the airport, mailed our postcards, and exchanged just enough money to get us to the airport. We walked back to the Danube for one last look, strolled by the craftsmen stalls, and then said a fond farewell to Budapest. We checked out of our room and waited for our taxi in the lobby.

We arrived at the airport an hour and a half early. We went through passport control and customs without a problem. We spent our remaining time in the British Airways lounge. I wasn't even interested in duty-free. Did I say that?? I can't believe I said that. We read some London newspapers to catch us up on the news. At two o'clock our flight was posted. Before being allowed to board our plane, our boarding passes and passports were checked. Once onboard, we buckled up and prepared for liftoff.

Our flight to Heathrow was smooth. Once again we passed through passport control and customs. With that over, we caught the Pink Elephant bus to our car and drove home. It took us our usual sixty minutes to get home. It was nice to get back into our own bed and surroundings. A fabulous venture into Europe, especially Prague. I want to go back there someday.

52. Preparations to Return

By the middle of July preparations for our return were in full swing. Jim Austen, Comco's head of removals, either into or out of England, had surveyed our home to assess the number of crates, boxes, workers, and lorries that would be needed to complete our move. Again, I had to make out the itemized inventories of everything we owned that was being transported either by air or by sea. Oh, how I hated filling out those lists but they safeguarded the company as well as the removers and us. This time I had much more to inventory with the sets of china I had bought my girls, the abundance of collectibles in Hazel's "Nation of Shopkeepers" porcelain shop fronts, the David Winter houses, and the Lilliput Village shops. As I inventoried, I questioned why I had bought all this. Each purchase had meaning to me or to its recipient. Still, I said, "Ugh".

The end of August, Ron and I flew home to close on our new house. Ron had only seen it as a piece of land in March when he had returned stateside for meetings. At that time he chose the color of the bathroom and kitchen fixtures as well as the outside and fireplace bricking. Late April I had flown back to choose the paint, cabinets, countertops, carpet, and wood floor colors. I saw it only as a foundation. Everything else had been done via the international telephone wires. Exorbitant as our telephone bills were to the builder and to John and Laura, the telephone became our only source of communication to keep on top of everything. We were so fortunate our "kids" watched over the whole project – without them we could not have had the house we had dreamed of. I truly thank them for all their time and efforts on our behalf.

On August 26, we walked into our home for the first time and inspected it before the closing the following day. It was absolutely wonderful. The whole house was perfect in every way. I couldn't believe it. The following day we owned our new home lock, stock, and barrel.

With the house bought, I contacted the local mover to bring our stored things out of storage as quickly as possible. They arranged to deliver them the following Friday. We stayed with John, Laura, and Christopher until then. When the furniture came, we had a bed, family room furniture, an office desk and chair, and boxes full of dishes, books, and miscellaneous items. Ron returned to the UK while I stayed home putting things in order. Within two weeks I was back on a Northwest flight bound for London and the beginning of getting our house there ready for the removers.

Two weeks later with my lists in hand, one for us, one for the removers, and one for the company, the removers came and began the task of boxing and crating. It took them two days to box and rebox some boxes I had never opened, crate pictures, the dining room hutch, base, and table then check that everything was ready. The men made sure everything was packed correctly. After another two days the removers had placed all the boxes, crates, and furniture into huge wooden overseas shipping crates that would be transferred into the metal overseas cartons for transport to the U. S. and our home.

After the removal was complete, I flew home to await our air shipment that was due the following week. I did not expect the sea shipment until the second or third week in November but it arrived two weeks after the air shipment. The movers uncrated and placed all the furniture. I worked feverishly to unbox and place dishes, clothes, and necessities so I could return to England for the last two weeks of Ron's assignment that would be a special time for both of us.

By the first of December our new home looked ready for Ron and me to walk into and begin living as a couple again. Many boxes were still in the basement but the living areas were complete. I was physically exhausted but happy with the way things looked. I was eager to get back to him. How I ever would have lived three thousand miles away from him for a year with only visits in between, I don't know. Three hours before my scheduled flight, British Airways called to say my flight had been canceled due to a mechanical problem. I could fly the following night with an upgrade to business class or I could book another date in tourist class. I explained I needed to get to London so transfer me to the next night's flight with the upgrade. I couldn't wait to get on that plane and back to Ron. I had really missed him around the house, his broad smiles, and his wonderful kisses of delight when he came home from work. One tends to forget those little things in the routine of the day but being apart reminds spouses how much they miss each other.

The evening after I arrived back in London, a small group of our friends took us to dinner and to see *Smokey Joe's Cafe*. I couldn't believe I sat there singing along with most of the songs in it. What a treat. I spent the rest of the week visiting friends and old London haunts.

A week before we were to leave, Ron's group and their spouses took us to the Imperial Garden Restaurant in Brentwood. Their food was excellent. Two days before our departure, Ron hosted what is called a drink up (British for a going away party). Just about everyone he knew and worked with came to wish us well on our return. We were so pleased with the turnout. Many tears were shed on our part, as we knew some we might never see again. They presented us with a fantastic British travel book on places to visit here. Looking at some of the photographs of places I had visited and loved would make this book one full of remembrances for me. The group hoped we would return to them in the future. The party went late into the night.

The day morning before we flew home, the removers arrived at Ron's flat to pick up his last things for a final air shipment home. He had kept with him his golf clubs, clothes, laptop, and various papers he needed while working here. He had been living in the flat since we closed up our house. Later that afternoon we packed up our remaining belongings, said goodbye to George, the apartment landlord, turned in Ron's car, and took a taxi to London where we would spend our last night. Ron had booked a room in the luxurious Thistle Hotel in St. Katherine's Way. That night we went to see *Jesus Christ Superstar,* a play I wanted to see. Absolutely outstanding. The story, the actors, and especially the music were overwhelming.

After the show we returned to our hotel, had a late dinner, and then a short nap before taking our taxi to Heathrow. We were up at five and by six we were showered and dressed. Our breakfast came at half past six. Carrying our bags, we checked out of the hotel by eight then stepped into our taxi while waving goodbye to London. I found myself crying, as I was leaving a place I had lived in for five years. The tears meant sadness for my loss, but also joy for what was about to become my new life.

Arriving at the British Airways check-in, Comco, as company policy for returnees, had booked us into business class. Ron talked a manager into upgrading us into first-class using his British Air miles and prestige card. What a treat we were in for, as neither of us had ever flown first class before. The first class stewardess had only ten passengers to cater to and that she did. We were treated to champagne and appetizers then a choice of steak, chicken, or pasta dinners and finally various desserts from her storehouse of goodies. From her cache of videos, we chose the ones we personally wanted to view. Our seats reclined into almost twin-sized beds. Snacks were available to us at all times. We felt like royalty.

Eight hours later the wheels of our 747 touched down on the runway at Detroit Metropolitan Airport. We were home! Our new life was ahead of us! Our family was there to greet us. What a glorious moment! I did admit to myself that I would miss our British and European friends and our traveling.

53. My New Encounter with Life Begins

A new encounter with life was exactly that. We were "home" but adjusting to our new life was tough. When I heard our orientation leader five years before say that re-entry home would be more difficult than going on assignment, I thought he was as crazy as a loony bin. What I quickly learned was – he was perfectly correct.

I thought we could just plug back into our family and friends without any problem. What would be different? What would we have to adjust to? Well, let me put it this way. We now had to adjust to a way of life that was foreign to us. I had to reorient myself with all the new and varied food products available in the stores that I had forgotten about or were new to me. Instead of one or two British ketchup choices, I now had six or seven. Instead of choosing between fresh and long life orange juice and milk, I had a wide variety of fresh products but no long life ones. Instead of deli sliced meats and cheeses, I had them as well as all kinds of packaged ones. Since leaving the States, food manufacturers had created dinners and casseroles that could be taken off the shelf, placed in a microwave or a pan of boiling water, and be a full cooked meal in a manner of minutes. After having a small home in England, I had to get use to one twice the size. Cars were now back on the right side of the road instead of the left. Our church services were now Episcopalian rather than Anglican which had become familiar to us.

The hardest and most shocking part for us was reconnecting with family and friends. I thought we could just reenter their lives without a hitch. That wasn't the case. We had been away for five years. Our life had been quite different to theirs. Their lives and ours didn't match like it used to, making it hard to reconnect with them. They hadn't had the same life experiences and travels we had. so it was hard for them to understand what our life was like. Some people didn't even want to discuss what we had done and seen. Tough it was!! It took me almost two years to adjust to England but knew this would take much longer on this side of the "pond". Even three years after our return, we still haven't reconnected with some family members and friends. That is tough to take. Most relationships are healing but some may never recover.

Today after being home three years, I look back on those five years overseas and realize I received more than I ever wanted to admit to myself while on assignment. Because of Uwe and his telling me to go into Kaiserslauten, I became confident. I have lost my fear of going into an unknown city and language, getting around where I want and return to my starting place, making myself understood with people I do not know, and making a situation work for me. I have used this new found confidence in many other situations I have encountered. I have made friends all over Europe – some live there permanently and some assignment friends have returned. They are still my friends and I keep in touch with them whenever I can.

I have seen a world from the inside – the beauty of its landscapes, rivers, and vineyards, its bone-tired people working eighteen hours a day for a morsel of food to eat or put on their family's kitchen table. I have seen the atrocities left behind after World War II, the countries and people who only know how to fight amongst themselves and never seem to know how to negotiate a just settlement to a problem. Living with daily threats of IRA bombings has given me a new meaning about living or living in fear. Standing on Omaha Beach and reliving the slaughter of our men and boys on June 6, 1944 has given me new meaning. Life is precious and we must preserve it. These are moments I will never forget.

I also saw good in the world: the love families had for each other while they lived life, people who go out of their way to help others like the bicyclist in Amsterdam who took us to our hotel, the German man, a stranger to us, who navigated us onto the correct autobahn home, Jackie Lonercan, the loving Irish man, who trusted us with his prized family heritage so we could photocopy the Hurley information to have a start on Ron's family background. The Martins, our next door neighbors, who not only shared themselves with us but loaned their daughter, Niamh, to us, giving us a sense of home and family. I will never forget them. The caring and sharing friends who helped me adjust to our assignment are priceless to me. The love St. Mary the Virgin church showered on us when they didn't have to. The gracious people we met on our travels, whether business or vacation related, will always be in our thoughts and hearts.

Daily life on foreign service is hard because you are a world away from your loved ones, family, friends, and familiar surroundings but it can, at the same time, be a most rewarding time if you let it. I would never discourage anyone from going on foreign service. I would even encourage them to do – as they become better people for the experience. I would do everything I could to help them adjust to their new life of adventure and close encounters.

Remembering all my funny, sad, special, and magical moments has made me see that my time in "purgatory" was a time that expanded me because I learned who I was and am from all my experiences and travels and from all the people I met along the encounter.

Looking back, I want others to know the anger I had about going and being on foreign assignment, with its three extensions, blinded me to many experiences I could have had or could have enjoyed more fully. Don't let that happen to you – this is an encounter to take full advantage of. It is a trip of a lifetime. Ride out the highs and the lows you will ultimately have, and fulfill all you can be within yourself. You will enrich yourself, your life, and who you are by becoming a better, smarter, and wiser person for it. I know – I did.

This is my advice and wish for you.